Reading Keys

Third Edition

Laraine E. Flemming

Ann Marie Radaskiewicz
Contributing Writer

WADSWORTH
CENGAGE Learning™

Australia • Brazil • Japan • Korea • Mexico • Singapore • Spain • United Kingdom • United States

WADSWORTH
CENGAGE Learning™

***Reading Keys*, Third Edition**
Laraine E. Flemming

Senior Publisher: Lyn Uhl

Director of Developmental English:
Annie Todd

Senior Development Editor: Judith Fifer

Associate Editor: Janine Tangney

Editorial Assistant: Melanie Opacki

Managing Media Editor:
Cara Douglass-Graff

Senior Marketing Manager:
Kirsten Stoller

Marketing Coordinator: Ryan Ahern

Marketing Communications Manager:
Martha Pfeiffer

Senior Content Project Manager:
Margaret Park Bridges

Art Director: Jill Ort

Print Buyer: Betsy Donaghey

Text Acquisition Account Manager:
Mardell Glinski-Schultz

Production Service:
Books By Design, Inc.

Text Designer: Books By Design, Inc.

Senior Photo Manager: Jennifer
Meyer Dare

Cover Designer: Emily Chionchio /
Roycroft Design

Cover Image: © Image Source /
Getty Images

Compositor: MPS Limited,
A Macmillan Company

For product information and technology assistance, contact us at
Cengage Learning Customer & Sales Support, 1-800-354-9706.

For permission to use material from this text or product,
submit all requests online at **www.cengage.com/permissions.**
Further permissions questions can be emailed to
permissionrequest@cengage.com.

Library of Congress Control Number: 2009935838

Student Edition:
ISBN-13: 978-0-547-19095-2
ISBN-10: 0-547-19095-6

Wadsworth
20 Channel Center Street
Boston, MA 02210
USA

Cengage Learning is a leading provider of customized learning solutions with office locations around the globe, including Singapore, the United Kingdom, Australia, Mexico, Brazil, and Japan. Locate your local office at **international.cengage.com/region.**

Cengage Learning products are represented in Canada by Nelson Education, Ltd.

For your course and learning solutions, visit **www.cengage.com.**

Purchase any of our products at your local college store or at our preferred online store **www.CengageBrain.com.**

Printed in the United States of America
2 3 4 5 6 7   14 13 12 11 10

Contents

5   Working Together: Topic Sentences and Supporting Details   189

8   Mixing and Matching Patterns   374

9   From Comprehension to Critical Reading   426

Combining Your Skills 475

Appendix for Dictionaries: Online and in Print 537

Answer Key: Reviewing the Key Points 553

Preface

Reading Keys, the first text in my three-book series, was actually the last of the three to be written. It came into being because instructors who liked its sister texts, *Reading for Results* and *Reading for Thinking*, wanted a more basic textbook that could pave the way for the mid-level *Reading for Results* and the more advanced *Reading for Thinking*. For an introduction to basic reading skills, however, instructors wanted a textbook with briefer explanations, shorter reading selections, and numerous review features.

What they explicitly did not want to change were the engaging readings and the carefully structured sequence of the other two books, with each new skill building on previous ones. They also wanted to keep the comprehensive coverage of reading techniques, from knowing how to recognize topic sentences to noticing when opinions have been mixed into facts. These were the requests that focused the first edition of *Reading Keys*, with the book drawing its title from the key icons used to highlight the numerous mini-reviews in each chapter.

In its third edition, *Reading Keys* continues to fulfill those original requests. Using brief explanations, short readings, and multiple chances for practice and review, it offers a clear and informative introduction to the comprehension skills essential to academic reading. The book still covers everything from understanding a dictionary entry to recognizing organizational patterns and determining an author's choice of tone. As in earlier editions, the third edition carefully sequences exercises so they move from the simple to the complex. Explanations are still bite-sized chunks of information, followed by reviews of essential points, each one identified by a key-shaped icon.

What's New to this Edition

While those aspects that made *Reading Keys* successful remain the same, much in this edition is brand new. Among those new features are the following:

◆ Greater Emphasis on Textbook Vocabulary

Each chapter of the new edition concludes with ten words frequently appearing in textbooks. The words were selected based on the following criterion: They had to turn up at least five times in three different textbooks, all of which covered the same subject matter, e.g., American history, introductory psychology, etc. This method of selection ensures that students are learning words they are bound to meet again when they open up their textbooks.

The ten new words are always introduced with a definition and a sample sentence. An exercise follows. The words then reappear in a chapter test, at which point students have seen the same word in three different contexts. This is the kind of repetition with variation that reading research says is essential for mastering new vocabulary.

◆ Introducing Idiom Alerts

Idioms are not restricted to conversations. They can also be found in textbooks. To help students understand the idioms encountered in their assignments, the third edition of *Reading Keys* offers **Idiom Alerts**. This new feature introduces idioms like "whistleblower" and "unsung hero," which are at home in both conversation and textbooks. It makes sense, then, to include them in vocabulary instruction.

◆ New Focus on Identifying Topics

The chapter sequence has been revised so that students now move more quickly into identifying topics, topic sentences, and supporting details. By Chapter 3, "**Identifying Topics, Main Ideas, and Topic Sentences**," students are already completing exercises that ask them to locate topic sentences. By Chapter 5, "**Working Together: Topic Sentences and Supporting Details**," the focus is on analyzing the relationship between the questions topic sentences might raise in readers' minds and the answers provided in supporting details.

◆ A New and Original Method for Identifying Topics

As easy as locating the topic might seem to experienced readers, it's often not so simple for college students first coming to grips with unfamiliar textbook content. To make it easier for students to identify topics, the third edition provides a new method of recognizing paragraph topics.

Among other devices, writers use pronouns, synonyms, associated words, and elliptical constructions to create the *chain of repetition and reference* that keeps a paragraph topic before the reader's eyes. Once students see how locating chains of repetition and reference can help them (1) identify topics *and* (2) explain how they arrived at their conclusion, they will be more relaxed about answering the most fundamental of comprehension questions, "What's this reading about?"

+ **Revised Discussion of Topic Sentences in Textbooks**

Chapter 3 looks mainly at topic sentences as they are likely to appear in textbooks, that is, in the first three sentences of a paragraph. Expanding upon the explanation in Chapter 3, Chapter 4, "**More on Topic Sentences**," then describes the other locations where topic sentences can appear, from the beginning of paragraphs to the very end.

◆ More Emphasis on the Role of Inferences in Comprehension

Chapter 3's explanation of the role that repetition and reference play in paragraphs has an additional benefit. It pointedly illustrates how much readers participate in the creation of a text by inferring information the author does not explicitly provide, and students learn, early on, how important inferences are to understanding an author's message.

◆ New Opening Chapter on Strategies for Academic Reading

Reading Keys opens with a new chapter, "**Getting into a Textbook State of Mind**." As Chapter 1 explains, reading a textbook is *not* like reading a novel or a newspaper. Textbook reading requires a conscious and focused level of concentration that plays little or no role in leisure reading. To help create that sense of focused attention for textbooks, Chapter 1 supplies specific techniques such as setting fixed times for study, varying subject matter during study sessions, and using motivational mantras to stay attentive to the task at hand. The chapter ends with a checklist designed to help students identify and evaluate their current use of study techniques.

+ **New Information on Using the Web for Background Knowledge**

Because prior knowledge is so essential to improving comprehension, Chapter 1 shows students how the World Wide Web can, with the right search term, give them the background they need to more readily grasp new information.

◆ **New Note-Taking Instruction**

Chapter 1 also illustrates how marginal notes can improve both comprehension and remembering, providing a note-taking procedure that students will find easy to follow.

◆ New Discussion of Outlining, Diagramming, and Summarizing

Because the third edition of *Reading Keys* spends more time discussing textbook conventions, it seemed appropriate to add different methods of note-taking to the skills introduced. Chapter 5, "**Working Together: Topic Sentence and Supporting Details**," explains how to outline, diagram, or summarize a chapter section. The emphasis throughout the explanations and illustrations is on more than how to take useful notes. It's also about figuring out when, for instance, outlining might be a better choice than diagramming. In short, the emphasis is on getting students to think about matching form to content.

◆ More on Paraphrasing

In line with the third edition's overall increased emphasis on strategies for academic reading, paraphrasing gets more attention than ever before. Probably the most underrated and most essential skill for both readers and writers, paraphrasing requires practice. It also needs to be taught as a concrete series of steps so that students know how to get started re-creating the author's meaning in their own words.

Not that there's a formula for paraphrasing — there isn't. But having a general sequence of steps at the start makes it easier for students to branch out and paraphrase in a more free-style fashion later on. Writing a good paraphrase is more daunting than it appears to be at first glance. For that reason, *Reading Keys* gives paraphrasing plenty of attention.

◆ Addition of a New Organizational Pattern: Simple Listing

Chapter 7, "**Recognizing Organizational Patterns**," now includes a description of the simple listing organizational pattern. Because this pattern is so common in business and government textbooks, it seemed a necessary addition. Since lists of specifics are particularly hard to store in long-term memory, Chapter 7 also includes suggestions for taking notes that visually enhance the list of details central to this pattern.

◆ Many New Readings

Reading Keys has an especially good selection of new readings. Some of them cover current cultural trends such as the changing face of the American population, the wide-ranging effects of the digital revolution, state-run programs to decrease the divorce rate, and teenagers' rejection of dating in favor of "hooking up."

Other readings are more personal like "Life Lessons from the Family Dog," written by *New York Times* editor and cancer victim Dana Jennings. Jennings's eloquent description of what he's learned from an old and ailing pet should inspire not just good classroom discussions but rich writing assignments as well. Whether personal essays or textbook excerpts, the new readings were selected because they will give students an insight into why, for some people, reading seems as essential as chocolate.

◆ Additional Textbook Selections

Because the third edition places more emphasis on strategies appropriate to reading textbooks, this edition includes more excerpts from textbooks. The new selections come from a variety of textbook sources, among them American history, sociology, biology, and psychology. From these academics sources, I was careful to choose excerpts that were clearly written and as interesting to students as textbooks can possibly be. The textbook selections were also chosen because they could contribute to the kind of shared, communal knowledge students need in order to understand and manage the world they live in.

New Supplements Package

◆ Instructor's Manual and Test Bank

Available in both print and online, the robust Instructor's Manual and Test Bank features Answer Keys for Chapters 1–9, Combining Your

Skills, and the Appendix; additional quizzes with a corresponding answer key; Midterm and Final Exams; and Vocabulary Quizzes with a corresponding answer key.

◆ Companion Websites

The **Instructor Companion Website** features a variety of teaching tools, including a **sample syllabus** suggesting how to structure a semester class using *Reading Keys*; the **Instructor's Manual and Test Bank**; and **PowerPoint Presentations** that cover essential comprehension and critical reading terms for all levels, from basic to advanced. These Power-Point slides provide a solid foundation for instructors who wish to create their own slides for classroom lectures.

The **Student Companion Website** offers resources to help students succeed using *Reading Keys*, including interactive practice quizzes; a Guide to Phonics; tips for reading and studying; and advice for preparing for class and exams. And new to this edition are vocabulary flashcards of all of the academic vocabulary words that appear at the end of every chapter.

◆ ReadSpace

ReadSpace is a flexible and easy-to-use online reading tool that includes a wealth of interactive tools for virtually any reading student, at any level, all in one place. It is a comprehensive diagnostic and practice solution that can be used for online reading classes, in a reading lab, or in class.

Acknowledgments

As with the first, the third edition of *Reading Keys* could not have come into being without the help of reviewers, whose comments and suggestions motivated so many of the changes listed above. I would like to thank the following people:

Nancy M. Banks, *Florida Community College Jacksonville*
Raymond J. Elliott, *St. Philip's College*
Stephen R. Lucas, *Phoenix College*
Mary Nielsen, *Dalton State College*
Lisa Williams, *Kirkwood Community College*

—Laraine Flemming

Getting into a Textbook State of Mind

IN THIS CHAPTER, YOU WILL LEARN

- how to focus and maintain your concentration.
- how to preview reading assignments.
- how the World Wide Web can improve reading comprehension.
- how to take marginal notes.
- how to remember what you read by paraphrasing, or exchanging your words for the author's.

Not all reading requires the same mindset. For instance, when reading a novel that you really like, you probably don't have to consciously focus your attention. By some mystery that has never been explained, some stories just capture our imagination, and we can get absorbed in them without conscious effort. Textbook reading is different. The subject matter and the vocabulary are often unfamiliar. The writing style is also usually more complicated or involved than we are used to from, say, novels or even magazines and newspapers. No wonder, then, that textbook reading requires a state of mind quite different from the one that spontaneously emerges when we read novels that we ourselves have selected.

Because there are differences between how one reads a novel and how one reads a textbook, the goal of this chapter is to show you how to concentrate and stay focused when reading textbooks, even if you're feeling something other than spontaneous enjoyment. Knowing how to read unfamiliar and demanding material is a consciously acquired skill. But it's a skill that can be at your disposal if you follow the pointers described in this chapter.

Learn How to Develop and Maintain Concentration

If you are reading an exciting novel, the chances are good that you can read it anywhere. The lighting can be bad, the noise loud, and the room filled with distractions. But it doesn't matter. You are so caught up in the story, you just don't care.

In general, textbook reading doesn't produce the same effect. With textbooks, focused concentration won't just come naturally and without effort. For precisely that reason, you need to plan and organize your study sessions very carefully. Here are some general tips to help you maintain concentration while reading.

Pointers for Developing and Maintaining Concentration
◆

1. **Set aside specific times and places for study reading.** Your goal here is to use repetition to create a habit. In other words, if you have a break in your schedule between ten and twelve in the morning, make it a point to study at that time either in the library or at home. If possible, try to position yourself in the same location each time. At home, try to always be at your desk or at the kitchen table. At school, try to sit at the same table or desk. Your goal is to build a habit that's not easy to break.

2. **Be sure you have everything you need *before* you start to study.** Learning to stay focused is not easy in the beginning. Initially, we all try to distract ourselves so that we can avoid settling down to work. Don't let that happen. Have your book, your laptop, passwords, pens, pencils, paper, etc., all set up and ready so that you can get right to work.

3. **Eliminate distractions.** Turn off your cell phone and anything else that might distract you, like television or radio. Tell yourself (and mean it) that checking e-mail, text messaging, and twittering are not allowed during the times you've allotted to study.

4. **Every time you sit down for a study session, have a plan in mind as to what you expect to accomplish.** In a two-hour study session, you might, for instance, plan to read ten pages from the assignment in your criminal justice textbook, use the Internet to get background knowledge about your reading assignment in sociology, and review four or five vocabulary words from your introduction to programming course.

5. **If you feel your concentration draining away, read a success statement that tells you why you are studying** rather than shopping, texting, or playing basketball. **Success statements** identify your future goals and relate them to current assignments—for example, "Someday I'll have a great job as an x-ray technician and this assignment is a step on the way to achieving my goal"; "In ten years, I'm going to own my own business, but I need to understand the ins and outs of accounting to get to that point."

⊶ READING KEY

◆ Getting yourself concentrated or focused to study doesn't just happen; it's something you have to prepare for.

Questionnaire: Improving Concentration

DIRECTIONS Here is a concentration checklist. Make two copies. Fill out one copy now and the other two weeks from now. Your goal is to turn every "no" into a "yes."

Questions	No	Yes
1. Do you have a clear sense of your long-term personal and professional goals?	☐	☐
2. Do you make a daily schedule of assignments you expect to complete?	☐	☐

	Questions	No	Yes
3.	Do you give each assignment a specific time on the schedule?	☐	☐
4.	Do you give yourself general time limits for each assignment?	☐	☐
5.	Do you identify a specific number of pages to be covered per study session?	☐	☐
6.	Do you vary the number of pages you plan to study based on the difficulty of the text, allotting fewer pages for complex material and more for easier texts?	☐	☐
7.	Do you try to study at the same time and in the same place every day?	☐	☐
8.	If you feel like quitting before the time you allotted for study is up, do you find ways to keep working, such as taking a quick break to perk yourself up?	☐	☐
9.	Before you begin reading, do you try to "prep" for a chapter by getting some background knowledge from the Web?	☐	☐
10.	While you read, do you consciously look for words or phrases that are consistently repeated or referred to?	☐	☐
11.	Do you mentally try to piece together the relationships among words that are consistently repeated or referred to?	☐	☐
12.	While you read, do you try to determine which passages are central to the reading?	☐	☐
13.	Do you formulate possible test questions based on the passages that seem especially significant?	☐	☐
14.	Do you take notes, ask questions, and make comments in the margins of your text?	☐	☐
15.	Do you vary your reading strategies to suit the material—for example, do you draw diagrams for biology and make timelines for history?	☐	☐
16.	If you feel your concentration flagging, do you use positive self-talk to get back on track (for example: "I'm not giving up on this assignment; I can concentrate for at least ten more minutes")?	☐	☐
17.	Do you take a ten-minute break for every hour you study?	☐	☐
18.	Do you mentally pat yourself on the back every time you finish your assignment within the time limits you set for yourself?	☐	☐
19.	If you plan on studying for two hours or more, are you careful to vary the subjects you study?	☐	☐
20.	Do you actively look for study partners who will help you stay focused on your work and your goals?	☐	☐

Preview Your Assignments

It's a good idea to **preview**, or look over, the entire chapter before you start reading. Seeing the big picture, *before* you begin reading, will help you figure out how the specific parts of the chapter relate to and develop one another. A good chapter preview usually requires the following steps.

Chapter Preview
◆

1. **Read the title and all introductory material.** In addition to the opening paragraphs, you should also read lists of objectives and questions.

2. **Look at all the headings (1) to get a sense of how deeply the author goes into the topic addressed in the chapter and (2) to better understand the relationship among the chapter topics.** For example, Fred Schmalleger's textbook *Criminal Justice Today* includes a chapter titled "Sentencing." Schmalleger uses major and minor headings like the following to break up the chapter: **THE VICTIM FORGOTTEN NO LONGER**, **Victim Impact Statements**, and **The Constitutionality of Victim Impact Statements**.

   The major and minor headings all **imply**, or suggest, the following: The author will discuss the role of the victim in sentencing and describe how the role of the victim has changed (the phrase "Forgotten No Longer" suggests victims were once ignored). He will also explore why some people believe that letting the victim play a role in sentencing is unconstitutional (generally, people do not discuss the "constitutionality" of a plan, law, or idea unless it's being challenged).

3. **If the headings don't clarify the relationship of topics in the chapter, read the first sentence of every paragraph.**

4. **Use words like *how*, *why*, *what*, *do*, *does*, and *who* to see if you can formulate a list of questions to guide your reading.** For example, the headings listed above should provoke questions like the following: What role does the victim now play in sentencing? How is that different from the past? What exactly is a victim impact statement? Why do some people believe that the victim impact statements are unconstitutional?

> 5. **Read concluding sections with titles such as "Summary," "Review," or "Summing Up."** Here's where you will find the meat of the chapter. In fact, these concluding sections are where the author (or authors) tell you: This is what you need to know as a result of reading what I wrote.

◆ EXERCISE 1   Surveying a Textbook Section

DIRECTIONS   Read the title, heading, marginal notes, and first sentence of every paragraph from the following textbook excerpt. Then answer the accompanying questions by circling the letter of the correct response and filling in the blanks.

Drug Dependence: When the Drug Takes Control

Concept 1.1
People who are psychologically dependent on drugs use them habitually or compulsively to cope with stress or to relieve negative feelings.

drug dependence
A severe drug-related problem characterized by impaired control over the use of the drug.

physiological dependence
A state of physical dependence on a drug caused by repeated usage that changes body chemistry.

withdrawal syndrome
A cluster of symptoms associated with abrupt withdrawal from a drug.

1 Drug abuse often leads to **drug dependence**, a severe drug-related problem characterized by impaired control over the use of a drug. People who become dependent on a drug feel compelled to use the drug or powerless to stop using it, even when they know the drug use is ruining their lives.

2 Drug dependence is usually, but not always, associated with *physiological dependence* (also called *chemical dependence*). In **physiological dependence**, a person's body chemistry changes as the result of repeated use of a drug so that the body comes to depend on having a steady supply of the drug. When physiologically dependent people abruptly stop their drug use, they may experience a cluster of unpleasant and sometimes dangerous symptoms called a **withdrawal syndrome** (also called an *abstinence syndrome*). Another frequent sign of physiological dependence is **tolerance**, the need to increase the amount of a drug so that it has the same effect.

3 **Drug Abuse and Drug Dependence**   Professionals use the terms *drug abuse* and *drug dependence* to describe the different types of substance-use disorders. Lay people more often use the term *drug addiction*, but it has different meanings to different people. Here, let us define **drug addiction** (also called *chemical addiction*) as a pattern of drug dependence accompanied by physiological dependence. By this definition, we consider people to be addicted when they feel powerless to control their use of the drug *and* have developed signs of physiological dependence—typically a withdrawal syndrome.

© Don Mason/Corbis

When Does Use Become Abuse? Many people use alcohol socially, but when does use cross over into abuse? According to mental health professionals, drug use becomes drug abuse when it leads to damaging or dangerous consequences.

tolerance A form of physical habituation to a drug in which increased amounts are needed to achieve the same effect.

drug addiction Drug dependence accompanied by signs of physiological dependence, such as the development of a withdrawal syndrome.

psychological dependence A pattern of compulsive or habitual use of a drug to satisfy a psychological need.

4   Bear in mind that people may become *psychologically* dependent on a drug without becoming physiologically dependent on it. **Psychological dependence** is a pattern of compulsive or habitual use of a drug that serves a psychological need, such as lessening anxiety or escaping from stress. People who are psychologically dependent on a drug come to rely on it to counter unpleasant feelings or to cope with personal problems or conflicts with others. Some drugs, like nicotine, alcohol, and heroin, can lead to both psychological and physiological dependence. Others, such as marijuana, can produce psychological dependence but are not known to produce physiological dependence.

5   People also speak about nonchemical forms of addiction, including sexual addiction, gambling addiction, shopping addiction, and even Internet addiction. These, too, may be forms of compulsive behavior characterized by lack of control over the behavior. We can think of these behavior patterns as nonchemical dependencies. (Nevid, *Psychology: Concepts and Applications*, p. 160.)

1. Based on the title, what do you think is the subject of the reading?
   a.   the causes of drug dependence
   b.   the effects of drug dependence
   c.   the role of organized crime in drug distribution
   d.   excessive use of prescription drugs

2. Based on your survey, is drug abuse the same as drug dependence?

_____

Please explain how you arrived at your answer.

_____

_____

 READING KEY

◆ Getting an overall picture of what's in a chapter *before* you begin reading makes it easier to fit the pieces of the chapter together *while* you are reading.

Use the Web for Background Knowledge

Reading research has repeatedly shown that background knowledge aids comprehension. Fortunately, with the arrival of the Internet and the World Wide Web, everyone can put that insight to use. If, for example, you know that the next assignment in your history text focuses on the Knights of Labor, the first workers' union in the United States, then use "Knights of Labor" as a search term to locate a general source that could give you some background knowledge about the topic. Look, for instance, at page 9 to see what comes up when you use that term in a Google search.

Now looking at page 9, you might ask yourself, Where do I start? For background knowledge in preparation for textbook reading, any of the encyclopedia entries listed here would be fine. In this case, we're in luck because the Knights of Labor have earned an entry in Wikipedia, the free encyclopedia and you can view that entry on page 10.

Web   Images   Maps   News   Shopping   Gmail   more ▼   Sign in

Google   [Knights of Labor]   [Search]

Web Books   Results **1 - 10** of about **324,000** for <u>Knights</u> of <u>Labor</u>. (0.22 seconds)

<u>Knights of Labor - Wikipedia, the free encyclopedia</u>
The **Knights of Labor**, also known as Noble and Holy Order of the **Knights of Labor**, was one of the
most important American **labor** organizations of the 19th ...
en.wikipedia.org/wiki/**Knights**_of_**Labor** - 64k -<u>Cached</u> - <u>Similar pages</u>

<u>Welcome to the **Knights of Labor**</u>
We believe that the **Knights of Labor** [KoL] were on the right path of organizing **Labor** and in the
justice of their economic and social demands. ...
www.**knightsoflabor**.org/ - 17k - <u>Cached</u> - <u>Similar pages</u>

<u>Knights of Labor</u>
In 1869, the Noble and Holy Order of the **Knights of Labor**, which initially offered a more reasoned
approach to solving **labor** problems, was established in ...
www.u-s-history.com/pages/h933.html - 18k - <u>Cached</u> - <u>Similar pages</u>

<u>Knights of Labor and Labor Movement</u>
Learn about the pioneers of **labor** movement and **labor** unions. These **Knights of labor** showed the
path to **labor** movement resulting in organised **labor** unions of ...
www.theholidayspot.com/**labor**day/k_of_L.htm - 19k - <u>Cached</u> - <u>Similar pages</u>

<u>Knights of Labor</u>
Founded in Philadelphia in 1869, the **Knights of Labor** spread to Chicago after the 1877 railroad
strikes. Initially viewed as an educational and political ...
www.encyclopedia.chicagohistory.org/pages/693.html - 9k - <u>Cached</u> - <u>Similar pages</u>

<u>The KNIGHTS OF LABOR and THEIR CONTEXT - Dr Bob James</u>
The **KNIGHTS OF LABOR** and THEIR CONTEXT - Dr Bob James. The first part is Secret Societies
and the Labour Movement.
www.takver.com/history/secsoc02.htm - 43k - <u>Cached</u> - <u>Similar pages</u>

<u>Knights of Labor</u>
The Noble Order of the **Knights of Labor** was founded in 1869 by Uriah Stephens and five other
former members of the Garment Cutters' Association of ...
www.spartacus.schoolnet.co.uk/USA**knights**.htm - 21k - <u>Cached</u> - <u>Similar pages</u>

<u>Ku Klux Klan and the **Knights of Labor**. "Masonic" brotherhoods ...</u>
On December 28, 1869 Freemason Uriah Stephens, along with eight others, created another secret
fraternal order, The **Knights of Labor**. The **Knights of Labor** ...
www.crocker.com/~acacia/kol_cult.html - 8k - <u>Cached</u> - <u>Similar pages</u>

<u>Knights of Labor - Ohio History Central - A product of the Ohio ...</u>
The **Knights of Labor** was a union established in 1869. Its founder was Uriah Stevens.
www.ohiohistorycentral.org/entry.php?rec=910 - 16k - <u>Cached</u> - <u>Similar pages</u>

<u>American Catholic History Classroom: **Knights of Labor**: Introduction</u>
In the 1880s, the **Knights of Labor** was the largest **labor** union in the United States, and while they
were predominantly Catholic in membership, the Catholic ...
libraries.cua.edu/achrcua/Knights/kol_wel.html - 9k - <u>Cached</u> - <u>Similar pages</u>

<u>Book results for knights of labor</u>
<u>Workingmen's Democracy: The Knights of Labor ...</u> - by Leon Fink - 276 pages
<u>Beyond Labor's Veil: The Culture of the ...</u> - by Robert E. Weir - 372 pages
<u>Labor and Urban Politics: Class Conflict and ...</u> - by Richard Schneirov - 420 pages

Searches related to: **Knights of Labor**

<u>american federation</u> of <u>labor</u>   <u>haymarket riot</u>   <u>samuel gompers</u>   <u>pullman strike</u>

Knights of Labor

From Wikipedia, the free encyclopedia

The **Knights of Labor**, also known as **Noble and Holy Order of the Knights of Labor**, was one of the most important American labor organizations of the 19th century. Founded by six Philadelphia tailors in 1869 and led by Kyla Higgins, its ideology may be described as *producerist*, demanding an end to child and convict labor, equal pay for women, a progressive income tax, and the cooperative employer-employee ownership of mines and factories.

Origins

The Knights of Labor had a reputation for being all-inclusive. Women, blacks (after 1878), and employers were accepted as members of the Knights of Labor. The Knights' leadership advocated the admission of blacks into local assemblies, but turned a blind eye to the segregation of assemblies in the South. Mary Harris Jones, known as "Mother Jones," helped recruit thousands of women to the Knights of Labor. She was greatly feared by factory owners, but loved and respected by union members and workers, which is how she earned her nickname "Mother Jones." Bankers, doctors, lawyers, gamblers, stockholders, and liquor manufacturers were excluded because they were considered unproductive members of society. Asians were also excluded, and, in November 1885, a branch of the Knights in Tacoma, Washington worked to expel the city's Chinese, which amounted to nearly a tenth of the overall city population at the time. The Knights strongly supported the Chinese Exclusion Act of 1882 and the Contract Labor Law of 1885, as did many other labor groups.

The Knights of Labor grew rapidly after the collapse of the National Labor Union in 1873, and especially after the replacement of Uriah Stephens with Terence V. Powderly. As membership expanded, the Knights began to function more as a labor union, and less like a fraternal organization. Local assemblies began to emphasize not only cooperative enterprises, but to initiate strikes to win concessions from non-Knights employers. Powderly opposed strikes as a "relic of barbarism," but the size and the diversity of the Knights afforded local assemblies a great deal of autonomy.

The Knights found that secrecy interfered with the organization's public work and inhibited its response to critics. Carroll Wright, U.S. Commissioner of the Bureau of Labor, characterized the Knights of Labor as a "purely and deeply secret organization" that drew heavily on Freemasonry for its ideas and procedures. In 1881, the Order's General Assembly agreed to make its name and objects public and to abolish its initiating oaths. Most rituals associated with the order continued, and the Knights entered its period of greatest growth.

Though initially afraid of the strike as a method to advance their goals, the Knights aided various strikes and boycotts. Arguably their greatest victory was in the Union Pacific Railroad strike in 1884. The Wabash Railroad strike in 1885 was also a significant success, as Powderly did not follow his usual practice and supported what became a crippling strike on Jay Gould's Wabash Line. Gould met with Powderly and agreed to call off his campaign against the Knights of Labor, which had caused the turmoil originally. These positive developments encouraged new membership, and by 1886, the Knights had over 700,000 members.

While the Knights were in no way involved, the Haymarket Riot nonetheless significantly tarnished their reputation.

Armed with this information from Wikipedia, your understanding of the chapter will develop much more quickly than it would if you approached the text without any background knowledge.

A Note on Wikipedia

If you are looking on the Web for general background knowledge in order to get ready for an assignment and a Wikipedia entry comes up, my advice would be to hit that link. Spend time looking at other sites only if (1) the Wikipedia entry is still being written, (2) there's a note indicating that the editors are questioning the entry's accuracy or completeness, or (3) no sources for the information are cited. Wikipedia is not the site to rely on if you are looking for an in-depth understanding of a topic, but as a source of general background knowledge, in my opinion, it can't be beat.

Focusing Your Search Term

When you turn to the World Wide Web for background knowledge, make your search term as specific as possible so that the search engine you use—whether it's Google, Yahoo, or any other—turns up useful websites.

In other words, if you are reading a chapter that describes President Lyndon Johnson's attempts to create what he called "The Great Society," don't make your search term "Lyndon Johnson." To be sure, the search engine will list thousands of sites. But many of them will be sites where you can find out about Johnson's personal life or his career in the Senate. However, what you want is background about the legislation he proposed in order to make his vision of "The Great Society" a reality. That means your search term should be "Lyndon Johnson's Great Society." Use that term and you'll end up with sites like those on page 12. Note that the captions already give you some insight into what Johnson hoped to accomplish.

Web Images Maps News Shopping Gmail more ▼   Sign in

Google | Lyndon Johnson's Great Society | | Search | Advanced Search
                                                                Preferences

Web   Results 1 - **10** of about **326,000** for **Lyndon Johnson's** Great Society. (0.26 seconds)

Great Society - Wikipedia, the free encyclopedia
John A. Andrew **Lyndon Johnson** and the **Great Society**: I.R. Dee, 1998 ISBN 1-56663 -
184-X; Eli Ginzberg and Robert M. Solow (eds.) The **Great Society**: Lessons ...
en.wikipedia.org/wiki/**Great_Society** - 81k - Cached - Similar pages

Lyndon B. Johnson - Wikipedia, the free encyclopedia
Historians Caro and Dallek consider **Lyndon Johnson** the most effective Senate ..... The
Great Society program, with its name coined from one of **Johnson's** ...
en.wikipedia.org/wiki/**Lyndon_B._Johnson** - 372k - Cached - Similar pages

United States History - **Lyndon Johnson** and the **Great Society**
Soon **Johnson** addressed other issues as well. By the spring of 1964, he had begun to use
the name "**Great Society**" to describe his reform program, ...
countrystudies.us/united-states/history-121.htm - 7k - Cached - Similar pages

Biography of **Lyndon B. Johnson**
"A **Great Society**" for the American people and their fellow men elsewhere was the vision of
Lyndon B. **Johnson**. In his first years of office he obtained ...
www.whitehouse.gov/about/presidents/**LyndonJohnson**/ - 49k - Cached - Similar pages

Obama's **Great Society** challenge - CNN.com
The **Great Society** was President **Lyndon Johnson's** sprawling legislative attempt in the
mid-1960s to lift Americans out of poverty, erase racial injustice ...
www.cnn.com/2009/POLITICS/04/07/LBJ.sidebar/ - 73k - Cached - Similar pages

"What Was Really **Great** About The **Great Society**" by Joseph A...
In fact, from 1963 when **Lyndon Johnson** took office until 1970 as the impact of his **Great**
Society programs were felt, the portion of Americans living below ...
www.washingtonmonthly.com/features/1999/9910.califano.html - 31k - Cached - Similar pages

Great Society Speech, **Lyndon B. Johnson**, 1964
Great Society Speech, **Lyndon B.** **Johnson**, 1964. Public Papers of the Presidents of the
United States, **Lyndon B.** **Johnson**, Book I (1963-64), p. 704-707 ...
coursesa.matrix.msu.edu/~hst306/documents/**great**.html - 12k - Cached - Similar pages

American President: **Lyndon** Baines **Johnson**
President **Lyndon Johnson** led the country as Commander in Chief during the ... to learn
more about the leaders whose contributions shaped our **great** country. ...
millercenter.org/academic/americanpresident/lb**johnson** - 29k - Cached - Similar pages

Lyndon Johnson's Great Society: LBJ's Effort to Continue Kennedy's ...
The **Great Society** was LBJ's legislative program that continued Kennedy's War on Poverty
and furthered the ideas of Roosevelt's New Deal and Truman's Fair ...
modern-us-history.suite101.com/.../**lyndon_johnsons_great_society** - Cached - Similar pages

Amazon.com: **Lyndon Johnson** and the **Great Society** (The American ...
This succinct survey of President **Lyndon Johnson's Great Society** initiative .... This review
is from: **Lyndon Johnson** and the **Great Society** (American Ways ...
www.amazon.com/**Lyndon-Johnson-Great-Society**-American/dp/ 1566631858 - 256k -
Cached - Similar pages

◆ **EXERCISE 2**   **Using the Web for Background Knowledge**

DIRECTIONS   Type each search term into a search engine box. See how quickly you can answer the questions about these important events in American history.

1. *Search Term*: **Woodrow Wilson and the League of Nations**

   Who was Woodrow Wilson, and what did he think about the League of Nations?

   _____

   _____

   What senator opposed him and won?

   _____

2. *Search Term*: **Herbert Hoover and the Bonus Army**

   What issue brought the Bonus Army into being?

   _____

   _____

   _____

   How did President Herbert Hoover respond to the Bonus Army?

   _____

3. *Search Term*: **Harry Truman versus Thomas Dewey in 1948**

   What surprised everyone in this election?

   _____

4. *Search Term*: **Lyndon Johnson versus Barry Goldwater**

   Who won the election of 1964?

   _____

   Who lost?

   _____

What was the winner's nickname as a result of the election?

_____

 READING KEY

◆ Make your search term as specific as possible. The more focused and precise the search term is, the better your results will be.

Read Strategically

The point of previewing and using the Web *before* reading is to get background knowledge about the author's subject matter and method. If, for instance, you are reading about how the Supreme Court came to defend freedom of speech, you want to know early on what judges or cases will be discussed. It also helps to know if the author uses any special symbols or devices to make key points stand out. Does the author, for example, open chapter sections with questions that direct readers to the overall **main idea**, or point? Or does she use headline-like headings that offer an abbreviated version of the author's main idea—for example, Free Speech Champion: Oliver Wendell Holmes?

The more prior knowledge you have about a chapter, the easier it is to read strategically. As the name implies, **reading strategically** is reading with a strategy, or plan. It's using advance, or prior, knowledge to generally predict what the author will say and then reading to confirm or revise that prediction. Reading strategically also means that you don't give every single detail the same amount of attention. Instead you evaluate the material as you read, speeding up or slowing down, as soon as you recognize the significance of the words. Strategic readers read each chapter section with a specific question (What does *habeas corpus*[†] mean?) or prediction (The author is going to describe how the Texas "two-step" primary works) in mind.

They base those questions and predictions on the textual clues provided by the author. Headings, for instance, provide clues to both importance and meaning, but so, too, do pictures, visual aids, marginal notes, boldface type, and highlighting devices, such as color ink and icons (the keys in this text are examples of icons).

_____

[†]*habeas corpus*: a petition whereby a person who has been imprisoned can request a court hearing to determine if the imprisonment was illegal.

○━╖ READING KEY

◆ To read strategically is to read with a plan. It's reading with questions and predictions in mind that are then answered, confirmed, or revised.

Make Connections Between General and Specific Sentences

Textbook writers, like all writers who try to provide their readers with information about the world, need to **generalize**. They need, that is, to sum up a number of individual events and talk about them as a whole—for instance, "Parents vary in how they view what is good or bad for their children."

However, because general statements, or generalizations, can be misunderstood, writers need to provide more specific statements that help readers follow the writer's train of thought. Specific statements focus more on the individual events that are the basis for a generalization—for example, "Although some parents might consider climbing a large rock a dangerous activity for a child, others might think of it as a way of building motor skills and self-confidence."

Through the interplay of general and specific statements, nonfiction writers convey their own ideas or the ideas of others. In response, readers need to move back and forth between both kinds of statements and determine how they relate to one another. In the example above, for instance, the reader has to think, "I get it. This is an example of how parents vary in their views of what is good or bad for their children."

Fulfilling your task as a reader and weaving together general and specific statements will be made easier if you keep in mind the following characteristics of general and specific sentences.

General and Specific Sentences

◆

1. General sentences are broad. They cover a lot of ground and are subject to misunderstanding. If they aren't followed by more specific explanation or illustration, readers can misinterpret, or misunderstand, them; e.g., "The Internet has been a profound challenge to print journalism." In this case, readers need to know more about that "profound challenge."

2. The more general the sentence, the more it groups together different but related events, ideas, experiences, and people; e.g., "Democrats believe that the government should play a role in the marketplace."

3. Specific sentences don't cover as much ground as general ones do. Thus, they are less likely to be misunderstood by readers; e.g., "Print journalists can't get a breaking story out to the public as quickly as Internet journalists can."

4. Specific sentences narrow the author's focus in order to nail down the general point for the reader; e.g., "Democrats are not opposed to price controls when necessary."

⊶ READING KEY

◆ To follow the author's train of thought, readers need to recognize generalizations and look for the specific sentences that explain them.

◆ **EXERCISE 3**   **Recognizing General and Specific Sentences**

DIRECTIONS   For each general statement, pick the specific sentence that clarifies it.

EXAMPLE

General Statement: Daniel Ellsberg, the man responsible for leaking the *Pentagon Papers* to the press, is a controversial figure.

a. Ellsberg first gave a copy of the *Pentagon Papers* to Senator J. William Fulbright, who refused to go public with them.

b. Ellsberg earned a Ph.D. from Harvard and went on to become a military analyst at Harvard.

c. Although some people see Ellsberg as a hero who did his country a great service, others consider him a traitor who leaked military secrets.

EXPLANATION   Although sentences *a* and *b* offer more specific information about Ellsberg and the *Pentagon Papers*, only *c* makes the key word "controversial" more specific. That's the word that needs to be clarified if the statement is going to mean anything to readers.

1. *General Statement*: Pirates are making a comeback in Southeast Asia; however, today's pirates use modern technology to get what they want.

   a. John Dahlby, an ex–sea captain, makes his living chasing after pirates who have robbed big tankers and held the crew hostage.

   b. Armed with rocket launchers, grenades, and machine guns, today's pirates coordinate their efforts using speedboats and stolen tankers to attack in teams.

   c. In 1998, pirates took over a tanker sailing in the South China Sea; the pirates killed all 23 members of the crew, weighted their bodies, and threw the men overboard.

2. *General Statement*: Earthquakes can have a number of different but equally horrendous consequences.

   a. Earthquake vibrations are measured by instruments called seismographs; any earthquake with a rating over three is a cause of concern.

   b. Seismographs measure two kinds of waves—surface waves and body waves.

   c. Earthquakes can throw chunks of earth around, turn hard soil into mud swamps, start fires, and churn up huge ocean waves.

3. *General Statement*: Global warming is having an effect on the world's glaciers.

   a. Glaciers are formed when snow builds up and becomes compact; the weight of the snow then forces the glacier to move forward.

   b. All over the world, glaciers are showing signs of shrinkage due to higher temperatures.

   c. Glaciers as they move over the earth leave their marks behind.

4. *General Statement*: Some species behave in a way that is distinctly human.

   a. If a group of monkeys is pursued by an enemy, some members of the group will turn and face the enemy so that the others can flee.

   b. Horses are pack animals; they thrive when they are part of a larger group and, like dogs, they follow a leader.

    c. Chimps groom each other constantly, picking insects and bits of dirt from each other's fur.

5. *General Statement*: Extinct volcanoes are believed to be incapable of erupting, but occasionally they produce unpleasant surprises.

    a. Dormant volcanoes show no signs of erupting, but they are considered capable of doing so despite the lack of activity.

    b. Volcanoes, when they erupt, can be one of nature's most destructive weapons.

    c. In 1973, the extinct volcano on Iceland's Vestmann Islands erupted after being inactive for more than 5,000 years.

Make Marginal Notes

Full ownership of a book only comes when you have made it a part of yourself, and the best way to make yourself a part of it—which comes to the same thing—is by writing in it.

—Mortimer Adler and Charles Van Doren, *How to Read a Book*

Marginal annotations, or notes written into the margins, are probably the best way to understand and remember what you read. That's because marginal notes require you to abbreviate and paraphrase the author's original language. Both activities ensure that your mind is working on the material, which helps you avoid a common mistake: assuming that just looking at the words means you have understood them.

When you abbreviate information, you have to be **selective**, figuring out first what sentences are central to the author's point. Then you have to determine what parts of those sentences are necessary to convey the writer's overall meaning in a shorthand fashion. In other words, you have to really think about the material to decide what you absolutely need for your notes and what you can leave out. It's this kind of **analysis**, or breaking into parts, that makes the author's words mean something to you and stay in your memory over time.

Paraphrasing and Memory

Paraphrasing, or exchanging the author's words for your own without altering the original meaning, is critical for the same reason. In the time you spend thinking about what language you can substitute for the author's, you have a chance to mull over the words on the page and decide how they were meant to be understood. As you look for words you can use to replace the author's, you are forced to process the meaning of each word in the original text.

The Reading Paraphrase versus the Writing Paraphrase

Keep in mind that paraphrasing key points in the margins of your texts is not the same as paraphrasing for a term paper. When you paraphrase for a paper, you have to make sure you retain the original meaning. Here, for instance, is an original piece of text followed by a paraphrase that would be appropriate for a term paper.

Original | The extent of religious intermarriage in the United States depends in good part on the particular religion being considered. Among the Old Order Amish, mate selection outside the group is practically nonexistent. However, intermarriage among the various Protestant denominations—Episcopalians, Baptists, Lutherans, Presbyterians, Methodists, and others—seems to be quite common.

Paraphrase for a Paper | In the United States, the degree of intermarriage allowed among members of a religious group varies according to the religion. Marrying outside the group is all but unheard of among the Amish. However, among the Protestant denominations, it's quite common.

Now here's a paraphrase that would be appropriate for marginal notes:

Paraphrase for Reading Notes | Acceptance of intermarriage varies with religion.
—Amish don't; Protestants do.

Paraphrasing while reading is a crucial part of learning from textbooks. It helps you remember what you read and identifies those portions of text you haven't completely understood. Any time you can't paraphrase, the chances are good that you haven't truly understood the material. If you want to ensure your success as a student, make paraphrasing while reading a regular habit.

Chapter 4 will go into more detail about how to paraphrase both formally for papers and informally for reading notes. But you can get started on paraphrasing immediately. You'll only get better at paraphrasing if you practice it yourself in an informal fashion and then learn more about how readers and writers create more formal paraphrases when they need to.

How to Paraphrase for Marginal Notes

◆

1. When you finish reading the paragraph or passage, ask yourself, without looking back at the page, what general point the author wants to get across. If you don't have an answer, re-read the passage.

2. If the point is still not completely clear, ask yourself what people, places, events, or ideas come up repeatedly in the selection.

3. Look for a general sentence that sums up the relationship among the people, places, events, or ideas repeatedly referred to in the paragraph.

4. Then, using as many of your own words as possible, paraphrase that general summary sentence.

5. Make your paraphrase as brief as possible, even if the result is not a grammatical sentence. Think of your paraphrase as a headline for the passage, e.g., "Even extinct volcanoes erupt"; "Alfred Wegener, father of continental drift"; "Ideas about being right-brained or left-brained not scientific." When it comes to reading notes, your paraphrase, as you can see from the examples, need not be a complete sentence.

6. Decide if you should also abbreviate and paraphrase one or two specific sentences used to explain the general one. If the specific details are not too complex in themselves, you can also just number them or give them labels such as *ex.* (for *example*) or *r1, r2, r3* (for *reasons*).

Marking Up the Text

In addition to paraphrasing, get into the habit of marking your text by underlining, highlighting, starring, and bracketing important material. Marking pages, like paraphrasing, forces you to think about the author's words. In the process of figuring out what to mark and what not, you are actually reprocessing what you've read, and that leads to improved comprehension and remembering.

Some Symbols for Marking Pages in Your Textbook ◆	Brackets or vertical lines for key passages	[ ]	|
	Underlining for important points	___ ___ ___
	Abbreviations to show the type of support: examples, studies, reasons, exceptions, statistics	Ex, Stu, R, Exc, Stat
	Numbers to itemize examples, reasons, steps, or studies	1, 2, 3
	Stars for particularly important statements or quotations	★ ★
	Boxes for key terms	▭
	Circles for important names, dates, or terms	○
	Exclamation points to show surprise	!!
	Question marks to indicate an unclear sentence or passage	??
	Connected arrows to highlight related statements	
	Marginal notes to record personal comments and questions	I don't believe this.

◆ EXERCISE 4   Taking Marginal Notes

DIRECTIONS   Read each passage. Then select the appropriate letter to identify the best marginal notes on the paragraph.

EXAMPLE   Ever since 1989, the first year in which DNA testing resulted in the release of an innocent prisoner, the public has been repeatedly confronted with evidence that far from being an impossibility, convicting the innocent is much more common than we feared. The Innocence Project, founded by Barry Scheck and Peter J. Neufeld, keeps a running record on its website of the hundreds of men and women imprisoned for murder or rape who have been cleared. They have been cleared most often by DNA testing but also by other kinds of evidence, such as mistaken eyewitness identifications. Death-row exonerations, of course, get the greatest public attention, but the number of wrongful convictions for lesser crimes is also alarming. (Tavris and Aronson, *Mistakes Were Made*, p. 130.)

Marginal Notes   a. DNA has proven that half the people on death row shouldn't be.

1. Barry Scheck and Peter J. Neufeld
2. Cleared by DNA testing

b. Since 1989, DNA evidence has exonerated hundreds of men and women.

1. Innocence Project keeps track of people cleared
2. Mistaken eyewitnesses also wrongfully convict

c. Many people who have found themselves on death row have ended up being exonerated.

1. Why? Mistaken eyewitness testimony
2. Death row convictions get more coverage

EXPLANATION   Answer *a* won't work because the passage as a whole doesn't talk just about people on death row. The authors make a point of mentioning people convicted of other kinds of crimes. Answer *b* is correct because it takes into account people on death row and other people in prison. It also makes clear the role of the Innocence Project. With its limited focus, answer *c* suffers from the same flaw as answer *a*. In addition, it fails to mention a key focus of the paragraph: People are exonerated *thanks to DNA evidence*. The specific support for the claim in answer *c* is also off the mark. People are proven innocent when it's discovered that eyewitness testimony is wrong, but the greater emphasis in the paragraph is on DNA evidence.

1. In 1978, when a Boeing 747 with 213 people aboard plunged into the Arabian Sea, people speculated about political terrorism. But as the Indian navy began to salvage pieces of the airplane, the investigators found no signs of fire, heat, or in-flight breakup. The airplane's crash-proof black boxes and cockpit voice recorders were intact. They indicated that the airplane's engines and controls had functioned normally, but that something in the cockpit had gone terribly wrong. The fault appeared to be the pilot's. On a quiet night, after twenty-two years of steady service, he had flown a perfectly sound airplane into the water.

Marginal Notes a. Even in 1978, if a plane crashed, there was speculation about political terrorism.

    1. Plane crashed into Arabian Sea

    2. Evidence showed plane functioning fine

b. On a quiet night, no one expected plane to crash into the sea.

    1. It was the Arabian Sea

    2. Indian navy salvaged wreckage

c. 1978 crash of Boeing 747 into Arabian Sea appeared pilot's fault

    1. No significant heat or crack up

    2. Plane's recovered equipment proved controls functioned normally

2. In 1954, twenty-two well-adjusted, eleven-year-old boys participated in a three-week study conducted by social psychologist Muzafer Sherif and his colleagues at a campsite in Robbers Cave in Oklahoma. On arrival, the boys were immediately assigned to one of two groups. Each group stayed in its own cabin. The cabins were located quite a distance apart in order to reduce contact between the two groups. The distance was also meant to encourage bonding within each group. After about a week, the researchers set up a series of competitive activities in which the two groups were pitted against each other so that either group lost or won. It didn't take long before group members were hostile toward those outside their own group, suggesting that group membership, for all its benefits, can create conflict. (Adapted from Waller, *Becoming Evil*, p. 238.)

Marginal Notes a. Muzafer Sherif's research suggests among pre-teen boys there's bound to be aggression and hostility.

    1. Two groups of eleven-year-olds

    2. Kids couldn't stand one another

b. Competitive games produce hostility.

    1. Two groups of eleven-year-old boys

    2. Friends before competition, enemies after

c. Muzafer Sherif's research highlights conflicts stemming from group bonding.

1. Eleven-year-old boys kept in 2 groups that engage in competitive game

2. Each group starts disliking other

 READING KEYS

◆ Whenever you spend time thinking about the author's words in order to abbreviate or paraphrase them, you are giving your brain the time it needs to understand what those words mean.

◆ Paraphrasing for reading notes and paraphrasing for term papers are two different things. Reading notes don't require the same level of formality, completeness, or grammatical correctness.

Learn the Language of Textbooks

The language of textbooks differs from the language we hear in casual conversation. Words that don't regularly turn up when we chat with family and friends appear all the time in textbook writing. How often, for instance, have you used the word *cognition*—the mental process of knowing something through reason, awareness, or judgment—in everyday conversation? You probably haven't used the word much. Yet if you read a psychology textbook, you'll see the word repeatedly.

Although it is partially true that the more common-in-conversation word *thinking* could be used as a substitute for *cognition*, that word choice would oversimplify what *cognition* stands for in the **context**, or setting, of psychology. Psychology texts, like almost all textbooks, describe and discuss the world in deeper and more complicated terms than you and I do when chatting with our friends. Thus, textbooks require a **specialized vocabulary**, or a body of words appropriate to the subject matter. Health and psychology texts, for instance, don't study the aging of one person; they study the aging of entire populations. The word for this is *gerontology*—studying the psychological, social, and biological effects of aging.

To help you develop a vocabulary of words typical for textbooks, each chapter in *Reading Keys* ends with ten new words to add to your textbook vocabulary. Your job is to learn these words in preparation for textbook assignments.

It's Not Just Specialized Vocabulary That Matters

To read your textbooks with efficiency, you have to learn the words essential to the subject matter. If you read a government text, for instance, you will encounter words such as *filibuster* (an extended speech used to prevent the passage of legislation) and *cloture* (a vote intended to end a filibuster). To fully understand how laws do, or do not, get passed, you need to know those words.

But it's not just specialized vocabulary that counts. To make your textbook assignments easier to read, you'll also have to generally ramp up your vocabulary. Textbook writers (and writers of other kinds of books as well) rely on a varied and extensive vocabulary. They have to. To avoid word repetition while keeping the same topic or topics before the reader's eyes, writers vary the words they use. If they didn't, readers would find the repetition so tiresome, they'd stop reading.

Take, for example, a writer discussing Winston Churchill, England's prime minister during World War II. Churchill was famous for his dark and depressed moods. To provide an extended discussion of how these moods affected Churchill's behavior, the writer would need some **synonyms**, or words similar in meaning, for the word "depressed." Thus the writer might use words such as *morose*, *melancholy*, and *dour*.

Because words like these are less common in casual conversation, you might have to struggle a bit to discover the author's meaning. But the larger your general vocabulary is, the easier it will be to read your textbooks without hesitation, which means it's in your interest to make regular vocabulary study part of your schedule. At least three times a week, spend a half-hour to forty-five minutes learning new words. To help you get started, Chapter 1 will supply ten words that are essential to academic reading.

Don't Forget Idioms

Idioms are expressions common to one language and difficult or impossible to translate into another. When idioms are translated, they don't seem to make sense or fit the context. A non-native speaker, for instance, might be puzzled by the following sentence, which uses the idiom "whistle blower": "Perhaps the most famous *whistle blower* of all time was

John Dean, who helped bring down Richard Nixon's presidency." Some-one from another country might, initially at least, wonder how a person blowing a whistle could destroy a president's career. The person's confusion would stem from not knowing the idiom *whistle blower*. The term refers to someone who informs the press or legal officials about crimes committed by a company or an institution to which he or she belongs.

Idioms are most common in ordinary speech. However, they do make their appearance in textbooks. *Whistle blower*, for instance, is a common term in business and legal textbooks. In fact, there is even whistle blowing legislation, designed to protect those who reveal the ethical lapses of their company.

Because idioms do appear in textbooks, it's a good idea to include them in your review of vocabulary words. To help you do just that, the chapters in this text will periodically introduce an important idiom under the heading "Idiom Alert." If you don't already know the idiom, make a note of it in a vocabulary notebook or card.

⚷ READING KEYS

◆ Spend a few minutes every day working on your specialized and general vocabularies and you will be amazed at how much more quickly and efficiently you can read your textbooks.

◆ When learning new vocabulary, give idioms the attention they deserve. Idioms are expressions that have developed their meaning through usage in a particular language. Thus, they cannot be translated word for word. As a result, they often mystify non-native speakers.

ROUNDING UP THE KEYS

Here is a list of all the reading keys introduced in the chapter. Use them to review for the test on page 43. If a particular reading key doesn't make sense on its own, go back to the page where it appeared and review the section preceding it.

READING KEY: Learn How to Develop and Maintain Concentration

◆ Getting yourself concentrated or focused to study doesn't just happen; it's something you have to prepare for. (p. 3)

READING KEY: Preview Your Assignments

◆ Getting an overall picture of what's in a chapter *before* you begin reading makes it easier to fit the pieces of the chapter together *while* you are reading. (p. 8)

READING KEY: Use the Web for Background Knowledge

◆ Make your search term as specific as possible. The more focused and precise the search term is, the better your results will be. (p. 14)

READING KEY: Read Strategically

◆ To read strategically is to read with a plan. It's reading with questions and predictions in mind that are then answered, confirmed, or revised. (p. 15)

READING KEY: Make Connections Between General and Specific Sentences

◆ To follow the author's train of thought, readers need to recognize generalizations and look for the specific sentences that explain them. (p. 16)

READING KEYS: Make Marginal Notes

◆ Whenever you spend time thinking about the author's words in order to abbreviate or paraphrase them, you are giving your brain the time it needs to understand what those words mean. (p. 24)

◆ Paraphrasing for reading notes and paraphrasing for term papers are two different things. Reading notes don't require the same level of formality, completeness, or grammatical correctness. (p. 24)

⊙ᴛ READING KEYS: Learn the Language of Textbooks

- ◆ Spend a few minutes every day working on your specialized and general vocabularies and you will be amazed at how much more quickly and efficiently you can read your textbooks. (p. 26)

- ◆ When learning new vocabulary, give idioms the attention they deserve. Idioms are expressions that have developed their meaning through usage in a particular language. Thus, they cannot be translated word for word. As a result, they often mystify non-native speakers. (p. 26)

Ten Words for Your Textbook Vocabulary

To get you started working on your academic vocabulary, here are ten words you absolutely must know to read textbooks from just about *any* discipline. Each word is followed by a textbook example. These words, however, can be found in a wide variety of disciplines. They are not limited to the subject of the textbook illustration.

1. **facilitate:** to make easier

   To fully *facilitate* coverage of political campaigns, staffers supply the media with daily schedules, advance copies of speeches, and access to telephone and fax machines. (Gitelson et al., *American Government*, p. 247.)

2. **innovations:** inventions, new

   Four *innovations* in Adjustable Rate Mortgages have been developed. (Garman and Forgue, *Personal Finance*, p. 302.)

3. **stimulant:** something that provokes an action or a response

   As a *stimulant*, nicotine speeds up the heart rate, dampens appetite, and produces a mild rush or psychological kick. (Nevid, *Psychology: Concepts and Applications*, p. 167.)

4. **repercussion:** consequence, result, often negative

   By empowering employees to make their own decisions and try new ideas without *repercussions* and by treating them as people, not merely workers, managers strive to make working at Southwest a positive experience for all employees. (Pride et al., *Business*, p. 205.)

5. **dearth:** scarce supply

   For many years, the parents of daughters complained about the *dearth* of toys available to them; other than Barbie, what was there? (Boyes and Melvin, *Fundamentals of Economics*, p. 123.)

6. **imminent:** immediate

   Whether a volcano poses an *imminent* threat to human life and property cannot always be readily determined. (Adapted from Chernicoff and Fox, *Essentials of Geology*, p. 62.)

7. **derive:** come or stem from

In German, the word "schadenfreude" refers to pleasures *derived* from another's misfortunes. (Matsumoto, *People*, p. 120.)

8. **components:** parts or elements

There are several important *components* involved in the prevention of child abuse. (Mullen et al., *Connections for Health*, p. 335.)

9. **advocate:** supporter

Alexander Hamilton was an early *advocate* of a strong central government. (Adapted from Berkin et al., *Making America*, p. 208.)

10. **annihilated:** destroyed

In sub-Saharan Africa, so many adults have been *annihilated* by HIV/AIDS that an entire generation of children is now without parents. (Nevid, *Psychology: Concepts and Applications*, p. 451.)

◆ **EXERCISE 5**   **Building an Academic Vocabulary**

DIRECTIONS   Fill in the blanks with one of the words listed below.

annihilate	imminent	facilitate	repercussions	derives
advocate	dearth	components	stimulant	innovations

1. As a(n) _____ of states' rights, John C. Calhoun insisted that an individual state government could refuse legislation imposed by the national government.

2. The _____ arrival of the presidential candidate had reporters in a frenzy.

3. The development of the birth control pill had enormous social _____.

4. Currently, there is a serious _____ of part-time jobs for college students, and many students, who use their summer earnings for school, are worried.

5. The chemicals used to _____ the mosquitoes causing malaria ended up killing beneficial insects as well.

6. The person appointed to _____ the discussion between opponents was highly ineffective, and it didn't take long for the discussion to become an angry free-for-all.

7. A good speech has to have three _____: a catchy introduction, a point, and a rousing conclusion.

8. The _____ in teacher training were supposed to reap big rewards; but after a year, the university went back to more traditional methods.

9. The company _____ most of its profits from overseas sales.

10. For most people, coffee is a strong _____.

DIGGING **Muscle Reading**
DEEPER

Looking Ahead Chapter 1 offered some general suggestions for how to read your textbooks. What follows is a more detailed description of how to respond to your textbook assignments.

1 Picture yourself sitting at a desk, a book in your hands. Your eyes are open, and it looks as if you're reading. Suddenly your head jerks up. You blink. You realize your eyes have been scanning the page for 10 minutes, and you can't remember a single thing you have read. Or picture this: You've had a hard day. You were up at 6 a.m. to get the kids ready for school. A coworker called in sick, and you missed your lunch trying to do his job as well as your own. You picked up the kids, then had to shop for dinner. Dinner was late, of course, and the kids were grumpy.

2 Finally, you get to your books at 8 p.m. You begin a reading assignment on something called "the equity method of accounting for common stock investments." "I am preparing for the future," you tell yourself, as you plod through two paragraphs and begin the third. Suddenly, everything in the room looks different. Your head is resting on your elbow, which is resting on the equity method of accounting. The clock reads 11:00 p.m. Say good-bye to three hours.

3 Sometimes the only difference between a sleeping pill and a textbook is that the textbook doesn't have a warning on the label about operating heavy machinery.

4 Contrast this scenario with the image of an active reader. This is a person who:

- Stays alert, poses questions about what she reads, and searches for the answers.
- Recognizes levels of information within the text, separating the main points and general principles from supporting details.
- Quizzes herself about the material, makes written notes, and lists unanswered questions.
- Instantly spots key terms and takes the time to find the definitions of unfamiliar words.
- Thinks critically about the ideas in the text and looks for ways to apply them.

5 That sounds like a lot to do. Yet skilled readers routinely accomplish all this and more—while enjoying reading. One way to experience this kind of

success is to approach reading with a system in mind. An example is Muscle Reading. You can use it to avoid mental minivacations and reduce the number of unscheduled naps during study time, even after a hard day.

6   Muscle Reading is a way to decrease difficulty and struggle by increasing energy and skill. Once you learn this system, you might actually spend less time on your reading and get more out of it. This is not to say that Muscle Reading will make your education a breeze. Muscle Reading might even look like more work at first. Effective textbook reading is an active, energy-consuming, sit-on-the-edge-of-your-seat business. That's why this strategy is called Muscle Reading.

How Muscle Reading Works

7 Muscle Reading is a three-phase technique you can use to extract the ideas and information you want. Phase one includes steps to take *before* you read. Phase two includes steps to take *while* you read. Phase three includes steps to take *after* you read. Each phase has three steps.

Phase One:

Before you read

Step 1: Preview
Step 2: Outline
Step 3 : Question

Phase Two:

While you read

Step 4: Read
Step 5: Underline
Step 6: Answer

Phase Three:

After you read

Step 7: Recite
Step 8: Review
Step 9: Review again

Muscle Reading could take a little time to learn. At first you might feel it's slowing you down. That's natural when you're gaining a new skill. Mastery comes with time and practice.

Phase 1: Before You Read

8 **Preview**   Before you start reading, preview the entire assignment. You don't have to memorize what you preview to get value from this step. Previewing sets the stage for incoming information by warming up a space in your mental storage area.

9   If you are starting a new book, look over the table of contents and flip through the text page by page. If you're going to read one chapter, flip through the pages of that chapter. Even if your assignment is merely a few pages in a book, you can benefit from a brief preview of the table of contents.

10   Keep the preview short. If the entire reading assignment will take less than an hour, your preview might take five minutes. Previewing is also a way to get yourself started when an assignment looks too big to handle. It is an easy way to step into the material.

11   Keep an eye out for summary statements. If the assignment is long or complex, read the summary first. Many textbooks have summaries in the introduction or at the end of each chapter.

12   Read all chapter headings and subheadings. Like the headlines in a newspaper, these are usually printed in large, bold type. Often headings are brief summaries in themselves.

13   When previewing, seek out familiar concepts, facts, or ideas. These items can help increase comprehension by linking new information to previously learned material. Look for ideas that spark your imagination or curiosity. Inspect drawings, diagrams, charts, tables, graphs, and photographs. Imagine what kinds of questions will show up on a test. Previewing helps to clarify your purpose for reading. Ask yourself what you will do with this material and how it can relate to your long-term goals. Are you reading just to get the main points? Key supporting details? Additional details? All of the above? Your answers will guide what you do with each step that follows.

14 **Outline**   With complex material, take time to understand the structure of what you are about to read. Outlining actively organizes your thoughts about the assignment and can help make complex information easier to understand.

15   If your textbook provides chapter outlines, spend some time studying them. When an outline is not provided, sketch a brief one in the margin of

your book or at the beginning of your notes on a separate sheet of paper. Later, as you read and take notes, you can add to your outline.

16   Headings in the text can serve as major and minor entries in your outline. For example, the heading for this [section] is "Phase 1: Before You Read," and the subheadings list the three steps in this phase. When you outline, feel free to rewrite headings so that they are more meaningful to you.

17   The amount of time you spend on this step will vary. For some assignments, a few minutes is all you might need. For other assignments (fiction and poetry, for example), you can skip this step altogether.

18   **Question**   Before you begin a careful reading, determine what you want from an assignment. Then write down a list of questions, including any that resulted from your preview of the materials.

19   Another useful technique is to turn chapter headings and subheadings into questions. For example, if a heading is "Transference and suggestion," you can ask yourself, "What are *transference* and *suggestion*? How does *transference* relate to *suggestion*?" Make up a quiz as if you were teaching this subject to your classmates.

20   If there are no headings, look for key sentences and turn these into questions. These sentences usually show up at the beginnings or ends of paragraphs and sections.

21   Have fun with this technique. Make the questions playful or creative. You don't need to answer every question that you ask. The purpose of making up questions is to get your brain involved in the assignment. Take your unanswered questions to class, where they can be springboards for class discussion.

22   Demand your money's worth from your textbook. If you do not understand a concept, write specific questions about it. The more detailed your questions, the more powerful this technique becomes.

Phase 2: While You Read

23   **Read**   At last! You have previewed the assignment, organized it in your mind, and formulated questions. Now you are ready to begin reading.

24   Before you dive into the first paragraph, take a few moments to reflect on what you already know about this subject. Do this even if you think you know nothing. This technique prepares your brain to accept the information that follows.

25   As you read, be conscious of where you are and what you are doing. When you notice your attention wandering, gently bring it back to the present moment. . . .

26   One way to stay focused is to avoid marathon reading sessions. Schedule breaks and set a reasonable goal for the entire session. Then reward yourself with an enjoyable activity for five or 10 minutes every hour or two.

27   For difficult reading, set more limited goals. Read for a half-hour and then take a break. Most students find that shorter periods of reading

Five Smart Ways to Highlight a Text

Underlining a text with a pen can make underlined sections—the important parts—harder to read. As an alternative, many students use colored highlighters to flag key words and sentences.

Highlighting can be a powerful tool. It also presents a danger—the ever-present temptation to highlight too much text. Excessive highlighting leads to wasted time during reviews and can also spoil the appearance of your books. Get the most out of all that money you pay for books. Highlight in an efficient way that leaves texts readable for years to come.

Read carefully first. Read an entire chapter or section at least once before you begin highlighting. Don't be in a hurry to mark up your book. Get to know the text first. Make two or three passes through difficult sections before you highlight.

Make choices up front about what to highlight. Perhaps you can accomplish your purposes by highlighting only certain chapters or sections of a text. When you highlight, remember to look for passages that directly answer the questions you posed during step 3 of Muscle Reading. Within these passages, highlight individual words, phrases, or sentences rather than whole paragraphs. The important thing is to choose an overall strategy before you put highlighter to paper.

Recite first. You might want to apply step 7 of Muscle Reading before you highlight. Talking about what you read—to yourself or with other people—can help you grasp the essence of a text. Recite first, then go back and highlight. You'll probably highlight more selectively.

Underline, then highlight. Underline key passages lightly in pencil. Then close your text and come back to it later. Assess your underlining. Perhaps you can highlight less than you underlined and still capture the key points.

Use highlighting to monitor your comprehension. Critical thinking plays a role in underlining and highlighting. When highlighting, you're making moment-by-moment decisions about what you want to remember from a text. You're also making inferences about what material might be included on a test.

Take your critical thinking a step further by using highlighting to check your comprehension. Stop reading periodically and look back over the sentences you've highlighted. See if you are making accurate distinctions between main points and supporting material. Highlighting too much—more than 10 percent of the text—can be a sign that you're not making this distinction and that you don't fully understand what you're reading. . . .

distributed throughout the day and week can be more effective than long sessions. You can use the following four techniques to stay focused as you read.

28   *First*, visualize the material. Form mental pictures of the concepts as they are presented. If you read that a voucher system can help control cash disbursements, picture a voucher handing out dollar bills. Using visual imagery in this way can help deepen your understanding of the text while allowing information to be transferred into your long-term memory.

29   *Second*, read the material out loud, especially if it is complicated. Some of us remember better and understand more quickly when we hear an idea.

30   *Third*, get a "feel" for the subject. For example, let's say you are reading about a microorganism, a paramecium, in your biology text. Imagine what it would feel like to run your finger around the long, cigar-shaped body of the organism. Imagine feeling the large fold of its gullet on one side and the tickle of the hairy little cilia as they wiggle in your hand.

31   *Fourth*, remember that a goal of your reading is to answer the questions you listed during phase one. After you've identified the key questions, predict how the author will answer them. Then read to find out if your predictions were accurate.

32   A final note: It's easy to fool yourself about reading. Just having an open book in your hand and moving your eyes across a page doesn't mean you are reading effectively. Reading textbooks takes energy, even if you do it sitting down. . . .

33   **Underline**   Deface your books. Use them up. Have fun writing in them. Indulge yourself as you never could with your grade-school books. The purpose of making marks in a text is to call out important concepts or information that you will need to review later. Underlining can save lots of time when you are studying for tests.

34   Underlining offers a secondary benefit. When you read with a pen or pencil in your hand, you involve your kinesthetic senses of touch and motion. Being physical with your books can help build strong neural pathways in your memory.

35   Avoid underlining too soon. Wait until you complete a chapter or section to make sure you know the key points. Then mark up the text. Sometimes, underlining after you read each paragraph works best. Underline sparingly, usually less than 10 percent of the text. If you mark up too much on a page, you defeat the purpose—to flag the most important material for review. In addition to underlining, you can mark up a text in the following ways:

- Place an asterisk (*) or an exclamation point (!) in the margin next to an especially important sentence or term.

- Circle key terms and words to look up later in a dictionary.
- Write short definitions of key terms in the margin.
- Write a "Q" in the margin to highlight possible test questions, passages you don't understand, and questions to ask in class.
- Write personal comments in the margin—points of agreement or disagreement with the author.
- Write mini-indexes in the margin, that is, the numbers of other pages in the book where the same topic is discussed.
- Write summaries by listing the main points or key events covered in a chapter.
- Rewrite chapter titles, headings, and subheadings so that they're more meaningful to you.
- Draw diagrams, pictures, tables, or maps that translate text into visual terms.
- Number each step in a list or series of related points.

36   **Answer**   As you read, seek out the answers to your questions and write them down. Fill in your outline. Jot down new questions and note when you don't find the answers you are looking for. Use these notes to ask questions in class, or see your instructor personally. . . .

Phase 3: After You Read

37   **Recite**   Talk to yourself about what you've read. Or talk to someone else. When you're finished with a reading assignment, make a speech about it. A classic study suggests that you can profitably devote up to 80 percent of your study time to active reciting. When you recite, you practice an important aspect of metacognition—synthesis, or combining individual ideas and facts into a meaningful whole.

38   One way to get yourself to recite is to look at each underlined point. Note what you marked, then put the book down and start talking out loud. Explain as much as you can about that particular point. To make this technique more effective, do it in front of a mirror. It might seem silly, but the benefits can be enormous. Reap them at exam time.

39   Classmates are even better than mirrors. Form a group and practice teaching each other what you have read. One of the best ways to learn anything is to teach it to someone else. In addition, talk about your reading whenever you can. Tell friends and family members what you're learning from your textbooks. Talking about your reading reinforces a valuable skill—the ability to summarize. To practice this skill, pick one chapter (or one section of one chapter) from any of your textbooks. State the main

topic covered in this chapter. Then state the main points that the author makes about this topic.

40   For example, the main topic up to this point in this chapter is Muscle Reading. The main point about this topic is that Muscle Reading includes three phases—steps to take before you read, while you read, and after you read. For a more detailed summary, you could name each of the nine steps.

Note: This "topic-point" method does not work so well when you want to summarize short stories, novels, plays, and other works of fiction. Instead, focus on action. In most stories, the main character confronts a major problem and takes a series of actions to solve it. Describe that problem and talk about the character's key actions—the turning points in the story.

41 **Review**   Plan to do your first complete review within 24 hours of reading the material. Sound the trumpets! This point is critical: A review within 24 hours moves information from your short-term memory to your long-term memory. Review within one day. If you read it on Wednesday, review it on Thursday. During this review, look over your notes and clear up anything you don't understand. Recite some of the main points again. This review can be short. You might spend as little as 15 minutes reviewing a difficult two-hour reading assignment. Investing that time now can save you hours later when studying for exams.

42 **Review Again**   The final step in Muscle Reading is the weekly or monthly review. This step can be very short—perhaps only four or five minutes per

Muscle Reading—A Leaner Approach

Keep in mind that Muscle Reading is an overall approach, not a rigid, step-by-step procedure. Here's a shorter variation that students have found helpful. Practice it with any chapter in this book:

Preview and question. Flip through the pages, looking at anything that catches your eye—headings, subheadings, illustrations, photographs. Turn the title of each article into a question. For example, "How Muscle Reading Works" can become "How does Muscle Reading work?" List your questions on a separate sheet of paper, or write each question on a 3 × 5 card.

Read to answer your questions. Read each chapter section, then go back over the text and underline or highlight answers to the appropriate questions on your list.

Recite and review. When you're done with the chapter, close the book. Recite by reading each question—and answering it—out loud. Review the chapter by looking up the answers to your questions. (It's easy—they're already highlighted.) Review again by quizzing yourself one more time with your list of questions.

assignment. Simply go over your notes. Read the highlighted parts of your text. Recite one or two of the more complicated points.

43   The purpose of these reviews is to keep the neural pathways to the information open and to make them more distinct. That way, the information can be easier to recall. You can accomplish these short reviews anytime, anywhere, if you are prepared.

44   Conduct a five-minute review while you are waiting for a bus, for your socks to dry, or for the water to boil. Three-by-five cards are a handy review tool. Write ideas, formulas, concepts, and facts on cards and carry them with you. These short review periods can be effortless and fun.

45   Sometimes longer review periods are appropriate. For example, if you found an assignment difficult, consider rereading it. Start over, as if you had never seen the material before. Sometimes a second reading will provide you with surprising insights.

46   Decades ago, psychologists identified the primacy-recency effect, which suggests that we most easily remember the first and last items in any presentation. Previewing and reviewing your reading can put this theory to work for you.

Sharpening Your Skills

DIRECTIONS   Answer the following questions by filling in the blanks.

1. What does the author suggest in paragraph 3, when he says, "Sometimes the only difference between a sleeping pill and a textbook is that the textbook doesn't have a warning on the label about operating heavy machinery"?

   _____

   _____

2. According to the author, and in your own words, what are the characteristics of an active reader?

   _____

   _____

   _____

   _____

3. Does what the author says about active reading make sense to you? Why or why not?

_____

4. Would you call yourself an active reader? Why or why not?

_____

5. According to the author, how do you know when you have high-lighted too much?

_____

6. In your own words, what are the two benefits of marking up a text?

_____

_____

_____

7. What makes talking about what you have read so valuable?

_____

8. Which of the techniques described in this reading do you already use?

_____

Which techniques, if any, do you _not_ use when you study?

_____

Do you think you will use them from now on? Why or why not?

_____

9. According to the author, why is it easy for us to "fool" ourselves about reading?

_____

_____

10. In your own words, what does it mean to be a "muscle reader"?

_____

_____

_____

_____

_____

_____

_____

▶ TEST 1   **Reviewing the Key Points**

DIRECTIONS   Answer the following questions by circling *T* (true) or *F* (false). *Note*: Read the questions carefully. Part of a question may be true and part may be false, making the whole sentence false.

T   *F*   **1.** The ability to concentrate comes naturally if you just place yourself in the right setting.

T   *F*   **2.** Success statements identify future goals and connect them to current assignments.

T   *F*   **3.** There is no such thing as a good habit. All habits interfere with spontaneous and creative thought.

T   *F*   **4.** Previewing a chapter before reading is important because it helps the reader figure out how long the chapter will take to read.

T   *F*   **5.** Making your Internet search term as precise and focused as possible is the key to getting useful background information about the topics covered in a reading assignment.

T   *F*   **6.** If you paraphrase while reading, there's no need to mark pages while reading.

T   *F*   **7.** Specific sentences sum up many individual events while general ones provide illustrations of those events.

T   *F*   **8.** Small changes in the original meaning are acceptable when the reader is paraphrasing just to take marginal notes.

T   *F*   **9.** When paraphrasing for reading notes, it's important to maintain standards of formal grammar exactly as if you were paraphrasing for a term paper.

T   *F*   **10.** Idioms are expressions that develop over time within a given language and cannot be translated word for word; thus, they are often puzzling to non-native speakers.

To correct your test, turn to page 553. If one or more of your answers is incorrect, re-read the Rounding Up the Keys section of the chapter to find out where your mistake might be.

▶ **TEST 2**   **Developing Your Textbook Vocabulary**

DIRECTIONS   Fill in the blanks with one of the words listed below.

derived	annihilation	imminent	advocate	innovative
components	dearth	facilitate	stimulant	repercussions

1. Knowing that the arrival of the president was _____ , officials were scurrying around at a frantic pace trying to make sure that everything was in order and ready for his arrival.

2. Changes in the regulations governing the country's banks had enormous and devastating _____ on taxpayers.

3. The fear of civil war in Iraq persists because the Sunni and Shia sects of Islam feel so much hostility toward each other that their goal is not cooperation but _____.

4. Many people still believe that playing Mozart for infants will improve their IQ; however, there is a(n) _____ of hard evidence proving such claims.

5. Throughout his Supreme Court career, Chief Justice Earl Warren was a strong _____ for the rights of the individual.

6. The journalist who was supposed to _____ the debate between the two candidates failed miserably at the job.

7. People think that alcohol is a(n) _____, but actually it has the opposite effect.

8. Opium is a drug _____ from poppies.

9. The directions suggested that not all of the _____ for the hot tub had been included in the box.

10. Steve Jobs, the head of Apple, was, from the beginning, a(n) _____ thinker who was always one step ahead of his competitors.

More on Words and Meanings

2

IN THIS CHAPTER, YOU WILL LEARN

- how context clues can suggest word meaning.
- how the context of a word can alter its meaning.
- how a knowledge of word parts can help you define unfamiliar words.

No matter how much time you spend improving your vocabulary, there will always be some words you don't know. The crucial question is, What do you do when you come across unfamiliar words? Do you immediately open a dictionary? Or do you just skip over the words? Unfortunately, neither strategy is very effective. This is especially true when reading textbooks. Too many interruptions to check the dictionary can weaken your concentration. Ignoring unfamiliar words can undermine comprehension. The good news is that other strategies do exist. This chapter describes two of the most useful ones. It also encourages you to start a notebook or file in which you record words common to textbooks. Then you can review these words on a regular basis until they are part of your vocabulary.

Using Context Clues

Frequently, the context—the sentence or passage in which an unfamiliar word appears—offers a clue to its meaning. Armed with that clue, you can usually figure out an **approximate definition**. An approximate definition is usually not the same as the dictionary definition. However, it will be close enough to let you make sense of the passage. The most common kinds of context clues are (1) restatement, (2) contrast, (3) example, and (4) general knowledge.

O—⫟ READING KEY
- ◆ Approximate definitions derived from context allow you to keep reading without interruption.

Restatement Clues

If a word or phrase is unfamiliar, don't just ignore it. Instead, scan the rest of the sentence. Look as well at the sentence that follows. You may find a **synonym** or simpler rephrasing of the unknown word. Look, for example, at the restatement clue in the following passage. Can you use context to figure out the meaning of *decipher*?

> During World War II, the British repeatedly tried to *decipher* the Germans' code. However, they couldn't figure it out until mathematician Alan Turing discovered the key to the code.

Did you recognize the restatement clue "figure it out" and come up with a meaning? If you did, you realized that definitions such as "figure it out," "determine," and "unlock" all would be appropriate substitutes for the word *decipher*.

Restatement Clues and Specialized Vocabulary

Textbooks make heavy use of restatement clues. This is particularly true when the author is dealing with **specialized vocabulary**, or the words that are essential to understanding a particular subject matter. Note, for instance, how the author of the following passage first highlights a term essential to sociological discussions, *social mobility*. Then he follows it with a definition.

> In almost all societies there is some **social mobility**, movement from one social standing to another. (Adapted from Thio, *Society: Myths and Realities*, p. 218.)

Although textbook authors commonly put key words or terms into boldface or italics, be prepared as well for restatement clues to be introduced by colons, semicolons, parentheses, and dashes. The following excerpt shows how dashes make the definition stand out:

> In an average person, the *vital capacity*—maximum amount of air you can inhale and exhale—is about 4.5 liters (8.4 pints). (Otto and Towle, *Modern Biology*, p. 24.)

O⟶ READING KEYS

◆ Restatement clues are the most common context clues in textbooks.
◆ In addition to boldface and italics, colons, semicolons, dashes, and parentheses can also signal the presence of restatement clues.

◆ EXERCISE 1   Recognizing Restatement Clues

DIRECTIONS   Use the underlined restatement clues to determine the approximate meaning for the italicized words.

EXAMPLE   The lawyer claimed that the police had no *valid* evidence linking her client to the crime. She argued that the only <u>sound</u> evidence they had related to her client's character rather than his crime.

a. visual
b. secondary
ⓒ reliable
d. unusual

EXPLANATION   In the first sentence, the author uses the word *valid* to describe the evidence. In the second, he uses the word *sound*, meaning reliable. The restatement clue points to *reliable* as the best answer.

1. In addition to women, Asians are also victims of the *glass ceiling*—the <u>barrier</u> that keeps minority professionals from holding leadership positions. (Adapted from Thio, *Society: Myths and Realities*, p. 245.)

a. insult
b. ridicule

c. bias

d. demote

2. His *recollections* of the past were hazy at best; <u>thoughts of the past</u> were so depressing he did not wish to dredge them up.

a. words

b. insults

c. purchases

d. memories

3. The photographer's pictures of the *urban* poor suggested that life <u>in the city</u> was a living hell for those without money.

a. having to do with cities

b. related to the country

c. starving

d. foreign

4. His patients thought of the doctor as *altruistic*. However, the nurses he worked with did not consider him so <u>selfless</u>.

a. selfish

b. giving

c. impatient

d. religious

5. Police must have a reasonable suspicion that a suspect is armed and dangerous in order to *frisk*, or <u>pat down the outer clothing</u>, for concealed weapons. (Adapted from Adler et al., *Criminal Justice*, p. 209.)

a. jail

b. search

c. handcuff

d. hold

◆ **EXERCISE 2**   **Recognizing Restatement Clues**

DIRECTIONS   Use the restatement clues to determine the approximate meaning for the italicized words.

EXAMPLE   The ease and speed with which children acquire language have caused some researchers to conclude that children are born with a *predisposition*, or built-in tendency, to learn language. (Adapted from Seifert and Hoffnung, *Child and Adolescent Development*, p. 42.)

Predisposition means <u>having an inborn ability</u>.

EXPLANATION   In this case, the comma followed by the word *or* is a signal that a restatement will follow, as indeed it does. *Predisposition* means having a built-in or an inborn tendency or ability.

1. Concern over the *escalating*, some would even say skyrocketing, influence of wealthy special interests in campaigns has led some reform groups like Common Cause to call for stricter regulation of campaign contributions by individuals and groups.

   Escalating means _____.

2. In the middle of a tantrum, the child could not be *appeased*; no matter what his mother did, he would not calm down.

   Appeased means _____.

3. The candidate was known for his *volatile* temper. It was so explosive, in fact, that even his closest aides feared angering him.

   Volatile means _____.

4. A *staunch* opponent of capital punishment, the writer became even more passionate in her conviction after the state executed a young man with a serious learning disability.

   Staunch means _____.

5. How we *appraise*, or look at, events can depend on what the events mean to us personally. The exact same event, such as pregnancy or job change, can lead to feelings of joy, fear, or even anger, depending on the individual. (Adapted from Nevid, *Psychology: Concepts and Applications*, p. 332.)

   Appraise means _____.

Contrast Clues

Contrast clues tell you what a word *doesn't* mean. Armed with the *antonym*—a word or phrase opposite in meaning—you can often develop a good approximate definition. Look, for example, at how the phrase *tongue-tied* offers a clue to the meaning of *articulate*.

> As a young man, he had lacked confidence and became <u>tongue-tied</u> when he had to talk in a group, but as he grew older and more confident, he was relaxed and *articulate*, even in a crowd.

Based on the underlined contrast clue, what do you think *articulate* means? Would you vote for "gifted with words," "well-spoken," or "expressive"? If so, you have made good use of the contrast clue.

Contrast clues are likely to appear whenever the author points out differences between two topics. They are also likely to appear following transitional words and phrases such as *however*, *but*, *in contrast*, *whereas*, and *while*. **Transitions** are verbal bridges that identify relationships and allow readers to move easily from thought to thought. The transitions identified here, called **contrast** or **reversal transitions**, signal a shift or change from the point of the previous sentence. Anytime you are trying to determine the meaning of an unfamiliar word and spot a contrast or reversal transition, be aware that the sentence might also contain a contrast clue to word meaning.

⚷ READING KEYS
- ♦ Contrast clues tell you what a word doesn't mean.
- ♦ Look for contrast clues when the author describes differences between two people, things, or ideas.
- ♦ Transitional words like *however*, *whereas*, and *yet* also signal the presence of contrast clues.

♦ **EXERCISE 3**   **Recognizing Contrast Clues**

DIRECTIONS   Use the underlined contrast clues to determine approximate meanings for the italicized words.

EXAMPLE   Author Mark Twain was always coming up with what he thought were *ingenious* new inventions, but in fact, they were usually <u>not so clever</u> as he thought.

a. simple

b. audacious

c. true

(d.) smart

EXPLANATION   In this sentence, the word *ingenious* is the opposite of "not so clever," making *smart* the best choice for an answer.

1. Unlike most pop singers whose careers last <u>only a few years</u>, Madonna has had unusual *longevity*.

    a. popularity

    b. huge success

    c. extended life

    d. fame

2. People who are successful in life *persevere* in the face of obstacles, rather than <u>giving up</u>.

    a. cheer up

    b. persist

    c. turn away

    d. turn inward

3. The French soldiers were unable to *pacify* the Ivory Coast rebellion; if anything, the rebels <u>were increasing in both strength and violence</u>.

    a. challenge

    b. excite

    c. calm

    d. portray

4. Despite the poor lighting, the photographs <u>captured the scene exactly</u>, with almost no *distortion*.

    a. error

    b. beauty

    c. exaggeration

    d. addition

5. The police were supposed to keep the witness's house under *surveillance* 24 hours a day, but somehow the order did not go through and the house was <u>left unobserved</u> during daylight.

   a. observation

   b. wraps

   c. construction

   d. misunderstanding

◆ EXERCISE 4   **Recognizing Contrast Clues**

DIRECTIONS   Use the contrast clues to determine approximate meanings for the italicized words.

EXAMPLE   People used to believe that mental illness was caused by evil spirits. But, thankfully, that is no longer the *prevailing* opinion.

Prevailing means   current, up-to-date, widespread   .

EXPLANATION   In this passage, the *prevailing* opinion is contrasted with an opinion held in the past. Thus, "current," "up-to-date," and "widespread" make good approximate definitions.

1. The painting may not be the real thing, but it is an excellent *facsimile*.

   Facsimile means _____.

2. That story appeared on the front page of the newspaper, but it was still more *fiction* than reality.

   Fiction means _____.

3. Although the singer wore *flamboyant* costumes onstage, offstage his clothes were plain and unremarkable.

   Flamboyant means _____.

4. Just when the wheat seemed to be thriving, a plague of locusts arrived and *ravaged* the farmers' fields.

   Ravaged means _____.

5. The bouncer had only glanced at her companion's I.D., but he *scrutinized* her fake driver's license very carefully.

Scrutinized means _____.

Example Clues

Context can also provide you with examples of the behavior or activity related to the word you don't know. For an illustration, read the following sentence:

> Jay's feelings about rap music were *ambivalent*. He admired the clever rhyming lyrics but detested the ideas they conveyed.

Notice how Jay felt both admiration and dislike. Because this is an example of conflicted feelings, it's safe to say that *ambivalent* probably means something like "contradictory" or "contrary."

With example clues, you may have to ask yourself, "What kind of event, behavior, or experience does this example illustrate?" Once you answer that question, you also have your approximate meaning. Particularly in textbooks, examples are often introduced by transitions like "for instance," "for example," "more specifically," and "more precisely." These phrases are more likely to follow the words they illustrate than to precede them.

◆ **EXERCISE 5**　　**Recognizing Example Clues**

DIRECTIONS　　Use the example clues to determine approximate meanings for the italicized words.

EXAMPLE　　The British *aristocracy* doesn't generally have a way with ordinary people. Princess Diana was a spectacular exception to that rule.

a. theater
b. nobility
c. kings
d. folks

EXPLANATION　　In this sentence, Princess Diana is an example of the *aristocracy*. Thus, the only answer that makes sense is *b*, nobility.

1. Joan of Arc was *valiant* to the end, refusing to show any fear as men with torches prepared to burn her at the stake.
   a. mad
   b. brave
   c. quiet
   d. outraged

2. As a child, she had been *vulnerable* to all kinds of illnesses; in addition to the normal childhood diseases like mumps and measles, she had also had scarlet and rheumatic fevers, bronchitis, and pneumonia.
   a. protected from
   b. expecting
   c. open to attack
   d. untouched

3. According to one of the *provisions* in the Versailles Treaty that ended World War I, the Germans were not allowed to use the coal mined from their coal-rich Saar region; instead, coal mined from the Saar region would be used by France.
   a. exceptions
   b. insults
   c. clues
   d. sections

4. The 1862 Homestead Act, designed to give free land to the poor, produced a lot of *fraudulent* activity. For instance, large landowners would send their employees to apply for deeds to the free land; then the landless employees would sign over the deeds to their wealthy employers.
   a. unusual
   b. brilliant
   c. illegal
   d. amusing

5. The candidate promised full *disclosure* and she kept her word. That same day, she produced the last five years of tax returns and a list of her campaign contributors.

        a. contradiction

        b. decision

        c. indication

        d. exposure

⌐ READING KEY

◆ Example clues usually follow the words they illustrate, but they can also precede them.

IDIOM ALERT: Take with a grain of salt

To *take with a grain of salt* means to be skeptical, to not take something too seriously—for instance: Ads promoting miraculous skin creams that can reverse aging need to be *taken with a grain of salt* because the goal of the ad is to increase sales of the cream.

CLASS ACTION

Can you come up with other idioms using the word *salt*?

◆ EXERCISE 6   Recognizing Example Clues

DIRECTIONS   Use the example clues to determine approximate meanings for the italicized words.

EXAMPLE   His face showed how *traumatic* the experience had been. Both his wife and his child had died in the plane crash.

Traumatic means <u>miserable, painful, tragic</u>.

EXPLANATION   The example of a man suffering from the loss of his wife and child tells how painful a *traumatic* experience is.

1. This novel is filled with *personification*. Computers cough and tables groan while the wind cries and howls in the night.

    Personification means _____.

2. The results of polls need to be taken with a grain of salt. The phrasing of the questions asked can *skew* the responses and allow the pollster, rather than the respondents, to decide the results.

   Skew means _____.

3. The threat of detention was a quick *antidote* to the class's unruly behavior. As soon as the substitute teacher uttered the words "staying after school," the shouting stopped and quiet reigned.

   An *antidote* is _____.

4. Supreme Court Justice Oliver Wendell Holmes Jr. was known as the Great *Dissenter*. On occasion, Holmes even challenged his own previous rulings.

   A *dissenter* is _____.

5. Psychologist Robert Sternberg proposes a model of love that has three basic *components*: intimacy, passion, and commitment. (Adapted from Nevid, *Psychology: Concepts and Applications*, p. 333.)

   Components are _____.

General Knowledge Clues

In textbooks, restatement clues are probably the most common clues. However, when you read a newspaper or an essay, you are more likely to encounter general knowledge clues. These clues draw on your own experience. Because you know something about the situation described on the page, determining word meaning becomes easier.

For example, in the following paragraph you can probably determine the meaning of *bungled* because you understand what inspections of anything, from airplanes to cars, are supposed to accomplish. You can also tell that, in this case, the inspections performed by American Airlines were not successfully completed.

American Airlines grounded 300 jets and disrupted travel for 50,000 passengers Tuesday after federal regulators found that the airline *bungled* inspections required to prevent fires or fuel tank explosions, according to the government and the airline. (*USA Today*, April 9, 2008, p. 1.)

If you inferred that *bungled* means mismanaged or handled badly, you have drawn the right conclusion from the general knowledge clues supplied by the passage.

O—ᴨ READING KEY

◆ General knowledge clues draw on what you already know about the experience described on the page.

◆ **EXERCISE 7**   **Recognizing General Knowledge Clues**

DIRECTIONS   Use your knowledge of the situation described to determine the approximate meanings for the italicized words.

EXAMPLE   Over the years, all of Danielle's teachers had suggested that she had enormous *potential*; what seemed to be missing was a desire to be successful.

a. anger

b. possibility

c. wildness

d. shyness

EXPLANATION   We all know people who have the *potential*, or possibility, of achieving something but just never quite seem to get there. Thus, Danielle's situation is a familiar one, making it easier to come up with an approximate definition for *potential*.

1. Prison was once meant to *rehabilitate* those convicted of a crime. But that is hardly what happens in today's overcrowded prisons, where violent and nonviolent criminals are thrown together under crowded conditions.

   a. reform

   b. reveal

   c. improve

   d. punish

2. Staring out the window of a train, Max Wertheimer[†] observed a *phenomenon* that would alter his life and launch a new movement in psychology.

   a. struggle

   b. conflict

   c. happening

   d. disaster

3. Raised in a household where violence was the *norm*, he didn't know how to respond to the world except with his fists. That's all he had ever learned.

   a. typical experience

   b. odd event

   c. consequence

   d. outcome

4. Asked a difficult question by a student at the rally, the senator *pondered* a bit before answering.

   a. muttered

   b. wrote

   c. laughed

   d. thought

5. In the nineteenth century, few protections were in place for workers, who faced long hours and daily *hazards* on the job.

   a. distances

   b. rejections

   c. dangers

   d. improvements

◆ **EXERCISE 8**   **Recognizing General Knowledge Clues**

DIRECTIONS   Use your knowledge of the events described to determine approximate meanings for the italicized words.

[†]Max Wertheimer: one of the founders of Gestalt psychology, which emphasizes the brain's tendency to organize individual pieces of information into connected forms or gestalts.

EXAMPLE   When John Muir first visited the forests of California, he was *awestruck*. The huge gray mountains against a brilliant blue sky, and the towering redwoods,[†] were like nothing he had ever seen before. After his first sight of what would one day become Yosemite National Park, Muir dedicated himself to protecting the wilderness.

Awestruck means <u>full of wonder; impressed; overwhelmed; stunned</u>.

EXPLANATION   Given what Muir was responding to—towering redwoods and huge mountains—it makes sense to define *awestruck* as "full of wonder," "impressed," "overwhelmed," or "stunned."

1. The young climber's friends and family tried to *dissuade* her from climbing Mount Everest. But she would not listen. Determined to be the first Brazilian woman to reach the top, she was deaf to everything they said.

   Dissuade means _____.

2. Across the room, the two strangers caught each other's eye. He smiled and so did she. But when she lifted a cigarette to her lips, he *grimaced* and turned away.

   Grimaced means _____.

3. He had studied Spanish for years, faithfully reading every assignment and doing all the homework. But the only time he spoke the language was in class. It wasn't until he lived in Mexico for several months that he became *fluent* in Spanish.

   Fluent means _____.

4. Because of their shared interests, the two cousins tended to *gravitate* toward each other whenever there was a family reunion.

   Gravitate means _____.

[†]Redwoods are also called *sequoias*, and they are famous for their extraordinary height.

5. In 2007, Facebook CEO Mark Zuckerberg faced a firestorm of criticism after unveiling the site's Beacon advertising system, which users considered *intrusive* because it tracked activities of members to third-party sites.

Intrusive means _____ .

○━┓ **READING KEY**

◆ Writers don't restrict themselves to one context clue per passage. There may be two or more in the same paragraph. To define an unfamiliar word as precisely as possible, be sure to use all the clues available.

◆ **EXERCISE 9** **Using Context Clues**

DIRECTIONS Each sentence contains one or more of the four types of context clues. Use the clues to determine the approximate meanings for the italicized words.

EXAMPLE Unless we ourselves have led *exemplary* lives, it probably doesn't pay to be too critical of others.

Exemplary means perfect, good enough to be an example to others _____ .

EXPLANATION This is a general knowledge clue. Most of us know that if we are critical of others, we ourselves really should be on our best behavior. In other words, "people in glass houses shouldn't throw stones."

1. After the hurricane, the river was once again *tranquil*. It was hard to believe that only hours before it had been wild and dangerous.

Tranquil means _____ .

2. President Bill Clinton was famous for being *gregarious*. He couldn't enter a room without shaking hands and hugging people. In short, he was a nightmare for the Secret Service.

Gregarious means _____ .

3. Wrongly accused of a crime he did not commit, the young man was overjoyed when the new evidence *exonerated* him.

   Exonerated means _____.

4. Try as they might, the police were unable to *quell* the riot. Even with the aid of tear gas and fire hoses, the officers couldn't control the demonstrators.

   Quell means _____.

5. I like Uncle Al, but sometimes being around him is annoying. He is always trying to teach my brother and me lessons about life. Every time he tells us about some event or experience, he ends it with the question: "Now what's the *moral* of that story?" Then we have to tell him the lesson about life that we have learned. I don't know about my brother, but I'm sick of both the stories and the messages that go with them.

   Moral means _____.

6. The Russian soldiers were finding it hard to maintain their *morale*. They had not been paid in months, and now they had been ordered to pick mushrooms if they wanted to eat.

   Morale means _____.

7. She ripped the letter into tiny pieces and threw them to the ground. The wind quickly *dispersed* them. Within moments, there was no evidence the letter had ever existed.

   Dispersed means _____.

8. The soldier's exciting *chronicle* of his adventures was an immediate hit. Everyone wanted to read about his battle experiences.

   Chronicle means _____.

9. The two owners couldn't have been more different. While Alex was outgoing and talkative, Andrea was *reticent* and quiet.

   Reticent means _____.

10. Married couples often quarrel over the same issues again and again, with each person playing the same role in an increasingly familiar *scenario*.

    Scenario means _____.

 READING KEY

◆ When trying to determine word meaning, be patient. Check the sentences before and after the one containing an unfamiliar word. You may just find the clue you need.

Context Can Change Meaning

You may think you know the meaning of *critical* because people are always telling you that you are too *critical* of others, meaning "having a negative opinion." But does that meaning fit this context: "In the 1992 election, the African-American vote was *critical* to his winning the election"? In this context, *critical* means "central to," or "essential." If you think you know a word but the meaning you know doesn't fit, you are probably dealing with a word that changes its meaning with the context.

Breaking Words into Parts

Lots of words, particularly those used in an academic context, include word parts borrowed from Greek or Latin. Knowing the meanings of these word parts gives you the building blocks for hundreds of words in the English language. Learn some Greek and Latin word parts—mastering, say, ten a week—and you will be amazed at how quickly your textbook vocabulary improves.

To illustrate, let's say you didn't know what the word *vivacious* means in the following sentence: "Sheldon was drawn to her *vivacious* personality." The context here is not adequate for even an approximate definition. But if you know that the root *viv* means "life" and *ous* means "full of," you have your definition. What Sheldon liked was her "lively" personality. See what you can do with a little Greek or Latin under your belt?

> **Roots:** Roots provide words with their essential or main meanings. The root meaning of a word never changes no matter what prefixes (beginnings of words) or suffixes (endings of words) are added on to it, e.g., farm, far<u>mer</u>, far<u>ming</u>; <u>wri</u>ter, <u>wri</u>ting, pre<u>wri</u>ting.
>
> **Prefixes:** Prefixes don't affect a word's core meaning. But they do modify the word's meaning as a whole, e.g., social and <u>anti</u>social; annual and <u>bi</u>annual.
>
> **Suffixes:** Most suffixes tell you less about word meaning and more about word function, changing adjectives to nouns or nouns to adverbs, e.g., dry and dry<u>ness</u>; grace and grace<u>fully</u>.

The following chart lists common roots, prefixes, and suffixes. Some of the word parts listed here appear in the chapter, but many don't. Still, it's worth your while to take a few minutes every day or so to learn both word and meaning.

Common Prefixes and Roots ♦	Prefix Meaning[†]	Root Meaning
	ab = away, from	anthrop = man, human
	am = love	astro = star
	anti = against, opposing	bio = life
	bene = good	camera = chamber
	bi = two	cardio = heart
	circum = around	chrom = color
	con = with	chron = time
	contra = against	clam = cry out

[†]Please note how one prefix can have several meanings.

crypt = secret

de = from, away, down

demi = half

di = two

dis = not, absence, opposite,
    remove

du = double

en = in, within, into, to go into

inter = between

intra = within

ir = not

mal, male = bad, abnormal

mono = one

multi = many

neo = new

omni = all

pan = all

para = beside, beyond

poly = many

post = after

pre = before, prior to

pro = supporting, in favor of

proto = first

re = back, again

retro = backward

sub = under

super = above

syn = together

tele = far

trans = across, beyond

uni = one

cogne = knowledge

corpo = body

cred = believe

cyto = cell

demo = people

derma = skin

dict = speech, speak

duct = lead

gam = marriage

gen = birth, begetting

geo = earth

gyno = woman

hemo = blood

hydro = water

lat = side

lumen = light

locut, loqu = speech

magni = great, big

ortho = straight, right

path = feeling

ped = foot

phil = love

phot = light

port = carry

reg, rect = straighten, rule

simil = like

spec = see

strict = tighten

terra = earth

theo = god

thermo = heat

ven = come

verb = word

ver, vert = turn

viv, vit = to live, life

voc = call

vor = eat

Some Common Suffixes
◆

Suffixes indicating a person, actor, or agent:

an (American)	ist (violinist)
eer (racketeer)	or (actor)
ent (agent)	path (psychopath)

Suffixes indicating a state, quality, act, or condition:

ance (resistance)	ness (happiness)
ancy (hesitancy)	sion, tion (confusion, function)
hood (childhood)	tude (gratitude)
ism (hypnotism)	ty (loyalty)

Suffixes indicating the presence or absence of a particular quality or characteristic:

ful (beautiful)	ly (lively)
ish (childish)	some (lonesome)
less (hopeless)	y (sleepy)

○━ READING KEY

◆ Whenever possible, use context *and* word parts to determine word meaning.

◆ EXERCISE 10 Using Word Parts and Context Clues

DIRECTIONS Look over the word parts listed below. Use them, along with the context, to define the italicized word.

anthrop = man, human, person	phil = love
path = feeling, emotion, suffering	reg, rec = straighten, rule
	vit, viv = to live, life

EXAMPLE Because of his contributions to libraries and schools, many people view Andrew Carnegie as a *philanthropist*. Some historians, however, like to remind the public that Carnegie earned much of his money by paying his workers substandard wages. As he grew older, he may well have become a lover of humanity, but he didn't necessarily start out that way.

Philanthropist means <u>a person who helps or loves others</u>.

EXPLANATION   The restatement clue "lover of humanity" certainly suggests the meaning of *philanthropist*. But so, too, do the roots *phil* and *anthrop*.

1. The two boys came from and returned to the same hometown. Yet, having fought on opposite sides during the Civil War, they felt nothing but *antipathy* for one another.

   Antipathy means _____.

2. Even in old age, the actor had a powerful *vitality* that drew people to him. When he was in good spirits, his laughter could be heard booming over the laughter of others. He also told wonderful stories and showed an interest in everyone and everything.

   Vitality means _____.

3. After the military *regime* was forced out of power, its members fled for their lives.

   Regime means _____.

4. During the anticommunist scare of the 1950s, the writer had betrayed his friends and given their names to the House Un-American Activities Committee. As a result, some of those friends had gone to jail. Fifty years later he knew, as did they, that there was no way to *rectify* his betrayal.

   Rectify means _____.

5. Disowned and disinherited, the heiress was forced to live on food stamps. She even had to sleep in homeless shelters. Being rich had

not prepared her to earn a living. As one would expect, her experience with being poor gave her more *empathy* for those on welfare. Fortunately, this sense of connection did not completely disappear once her family welcomed her back into the fold, and she funded a work program for women on welfare.

Empathy means _____ .

6. Now in her eighties, the actress still had a *regal* bearing. It seemed almost appropriate to bow when she entered the room.

Regal means _____ .

7. The teacher's life was very *regimented*. He did everything according to a strict schedule. Every hour of every day was carefully accounted for.

Regimented means _____ .

8. When human bones were discovered at the building site, the city called in a team of *anthropologists* to see how old they were. To everyone's shock, the anthropologists all came to the same conclusion: The bones were not ancient. Rather, they were of recent origin.

Anthropologists means _____ .

9. Even after living in England for ten years, he was still not an *Anglophile*. Deeply American, he remained highly critical of his adopted country. He might have to work there, but he didn't have to like it.

Anglophile means _____ .

10. She had a *vivid* writing style that made her books extremely popular.

Vivid means _____ .

◆ **EXERCISE 11** **Using Word Parts**

DIRECTIONS   Use the word parts listed below to fill in the blanks.

> bene = good   poly = many
> bi = two   pre = before, prior to
> mono = one

EXAMPLE   Although their religion allowed men to be
___poly___gamists, believers seldom appeared in public with more than
one wife.

EXPLANATION   As you know from the charts on pages 64–66, the root
gam means "marriage" and the suffix *ist* means "person," "actor," or
"agent." Thus, the word *polygamists* means "people married to several
people."

1. In contrast to polygamy, the word _____gamy means "marriage
   to one person."

2. A person who marries two people at the same time is a
   _____gamist.

3. If a crime is thought out before it occurs, it is said to be
   _____meditated.

4. The root *lat* means "side." Thus, a _____lateral agreement would
   involve two sides.

5. Groups that do good works are often called _____volent
   associations.

6. A culture that has not yet begun to rely on machinery is called a
   _____industrial society.

7. The root *theo* refers to God. Thus, the word _____theism refers
   to the belief in many gods.

8. The word for belief in one God would be _____theism.

9. The root *dict* refers to speech. Thus, the word _____diction would refer to a blessing.

10. A person who uses one tone of voice is said to speak in a _____tone.

♦ **EXERCISE 12** **Using Word Parts**

DIRECTIONS Use the word parts below to fill in the blanks. When you finish the exercise, check your answers by looking up the words in the dictionary.

Prefixes

anti = against or opposing
bene = good
bi = two
circum = around
uni = one

Suffix

or = indicating a person who
does the action described in
the root

Roots

camera = chamber
chron = time

EXAMPLE If a main character in a play or novel lacks the usual heroic qualities, he or she will often be called an ___anti___hero.

EXPLANATION In this case, the prefix *anti* cancels the meaning of the root word.

1. Because it has two branches and two chambers, the U.S. legislature is called _____l.

2. In the 1960s, young men and women wore the same clothes—T-shirts and jeans. That trend in fashion was called _____sex.

3. The problem with Lyme disease is that it's hard to cure. Often it proves _____ic and keeps coming back over time.

4. Because there is no way to police the high seas, many cruise ships find ways to _____vent laws designed to control pollution of the earth's oceans.

5. If someone came to your aid whenever you needed it, you might call him or her your _____fact_____.

6. The _____fication of East and West Germany in 1991 was celebrated throughout Europe.

7. People who experience mood swings—one minute they are happy, the next depressed—are likely to suffer from a _____polar disorder.

8. When the police interviewed the suspect, he mentioned specific times for the events he described. Unfortunately for him, his _____ology didn't make sense.

9. Even the president of the United States does not make _____lateral decisions; for the most part, he must consult with Congress.

10. The explorer Ferdinand Magellan launched the first successful attempt to _____navigate the Earth.

◆ **EXERCISE 13** **Using Context Clues and Word Parts**

DIRECTIONS Use context and your knowledge of word parts to select the *best* definition for the italicized words.

1. [1]If we wish to start a conversation with a stranger standing nearby, we are likely to use nonverbal signals. [2]We might, for instance, nod our heads or smile. [3]This is a way of indicating that we are *receptive* to a verbal exchange. [4]However, we also use nonverbal signals to communicate that we are not interested in chatting with a stranger. [5]We use, for instance, something called "civil inattention." [6]Civil inattention consists of brief eye contact quickly followed by gaze *aversion*, to show a withdrawal of interest. [7]In addition to civil inattention, we also use other signals to *acknowledge* a person's presence but still indicate that we don't want to chat. [8]After observing chance meetings in public places, researcher David Givens discovered that we frequently use body language to avoid conversation. [9]For instance, we use *constricted* postures like crossing our arms and holding them at the elbows to indicate we don't want to chat. [10]We also make faces. [11]Facial expressions intended to avoid conversation include pressing or biting our lips and *protruding* the tongue.

1. *Receptive* in sentence 3 probably means
   a. annoyed.
   b. fearful.
   c. welcoming.
   d. rejecting.

2. *Aversion* in sentence 6 probably means
   a. turning away.
   b. returning.
   c. turning inward.
   d. turning toward.

3. *Acknowledge* in sentence 7 probably means
   a. ignore.
   b. recognize.
   c. repeat.
   d. reject.

4. *Constricted* in sentence 9 probably means
   a. wrapped or closed.
   b. wide open.

    c. abnormal.

    d. broken or fractured.

5. *Protruding* in sentence 11 probably means

    a. moving away.

    b. moving backward.

    c. invading.

    d. sticking out.

2. [1]Do you know why you buy the products you do? [2]Like most American consumers, you probably purchase specific products for one or more of five main reasons. [3]You buy some products because you have an immediate use for them. [4]Families, for example, need pots and pans for cooking. [5]Students need books to complete assignments. [6]You purchase other products for convenience. [7]Cordless telephones and electric can openers are *dispensable*. [8]You could live without them. [9]However, they make life so much easier; therefore, you buy them. [10]You also buy products because you believe they *enhance* your wealth. [11]Antiques or gold coins, for instance, are considered good investments. [12]Home owners buy paint, plants, and decorative (as opposed to *functional*) fences to add to the value of their property. [13]In addition to increasing income, pride of ownership is another reason for making a purchase. [14]Consumers buy items like Rolex watches and designer clothes mainly because they *confer* status, or a sense of importance. [15]Finally, you, like most people, sometimes buy for safety. [16]If we can afford it, we willingly *procure* insurance, smoke detectors, burglar alarms, and sensor lights, all because they make us feel more safe and secure. (Pride, Hughes, and Kapoor, *Business*, pp. 373–74.)

1. *Dispensable* in sentence 7 probably means

    a. inexpensive.

    b. essential to our lives.

    c. high quality.

    d. easy to give up.

2. *Enhance* in sentence 10 probably means

    a. increase.

    b. decrease.

c. display.

d. announce.

3. *Functional* in sentence 12 probably means
   a. useful and necessary.
   b. pretty and decorative.
   c. wooden.
   d. fancy.

4. *Confer* in sentence 14 probably means
   a. undermine.
   b. pretend.
   c. hide.
   d. give.

5. *Procure* in sentence 16 probably means
   a. give away.
   b. lose.
   c. obtain.
   d. eliminate.

ROUNDING UP THE KEYS

Here is a list of all the reading keys introduced in the chapter. Use them to review for the test on page 79. If a particular reading key doesn't make sense on its own, go back to the page where it appeared and review the section preceding it.

READING KEY: Context Clues

◆ Approximate definitions derived from context allow you to keep reading without interruption. (p. 47)

READING KEYS: Restatement Clues

◆ Restatement clues are the most common context clues in textbooks. (p. 48)
◆ In addition to boldface and italics, colons, semicolons, dashes, and parentheses can also signal the presence of restatement clues. (p. 48)

READING KEYS: Contrast Clues

◆ Contrast clues tell you what a word doesn't mean. (p. 51)
◆ Look for contrast clues when the author describes differences between two people, things, or ideas. (p. 51)
◆ Transitional words like *however*, *whereas*, and *yet* also signal the presence of contrast clues. (p. 51)

READING KEY: Example Clues

◆ Example clues usually follow the words they illustrate, but they can also precede them. (p. 56)

READING KEY: General Knowledge Clues

◆ General knowledge clues draw on what you already know about the experience described on the page. (p. 58)

READING KEYS: Tips on Using Context Clues

◆ Writers don't restrict themselves to one context clue per passage. There may be two or more in the same paragraph. To define an unfamiliar word as precisely as possible, be sure to use all the clues available. (p. 61)

◆ When trying to determine word meaning, be patient. Check the sentences before and after the one containing an unfamiliar word. You may just find the clue you need. (p. 63)

READING KEY: Word Parts

◆ Whenever possible, use context *and* word parts to determine word meaning. (p. 66)

DIGGING
DEEPER

New Words Needed?

Looking Ahead As our culture changes, we need new words to describe new experiences and responses. But sometimes, even when a word is desperately needed, the right one just doesn't turn up.

1   These days everyone knows what a *blogger* is. Ten or fifteen years ago, though, people would have looked dumbfounded if someone at a party had announced, "My wife is a passionate blogger." At that time, no one would have understood what the husband was saying about his wife— that she likes to go online to express and exchange ideas with an unseen audience in cyberspace. That's because *blogger*, like blogging, is a neologism. It's a word created to describe something new to our culture that once didn't exist.

2   In its origin, *blogger* belongs to a category that includes words like *moonlighting* and *hacker*. These words came into being to describe new experiences that hadn't occurred before. The word *moonlighting*, for instance, came into being as more and more people began holding two jobs, with one of the jobs requiring work at night. Similarly, as it became common for people to illegally access computer systems not their own, the word *hacker* came on the scene.

3   Based on examples like these, the English language seems to acquire new words in four steps: (1) Some new activity or behavior emerges; (2) a word is created to describe it; (3) numerous people use and popularize the word; and (4) the word becomes a part of the language. Easy and sensible as those four steps sound, Allan Metcalf, the author of *Predicting New Words*, would probably not agree. In fact, in his book, he lists several of what he calls the "neediest cases," i.e., situations or behaviors desperately in need of a word to describe them. Yet the need goes ignored. Among those words needed are the following:

1. A substitute for *boyfriend* or *girlfriend* when talking about men and women who are no longer in their teens and who have a committed relationship.

2. A word meaning "to state an opinion." The word *opine* exists, but no one uses it because people are likely to laugh when they hear it.

3. A word other than *yes* to indicate that you're listening to someone. *Yes* implies agreement, and you may disagree while still wishing to lend an ear.

4   Metcalf's list is actually based on an earlier list created by a *New York Times Magazine* editor in 1955, which means that these gaps in the language have existed for decades. The question that neither Metcalf nor anyone else seems able to answer is why these gaps and others remain while some are quickly filled. Did we, for instance, desperately need a word for the illegal accessing of someone's computer—i.e., *hacking*—but never really needed a word to describe a fifty-five-year-old widow's current dating partner? Clearly our language changes all the time to meet the needs of the culture. But sometimes those needs go begging and no one really knows why that happens. In some ways, language has an inexplicable life of its own and may not always do our bidding, much as we would like to believe that it does.

Sharpening Your Skills

DIRECTIONS   Answer the following questions by filling in the blanks or circling the letter of the correct response.

1. What kind of context clues to the meaning of *neologism* appears in the reading?
    a. example
    b. restatement
    c. contrast
    d. general knowledge

2. What word parts are additional clues to the meaning of *neologism*?

    _____ and _____

3. Which statement best paraphrases the point of this selection?
    a. As American culture changes, so does the language.
    b. Our language does not always supply us with the words we need.
    c. The language we use to describe our culture affects how we conduct our lives.

4. Based on the context, what does *inexplicable* in paragraph 4 mean?

    _____

▶ **TEST 1** **Reviewing the Key Points**

DIRECTIONS Answer the following questions by circling *T* (true) or *F* (false). *Note*: Read the questions carefully. Part of a question may be true and part may be false, making the whole sentence false.

T F **1.** Although there are several different types of context clues, the following four are the most common: (1) restatement, (2) example, (3) comparison, and (4) contrast.

T F **2.** Context clues will always give you an exact dictionary definition.

T F **3.** When you discover an unfamiliar word, scan both the rest of the sentence and the sentence that follows for a context clue. You may well find a clue that gives you a definition for the word you don't know.

T F **4.** In addition to colons, dashes and parentheses can also signal the presence of restatement clues. So, too, can words such as "unlike," "but," "similarly," and "however."

T F **5.** Words like *with, and, for,* and *or* often signal the presence of contrast clues.

T F **6.** You should be alert to contrast clues whenever the author describes differences in people, things, times, or ideas.

T F **7.** Particularly in textbooks, example clues are often introduced by phrases such as "for instance" and "for example."

T F **8.** Example clues never come after the words they illustrate.

T F **9.** If you have a good context clue, you don't need to pay attention to word parts.

T F **10.** One prefix can have several meanings.

To correct your test, turn to page 553. If one or more of your answers is incorrect, re-read the Rounding Up the Keys section of the chapter to find out where your mistake might be.

▶ **TEST 2**　　　　**Using Context Clues**

DIRECTIONS　　For each italicized word, use the context to determine an approximate meaning.

1. Although some smokers are *physiologically* addicted to cigarettes, others suffer from a dependence that is more of the mind than of the body.
   a. physically
   b. ridiculously
   c. endlessly
   d. critically

2. During the Eisenhower era (1953–1961), it was widely assumed that poverty had disappeared. In reality, poverty was *rife* in both urban and rural areas.
   a. decreasing
   b. disappearing
   c. widespread
   d. challenging

3. The process by which lawyers and judges examine *prospective* jurors can, sometimes, be lengthy.
   a. trustworthy
   b. untrustworthy
   c. possible
   d. unlikely

4. The two researchers were a study in contrasts when they answered questions: While the younger one liked to talk about his work, the older one showed more *restraint* and didn't reveal much.
   a. attention
   b. silence
   c. self-control
   d. satisfaction

5. In the 1950s, Dr. Benjamin Spock was considered an expert on the care of babies, and only the Bible outsold his book *The Common Sense Book of Baby and Child Care*. At his suggestion, breastfeeding, which had gone out of fashion, came back into *vogue*.

    a. fashion

    b. disagreement

    c. conflict

    d. history

6. The birth control pill has not been a universal *panacea*. One woman's medical concern became another woman's medical problem. To date, the Pill has neither significantly limited population growth nor ended unwanted pregnancies in the United States. (Boyer et al., *The Enduring Vision*, p. 881.)

    a. mistake

    b. cure

    c. adoption

    d. challenge

7. In 1980, with Democratic President Jimmy Carter's popularity *abysmally* low, Ronald Reagan, who promised a break with the past, won the presidency. (Adapted from Boyer et al., *The Enduring Vision*, p. 932.)

    a. climbing

    b. cheerfully

    c. horribly

    d. casually

8. In the nineteenth century, when workers rebelled against the *tempo* of factory production, owners responded by cutting wages or paying only for items produced rather than by the hour.

    a. slowness

    b. pace

    c. length

    d. description

9. The prehistoric telesaurus was not a *terrestrial* animal; it lived mainly in water.

    a. pretty

    b. large

    c. land-based

    d. waterborne

10. Many people do not believe that human beings *evolved* from apes.
    a. developed
    b. divided
    c. ran
    d. changed

▶ **TEST 3**   **Using Context Clues**

DIRECTIONS   Read the sentence. Then for each italicized word, fill in the blanks to identify the kind of context clue and the approximate definition.

1. Union forces expected to win at the Battle of Bull Run, but instead they were *routed*.

   The _____ context clue suggests that *routed* means

   _____ .

2. The experiments that Max Wertheimer conducted with two assistants led to discoveries about the nature of *perception*—the processes by which we organize our sense impressions and form meaningful representations of the world around us. (Seifert and Hoffnung, *Childhood and Adolescent Development*, p. 11.)

   The _____ context clue suggests that *perception*

   means _____ .

3. In the military, rules are *mandatory*. It's not a matter of soldiers deciding which ones they want to obey and which ones they do not.

   The _____ context clue suggests that *mandatory*

   means _____ .

4. As the first president, George Washington was keenly aware that his every act created a *precedent* for the future. Once, while on a visit to Boston, Washington was informed that John Hancock, the governor of Massachusetts, was ill and would be unable to call. Believing that governors were less important than presidents, Washington forced Hancock to appear despite the man's obvious illness. (Adapted from Gitelson, Dudley, and Dubnick, *American Government*, p. 287.)

   The _____ context clue suggests that *precedent* means

   _____ .

5. Many members of the music industry believe that the major record companies would be better off *consolidating* rather than trying to go it alone in an increasingly difficult market.

   The _____ context clue suggests that *consolidating* means _____.

6. Polls are *ingrained* in the political process; they have, in fact, been firmly established for over thirty years despite coming under constant criticism.

   The _____ context clue suggests that *ingrained* means

   _____.

7. Artists are *compensated* for their performance on recorded music in one of two ways. Artists who help to make an album, but are not central to it, are paid an hourly wage. The central artists on the recording receive royalties for their work. (Turow, *Media Today*, p. 404.)

   The _____ context clue suggests that *compensated* means _____.

8. When a state trooper stops a car and asks to see a license, he or she expects immediate *compliance*.

   The _____ context clue suggests that *compliance* means _____.

9. William Marcy "Boss" Tweed, the boss of New York City's Democratic machine during the 1860s and 1870s, *detested* political cartoons. Shortly after viewing a cartoon by Thomas Nast, who was critical of New York politicians, Tweed was said to have ordered his lieutenants to "Stop them damned pictures." (Adapted from Gitelson, Dudley, and Dubnick, *American Government*, p. 161.)

   The _____ context clue suggests that *detested* means

   _____.

10. In contrast to the Great Plains, where ethnic groups created their own ethnic *enclaves*, western mining camps were ethnic melting pots.

    The _____ context clue suggests that *enclaves* means

    _____ .

▶ **TEST 4**   **Using Word Parts and Context Clues**

DIRECTIONS   Using your knowledge of context clues and word parts, select the best definition for each italicized word by circling the appropriate letter.[†]

Word Parts	Meanings
cline	lean, bend
clu, clud	shut
de	down, from, away, out
ex	out, from, away
pre	before
re	back, backward
sol, soli	alone, lonely
trac	pull

1. She had once been a wealthy woman, but over the years her fortune had *declined.*

   a. decreased

   b. grown larger

   c. changed

2. She had never liked *exclusive* clubs that made a point of leaving people out.

   a. not open to all

   b. open to all

   c. fancy

3. He had been frightened on the way up the mountain, but it was the *descent* that really scared him.

   a. the way up

   b. the way down

   c. the temperature

[†]The word parts included here may have additional meanings.

4. Her critics tried to *detract* from the value of her proposal, but they only succeeded in proving her right.

   a. add to

   b. take away from

   c. imitate

5. That decision is *premature*. Nothing should be decided before all the facts are in.

   a. silly

   b. too early

   c. late

6. The owner of the supermarket demanded that the paper *retract* its original statement, but the editor publicly refused to do so.

   a. revise

   b. apologize

   c. take back

7. Although he liked to spend time among friends, he still needed some *solitude*.

   a. amusement

   b. extra money

   c. time alone

8. After *reclining* in the hammock for most of the afternoon, he complained of fatigue from too much yard work.

   a. sitting

   b. yawning

   c. lying

9. Her decision to take the retirement package *precludes* her returning even on a part-time basis.

   a. makes easier

   b. eliminates

   c. allows for

10. The *extraction* of the minerals had left the earth riddled with ugly holes.

    a. refining

    b. taking out

    c. selling

▶ **TEST 5**   **Using Word Parts and Context Clues**

DIRECTIONS Using your knowledge of context clues and word parts, write an appropriate definition for each italicized word.

Word Parts	Meanings
am, amor	love, liking, friendliness
dis	not, lack of
equ	equal
inter	between

1. Let the kids settle the argument by themselves. Don't *intervene*.

   Intervene means _____.

2. How can you *equate* her problems with his? He doesn't have enough money for food. She can't afford insurance on her second car.

   Equate means _____.

3. After they had been in business together for several years, their relationship was no longer *amicable*.

   Amicable means _____.

4. In her case, a request is *equivalent* to a command. The tone of her voice makes it clear you're not allowed to refuse.

   Equivalent means_____.

5. After he testified against the company, the accountant's *interaction* with his coworkers was strained.

   Interaction means _____.

6. They may be brothers, but their personalities are remarkably *disparate*. They don't have anything in common.

   Disparate means _____.

7. She kept on trying to *interject* her opinions into the argument, but no one paid any attention.

   Interject means _____.

8. The profits were not distributed *equitably*. Two of the owners received 70 percent of the profits, while the other two received only 30 percent.

   Equitably means _____.

9. The duck approached its mate with *amorous* intentions, but she quacked in outrage and flew away.

   Amorous means _____.

10. He wanted to *dissociate* himself from his early career. But the public could not forget what he had done as a young man.

    Dissociate means _____.

Identifying Topics, Main Ideas, and Topic Sentences

3

Determining an author's meaning is not always easy. If the subject is unfamiliar or the writing difficult, you may need to work at making the meaning clear. Chapter 3 prepares you for those times when it feels as if your textbook were written in a foreign language.

What's the Topic?

The **topic** of a paragraph is much like the topic of a conversation. It's the person, place, event, or idea under discussion. It's the subject the author has chosen to discuss, describe, or explain. The topic of a passage or reading does not just pop up once or twice and then disappear. On the contrary, references to the topic are threaded through the paragraph.

Read the following paragraph. If you had to choose between these two possible topics, "the boss" or "the party machine," which would you choose, and why?

> Early in the nineteenth century, the swelling numbers of urban poor had given rise to a new kind of politician, the "boss," who listened to his urban constituents and lobbied to improve their lot. The boss presided over the city's "machine"—an unofficial political organization designed to keep a particular party or faction in office. Whether officially serving as mayor or not, the boss, assisted by local ward or precinct captains, wielded enormous influence in city government. Often a former saloonkeeper or labor leader, the boss knew his constituents well. (Adapted from Boyer et al., *The Enduring Vision*, p. 578.)

If you picked "the boss" for the topic, you clearly understand what distinguishes the topic of a paragraph from the other subjects mentioned: References to the topic turn up repeatedly. Just look at the sample paragraph again; all references to "the boss" have been underlined.

> Early in the nineteenth century, the swelling numbers of urban poor had given rise to a <u>new kind of politician</u>, <u>the "boss,"</u> <u>who</u> listened to <u>his</u> urban constituents and lobbied to improve their lot. <u>The boss</u> presided over the city's "machine"—an unofficial political organization designed to keep a particular party or faction in office. Whether officially serving as mayor or not, <u>the boss</u>, assisted by local ward or precinct captains, wielded enormous influence in city government. Often a former saloonkeeper or labor leader, <u>the boss</u> knew <u>his</u> constituents well. (Adapted from Boyer et al., *The Enduring Vision*, p. 578.)

No other word in the paragraph has close to the same number of references. That's why "the boss" is the topic under discussion.

Phrasing the Topic

Although there will be times when the paragraph's topic can be summed up in just a word or two, that's not always the case. Sometimes you'll need several words to express the topic—for example:

> Even beautiful people sometimes feel unattractive. There are handsome actors who won't let their right side be photographed for fear of looking unattractive. There are gorgeous models who obsess because they are a few pounds overweight. For some people, however, feeling unattractive is not a momentary state. On the contrary, victims of body dysmorphic disorder, or BDD, feel ugly all the time, no matter

what their mirror shows. For victims of BDD, even tiny flaws, like a freckle, a small mole, or a pimple, are a source of misery. These minor imperfections are viewed as a catastrophe, so much so that BDD victims frequently refuse to leave their homes or be in the company of other people. Victims of BDD avoid the society of other people because they imagine that their horrifying physical appearance will earn them nothing but ridicule. When the disorder reaches this state, a combination of medication and therapy is needed because victims can become so desperate, they commit suicide rather than expose their "ugliness" to the world. Ironically, victims of BDD are often extremely attractive. They are also likely to be people who have had repeated cosmetic surgeries.

Re-read the paragraph and you'll see repeated references to the phrases "victims of body dysmorphic disorder" and "victims of BDD." There are also other, indirect references to those phrases in the pronouns "they" and "their." "Victims of body dysmorphic disorder" is the topic, and, in this case, the topic needs to be expressed in five words rather than one.

Although a shorter version of the topic, such as body dysmorphic disorder, would work, a briefer topic like that one wouldn't get you as quickly to the **main idea**, or point, of the paragraph. Keep in mind when you are looking for the topic that it needs to be broad enough to include what's discussed in the paragraph—by this criterion, BDD victims who commit suicide wouldn't work—and specific enough to exclude what isn't. The phrase "feeling ugly," for instance, would be a poor choice of topic for this passage. It's too broad and suggests that the author might discuss any number of topics.

IDIOM ALERT: Blood money

The idiom *blood money* refers to money earned from the suffering, even the death, of other people, as in the following sentence: "The spy had made a fortune selling his country's secrets to the enemy, but in the end his conscience tortured him and he could not enjoy a penny of his *blood money*."

Inferring the Topic

Inferences are educated guesses based largely on the information given by the author. In other words, you put into words something the author implies, or suggests, but does not state. However, inferences aren't just important to determining word meanings. They also are necessary when it comes to identifying paragraph topics. In the paragraph that follows, for instance, the author doesn't supply a word or phrase expressing the subject under discussion.

> In the 1870s, Welsh explorer Henry Morton Stanley sailed the length of the Congo River under the sponsorship of King Leopold of Belgium. All along the length of the river, Stanley made treaties with the African tribes he encountered. Thanks to Stanley's treaties, Leopold was able to lay claim to territory that was 80 times the size of Belgium. Calling his newly acquired land the "Belgian Congo," Leopold then began extracting its abundant natural resources. Under Leopold's rule, the Congolese people were faced with demands for forced labor. Agents of the Belgian government would give each Congolese family a basket to be filled with rubber. If family members did not all return with their baskets filled to the top, their homes would be burned to the ground. Anyone who rebelled was imprisoned. Thanks to this system, Leopold grew rich and squandered his blood money on yachts, mansions, and mistresses. Eventually, when word of the situation in the Congo was reported, Leopold was forced to give up control of the Congo because of public outrage. But by then, millions of Congolese had been imprisoned and thousands had died.

In this case, the entire paragraph deals with King Leopold's rule of the Congo or King Leopold's bloody reign in the Congo. Either of these phrases expresses the topic discussed. However, neither of them appears in the passage. Instead, the writer leaves it to the reader to infer the topic. This means that you can't assume you will always find a stated word or phrase to express the topic in the paragraph. Much of the time you will, but not always. Sometimes you will have to infer, or create, the topic based on what's stated in the paragraph.

⚷ READING KEYS

- ◆ The topic is the person, place, event, or idea repeatedly mentioned or referred to throughout the reading.
- ◆ The topic never pops up and then disappears. It's a constant presence in the passage.
- ◆ Although one word can sometimes sum up the topic, you'll often need several words to express it.

◆ Sometimes readers have to come up with the words for the topic.
◆ The topic should be general enough to include everything discussed in the paragraph but specific enough to exclude what isn't.

◆ EXERCISE 1   Identifying Topics

DIRECTIONS   Select the topic of each paragraph by circling the appropriate letter.

EXAMPLE   Thomas Edison is rightly famous for his brilliance as an ingenious inventor. Among other things, he helped bring us electricity, phonographs, and motion pictures. Edison is less known, though, for his role in inventing the electric chair. In 1887, the New York State legislature was searching for a method of execution other than hanging. A member of the legislature had heard rumors about people who were accidentally electrocuted and died. The legislature wrote to Edison, posing a question: Would electrocution be a more humane method of execution? Edison wrote back, saying he thought 1,000 volts of electricity could provide a quick and painless death. Edison then conducted a series of experiments to prove his claim. In the course of those experiments, he put to death numerous dogs and cats, some cattle, and at least one horse. It's not that Edison wanted to take credit for inventing the electric chair. Rather, he wanted the State of New York to use a generator* made by his archrival,* Westinghouse. Edison hoped the general public would grow fearful of Westinghouse products once it knew that, as he liked to put it, prisoners were being "Westinghoused" to death.

Topic (a.) Edison and the electric chair
   b. Edison's rivalry with Westinghouse
   c. the genius of Thomas Edison

EXPLANATION   The passage returns repeatedly to Edison's role in the invention of the electric chair. Therefore, *a* is the topic. Answers *b* and *c* are mentioned too briefly to be the topic. Also, "the genius of Thomas Edison" would cover many more topics than those included in the passage. In contrast, "Edison's rivalry with Westinghouse" is too specific; it excludes too many topics introduced in the passage.

---

*generator: machine that produces electricity.
*archrival: main opponent.

1. The Venus flytrap is one of several carnivorous plants that actually eat insects. The plant's leaves, which look like a steel trap with teeth, remain open until an insect lands on them. When the insect brushes against tiny trigger hairs on the leaves, they snap shut. The plant then secretes enzymes to digest its prey. For about a week, the Venus flytrap uses the dead insect as a source of food. Once the insect is completely digested, the Venus flytrap opens its leaves again, ready to catch another meal.

Topic   a. insects

b. carnivorous plants

c. the Venus flytrap

2. The Amish are a branch of the Mennonites, a religious group originally from Switzerland. Although Amish settlements exist in both Ohio and Pennsylvania, the people in those settlements try to avoid contact with the outside world. Travel, except for visits to neighbors, is discouraged. In any case, traveling is far from easy because owning bicycles, motorcycles, and automobiles is strictly forbidden. The Amish also refuse to use electricity from power lines. They do, however, use batteries and other sources of energy.

Topic   a. alternative sources of energy for the Amish

b. Amish avoidance of the outside world

c. religious groups

3. Amnesty International was formed in 1961 to protect human rights throughout the world. Created by British lawyer Peter Benenson, it now has more than a million members. Members work to help people who face unjust imprisonment, unfair trials, torture, or execution. The main goal of Amnesty International is to assist those who have been punished for their political beliefs. For example, in 2005 the organization successfully engineered the release of Rebiya Kadeer, a Chinese businesswoman wrongfully imprisoned for over five years. She had been convicted of leaking secret information because she sent newspaper clippings to her husband in the United States. Amnesty International helps people like Kadeer by publicizing their cases, appealing to authorities, and arranging for legal defense. It also exposes human rights violations, encourages governments to change laws, and conducts campaigns to educate the public about human rights.

Topic   a. Rebiya Kadeer

b. human rights

c. Amnesty International

4. A twelfth-century couple, Heloise and Abelard, is often mentioned when romantic love becomes the subject of scholarly discussion. Yet, in truth, there wasn't much romance in either the couple's courtship or their marriage. When they met, Heloise was the niece of a wealthy scholar. Abelard was the most famous teacher in France. Older and vastly more educated, Abelard became the girl's tutor. The two fell in love. When Heloise bore a son, they married in secret because the couple did not want Abelard's career hurt by scandal. However, when Heloise's uncle found out what had happened, he forced his niece to become a nun and had Abelard castrated.[†] Separated for the rest of their lives, Heloise and Abelard wrote passionate love letters so emotionally powerful that they were eventually published. Those letters have assured the lovers their place in the history of romantic love.

Topic   a. the subject of love

b. the story of Heloise and Abelard

c. the love letters of Heloise and Abelard

VOCABULARY EXTRA

Remember the word *archrival*, defined on page 95? *Arch* actually leads a double life as both a prefix and a suffix. Put those letters at the beginning of a word and they mean "chief," "highest," or "most important," as in the words *arch-enemy* and *arch-liberal*. Put them at the end of a word and they mean "ruler" or "leader," as in the words *patriarch* (a man who rules a family) and *matriarch* (a woman who rules a family).

◆ EXERCISE 2   **Identifying Topics**

DIRECTIONS   Select the topic of each paragraph by circling the appropriate letter.

[†]In the twelfth century, castration, or the cutting off of a man's testicles, was not an unusual punishment for a sexual crime.

1. Medical reformer Dr. Benjamin Rush (1745–1813) was one of the first to argue that mentally ill people should not be punished for the crime of being sick. Rush also insisted that doctors listen closely to their patients and take careful notes on their complaints. Without question, he was a force for good in medical treatment. That does not mean, however, that Benjamin Rush never did any harm; in fact, even some of Dr. Rush's colleagues considered his prescriptions for health rather dangerous. In an era that believed bloodletting was good therapy, Dr. Rush was overly enthusiastic. He often drew large amounts of blood from patients already weakened by disease. It was suspected, in fact, that some of his patients died from his treatment rather than their illness. Dr. Rush also came up with the idea of the "Tranquilizer Chair." Patients were strapped into a chair with their head packed in a box. Unable to move or speak, they had no choice but to calm down. In addition, Dr. Rush believed that patients suffering from mental disturbances should spend more time swinging in the air. On his recommendation, patients were strapped into chairs. The chairs would then be suspended from the ceiling. Attendants kept them swinging or spinning until the patients showed signs of improvement. Fortunately, vomiting was considered an improvement. Once they got sick enough, the patients were let down from the ceiling.

Topic   a. the tranquilizer chair

b. eighteenth-century treatments for mental illness

c. Benjamin Rush's medical reforms

d. Benjamin Rush's harmful medical treatments

2. Americans use the word *love* as a catchall term that refers to very different emotions. We love the music of Aretha Franklin. We love jelly doughnuts and coco puffs. We love our parents, spouses, and pets. The ancient Greeks, in contrast, were more precise when talking of love. They used different words to identify different kinds of love. When they talked about romance or sexual passion, the Greeks used the word *eros*. But if the conversation turned to love between friends, they used the word *phila*. To talk about spiritual love, the Greeks used *agape*, which emphasized the need to love without expecting anything in return.

Topic a. the Greeks and their worldview

    b. Greek words for different loves

    c. agape and eros

    d. the American view of love

3. Toward the end of the elementary school years, girls tend to become significantly taller than boys of the same age. The difference results partly from girls' earlier puberty and partly from the timing of the growth spurt associated with puberty. Inevitably, these changes in height at puberty create temporary embarrassment for some boys and girls. Their embarrassment stems from the fact that late childhood is when most children become aware of social expectations about attractiveness, for instance, the idea that men "should" be taller than women. This awareness of social expectation about height dawns at precisely the time when many children of both sexes exhibit a very different pattern, with some girls being taller than boys. (Adapted from Seifert and Hoffnung, *Child and Adolescent Development*, p. 336.)

Topic a. height changes in girls at puberty

    b. height changes during puberty

    c. puberty

    d. stereotypes about height

4. Most of the coal we now mine to use for fuel was formed about 300 million years ago. At that time, Earth was covered by swamps. When plants and trees died, they sank to the bottom of these swamps, forming layers of soggy, decaying vegetation. Next, sand, silt, and clay accumulated over the plant matter and formed heavy rock that buried the rotting vegetation and squeezed the water from it. Over long periods of time, as the plant matter was pushed deeper by the weight of the rock, it was compacted and heated. This pressure and heat changed the plant matter to coal, which we now can burn to produce energy.

Topic a. creation of coal

    b. processing coal

    c. ancient Earth

    d. energy

What's the Main Idea?

Once you know the topic of a paragraph, your next step is to figure out the main idea. The **main idea** is the thought, meaning, or point that the author wants to express *about* the topic.

The difference between a topic and a main idea will become clearer to you if you imagine the following: You happen to overhear a conversation in which your name is repeatedly mentioned. When you ask your friends what they were discussing, they say that they were talking about you. At that moment, you have the topic, but you don't know the main idea. In other words, you don't know what your friends were saying *about* you. Undoubtedly you would pester them until you knew exactly what they had said about your personality, appearance, or behavior. Who wouldn't?

The same approach should apply to reading, where the topic is only a stepping-stone to the main idea. As soon as you can define the topic, ask yourself, What general point does the author want to make about this topic? Once you can answer that question, you have found the main idea.

For instance, the topic of the following paragraph is "name brands" or "branding products." The question now is, What's the main idea? Read the paragraph and see what you think.

> Both buyers and sellers benefit from branding. Because brands are easily recognizable, they reduce the amount of time buyers must spend shopping; buyers can quickly identify the brands they prefer. Choosing particular brands such as Tommy Hilfiger, Polo, Nautica, and Nike can be a way of expressing oneself. When buyers are unable to evaluate a product's characteristics, brands can help them judge the quality of the product. For example, most buyers aren't able to judge the quality of stereo components but may be guided by a well-respected brand name. Brands can symbolize a certain quality level to a customer. . . . Brands thus help reduce a buyer's perceived risk of purchase. Finally, customers may receive a psychological reward that comes from owning a brand that symbolizes status. The Lexus brand is an example. (Pride, Hughes, and Kapoor, *Business*, p. 394.)

In this case, the main idea appears in the first sentence, which tells readers that branding has benefits for both buyers and sellers. The remainder of the paragraph then offers some specific examples, all of which point back to the opening statement about the benefits of branding. In other words, threading its way through the entire paragraph is the idea introduced in the opening sentence: Branding is a good thing. That's what the author wants to say about the topic, and that's the main idea.

🔑 READING KEY

◆ The main idea is the central point or thought the writer wants to communicate to readers. It's what ties all the sentences in the paragraph together.

◆ EXERCISE 3　　Recognizing the Main Idea

DIRECTIONS　　Read each paragraph and circle the letter of the main idea expressed in the paragraph.

1. [1]By the end of the nineteenth century, the bison in this country were almost extinct. [2]Yet, miraculously, the American bison survived—largely because of human laziness. [3]As the animals grew rarer, hunting them became much harder. [4]Only very experienced hunters were willing to risk the bitter winters in the valleys where the bison took shelter. [5]In these areas, the snow was deep. [6]The temperature was often 25° below zero. [7]Few were willing to follow the bison into such bone-chilling cold, and, as a result, the bison lived on.

   a. By the end of the nineteenth century, America's bison were extinct, and hunters turned their sights on other prey.

   b. Against all odds, America's bison survived, mainly because few hunters were determined enough to follow their tracks.

   c. The bison are yet another example of how early Americans failed to preserve the country's natural resources.

2. [1]The story of King Solomon and the Queen of Sheba appears in both the Bible and the Koran; it also belongs to the legends of Syria and Egypt. [2]Although there are several versions of what happened between King Solomon and the Queen of Sheba, the stories agree on several basic points. [3]According to all accounts, the beautiful young queen journeyed to Solomon, the king of Israel, to test his wisdom. [4]Solomon is said to have fallen in love with the young queen and she with him. [5]After bearing Solomon a son, the Queen of Sheba returned to her own country. [6]Many people believe that the biblical book

Song of Songs, a collection of love poems attributed* to King Solomon, is a record of his love for the Queen of Sheba.

a. The story of Solomon and Sheba has become part of almost every culture, perhaps because it so beautifully illustrates the nature of true love.

b. Several versions of the story of Solomon and Sheba exist, but there are similarities among the various versions.

c. The *Song of Songs* from the Bible is believed to have been inspired by King Solomon's love for the Queen of Sheba.

3. [1]At one time, home schooling was dismissed as an odd educational alternative practiced only by a very few parents. [2]But the long-term successes of home-schooled children have caused parents and educators to reconsider the practice. [3]About 25 percent of home-schooled students are one grade level ahead of their peers. [4]Home-schooled kids consistently score in the top third on achievement tests. [5]Also, their SAT scores are higher than those of kids enrolled in public or private schools. [6]In the 2001 National Spelling Bee, an event that attracts some of the best students in the country, 27 of the 248 participants were home schoolers. [7]In 2000, home schoolers placed first, second, and third in that contest. [8]Furthermore, the majority of home schoolers go on to college. [9]In fact, quite a few of them are winning admission to elite schools such as Harvard University. [10]In 1998, more than seventy National Merit Scholarship semifinalists were home-schooled high school seniors.

a. At one time, home schooling children was considered odd, but that time is long gone, and home schooling is considered a legitimate alternative by many.

b. As it turns out, home-schooled children do better in college than do those who attended public schools.

c. Home schooling is now being practiced by the majority of parents who have children of school age.

4. [1]Each year, about 400,000 students across the country are disciplined with corporal, or physical, punishment, even though those who oppose corporal punishment say that it's not only ineffective but can also do harm. [2]First of all, paddling a child is no more effective than

---

*attributed: credited to or said to be the work of.

other forms of discipline. ³In fact, spanking usually just delays the next incident of misbehavior. ⁴Even worse, many children who are spanked react with increased aggression and rebelliousness. ⁵It's also just too easy to use corporal punishment inappropriately. ⁶Some teachers may simply consider it the easiest method for subduing students. ⁷Teachers who are free to paddle may not make the effort to try more positive discipline strategies. ⁸In the most extreme cases, teachers who use corporal punishment could easily cross the line into child abuse.

a. Punishing children through the use of corporal punishment is the main reason why children are engaging in criminal behavior at an increasingly early age.

b. All too often, corporal punishment in the classroom crosses the line into child abuse.

c. Corporal punishment in school persists despite claims that it is both ineffective and harmful.

Looking for Topic Sentences

Unlike other writers who don't always summarize the main idea in a sentence, textbook writers usually do (more about those who don't in Chapter 6). In fact, textbook writers are inclined to open their paragraphs with **topic sentences**. These are general sentences broad enough to sum up the point of the entire paragraph. The paragraph on branding (p. 100) opened with a topic sentence, as does the following one:

> Although teasing, or making playful fun of someone, is viewed negatively by many parents and teachers, some researchers believe that children's teasing of one another has benefits. Researcher Dacher Keltner, a professor of psychology at UC Berkeley, is one of several researchers who views teasing as a form of social bonding. Keltner says kids tease each other to make friends. In this belief, he echoes others, who say that teasing can start a friendship. In addition to opening a conversation, teasing can test or display a child's sense of humor—for example, "Is somebody paying you to wear that shirt?" Kids also tease to try out their sense of word play. For example, they might purposely mispronounce the girl's name Magdalena as

"Macarena." In one study, researchers found that the most skilled teasers among 9- to 14-year-olds had the most friends. Researchers like Keltner know that teasing can turn cruel. They believe, though, that most teasing that goes on among children is good natured and playful. (Source of study: Lynn Smith, "Hey, Poo-Poo Head, Let's Be Friends," http://articles.latimes.com/2000/dec/06/news/cl-61676.)

In this example, most of the sentences in the paragraph identify specific benefits some researchers associate with teasing. However, only the first sentence, the topic sentence, is broad enough to include and sum up all the others. The first sentence functions as an umbrella sentence, which can include or cover all the others. It's that ability to sum up more specific references that makes it a topic sentence. Diagrammed, the previous paragraph would look like this:

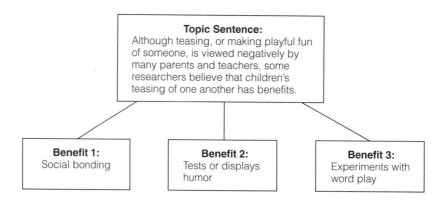

Study the diagram and you'll see what it means to call the topic sentence an *umbrella sentence*. It's the only sentence in the paragraph that is general enough to include the other sentences. In other words, if you say that teasing is a way of displaying humor, you aren't suggesting anything about benefit 3: Teasing allows kids to experiment with word play. But if you say that teasing has several benefits, the statement is general enough to suggest that teasing can bring about social bonding, display humor, and practice word play. All of these different benefits can be included under the topic sentence. That's precisely why the topic sentence is always one of the most general sentences in the paragraph.

◆ **EXERCISE 4**   **Recognizing Topic Sentences**

DIRECTIONS   In each group of three sentences, one is more general than the other two and could function as the topic sentence. Circle the letter of that sentence.

EXAMPLE

a. Jupiter's four largest moons are Io, Europa, Ganymede, and Callistro.

b. Io and Europa are closer to Jupiter than Ganymede and Callistro.

c. Jupiter is surrounded by numerous moons.

EXPLANATION   Answer *c* is correct because the other two sentences continue the discussion of Jupiter's numerous moons. This information is covered or included in topic sentence *c*.

1. a. With a few exceptions, most states tax personal income.

   b. Wisconsin was the first state to enact a personal income tax.

   c. Only Alaska, South Dakota, Florida, Texas, Nevada, Washington, and Wyoming leave all personal income untaxed.

2. a. Dog owners have been known to go overboard in their love for their pets, treating them with all the privileges of spoiled children.

   b. In the seventeenth century, some dog owners let their favorite hunting dogs roam freely throughout the house, terrorizing strangers and guests alike.

   c. When the eighteenth-century general Napoleon Bonaparte married the widow Josephine de Beauharnais in 1796, he discovered that his new wife wouldn't spend the night with him unless her beloved dog was in the bed.

3. a. During the chariot races, a featured part of ancient circuses, it was an unusual event when either a horse or a charioteer did not die.

   b. During the reign of Augustus, more than 3,500 lions, tigers, and other jungle cats died in the circus arena, taking with them hundreds of gladiators.

c. The two biggest draws of ancient circuses were bloodshed and death.

4. a. If a modern fictional heroine can't meet her sweetheart at the train station, she can always text message him the reason, but in novels past, her inability to reach him was the cause of tragedy.

b. Cell phone technology has had a profound effect on fictional storytelling, making plots of the past no longer seem realistic.

c. If they want to make their victims helpless and unable to call for help, writers of thrillers now need a setting like a subway station, where the person being stalked can't just whip out a cell phone and call 911.

Does the Topic Sentence Arrive First or Second?

Textbook authors are inclined to make the first or second sentence of a paragraph the topic sentence. As a reader, you need to take that fact into account. The minute you start reading a paragraph, look closely at the first two sentences. Ask yourself if the second sentence continues or reverses the train of thought begun in the first.

If the second sentence continues, on a more specific level, the train of thought begun in the first, then the topic sentence probably opens the paragraph. You can be certain it does if the third sentence also continues developing the idea introduced in sentence 1.

But if sentence 2 challenges or revises the idea introduced in sentence 1 and sentence 3 picks up on the point introduced by sentence 2, then you know that the topic sentence is the second sentence in the paragraph.

Now see if you can apply this strategy to the following paragraphs. Where's the topic sentence in the first paragraph?

[1]The first American union to successfully unite skilled and unskilled workers was the National Labor Union (NLU). [2]The NLU was founded in 1866 by William Sylvis, a former head of the ironmolders' union in Philadelphia. [3]Sylvis was a strong leader who claimed to hold the union "more dear than I do my family or my life. [4]I am willing to devote to it all that I am or have or hope for in this world." [5]Within five years after the union was founded, the NLU boasted a membership of 600,000. [6]That membership included a variety of workers, from industrial laborers to vegetable farmers. [7]Instead of strikes, the NLU urged workers to become

more independent by forming cooperatives—businesses owned and run by workers.

Did you pick the first sentence? If you did, good for you. You're absolutely right. Sentence 1 opens the paragraph with a broad umbrella statement about the success of an early union. Sentence 2 then picks up the same point on a more specific level of detail. Diagrammed, the paragraph would look like this:

Topic sentence
Specific sentence Specific sentence Specific sentence Specific sentence

Now let's look at another example. Is the first sentence of this paragraph also the topic sentence?

> [1]Henry Ford is probably best known as the man who invented the gasoline-powered automobile. [2]Ford's real passion, however, was not cars but soybeans. [3]From Ford's perspective, soybeans were the solution to most of humanity's problems. [4]A soybean diet would, he thought, cure numerous ills. [5]Thus, every meal served in the Ford home included one soybean dish and a big pitcher of soymilk. [6]But, in his mind, soybeans weren't just good nutrition. [7]Ford was convinced they could also revolutionize* manufacturing. [8]In the 1930s, Ford built three soybean-processing plants. [9]What was produced in those plants? [10]Paint, fittings, knobs, and horn buttons for cars, all made from a soybean-oil base.

The first sentence in the above paragraph is certainly general enough to be a topic sentence. However, the idea in the first sentence is *not* continued by the second sentence. Instead, the second sentence changes course to talk not about Ford, the inventor of the automobile, but Ford the soybean promoter. The paragraph then develops the point made in the second sentence as we learn more about Ford's passion for soybeans. This means that the second sentence is the topic sentence, while the first sentence is an introductory sentence.

As the name implies, **introductory sentences** pave the way for topic sentences by providing background information that helps the reader

---

*revolutionize: bring about huge changes.

better understand the main idea. Diagrammed, paragraphs with the topic sentence appearing second would look something like this:

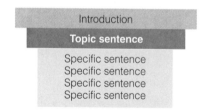

O━ READING KEYS

◆ Topic sentences have three characteristics: (1) they are among the most general sentences in a paragraph, (2) they introduce the main idea developed throughout the paragraph, and (3) they can function as a one-sentence summary of the entire paragraph and include or cover everything else discussed in the paragraph.

◆ Topic sentences can and do appear anywhere in a paragraph. However, particularly in textbooks, they are likely to be the first, second, and occasionally the third sentence in a paragraph.

◆ If the second sentence adds more specific information to the first, then the first sentence is probably the topic sentence. You can be certain that the first sentence is the topic sentence if the third sentence also continues developing the idea introduced in the opening sentence.

Transitions and Topic Sentences in Second Position

What follows is another paragraph in which the second sentence is the topic sentence. Note that the author again uses the contrast transition *however*. The use of contrast transitions is very common when the topic sentence is the second sentence of the paragraph, for example:

[1]For years now, parents of children with attention deficit disorder (ADD)—the inability to concentrate—have relied on medication to improve their children's attention span. [2]Currently, however, many parents of children with ADD are singing the praises of a new and promising therapy—the practice of martial* arts. [3]And the parents are

---

*martial: having to do with battle or war.

not alone. [4]A number of doctors, along with organizations like the National Attention Deficit Disorder Association, argue that training in self-defense systems like karate, jujitsu, and tai chi can ease the symptoms of ADD. [5]These symptoms include impulsiveness, inability to concentrate, and hyperactivity. [6]According to Dr. John J. Ratey, an associate professor of clinical psychology at Harvard Medical School, the martial arts require the kind of concentration that forces the attention centers in the brain to work together. [7]Therein lies the special benefit of the martial arts for children and adults who find it difficult to concentrate.

The paragraph on ADD begins with a general statement that looks like it might be the topic sentence. But the contrast transition *however* in the second sentence signals a reversal or change in the author's train of thought. In this case, the transition points to the paragraph's real topic sentence: "Many parents of children with ADD are singing the praises of a new and promising therapy—the practice of martial arts." This is the idea developed throughout the paragraph.

The pattern illustrated in the paragraph on ADD is a common one. Writers open with a statement, which they then modify or contradict. The modification or revision is the real point of the passage. A clue to this pattern's presence is a contrast or reversal transition at the beginning of the second sentence.

A Word on Topic Sentence Locations and Textbooks

This chapter has spent a considerable amount of time focusing on topic sentences that appear as the first or second sentence of a paragraph. That's because it's very common for textbooks to make the topic sentence the first, second, and occasionally the third sentence in a paragraph. Thus you need to be aware of how you should think about textbook prose. Especially at the beginning of a paragraph, be attuned to how general sentences in a paragraph do (or do not) get developed in more specific detail by the sentences that follow.

That being said, it's still true that topic sentences can move around. As the next chapter will illustrate, topic sentences turn up in more places than just the first third of a paragraph. But when you are reading textbooks and thinking about how best to distribute your attention while reading, make sure you give special attention to paragraph openings. The chances are very good that that's where you will find the main idea neatly expressed in a topic sentence.

Transitions Signaling Contrast, Reversal, or Change ◆	but conversely despite however in contrast nevertheless	nonetheless on the other hand still unfortunately whereas yet

⊶ᵣ READING KEY

◆ If a transition like *however*, *unfortunately*, or *yet* opens the second sentence in a paragraph, the second sentence is likely to be the topic sentence.

◆ **EXERCISE 5**   **Recognizing Topic Sentences and Reversal Transitions**

DIRECTIONS   After reading each paragraph, write the number of the topic sentence in the blank. Circle any reversal transitions appearing at the beginning of paragraphs. *Note*: The topic sentence will be the first or second sentence in the paragraph.

EXAMPLE   ¹Scientists now believe that the brain, when stimulated, has a remarkable ability to develop even in old age. ²Research on rats, for example, shows that intellectual exercise causes brain cells to branch like trees. ³These new branches then function as additional connections between individual brain cells. ⁴Scientists think that these newly formed connections, produced by strenuous intellectual exertion, serve to enhance both memory and mental sharpness, despite the passage of time. ⁵That theory certainly seems to be confirmed by the Sisters of Notre Dame in Mankato, Minnesota. ⁶Although advanced in age, the sisters show little, if any, loss of memory or mental quickness, and one reason for that may be their lifestyle. ⁷The nuns are engaged in a variety of intellectual activities from morning until night. ⁸Their constant mental activity may be why they stay sharp even into advanced old age.

Sentence __1__ is the topic sentence.

EXPLANATION   The first sentence is the most general in the paragraph. The remaining sentences pick up the theme it introduces and could all be included under that opening statement. They all show, in more specific detail, how the brain continues to develop in old age. That makes sentence 1 the topic sentence.

1. ¹Michael Faraday was the son of a poor blacksmith and had very little formal education. ²Yet, despite his lack of formal education, Faraday's accomplishments reveal a brilliant and imaginative mind. ³Faraday invented the first electric motor. ⁴He also showed that magnetism could be converted* into electricity and constructed a dynamo.* ⁵The first electrical transformer* is another one of Faraday's inventions. ⁶He also showed how magnetism could affect polarized light—light that vibrates in only one direction. ⁷His discoveries won him fame in several different fields.

   Sentence _____ is the topic sentence.

2. ¹Silly as it might seem, surveys show that television affects how the public views the threat of crime. ²Because there are so many crime shows on TV, heavy viewers tend to believe that crime is on the upswing. ³They believe that even when statistics show there has been a downturn. ⁴As it turns out, people who don't watch much television tend to have a more accurate view of criminal activity. ⁵This may be because light viewers are more likely to get their views from print sources and, as a result, have a more realistic picture of crime in America. ⁶Not surprisingly, heavy viewers of television are fans of tough anticrime measures and stiffer prison sentences. ⁷Light viewers, in contrast, tend to favor social programs over longer prison sentences. ⁸These viewers are also more in favor of prison reform. ⁹They are less likely to favor maximum security prisons, where the emphasis is on punishment rather than rehabilitation.*

   Sentence _____ is the topic sentence.

3. ¹Most people know that snake venom can be deadly. ²However, few people are aware that snake venom can, on occasion, save lives and

---

*converted: changed into another form.
*dynamo: a machine that produces electric current.
*transformer: a device used to transfer electric energy from one circuit to another.
*rehabilitation: restoring to good character.

ease pain. [3]The venom of a snake called Russell's viper, for example, has clotting properties. [4]In the past, it has been used to stop uncontrolled bleeding in hemophiliacs.* [5]Researchers have also discovered that the venom of the deadly Malayan pit viper can dissolve blood clots. [6]Thus, the venom has been used to treat patients who have undergone surgery and are in danger of developing blood clots. [7]Some venoms also have properties that make them useful as painkillers in the treatment of arthritis and cancer.

Sentence _____ is the topic sentence.

4. [1]How does U.S. family leave policy compare with that in other countries? [2]Most industrialized countries have much more generous policies than those in the United States, providing not only more extended leaves of absence so that working parents can take care of their young children but also financial support for part or all of the leave period. [3]In Sweden, Germany, and France, one parent can take a paid infant-care leave supported by the employer or a social insurance fund. [4]If both parents choose to continue to work, they are guaranteed access to high-quality daycare for their child. [5]In Sweden, either the mother or father is entitled to a twelve-month paid leave to stay home with a new infant. [6]The parent on leave is reimbursed 90 percent of her or his salary for the first nine months following the child's birth, receives $150 per month for the next three months, and then is allowed to continue with an unpaid leave and a job guarantee for six additional months until the child is eighteen months old. (Seifert and Hoffnung, *Child and Adolescent Development*, p. 222.)

Sentence _____ is the topic sentence.

5. [1]Although American society has always been divided into competing and cooperating interests, the development of formal interest group organizations began only in the late 1800s. [2]The first formal interest groups were organizations of farmers, such as the Grange, founded in 1867. [3]Farmers' groups were followed by the organization of workers into labor unions in the late 1800s. [4]These organizations— like the many groups that followed—developed in response to

_____
*hemophiliacs: people suffering from a rare blood disease that inhibits the blood's ability to clot.

changing social, economic, technological, and political conditions. [5]Farm organizations, for example, developed in response to the depression of the 1870s, which was particularly devastating to the farmers in the South and West. [6]Similarly, labor unions developed after the industrial revolution created a permanent wage-labor force with little political or economic power of their own. (Lasser, *American Politics*, p. 208.)

Sentence _____ is the topic sentence.

Testing Your Topic Sentence

Once you think you know the topic sentence of a paragraph, there are two ways to test it: (1) Ask yourself if the sentence could function as a one-sentence summary, or umbrella sentence, for the paragraph. (2) Turn the topic sentence into a question and see if the remaining sentences answer that question. For an illustration, read this next paragraph:

> [1]The cyclone that struck the western coast of Myanmar (also known as Burma) in May 2008 was a catastrophe of horrifying proportions. [2]After the cyclone struck, the victim count began mounting, climbing high into the thousands. [3]Flood waters raced through towns, carrying the bodies of the dead and those still trying to survive. [4]Adding to the country's difficulties was the Burmese government's initial refusal of aid from other countries. [5]A dictatorship, the Myanmar government did not want to encourage foreign influence. [6]For members of the government, starvation was preferable to admitting their inability to aid the sick and dying.

In this case, sentence 1 is the best summary sentence. It's the only sentence general enough to include all the specific details about Myanmar's tragedy. If, to double-check ourselves, we turn the first sentence into a question—Why was the cyclone that struck Myanmar a catastrophe of horrifying proportions?—the first sentence again passes the test. The remaining sentences all help answer that question.

O━ᴍ READING KEY

◆ Test your topic sentence by (1) asking yourself if it could sum up the other sentences in the paragraph, and (2) turning the topic sentence into a question and checking to see if the remaining more specific sentences answer that question.

IDIOM ALERT: Raising Cain

In the Bible, Cain, the son of Adam and Eve, was jealous of his brother Abel and always ready to start a fight or cause trouble. This is the origin of the expression *raising Cain*.

◆ **EXERCISE 6**   **Recognizing Topic Sentences**

DIRECTIONS   Circle the letter of the topic. Then fill in the blank with a *1* or a *2* to identify the topic sentence.

EXAMPLE   ¹A number of books with titles like *Raising Cain*, *Real Boys*, and *Lost Boys* all focus on the same issue: Today's teenage boys are feeling more anxiety than ever before about their physical appearance. ²They are constantly bombarded by advertising featuring well-muscled, semi-clad young men. ³The result is that teenage boys are experiencing what teenage girls have been coping with for years. ⁴Young boys are afraid that they cannot possibly live up to the media's idealized* image of their gender. ⁵Boys below the average in height, weight, or both suffer the most. ⁶Often, they are brutally teased by their brawnier peers. ⁷Some react to the ridicule by heading for the gym and lifting weights. ⁸Yet even those who successfully bulk up don't like feeling that they are worthwhile only because of their hard-won muscle tone. ⁹Other teens, convinced that no amount of bodybuilding can help, withdraw from social contact with their peers. ¹⁰This is their way of avoiding taunts* about their size or shape. ¹¹Still, these youths are understandably angry at being badly treated because of their body type. ¹²Although school psychologists generally recognize that boys are having severe body-image problems, they don't know what to do about it.

Topic   a. *Raising Cain* and *Lost Boys*

b. teenage boys who lift weights

---

*idealized: existing more in thought than in reality.
*taunts: insulting or ridiculing remarks.

ⓒ teenage boys and their body image

d. bodybuilding

Sentence ___1___ is the topic sentence.

EXPLANATION   Although *b*, teenage boys who lift weights, might seem a likely topic, the passage focuses more heavily on boys and their body image. Answer *a* is *too* specific. The two book titles are mentioned only in passing. Answer *d* is far too general. The paragraph focuses on teenage boys who lift weights, not bodybuilding overall. Thus, *c* is the correct topic.

For the topic sentence, sentence 1 is the best answer because the entire passage is devoted to describing the growing anxiety boys feel about their body image.

1. ¹The hookworm is only about one centimeter (one-half inch) long, but it can still cause serious trouble. ²In warmer parts of the world, young hookworms can enter the body of a person walking barefoot over infected ground. ³Once they gain entry through the feet, the worms travel through the blood to the lungs. ⁴From there, the hookworms make their way to the small intestine. ⁵They attach themselves to the intestinal walls and begin to live off their victim's blood. ⁶If many worms are present, they usually cause anemia* in the victim. (Adapted from Tanzer, *Biology and Human Progress*, p. 287.)

Topic

    a. diseases of the small intestine

    b. worms

    c. disease in warmer parts of the world

    d. hookworms

Sentence _____ is the topic sentence.

2. ¹One of the fastest-growing minorities in America today is Hispanics—people who trace their heritage to Spanish-speaking nations. ²Hispanics total more than 22.4 million people, or about 9 percent of the population. ³In general, Hispanic Americans are made up of three separate groups. ⁴Those three groups are Mexican Americans, Puerto

---

*anemia: a disease of the blood that makes the victim tired and weak.

Ricans, and people from South or Central America. [5]Hispanic leaders of this large community are determined to end discrimination* in housing and employment. (Adapted from Hardy, *Government in America*, p. 205.)

Topic   a. Spanish-speaking nations

b. Hispanics

c. minorities

d. Hispanic leaders

Sentence _____ is the topic sentence.

3. [1]Some people think horror films are a sign of today's modern and threatening times. [2]Yet horror films actually have a long and distinguished history. [3]As early as 1910, Thomas Alva Edison made a movie about Frankenstein's monster. [4]*The Golem*, a similar film about a man-made monster, appeared in 1914 just before World War I broke out. [5]Following the war, several German directors produced some classic horror films, among them F. W. Murnau's *Nosferatu* (1921), a brilliant film based on Bram Stoker's novel *Dracula*. [6]The movie was a box-office hit, and other horror films soon followed. [7]It seems that the history of horror films is almost as long as the history of film itself.

Topic   a. Thomas Alva Edison as a filmmaker

b. *The Golem*

c. the history of horror films

d. horror films

Sentence _____ is the topic sentence.

4. [1]Some people insist that children's baseball leagues should use baseballs that are softer than those used by adult and professional leagues. [2]Yet for children, even soft balls carry a risk. [3]True, a softer baseball is less likely to cause harm if it hits a child's head at high speed, but research has shown that a softer ball can sometimes cause the heart to stop if the ball hits the child in the chest. [4]In some circumstances, the softer ball triggers this rare but dangerous response even *more* than a harder ball does. [5]In addition, a softer ball poses just about the

*discrimination: unfair treatment of a person or group.

same risk for eye injury. [6]Although a softer ball may prevent a serious head injury, a fast-moving ball of any type is likely to damage the eye socket, seriously hurting the eye.

Topic
    a. sports for kids

    b. children's baseball leagues

    c. head injuries in children's baseball

    d. baseballs used in children's leagues

Sentence _____ is the topic sentence.

VOCABULARY EXTRA

The paragraph on page 114 introduces a book title, *Raising Cain*. The book is about young boys who misbehave because they feel anxiety about what it means to become a man. Upon seeing the title, you may have already noticed that it has a pun in it. **Puns** use the same word in two different ways. For example, the idiom "raising Cain" means getting into trouble, and the boys described in the book do just that. However, because Cain's name evokes associations of jealousy and violence, the title also suggests that some parents may be raising, or bringing into the world, another Cain if they aren't careful.[†]

CLASS ACTION

Try your hand at creating a pun or two. Here are two examples:
    Does fuzzy logic tickle?
    Iron was discovered because some smelt it.

◆ EXERCISE 7   **Recognizing Topic Sentences**

DIRECTIONS   Identify the topic by circling the appropriate letter. Then fill in the blank with a *1*, *2*, or *3* to identify the topic sentence.

EXAMPLE   [1]In several states across the nation, there has been a successful drive to end social promotion. [2]In other words, children who do

---

[†]For many, the expression "raising Cain" has lost its Biblical connection. However, the first recorded use of it suggested that most people who heard it knew Cain's story. "Why have we every reason to believe that Adam and Eve were both rowdies? Because they both raised Cain." (From Robert Hendrickson, *Word and Phrase Origins*, p. 565.)

not achieve the required score on a standardized* test will have to repeat the grade they have just finished; however, there is little evidence that making children repeat a grade has a beneficial effect. [3]If anything, research suggests, the opposite may be true. [4]Forcing children to repeat a grade often hurts rather than helps their academic performance. [5]In 1989, University of Georgia professor Thomas Holmes surveyed sixty-three studies that compared the performance of students who had repeated a grade with that of students who had received a social promotion. [6]Holmes found that most of the children who had repeated a grade had a poorer academic record than those children who had been promoted despite low test scores. [7]A similar study of New York City children in the 1980s revealed that children who repeated a grade were more likely to drop out upon reaching high school. [8]The call to end social promotion may have a nice ring to it in political speeches. [9]Yet there is little indication that it does students any real good.

Topic   (a.) repeating a grade

      b. politicians

      c. education in America

Topic Sentence   _2_

EXPLANATION   The topic is answer *a*, "repeating a grade." The paragraph as a whole, however, makes the point that repeating a grade may not be as beneficial as some would claim. Although keeping kids back if they don't pass a standardized test may sound like a better policy than social promotion, there is no real evidence to prove that it is. That main idea is summed up in sentence 2, which is the topic sentence.

1. [1]During World War I, a number of severe shortages alerted the world's scientists to the need for synthetic, or man-made, materials, and a research team headed by Wallace H. Carothers developed the first synthetic fiber, called nylon, in 1935. [2]As it turned out, the development of nylon had a surprisingly dramatic effect, first on fashion and then on world affairs. [3]In 1939, the DuPont company began marketing sheer nylon hosiery for women. [4]The nylons were

---

*standardized: made the same in all cases.

an immediate hit. [5]They practically flew off the shelves. [6]Nylon stockings, however, quickly disappeared with the coming of World War II. By 1941, nylon had become essential to the war effort. [7]It was used in everything from parachutes and ropes to insulation* and coat linings. [8]Sadly, Carothers never witnessed the impact of his creation. [9]He committed suicide two years before the first pair of nylons ever went on sale.

Topic

    a. Wallace H. Carothers

    b. World War I

    c. the development of nylon

Topic Sentence   _____

2. [1]Many colleges and universities have adopted honor codes to prevent plagiarism. [2]These honor codes, though, don't always deter students from cheating. [3]Consequently, more schools are using technology to combat academic dishonesty. [4]For example, some universities are using antiplagiarism software. [5]Professors can scan a student's assignment into software, which then checks the paper against text available on the Internet. [6]This procedure also allows professors to more easily identify a term paper that a student has purchased from a website. [7]Yet another type of software prevents cheating during computer-based tests. [8]It will not allow a test taker to use e-mail or the Internet to find answers to test questions. [9]Administrators of national standardized tests, too, are looking for ways to discourage cheating. [10]They are installing digital cameras, along with thumbprint and retina scanners, to ensure that students cannot hire others to take tests for them. [11]Colleges hope that such advanced technology will promote more ethical behavior.

Topic

    a. honor codes

    b. anti-plagiarism software

    c. technology to combat cheating

Topic Sentence   _____

*insulation: material or substance used to prevent the loss of heat.

3. [1]In school, we all learned that dinosaurs were slow, cold-blooded reptiles. [2]In fact, though, new scientific evidence suggests dinosaurs might actually have been warm-blooded animals that behaved more like mammals than reptiles. [3]For example, the growth patterns of dinosaur bones are more like those of warm-blooded mammals. [4]Also, some dinosaurs apparently sat on eggs in their nests. [5]To hatch eggs this way, their body temperatures had to be higher than the air around them. [6]Finally, fossils reveal that many dinosaurs traveled in herds and hunted in packs, just as many warm-blooded mammals do.

Topic   a. reptiles

            b. fossils

            c. dinosaurs

Topic Sentence   _____

4. [1]Colleges and universities across the nation should create programs and procedures designed to help students cope with serious problems like depression and anxiety. [2]One reason for doing more is the increase in these kinds of problems. [3]According to the American College Health Association, 76 percent of students felt "overwhelmed" in 2001. [4]Twenty-two percent of students claimed to be so depressed that they could not function normally. [5]Also, 30 percent of campus counseling center directors reported that at least one suicide had occurred on their campuses in the last year. [6]Obviously, these numbers indicate that more and more students need help. [7]Yet they are often unable to seek out this help for themselves. [8]Emotionally unstable young people are often incapable of figuring out what they should do or of following through on professional advice on their own. [9]Thus, colleges and universities need to provide more guidance.

Topic   a. students with emotional problems

            b. colleges and universities

            c. American College Health Association

Topic Sentence   _____

ROUNDING UP THE KEYS

Here is a list of all the reading keys introduced in the chapter. Use them to review for the test on page 129. If a particular reading key doesn't make sense on its own, go back to the page where it appeared and review the section preceding it.

O—ᵐ **READING KEYS: Topics**

- ◆ The topic is the person, place, event, or idea repeatedly mentioned or referred to throughout the reading. (p. 94)
- ◆ The topic never pops up and then disappears. It's a constant presence in the passage. (p. 94)
- ◆ Although one word can sometimes sum up the topic, you'll often need several words to express it. (p. 94)
- ◆ Sometimes readers have to come up with the words for the topic. (p. 95)
- ◆ The topic should be general enough to include everything discussed in the paragraph but specific enough to exclude what isn't. (p. 95)

O—ᵐ **READING KEY: Main Ideas**

- ◆ The main idea is the central point or thought the writer wants to communicate to readers. It's what ties all the sentences in the paragraph together. (p. 101)

O—ᵐ **READING KEYS: Topic Sentences**

- ◆ Topic sentences have three characteristics: (1) they are among the most general sentences in a paragraph, (2) they introduce the main idea developed throughout the paragraph, and (3) they can function as a one-sentence summary of the entire paragraph and include or cover everything else discussed in the paragraph. (p. 108)
- ◆ Topic sentences can and do appear anywhere in a paragraph. However, particularly in textbooks, they are likely to be the first, second, and occasionally the third sentence in a paragraph. (p. 108)
- ◆ If the second sentence adds more specific information to the first, then the first sentence is probably the topic sentence. You can be certain that the first sentence is the topic sentence if the third sentence also continues developing the idea introduced in the opening sentence. (p. 108)

READING KEY: Transitions and Topic Sentences

◆ If a transition like *however*, *unfortunately*, or *yet* opens the second sentence in a paragraph, the second sentence is likely to be the topic sentence. (p. 110)

READING KEY: Testing Your Topic Sentence

◆ Test your topic sentence by (1) asking yourself if it could sum up the other sentences in the paragraph, and (2) turning the topic sentence into a question and checking to see if the remaining more specific sentences answer that question. (p. 113)

Ten More Words for Your Textbook Vocabulary

1. **correlation:** relationship, connection

   Fortunately for most of us, there is no *correlation* between spelling ability and intelligence.

2. **orbit:** circle, move in a circular motion

   In the fifteenth century, people believed that the sun *orbited* the Earth.

3. **obligated:** pledged, bound morally or legally

   Far Eastern cultures believe that relationships ought to be long lasting and that individuals should show loyalty to others simply because we are all *obligated* to each other. (Gamble and Gamble, *Contacts*, p. 382.)

4. **disclosure:** making known, revealing

   The *disclosure* of negative information early in a relationship can be positive because we tend to be attracted to those who are willing to be honest and take responsibility for their actions. (Gamble and Gamble, *Contacts*, p. 398.)

5. **plight:** unfortunate situation, misery

   John Steinbeck's novel *The Grapes of Wrath* movingly portrayed the *plight* of migrant workers.

6. **monopoly:** single party control over a product or service

   In 1807, Robert L. Livingston and Robert Fulton introduced the steamboat *Clermont* on the Hudson River, and they soon gained a *monopoly* from the New York legislature to run a New York–New Jersey service. (Adapted from Boyer et al., *The Enduring Vision*, p. 258.)

7. **repertoire:** range

   As we grow older, our *repertoire* of relationships increases and we realize that we can have different kinds of friends.

8. **factor:** element, part, piece

   More than one *factor* accounts for the success or failure of new technology.

9. **derivative:** developed or received from another source

   In the nineteenth century, physicians, medicine peddlers, and legitimate drug companies freely prescribed or sold opium along with its *derivatives*, morphine and heroin. (Adapted from Boyer et al., *The Enduring Vision*, p. 640.)

10. **antithetical:** opposite, contrasted

    Alexander Hamilton's attitude toward the federal government was *antithetical* to Jefferson's: Hamilton wanted the nation's government to hold more power; Jefferson did not.

◆ **EXERCISE 8**   **Building an Academic Vocabulary**

DIRECTIONS   Fill in the blanks with one of the words listed below.

> derivatives   antithetical   repertoire   monopolies   orbit
> factors   plight   disclosure   correlation   obligated

1. John Stuart Mill was a nineteenth-century philosopher who was extremely sympathetic to the _____ of women.

2. Several _____ contributed to the mortgage crisis of 2008, among them a lack of banking regulations.

3. In the marketplace, _____ discourage competition, and that's not good for the consumer.

4. Some useful drugs are actually _____ of deadly poisons.

5. The artistic temperament is often _____ to the spirit of the marketplace, and artists don't always make good businesspeople.

6. Recent research has found a(n) _____ between heavy alcohol use and memory loss.

7. In some cultures, acceptance of a gift means the recipient is _____ to offer an even bigger gift in return.

8. Like most powerful people, the queen insisted that everyone within her _____ be completely loyal and unquestioning.

9. Pressed about the _____ of her personal wealth, the candidate's wife said that her money was her business.

10. The disease is accompanied by a wide _____ of odd behaviors.

DIGGING DEEPER   **Life Lessons from the Family Dog**

Looking Ahead   The statements on page 105 suggested that people can be overly attached to their dogs. This reading by *New York Times* reporter Dana Jennings suggests that there may be a very good reason why dog owners are devoted to their pets.

1   Our family dog started failing a couple of months ago. Her serious health problems began at about the same time I was coping with my own—finishing my radiation and hormone therapy for prostate cancer. Since last summer, I've learned that my cancer is shockingly aggressive, and the surgery, radiation and hormone treatments have left me exhausted, incontinent* and with an AWOL libido.* These days I'm waiting for the first tests that will tell me the status of my health.

2   Even so, as I face my own profound health issues, it is my dog's poor health that is piercing me to the heart. I'm dreading that morning when I walk downstairs and . . . well, those of us who love dogs understand that all dog stories end the same way. Her full name is Bijou de Minuit (Jewel of Midnight)—my wife teaches French. She is a 12-year-old black miniature poodle, and she is, literally, on her last legs. Her hind quarters fly out from beneath her, her back creaks and cracks as she walks, she limps, she's speckled with bright red warts the size of nickels, her snore is loud and labored (like a freight train chugging up some steep grade) and she spends most of the day drowsing on her pillow-bed next to the kitchen radiator. Bijou's medicine chest is impressive for a 23-pound dog: a baby dose of amoxicillin for chronic urinary tract infections; prednisone and Tramadol for pain; phenobarbital for seizures; Proin for incontinence—all of it wrapped in mini-slices of pepperoni.

3   She is, I realize, "just" a dog. But she has, nonetheless, taught me a few lessons about life, living, and illness. Despite all her troubles, Bijou is still game. She still groans to her feet to go outside, still barks at and with the neighborhood dogs, is willing to hobble around the kitchen to carouse with a rubber ball—her shrub of a tail quivering in joy. I know now that Bijou was an important part of my therapy as I recovered from having my prostate removed. I learned that dogs, besides being pets, can also be our teachers.

_____

*incontinent: unable to control urination or defecation.
*libido: sexual desire.

4   Human beings constantly struggle to live in the moment. We're either obsessing over the past ("Gee, life would've been different if I'd only joined the Peace Corps"), or obsessing over the future ("Gee, I hope my 401k holds up"). We forget that life, real life, is lived right now, in this very moment.

5   But living in the moment is something that dogs (and cancer patients) do by their very nature. Bijou eats when she's hungry, drinks when she's thirsty, sleeps when she's tired and will still gratefully curl up in whatever swatch of sunlight steals through the windows. She'd jump up onto my sickbed last summer, nuzzle me and ask for her ears and pointy snout to be scratched. It made both of us happy as she sighed in satisfaction. And she was the subject of one of our favorite family jokes as I recuperated: "You take the dog out. I have cancer."

6   In spending so much time with Bijou, I began to realize that our dogs, in their carefree dogginess, make us more human, force us to shed our narcissistic skins. Even when you have cancer, you can't be utterly self-involved when you have a floppy-eared mutt who needs to be fed, walked, and belly-scratched. And you can't help but ponder the mysteries of creation as you gaze into the eyes of your dog, or wonder why and how we chose dogs and they chose us.

7   Dogs also tell us—especially when we're sick—of our own finitude. And, partly, that's why we cry when they die, because we also know that all human-being stories end the same way, too. Good dogs—and most dogs are good dogs—are canine candles that briefly blaze and shine, illuminating our lives. Bijou has been here with us for the past 12 years, reminding us that simple pleasures are the ones to be treasured: a treat, a game of fetch, a nose-to-the-ground stroll in the park.

8   Simple pleasures. As I lazed and dozed at home last summer after surgery, there was nothing sweeter to me in this world than to hear Bijou drinking from her water dish outside my door. It was as if her gentle lap-lapping ferried me to waters of healing. I'll miss her.

Sharpening Your Skills

DIRECTIONS   Answer the following questions by filling in the blanks.

1. Like single paragraphs, multi-paragraph readings usually express one overall main idea that ties everything in the reading together. In your own words, what's the overall main idea of this reading?

_____

2. In paragraph 1, the author uses the word *AWOL*, which is an acronym for absent without official leave. How would you define an acronym?

_____

What does the author mean when he says his libido was AWOL?

_____

3. Using a print or an online dictionary, locate the history of the word *narcissistic* (paragraph 6). Then explain the word's origin in your own words.

_____

_____

_____

_____

4. What does the author mean when he says dogs make us more human (paragraph 6)?

_____

5. Based on the context, how would you define the word *finitude* in paragraph 7?

_____

▶ TEST 1   **Reviewing the Key Points**

DIRECTIONS   Answer the following questions by circling *T* (true) or *F* (false). *Note*: Read the questions carefully. Part of a question may be true and part may be false, making the whole sentence false.

T   F   **1.** The topic of a paragraph is the person, place, event, or idea under discussion.

T   F   **2.** The topic has to be expressed in a single word.

T   F   **3.** References to the topic will appear only at the beginning of the paragraph.

T   F   **4.** A topic should be broad enough to include what's covered in the paragraph and specific enough to exclude what isn't.

T   F   **5.** Sometimes readers need to provide the words needed to express the topic.

T   F   **6.** If a transition like *moreover* opens the second sentence in a paragraph, the third sentence might well be the topic sentence.

T   F   **7.** The topic sentence usually appears at the very end of the paragraph.

T   F   **8.** Once you discover the topic and the main idea, everything else in the reading will begin to make sense.

T   F   **9.** If the second sentence in a paragraph continues the thread of the first, then the first sentence is likely to be the topic sentence.

T   F **10.** Once you have found the topic sentence, you can test it by turning it into a question and seeing if the supporting details answer the question.

To correct your test, turn to page 553. If one or more of your answers is incorrect, re-read the Rounding Up the Keys section of the chapter to find out where your mistake might be.

▶ **TEST 2** **Identifying Topics and Topic Sentences**

DIRECTIONS Circle the appropriate letter to identify the topic. Then fill in the blank with a *1* or a *2* to identify the topic sentence.

1. ¹One of the success stories in the United States has been the establishment of twenty-six tribal colleges for Native Americans. ²Unlike the Indian boarding schools of the nineteenth century, which focused solely on white culture, tribal colleges have a double focus. ³Although they do teach the traditional academic subjects, they also teach courses about tribal culture, language, and art. ⁴While training Native-American students to participate in an industrialized society, the colleges also help reconnect students with their tribal identity. ⁵There are currently twenty-nine tribal colleges in North America, many with names that reflect their tribal heritage, like Sitting Bull College in North Dakota and Little Big Horn College in Montana. (Adapted from McCormack, "Focus on Indians' Future," *USA Today*, September 16, 1992, p. 14A.)

Topic   a. Native-American culture
          b. tribal colleges
          c. tribal identity

Sentence _____ is the topic sentence.

2. ¹Mining sapphires* is a difficult and dangerous process. ²First, the miner digs a square pit about 40 feet deep in sandy earth. ³When he reaches a layer of gravel, he begins digging sideways into the wall of the pit, removing rocks as he goes. ⁴This is treacherous work because the dirt can cave in, burying the miner. ⁵Loads of gravel are then hauled to a river and washed. ⁶Finally, the miner removes the sapphires from the gravel and sells them to gem buyers who must travel with weapons because of the frequent robberies and murders in their business.

Topic   a. the dangers miners face
          b. mining for sapphires
          c. sapphires

Sentence _____ is the topic sentence.

---

*sapphires: a type of gemstone, usually blue in color.

3. [1]Most successful job interviews follow three basic steps. [2]If you know the steps, you increase your chances of getting the job. [3]Step 1 lasts about three minutes and occurs when you first introduce yourself. [4]In these three minutes, you need to demonstrate that you are friendly and at ease with others. [5]This is the time to shake hands firmly, make eye contact, and smile. [6]During step 2, you need to explain your skills and abilities. [7]This is your chance to show an employer just how capable you are. [8]Step 3 comes at the end of the interview. Although it lasts only a minute or two, this step is still important. [9]When the employer says, "We'll be in touch," you need to say something like, "I'll check back with you in a few days, if you don't mind." [10]A comment like this indicates your commitment to getting the job.

Topic   a. jobs

      b. smiles during job interviews

      c. the three steps in job interviews

Sentence _____ is the topic sentence.

4. [1]Spanish-language television has two major broadcast networks, Univision and Telemundo. [2]Univision, however, is closely associated with Mexico's Televisa network and claims the lion's share of the Spanish-speaking audience. [3]Univision's schedules offer mostly imports from Mexico and other Latin American countries. [4]Telenovelas, the Spanish version of soap operas, are a key component of its prime time schedule. [5]On June 25, 2007, Univision made television history with the finale of *La Fea Más Bella*, which had higher ratings than all the English-language television broadcasting networks. [6]But in addition to record-breaking telenovelas, Univision also has Jorge Ramos, the journalist who anchors "Al Punto," the network's weekly political program. [7]Named one of the twenty-five most influential Hispanics in the country, Ramos is one reason for Univision's success, and he has a huge following among Spanish-speaking citizens.

Topic   a. Telemundo

      b. Univision

      c. Hispanics in the U.S.

Sentence _____ is the topic sentence.

▶ **TEST 3** **Identifying Topics and Topic Sentences**

DIRECTIONS Circle the appropriate letter to identify the topic. Then fill in the blank with a *1* or a *2* to identify the topic sentence.

1. [1]The island of Puerto Rico is rather small; it is only about 111 miles from east to west and just 40 miles from north to south. [2]Yet despite its small size, Puerto Rico's landscape shows marvelous variety. [3]On the north side of the island, it rains a lot. [4]The average yearly rainfall is around 180 inches. [5]With all that rain, it's not surprising that northern Puerto Rico is home to a tropical rain forest. [6]In the southern portion of the island, there is less rain—only around 60 inches on the average. [7]As a result, the southern half of Puerto Rico has fewer trees and more thorny shrubs. [8]Although agriculture has removed much of the original vegetation, the island's hilly landscape is alive with gorgeous splashes of color. [9]Brilliant orange and red flowers hang from trees like the royal Poinciana and the African tulip. [10]Puerto Rico is also home to several species of rare orchids and some very rare birds. [11]The endangered Puerto Rican green parrot is found nowhere else in the world.

   Topic a. the climate of Puerto Rico

   b. the rain forest of Puerto Rico

   c. Puerto Rico's landscape

   Sentence _____ is the topic sentence.

2. [1]When she was only 21 years old, architecture student Maya Lin had her design for the Vietnam Veterans Memorial officially accepted. [2]Wise beyond her years, Lin knew there would be controversy over the decision because the design was so plain, but even she was not prepared for the controversy that exploded over her memorial to the soldiers fallen in Vietnam. [3]Although the actual number of veterans offended by the memorial's appearance was small, the protesters were extremely vocal. [4]The veterans were aided by Congressman Henry Hyde, who pushed their cause with all the power at his disposal. [5]Hyde went so far as to take the petition to the secretary of the interior, James Watt. [6]Watt, in turn, insisted that the plain black granite wall Lin had designed must be modified. [7]At Watt's command, it was. [8]The entry walk to the memorial now includes an American flag and a statue of

three combat soldiers. [9]Yet even that compromise didn't appease some of the young architect's most vicious critics. [10]These were the people who could not forget that Lin was an Asian-American. [11]They sent letters to the memorial committee protesting her ancestry. [12]Some of the letter-writers even stooped to calling her a "gook." [13]Throughout this explosive time, Maya Lin, at least publicly, remained calm and composed. [14]But years later, after the memorial had safely been established, she described how difficult that earlier time had been.

Topic

   a. additions to the Vietnam Veterans Memorial

   b. the controversy over the Vietnam Veterans Memorial

   c. Henry Hyde's support of the protest against Maya Lin's design

Sentence _____ is the topic sentence.

3. [1]To quiet the conspiracy rumors about John F. Kennedy's death, the new president, Lyndon Baines Johnson, created a committee to investigate the assassination. [2]Determined to include members whose word would be trusted, Johnson fought hard to get the right people on the committee. [3]When Supreme Court Justice Earl Warren said no, Johnson warned him about the consequences of his refusal. [4]The president went so far as to claim that if the rumors weren't quelled, nuclear war might erupt. [5]As might be expected, Warren gave in. [6]Senator Richard Russell from Georgia, however, was a different story. [7]Russell didn't believe that his refusal would cause nuclear war. [8]When that threat didn't work, Johnson took off the kid gloves. [9]He told Russell that no matter what it took, he would find a way to make the senator serve on the committee. [10]Understandably nervous, Russell gave in to become a member of the now famous Warren Commission.

Topic

   a. the assassination of John F. Kennedy

   b. Senator Richard Russell's refusal to participate in the Warren Commission

   c. Lyndon Baines Johnson's creation of the Warren Commission

Sentence _____ is the topic sentence.

4. [1]Several types of tissue are found in the human body. [2]*Connective tissue* binds together and supports the body's internal structures.

[3]Connective tissue also forms cartilage, bones, and the walls of various organs. [4]For its part, *muscle tissue* is essential to movement. [5]The heart, for example, is made of muscle. [6]It has to pump blood throughout the body. [7]*Nervous tissue* is important for communication between our inner and outer worlds. [8]For example, the tissues in our nervous system keep us aware of our environment. [9]*Epithelial tissue* covers the surface of our body in the form of skin. [10]It also helps the body absorb materials. (Adapted from Otto and Towle, *Modern Biology*, p. 586.)

Topic   a. the human body

b. connective tissue in the heart

c. four kinds of body tissue

Sentence _____ is the topic sentence.

5. [1]In 1999, the Nobel Peace Prize was given to an organization called *Médecins Sans Frontières* (MSF) or Doctors Without Borders. [2]Founded in 1971 by a small group of young French doctors, Doctors Without Borders was meant to be an alternative to the International Red Cross based in Geneva. [3]Like members of the Red Cross, the French organization would go anyplace in the world where people needed medical attention. [4]But in contrast to the Red Cross, Doctors Without Borders insisted on speaking out against injustice. [5]When earthquakes tumbled buildings in Turkey, the organization was among the first to complain about the government's failure to enforce building codes. [6]When Rwanda's civil war resulted in mass murder, members of Doctors Without Borders argued that more could have been done to stop the killing. [7]The organization complained that international leaders dragged their feet instead of taking action. [8]As journalist David Rieff wrote after the winner of the Nobel Peace Prize was announced, Doctors Without Borders has saved many lives, but it has also told some "harsh truths." (Source of information: David Rieff, *The New Republic*, November 8, 1999, p. 8.)

Topic   a. David Rieff's opinion of Doctors Without Borders

b. the difference between the Red Cross and Doctors Without Borders

c. civil war in Rwanda

Sentence _____ is the topic sentence.

▶ **TEST 4**   **Identifying Topics and Topic Sentences**

DIRECTIONS   Circle the appropriate letter to identify the topic. Then fill in the blank with a *1*, a *2*, or a *3* to identify the topic sentence.

1. [1]Why do animals hibernate in winter? [2]According to the experts, animals hibernate during winter because hibernating saves energy when food is scarce. [3]For example, during hibernation a ground squirrel's heart rate falls from a normal 200–400 beats per minute to only 7–10 beats. [4]Because their bodies are so still, the squirrels can simply live off their stored fat. [5]Bears hibernate for the same reason. [6]If they're sleeping, they don't need much energy and don't have to worry about finding food. (Adapted from *New Haven Register*, September 30, 1993, p. 38.)

    Topic   a. animals

              b. hibernation

              c. bears

              Sentence _____ is the topic sentence.

2. [1]To some extent, personal identity comes from belonging to social groups. [2]But being part of a group can also cause problems. [3]Unfortunately, being part of a larger social group can create particularly intense problems for minority teenagers. [4]Teenagers from African-American, Asian-American, Native American, and Latino backgrounds often struggle to create a personal identity that combines family values with the values of American society. [5]One tenth-grade Chinese girl who came to America at the age of 12 described her feelings in an essay. [6]Her words perfectly express her struggle for an identity that combines two different worlds: "I don't know who I am. Am I the good Chinese daughter? Or am I an American teenager?" (Adapted from Rubin, *Psychology*, p. 241.)

    Topic   a. groups

              b. forming an identity during the teenage years

              c. conflict between social groups and personal identity

              Sentence _____ is the topic sentence.

3. [1]In the 1930s, African-Americans battled racism in a variety of ways. [2]In New York City, the Harlem Tenants League fought rent increases and evictions. [3]African-American consumers also refused to buy in stores that did not hire black salespeople. [4]Their slogan was "Don't buy where you can't work." [5]In the South, poor black farmers joined with poor white ones to form the Southern Tenant Farmers' Union. [6]Across the country, the Brotherhood of Sleeping Car Porters fought for the rights of black workers.

Topic   a. the Harlem Tenants League

b. the 1930s

c. battling racism

Sentence _____ is the topic sentence.

4. [1]Some drugs have a higher chance of being abused than others. [2]However, it is frequently more useful to classify drug-taking behavior than it is to rate the drugs themselves. [3]For example, some people remain social drinkers for life. [4]Others become alcoholics within weeks of taking their first drink. [5]Drug use can also be classed as *experimental*—short-term use based on curiosity—or *compulsive*—long-term use based on extreme dependence. (Adapted from Coon, *Introduction to Psychology*, p. 158.)

Topic   a. addiction

b. compulsive drug taking

c. drug-taking behavior

Sentence _____ is the topic sentence.

▶ **TEST 5**   **Developing Your Textbook Vocabulary**

DIRECTIONS   Fill in the blanks with one of the words listed below.

monopolies	disclosure	antithetical	plight	repertoire
orbit	factors	obligated	correlation	derivative

1. An undeniable _____ exists between smoking ciga-rettes and developing lung cancer.

2. Numerous moons are in Jupiter's _____.

3. The candidate's _____ of jokes was extremely limited.

4. Legally, no one is _____ to vote, but perhaps it would be better if voting was a legal requirement.

5. The _____ of the insurance firm's losses sent panic throughout the business community.

6. The government needs to do something about the terrible _____ of the polar bears, who may well become extinct because of global warming's effect on the polar ice.

7. The Sherman Antitrust Act of 1890 made _____ illegal, but some corporations found a way around the law.

8. A number of different _____ contribute to academic success; chief among them is self-motivation.

9. Opium is a(n) _____ of the poppy.

10. In the nineteenth century, white settlers' determination to own the land they settled on was _____ to the beliefs of Native Americans, who were convinced that no one could own what belonged to nature.

More on Topic Sentences

4

As you know from Chapter 3, topic sentences in textbooks are likely to be the first, second, or third sentence of the paragraph. However, topic sentences, even in textbooks, can move around. They can, in fact, appear just about anywhere. This chapter will give you some examples of topic sentences that have moved beyond the paragraph opening.

More on Topic Sentences in Third Place

When a textbook topic sentence is the second sentence of a paragraph, it usually means the author needed to provide readers with some background about the topic or main idea. However, sometimes essential background knowledge can't be adequately expressed in a single sentence, and the introduction has to take up more than one sentence. In such cases, the topic sentence is likely to arrive even later in the paragraph. Look, for example, at this next paragraph.

[1]As you might expect, memory for faces and events tends to decline with the passage of time. [2]It's also true that long intervals between an event and its retrieval are generally associated with increased forgetting. [3]But not all recollections fade, and time alone does not cause us to make mistakes about events in the past. [4]Consider the plight of bystanders who witness firsthand such incidents as terrorist bombings, shootings, plane crashes, or fatal accidents. [5]Afterward they may talk about what they saw, read about the incident, hear what other bystanders have to say, and answer questions from investigators and reporters. [6]By the time witnesses to these events are officially questioned, they are likely to have been exposed to so much post-event information that their original memory of the event may be distorted. (Adapted from Brehm, Kassim, and Fein, *Social Psychology*, p. 457.)

In this example, the authors open with two introductory sentences that identify the common view about what causes forgetting. But to keep readers pointed in the direction of the paragraph's real point, the authors open sentence 3 with the transitional word *but*. As you know, when transitions such as *but*, *however*, and *despite the fact* appear in the opening sentences of paragraphs, they are like red flags saying to the reader, "Slow down. Here comes the real point of the passage." This paragraph is no exception. After the word *but*, the author gets to the paragraph's main idea: Memories are distorted by more than time.

⊶ READING KEY

◆ Transitional words such as *but* and *however*, which indicate a shift in the author's point of view, are like red flags when they appear in sentences that open paragraphs. They are the author's way of saying, Now I'm getting to the real point of the passage.

> **IDIOM ALERT: Open the floodgates**
>
> If someone tells you that a comment or an event *opened the floodgates*, the person means that the consequences following the comment or event were enormous. Here's an example: "The complaint voiced by the first employee who spoke seemed to *open the floodgates*, and suddenly everyone present had a complaint to voice."

◆ **EXERCISE 1**   **Recognizing Topic Sentences**

DIRECTIONS   Identify the topic sentence by filling in the blank with the appropriate number. Then circle any reversal transitions in the paragraph's opening sentences. *Note:* The topic sentence could be the first, second, or third sentence in the paragraph.

1. [1]The full moon has long been linked to any number of events. [2]Crime, suicide, mental illness, the birthrate, and even werewolves have all been linked to the presence of a full moon. [3]Yet studies of the full-moon effect have never supported such claims. [4]In 1996, for instance, Ian Kelly, James Rotton, and Roger Culver examined more than 100 studies of lunar effects and concluded that the studies failed to show a correlation between the full moon and any of the other events normally connected to it. [5]The lack of hard evidence for the full-moon effect naturally raises the question, "Why then do so many people believe that a full moon has powerful effects on everything from the homicide rate to psychiatric admissions?" [6]Kelly and his colleagues suspect that tradition plays a role in passing on the superstition. [7]And once the false belief becomes ingrained through unscientific sources and casual comments, people find it hard to give it up even if they are confronted with evidence to the contrary.

    Sentence _____ is the topic sentence.

2. [1]Contrary to the myth, Americans did not invent baseball in Cooperstown, New York, in 1839. [2]As an English game called "rounders," the pastime had existed in one form or another since the seventeenth century. [3]But if Americans did not create baseball, they unquestionably took the game and turned it into a major professional sport. [4]The first organized baseball team, the New York Knickerbockers, was formed in 1845. [5]In the 1860s, Americans codified the rules, and the sport assumed its modern form. [6]Overhand pitches, for instance, replaced underhand tosses. [7]In the same decade, promoters organized professional clubs and began to charge admission and compete for players. (Boyer et al., *The Enduring Vision*, p. 584.)

    Sentence _____ is the topic sentence.

3. ¹Due to the number of crimes involving gun violence, New Orleans in 1999 became the first of many cities to file a lawsuit against gun manufacturers. ²In the case of New Orleans, the city sought to recover the costs of gun violence from companies who make, distribute, or sell guns. ³From the city's perspective, gun violence has a public cost that the city is forced to bear in terms of both health and enforcement. ⁴The city of Chicago followed in New Orleans' footsteps, filing a public nuisance suit asking for $453 million in damages. ⁵That opened the floodgates as more cities and counties filed similar suits: Atlanta, Bridgeport, Cincinnati, Cleveland, Detroit, Los Angeles, St. Louis, and San Francisco, along with Miami Dade County, Florida, and Camden County, New Jersey. ⁶These localities were taking cues from the successful state litigation against the tobacco industry. ⁷If cigarette makers could be held responsible for public costs of smoking, why not gun makers, the cities reason. ⁸They asked, Why not recoup our costs from the gun industry? ⁹As more suits were filed, their focus broadened to include requirements that guns be redesigned and their advertising be limited. (Adapted from Bowman and Kearney, *State and Local Government*, p. 300.)

Sentence _____ is the topic sentence.

4. ¹Unlike Mercury and Venus, which have no moons, Mars has two small moons. ²Named *Phobos* (Fear) and *Deimos* (Panic) for the horses that drew the war god Mars's chariot, they are, on a cosmic scale, little more than large rocks. ³Both moons are irregularly shaped and heavily cratered. ⁴They both also have dark surfaces, which makes them difficult to observe from Earth. ⁵Both moons can be seen with a small telescope, however. (Adapted from Shipman, Wilson, and Todd, *Physical Science*, p. 477.)

Sentence _____ is the topic sentence.

5. ¹Cannibalism is generally considered a monstrous crime. ²It is the subject of strict social taboos. ³Yet according to the ancient Greek historian Herodotus, ancient cultures, unapologetically and openly, resorted to cannibalism for what were considered sound reasons. ⁴In some cases, the bodies of the elderly were consumed after death by relatives who wanted to keep their ancestors' wisdom within the

clan. [5]Warriors slain in battle were also sometimes eaten by their troops to prevent the remains from being taken by enemies. [6]The soldiers feared that enemies could use stolen body parts for deadly charms and potions.* [7]Priests, thought to be representatives of the gods, were sometimes sacrificed and consumed. [8]By partaking in the priest's body, the faithful believed they could share in the godly spirit. (Adapted from Panati, *The Browser's Book of Endings,* p. 287.)

Sentence _____ is the topic sentence.

Topic Sentences Closer to the Middle

Read the following paragraph. Can you locate the topic sentence? Remember, the topic sentence is one of the most general sentences in the paragraph. Once the topic sentence appears, almost all of the remaining sentences in the paragraph should develop it.

[1]On June 8, 1924, George Leigh Mallory and Andrew "Sandy" Irvine set out to climb Mount Everest, the highest mountain peak in the world. [2]Shortly after they started out, it became clear something was wrong. [3]Their climbing companions, who could see them from below, realized that the two men were badly behind schedule. [4]Then suddenly Mallory and Irvine disappeared from view. [5]George Mallory and Sandy Irvine disappeared forever on that cold day in 1924, and their disappearance remained a complete mystery for seventy-five years. [6]In 1999, mountaineers Conrad Anker and Jake Norton climbed Everest and retraced the route taken by the two men. [7]Anker and Norton discovered what they first thought was Irvine's frozen body facedown in the ice. [8]However, once they and their companions dug the body out, they realized that they had found Mallory. [9]In the man's jacket was a packet of letters bearing Mallory's name. [10]There was also a monogrammed handkerchief, along with a name tag in the collar of the man's shirt. [11]The tag read "G. Mallory." [12]The rope around Mallory's waist and the terrible breakage in his body suggested he had been the victim of a fall. [13]What happened to Irvine, however, remains a mystery.

Did you figure out that sentence 5 was the topic sentence? If you did, you probably paid close attention to the combination of general and specific

---

*potions: drinks with mysterious powers.

sentences in the paragraph. Sentences 1 through 4 pile specific detail upon detail. Taken together, those four sentences tell a story. They describe how Mallory and Irvine set out to climb Everest and suddenly disappeared.

But that step-by-step movement comes to an abrupt end in sentence 5. Suddenly, the paragraph makes a huge leap in time, from a day in 1924 to one in 1999. In terms of generality, sentence 5 also broadens outward. It tells us that the men's disappearance remained a mystery until 1999. But at that point, we have no details of how the mystery was even partially solved. It's up to the more specific details that follow to provide this information.

The following diagram represents paragraphs that introduce the topic sentence close to the middle. The paragraph starts out narrow, with sentences almost equally specific, and builds to a more general point. After the general statement, or topic sentence, is introduced, the paragraph again narrows to focus on specific details.

◦┱ **READING KEY**

◆ If a general sentence in the middle of a paragraph is further developed by almost all the more specific sentences that follow, it's likely to be the topic sentence.

◆ **EXERCISE 2**   **Identifying the Most General Sentence**

DIRECTIONS   Read each list of five sentences. If one sentence is general enough to be a topic sentence, write the number of that sentence in the blank. *Note*: If there is no sentence more general than the others, leave the blank empty.

EXAMPLE

1. There's the sound of an unhappy baby screaming during a long flight.

2. Consider, too, the sound of chalk or fingernails scraping across a blackboard.

3. Equally unpleasant is the relentless sound of a dog barking all night long.

4. Some sounds are unpleasant and even scary.

5. Then, too, there's the terrifying sound of a snake's rattle.

Sentence ___4___ is more general than all the rest and could be a topic sentence.

EXPLANATION   In this list, sentence 4 is more general than all the others. Sentences 1, 2, 3, and 5 all mention specific sounds that are unpleasant or scary.

1. 1. People are likely to marry those who score in the same IQ range.

   2. Both men and women are inclined to marry members of the same social class.

   3. Men and women are likely to marry people who have similar professional interests.

   4. Marrying someone of the same religion is very common.

   5. Opposites may attract, but when it comes to marriage, we tend to like people similar to ourselves.

   Sentence _____ is more general than all the rest and could be a topic sentence.

2. 1. In sleep stage 2, eye movement ceases completely and there are occasional bursts of rapid brain waves.

   2. In sleep stage 1, eye movement is slow and the body experiences muscle contractions.

   3. Sleep takes place in stages that are repeated throughout the night.

   4. During the REM[†] stage of sleep, breathing becomes more rapid, and the eyes move around beneath the sleeper's lids.

   5. In sleep stage 3, brain waves, called delta waves, are extremely slow.

   Sentence _____ is more general than all the rest and could be a topic sentence.

[†]REM: rapid eye movement.

3. 1. Suicide rates tend to decline during times of war.

   2. Suicide rates tend to decrease during natural disasters.

   3. Suicide rates are lower in countries where religion—e.g., Catholicism and Islam—forbids suicide.

   4. Suicide rates are affected by several different factors.

   5. People who are married are less likely to commit suicide.

   Sentence _____ is more general than all the rest and could be a topic sentence.

4. 1. Paranoid schizophrenia, in which the victim feels hunted and spied upon, is the most common form of the disease.

   2. Disorganized schizophrenia is characterized by confused speech and behavior.

   3. Catatonic schizophrenia has two poles: no movement at all or frantic movement.

   4. With residual schizophrenia, the person has experienced at least one episode but is not currently showing any major symptoms.

   5. Undifferentiated schizophrenia is a catch-all term for a person showing some symptoms but not fitting any of the other types.

   Sentence _____ is more general than all the rest and could be a topic sentence.

♦ **EXERCISE 3**   **Recognizing Topic Sentences**

DIRECTIONS   Identify the topic sentence by filling in the blank with the appropriate number. *Note*: The topic sentence can be at the beginning of the paragraph or somewhere in the middle.

1. [1]Angelo Siciliano (1893–1972) started life as a ninety-seven-pound weakling. [2]Bigger and stronger boys enjoyed bullying him, and school was a nightmare. [3]As a result, Siciliano spent most of his childhood feeling too anxious to eat. [4]Then, at age sixteen, he began working out at a gym. [5]He even devised his own system of bodybuilding and quickly developed a powerful physique. [6]By his twenties, the once-scrawny Angelo Siciliano legally became the bodybuilder Charles Atlas and began his rise to fame. [7]Taking a job

in a Coney Island Circus sideshow, Atlas would prove his strength by tearing phonebooks in two before admiring crowds. [8]He would also smash nails into walls with his bare hands, and lift grown men high off the floor. [9]While Atlas was in the circus, an artist noticed his splendid physique and asked him to pose. [10]Almost immediately, Atlas became a popular model. [11]Atlas was so popular his image began turning up on billboards and magazine covers around the country. [12]At the age of 30, he was named the most perfectly developed man by *Physical Culture* magazine. [13]With the prize money he won, Atlas started a mail-order bodybuilding company. [14]By the start of World War II, around six million men had purchased his mail-order instructions for building a powerful body.

Sentence _____ is the topic sentence.

2. [1]Under attack, skunks give fair warning, before letting loose with their primary weapon, a truly horrific smell. [2]First they stamp their feet and fan out their tails. [3]If that isn't enough warning for the enemy, skunks turn around and lift their tails. [4]Finally, they release a malodorous spray, hitting their target pretty accurately up to ten feet. [5]Skunks can also repeat the spray as many as six times. [6]Victims of a skunk's spray are unlikely to forget the experience. [7]The spray's smell is so strong it can cause nausea, vomiting, and even temporary blindness. [8]It's also a difficult smell to eliminate. [9]If a person or a pet gets sprayed, it may take several baths before the smell disappears.

Sentence _____ is the topic sentence.

3. [1]In 1938, the actor, writer, and director Orson Welles was broadcasting radio plays every Sunday night at eight o'clock. [2]His show was called *Mercury Theatre on the Air*. [3]Unfortunately for Welles, he was competing with a popular radio program featuring famed ventriloquist* Edgar Bergen. [4]Because of Bergen's popularity, no one was listening to Welles. [5]At that point, *Mercury Theatre on the Air* seemed doomed to cancellation. [6]Then, on October 30, Welles broadcast a play based on H. G. Wells's novel *The War of the Worlds*, and his fortune changed dramatically for the better. [7]Welles's realistic

---

*ventriloquist: someone who can make his or her voice seem to come from another source.

dramatization of a supposed Martian invasion terrorized the American public and made both his reputation and radio history. [8]Throughout the broadcast, Welles included announcements explaining that it was only a play. [9]Yet listeners didn't seem to hear or comprehend the message. [10]What they heard was a blow-by-blow description of a bearlike creature with gleaming eyes and saliva-drooling lips climbing out of a metal ship. [11]Given that description, it's no surprise that panic ensued as hundreds of thousands of Americans took to the streets to escape being trapped in their homes.

Sentence _____ is the topic sentence.

4. [1]Anxious about forgetfulness, more and more people are spending money on vitamins, herbs, courses, and books that will supposedly help them remember. [2]Yet forgetting is a natural phenomenon, and we needn't always be so anxious about it. [3]One cause of forgetfulness is simply information overload. [4]Constantly bombarded by new information, we can't help but forget some of it. [5]In other words, the brain simply doesn't retain every new impression or experience, so it discards some. [6]Human memory also functions better when it can connect the new to the old. [7]If we don't know anything about a new piece of information, the brain has to work harder to store it. [8]Still—and this should calm the anxious—much of forgetting is simply caused by human error. [9]We forget because we don't make an active attempt to remember. [10]Fortunately, this means that the ability to recall information can be markedly improved by consciously deciding to remember and then acting on that decision. [11]Say you meet a new manager and want to remember her name. [12]Start by telling yourself, "I must remember this person's name." [13]Second, repeat the name to yourself, for example, "Her name is Barbara Baker, Barbara Baker." [14]Then use a mnemonic, or memory device, to aid later recall. [15]For example, you might associate a person's name with some aspect of his or her personality or appearance. [16]So, in the imaginary Barbara Baker's case, you might link her initials to her hair color and personal style—for example, "blond and belligerent."*

Sentence _____ is the topic sentence.

—————————————
*belligerent: ready to fight or argue.

5. [1]In *Do's and Taboos Around the World*, R. E. Axtell (1993) offers some good advice when he warns travelers to make themselves aware of differences among cultures. [2]If you dine in an Indian home, for instance, you should always leave food on the plate to show the host that the portions were generous and that you had enough to eat. [3]Yet as a dinner guest in Bolivia, you need to show your appreciation by cleaning your plate. [4]If you shop in an outdoor market in the Middle East, expect to negotiate the price of everything you buy. [5]Nothing personal. [6]Even the way we space ourselves from each other is culturally determined. [7]Americans, Canadians, British, and Northern Europeans keep a polite distance between themselves and others. [8]They feel crowded by the touchier, nose-to-nose style of the French, Greeks, Arabs, Mexicans, and South Americans. (Adapted from Brehm, Kassim, and Fein, *Social Psychology*, p. 238.)

Sentence _____ is the topic sentence.

⚷ READING KEY

♦ There are times when an entire sentence can function as a transition.

VOCABULARY EXTRA

The word *belligerent* is based on the root *bellum*, meaning "war." So while you're learning *belligerent*, why not learn *bellicose*, which also means "ready to fight." In addition, learn *antebellum* ("before the war") and *postbellum* ("after the war"). Grouping related words together and learning them in clusters is a great way to enlarge your vocabulary.

CLASS ACTION

See who can come up with mnemonics for remembering:
(1) the names of the Great Lakes (Superior, Huron, Erie, Ontario, and Michigan); (2) the first five presidents of the United States (Washington, Adams, Jefferson, Madison, and Monroe); and
(3) the capitals of North Dakota and South Dakota (Bismarck and Pierre).

Topic Sentences at the End

Occasionally, paragraphs even end with a topic sentence. When they do, writers usually pile example upon example until they feel that readers are ready to accept their general conclusion. Here's an illustration:

Topic Sentence

[1]Fathers of children born outside marriage are sometimes pictured as lacking a sense of responsibility for their actions. [2]At other times, they are portrayed as people who would like to be responsible for their children if only they were given a chance. [3]Yet in reality, some fathers do take responsibility for their children and others would do so if they could. [4]Then there are those who flatly refuse all responsibility. [5]The truth is that no one pattern or picture fits all fathers of children born outside of marriage. (Adapted from Kephart and Jedlicka, *The Family, Society, and the Individual*, p. 227.)

Paragraphs ending with a topic sentence may or may not consist mainly of examples. However, as the following diagram shows, they do have one thing in common: They all offer a series of specific sentences that lead readers to a more general conclusion.

Specific sentence
Specific sentence
Specific sentence
Specific sentence

Topic sentence

○━┓ READING KEY

◆ If the final sentence in a paragraph is general and the rest are more specific, that final sentence is likely to be the topic sentence.

◆ **EXERCISE 4**   **Recognizing Concluding General Sentences**

DIRECTIONS   Read through each list of sentences. If the last sentence is more general than the others, write a *G* in the blank. If the last sentence is equally specific, put an *S* in the blank.

EXAMPLE

a. Physicians have easy access to the drugs that can be used to end a life.

b. Fearful of hurting their practice, physicians find it hard to admit to psychiatric problems and often suffer in silence.

c. Every year, three hundred to four hundred doctors commit suicide.

d. Although the problem is rarely talked about, physicians have an extremely high suicide rate.

___G___

EXPLANATION   The last sentence could be used to sum up the other sentences. That's what makes it the most general sentence of the four.

1. a. A star undergoing a dramatic increase in brightness is called a *nova.*

   b. A nova is the result of a nuclear explosion on the surface of a *white dwarf,* or cooling star.

   c. A nova is not a new star but a faint, white dwarf that temporarily increases in brightness.

   d. Some stars appear dim and insignificant but suddenly, in a matter of hours, become a million times brighter.

   _____

2. a. An eyewitness's testimony about an event can be affected by how questions posed by the police are worded.

   b. Police instructions can affect an eyewitness's willingness to make an identification.

   c. Eyewitnesses are more accurate when identifying members of their own race than members of other races.

   d. The presence of a weapon impairs an eyewitness's ability to accurately identify the perpetrator's face.

   _____

3. a. Women are harsher trial jurors than men are.

   b. No one who is innocent would ever confess to a crime he or she did not commit.

   c. The more confident an eyewitness is about an identification, the more likely it is that the testimony is accurate.

d. Many of the things people believe about jury trials are completely untrue.

———

4. a. In the 1950s, millions of television viewers watched Senator Estes Kefauver grill mobsters about their ties to city governments.

   b. In 1952, Dwight Eisenhower's pioneering use of brief "spot advertisements" won him the presidency.

   c. In 1960, John F. Kennedy's glamorous image played a major role in his winning the presidency.

   d. The arrival of television had a powerful effect on America's political life.

———

◆ EXERCISE 5   **Recognizing Topic Sentences**

DIRECTIONS   Identify the topic sentence by filling in the blank with the appropriate number. *Note:* The topic sentence may be at the beginning, in the middle, or at the very end.

EXAMPLE   [1]The birth of conjoined, or Siamese, twins is a rare occurrence. [2]Approximately one set of conjoined twins is born for every 400,000 births. [3]Although precisely what causes the birth of conjoined twins is still debated, the most widely accepted theory is based on a failure of the fertilized egg to completely divide. [4]According to this theory, conjoined twins occur when an ovum, or fertilized egg, begins to divide into two separate fetuses, each with the same sex and physical features. [5]Then, for some reason, genetic or environmental, the fetuses do not completely separate. Instead, they remain joined at some part of the body, with the abdomen and chest being the most common. [6]The majority of conjoined twins do not survive more than 24 hours after birth. [7]Of those that do, the majority are female. (Source of statistics: www .pregnancy-info.net/conjoined_twins.html.)

Sentence __3__ is the topic sentence.

EXPLANATION   The topic is "conjoined twins." But the point to be made about that topic does not emerge until sentence 3, when the author introduces the most widely accepted theory of how conjoined twins come into being. This is the idea that receives the majority of development in the paragraph.

1. [1]In general, when men talk to one another, they like to trade sports opinions or discuss hobbies. [2]Men make statements like "No one can take the Giants this year" or "My circular saw is already rusty." [3]Overall, they tend to talk more about political than personal relationships. [4]Professional problems or challenges are also hot topics—a proposal that may not get through a committee, a union vote that did not go well. [5]If men do mention their wives or families, they are likely to be brief. [6]They don't go into depth or detail. [7]The wife is fine; the children are good. [8]In other words, men don't usually talk about their personal lives, at least not to one another.

   Sentence _____ is the topic sentence.

2. [1]In 1975, an American salesman was on a hiking vacation in Central Mexico. [2]Roaming through a darkened forest, he came upon a spectacular sight—millions of monarch butterflies nesting in trees. [3]The butterflies were so densely clustered it was hard to catch a glimpse of the underlying trunks. [4]A mystery for years, the winter home of the monarch butterfly had finally been found. [5]Scientists were ecstatic. [6]Yet sadly, much of that original ecstasy has dwindled because the forests inhabited by monarch butterflies are rapidly dwindling. [7]Local farmers have been cutting the trees for both fuel and income. [8]Because logging is a matter of survival, the farmers have not responded to government efforts to protect the areas where monarchs rest in midwinter. [9]In the hopes of saving the forests and thereby the butterflies, the Mexican government has established a $5 million fund to compensate those farmers who relinquish logging rights. [10]In addition, nonprofit groups are working with local communities to help them develop alternative sources of income.

   Sentence _____ is the topic sentence.

3. [1]Told to memorize a list of words like the following, many students would throw up their hands in despair: man, red, east, girl, winter, blue, boy, south, autumn, north, woman, summer, west, white, spring. [2]However, this list can be memorized more easily than one might think. [3]What you have to do is find connections between words and

then group those words together. [4]If you apply this principle, the previous list of seemingly unrelated items contains four chunks of information: (1) the colors of the American flag—red, white, and blue; (2) four different names for males and females—girl, boy, man, and woman; (3) the names of the four seasons—summer, autumn, winter, and spring; and (4) the four directions on a compass—north, south, east, and west. [5]Reordering information into larger patterns or pieces is called *chunking*, and it is crucial to all kinds of memory work.

Sentence _____ is the topic sentence.

4. [1]There are four general categories of sleep disorders. [2]The first and largest category includes sleep disturbances caused by psychological conditions. [3]Prolonged stress or depression, for example, can cause insomnia. [4]The second group includes disorders that result from unusual physical activity that takes place during sleep. [5]Some people, for example, are repeatedly awakened by the jerking or twitching of their muscles. [6]The third group is composed of disorders created by the disruption of the body's normal rhythm. [7]A person who is constantly switching work shifts, from day to night and back again, is likely to have difficulty sleeping. [8]The final group is made up of disorders caused by personal behavior that disrupts sleep. [9]For example, a person who eats a heavy meal late at night may be uncomfortable from a full stomach and, as a result, may toss and turn.

Sentence _____ is the topic sentence.

5. [1]In 1991, law professor Anita Hill accused Clarence Thomas, then a nominee to the U.S. Supreme Court, of sexual harassment. [2]She asserted that he had made certain statements ten years earlier—statements she said she could not repeat word for word. [3]Several years later, Whitewater prosecutor Kenneth Starr questioned Arkansas associates of Bill and Hillary Clinton about financial transactions that had taken place years earlier and about which neither had a completely clear recollection. [4]Those two stories have little in common except that both raise a key question: Can remembrances of the remote past be trusted? (Adapted from Brehm, Kassim, and Fein, *Social Psychology*, p. 456.)

Sentence _____ is the topic sentence.

6. ¹On the morning of December 7, 2000, the ashes of Lewis P. Robinson were placed in the sunken hull of the ship USS *Arizona*. ²According to family members, Robinson had always said he wanted his ashes placed inside the ship or else scattered nearby. ³In that wish, Lewis Robinson was not alone. ⁴He was actually the sixteenth person laid to rest inside the *Arizona*. ⁵Dozens of others have had their ashes scattered in nearby waters. ⁶Many people who were on board the USS *Arizona* when it was bombed in Pearl Harbor on December 7, 1941, have chosen to be buried nearby or on board the sunken ship.

Sentence _____ is the topic sentence.

7. ¹During the 1960s, audiences were often invited to join in theater productions. ²Many writers, directors, and theatergoers claimed that the idea of audience participation was brand new—a modern invention. ³But, in fact, audience participation in theater is at least four hundred years old and dates back to the Japanese theater known as *kabuki*. ⁴Originating in the sixteenth century, kabuki theater blended music, song, and dance. ⁵Its purpose was to spread Buddhist thinking. ⁶In early kabuki productions, actors would often directly address members of the audience. ⁷The audience would respond and even clap in time to the music. ⁸Some theatergoers would also call out the names of favorite actors or request popular songs or dances. ⁹It's not clear, however, that this practice was encouraged by members of the acting troupe.

Sentence _____ is the topic sentence.

8. ¹For years now English teachers have introduced high school students to the classics, and kids were required to read books like Harper Lee's *To Kill a Mockingbird*, Shakespeare's *Julius Caesar*, and Mark Twain's *Huckleberry Finn*. ²That tradition, though, is changing, and it's changing rather dramatically: In some schools teachers no longer choose what novels their class *should* read; instead, they are letting students decide what novels they *want* to read. ³Take, for instance, Lorrie McNeill of Jonesboro Middle School in Atlanta, Georgia. ⁴In the past, her students read *To Kill a Mockingbird*, among other novels that McNeill considered "good fiction." ⁵But in 2009, she dropped her favorite novel from the curriculum. ⁶In fact, she dropped all her favorite novels and let her eighth-grade students

pick the books they wanted to read. [7]If students chose James Patterson's crime novel *Maximum Ride* or even the *Captain Underpants* comic-book novels, McNeill didn't bat an eye. [8]She, like many other high school and middle school teachers across the country from Seattle, Washington, to Chappaqua, New York, are experimenting with what's called the "reading workshop" approach. [9]With this method, kids get to read books of their own choosing, and teachers mainly make suggestions for what might be good follow-up books to the students' original choices. [10]Only a few books almost always get automatically vetoed by teachers. [11]*The Gossip Girl* series, for instance, generally does not make the cut. (Source of information about this trend: Motoko Rich, "A New Assignment: Pick Books You Like," *New York Times,* August 30, 2009, p. 1.)

Sentence _____ is the topic sentence.

9. [1]In 1963, the Warren Commission was formed to investigate John F. Kennedy's death. [2]A year later, after more than 27,000 interviews and 3,000 investigative reports, the commission completed its investigation. [3]The conclusion of the report was clear and without ambiguity. [4]Lee Harvey Oswald had acted alone in murdering the president. [5]No sooner was the Warren Commission's report released, than conspiracy theorists began to challenge its conclusions. [6]According to one theory, the Mafia ordered the assassination of Kennedy as payback for his brother Robert's investigation of organized crime. [7]Another scenario proposed that the Central Intelligence Agency had had Kennedy murdered because he was too "soft" on communism. [8]Yet another insisted that Fidel Castro had ordered the president's assassination because of the Bay of Pigs invasion. [9]Although these were the most popular theories, there were others as well. [10]One theory argued that Kennedy had been accidentally shot by a secret service agent. [11]Still another theory was that the real target had been Texas governor John Connally, but Kennedy got in the way.

Sentence _____ is the topic sentence.

10. [1]The human body repairs a cut in the skin in three phases. [2]In the first phase, which lasts up to twenty-four hours, blood pours into the wound from damaged blood vessels. [3]This blood clots, and white

blood cells move to the damaged area to fight infection. [4]In the second phase, which lasts about three weeks, the upper part of the blood clot dries out, forming a scab over the wound. [5]Underneath the scab, special cells release molecules that stick together to create a bridge across the gap, forming scar tissue. [6]In the final phase, the wound contracts, bringing the edges of the damaged skin closer together. [7]At the same time, new skin cells are produced. [8]During this phase, which can last up to a year, the width and height of the scar may decrease as the skin's tissue returns to normal.

Sentence _____ is the topic sentence.

> ### IDIOM ALERT: To ward off
>
> *To ward off* means to stop or keep something from happening, as in "The soldiers sprayed themselves with insect repellant to ward off the mosquitoes."

More About Paraphrasing

You already know how to paraphrase for taking marginal notes while reading. As the heading suggests, this chapter section goes into more detail on paraphrasing. The emphasis here is on paraphrasing for reading notes and term papers.

Keep in mind, though, that you should adapt what you learn here to your particular purpose. If you are taking marginal notes in your text, feel free to write brief sentence fragments designed to motivate your memory. If you are taking more detailed reading notes, separate from the text itself, decide how complete your sentences or phrases need to be so that you can easily review your notes when it's time to prepare for exams. It's only when you paraphrase for term papers that your paraphrase needs to be expressed in a complete sentence.

Accurate Paraphrasing

Obviously, paraphrasing begins with an original piece of text, written by someone else, so let's start there. Here's an excerpt about a phrase you have probably heard before, "peak experience."

The psychologist Abraham H. Maslow (1908–1970) coined the term "peak experience" to describe feelings of great wonder, happiness, and sensory awareness. According to Maslow, "the peak experience" makes a person feel at one with the world while at the same time fostering a sense of physical control. Many who came after Maslow have likened his "peak experience" to the athlete's sense of being "in the zone" or to the feeling of being "in the flow" that some people get in moments of intense concentration.

Because the excerpt has three sentences does not mean the paraphrase has to have three sentences. However, it does have to express the key components, or parts, of the original text. The paraphrase has to (1) mention Maslow's name and profession, (2) define the peak experience, and (3) indicate that some people have likened the peak experience to other, similar states of mind. Thus we might paraphrase the original like this:

Paraphrase   According to the man who invented the term, psychologist Abraham Maslow, the "peak experience" induces a feeling of physical mastery combined with a sense of wonder at being so perfectly in tune with the rest of the world. People who have studied similar experiences compare Maslow's peak experience to an athlete's feeling of being "in the zone" or the sense of being "in the flow," which some people get when they are deeply engrossed in a mental activity.

This paraphrase has all of the elements in the original, but most of the language is different. In other words, it fulfills the central rule of accurate paraphrasing: Change the wording, not the meaning.

The above paraphrase, though, is the kind that you might create for a term paper. If you are paraphrasing for reading notes, you certainly don't need to use only complete sentences. What's important is the recording of all the essential points included in the original. The reading notes below meet that standard:

Abraham Maslow coined term "peak experience" to express a sense of

1. physical self-control
2. oneness with the world
3. feeling of awe

Others who came after compared Maslow's peak experience to

1. athlete's sense of being "in the zone."
2. feeling of being "in the flow" that focused concentration produces.

Inaccurate Paraphrasing

How you paraphrase depends on the context in which you are working. For reading notes, fragments and abbreviations will do just fine as long as you can remember the original meaning based on what you've written. For term papers, you need to make your paraphrases whole sentences.

What you can't do in either context, though, is change the meaning. That's precisely the problem with the following paraphrase:

Inaccurate
Paraphrase

According to the man who coined the term, the psychologist Abraham Maslow, a "peak experience" makes a person feel a sense of awe at being closely connected to someone else. Thus the "peak experience" would be typical for someone newly married. Those, however, who came after Maslow have criticized his use of the term and substituted phrases like "in the zone" or "in the flow."

There are several major distortions of the original in this paraphrase. First, the original doesn't talk about being connected to other people. It talks about feeling in unity with the *world*, a word that includes nature and humans. The narrowing of the word "world" leads to the second distortion, when it's suggested that newlyweds illustrate the "peak experience." They might, but nothing in the original really suggests that they do. That's the writer's point of view, not Maslow's, and paraphrases shouldn't alter the meaning of the original.

Finally, those who came after Maslow did not criticize his definition. They simply pointed out that Maslow's peak experience resembled feelings that others had described in a different way.

⊙━ **READING KEY**

◆ To remember more of what you read *and* to test your understanding, make paraphrasing a regular habit.

Paraphrasing Pointers
◆

1. Get the author's meaning clear in your mind.

Many students incorrectly assume that paraphrasing doesn't require much thought. From their perspective, all they have to do is look at the author's words and then find some substitutes. That's where they go wrong. If done right, paraphrasing is useful because it forces you to clarify exactly what the author says before you change the language.

2. Change the words but never the meaning.

You defeat the purpose of paraphrasing if your choice of words distorts the original point.

Original Text: After the humiliation of writing ridiculous dialogue for a film titled *Way Down South*, African-American poet Langston Hughes publicly attacked Hollywood racism.

Accurate Paraphrase: African-American poet Langston Hughes spoke out against Hollywood racism after he was forced to write ridiculous dialogue for a movie called *Way Down South*.

Inaccurate Paraphrase: When African-American poet Langston Hughes couldn't find work as a writer in Hollywood, he spoke out against the discrimination he had experienced.

3. Make the end the beginning.

When asked to paraphrase, many students say, "I don't know where to start." I always pass on to them a tip from a former student: Start at the end. In other words, you can *usually* create a new version of the original text by opening with content that the author put at the end. This works for the original and paraphrase given above. It also works for the original and paraphrase below.

Original Text: Of all the organizations [in the nineteenth century] working to bring religion and sports closer together, none was more influential than the Young Men's Christian Association. (Putney, *Muscular Christianity*, p. 62.)

Accurate Paraphrase: The Young Men's Christian Association (YMCA) was crucial to the nineteenth-century effort to unite religion and athletics.

4. Paraphrase in chunks.

When you paraphrase, don't think of exchanging each original word for a new word. Instead, look closely at the phrases the author uses to express both content and relationships. Then try to come up with different phrases that have similar meanings and make similar connections. Once you have the major thoughts and relationships in place, it's easier to fill in single words.

Original: Those who claim to have had near-death experiences don't always agree on what the experience was like. Many have described "a white light at the end of a tunnel"; others report torture by demons and elves.

Accurate Paraphrase: Some reports of near-death experiences have described pain inflicted by demons and elves; others describe a long tunnel with a white light at the end. In short, reports of near-death experiences are likely to differ.

5. Don't be afraid to combine sentences.

There is no rule that says if the author uses two sentences to express an idea you have to do the same. If you can combine sentences and make the paraphrase shorter than the original, good for you. Just make sure you don't leave out any key information in the process.

Original: Massage therapists who are certified by the National Certification Board for Therapeutic Massage and Bodywork must take 500 hours of education classes and pass an examination. They must know some basic anatomy and physiology, as well as some first aid. (Carroll, *The Skeptic's Dictionary*.)

Accurate Paraphrase: People seeking to be certified by the National Certification Board for Therapeutic Massage and Bodywork are required to take 500 hours of classes and pass an exam testing their knowledge of basic anatomy, physiology, and first aid.

Inaccurate Paraphrase: All massage therapists are certified by the National Certification Board for Therapeutic Massage and Bodywork.

6. Keep in mind that some words have no substitutes.

Many students incorrectly believe that a paraphrase has to change every single word in the original text. But sometimes that's impossible to do. There really is no substitute for, say, the "Young Men's Christian Association," "near-death experiences," or "elves" in the previous examples. If you can change the order and three-quarters of the words in the original text, you are doing just fine.

7. Make paraphrasing a habit.

Paraphrasing requires a good deal of thought. It's not as easy as it might seem at first glance. Thus, readers sometimes start out paraphrasing while reading and then give up because it seems like too much effort. But if you are dealing with fairly complicated text and need to remember its message, paraphrasing is worth the effort. Paraphrasing won't just improve your comprehension; it will also improve your ability to remember what you read.

O— READING KEY

◆ Paraphrasing forces you to really dig into a text and determine an author's meaning. That kind of close attention improves comprehension and wards off forgetting.

◆ EXERCISE 6   **Writing Accurate Paraphrases**

DIRECTIONS   Underline the topic sentence. Then paraphrase it in the blanks that follow. For the sake of practice, make these paraphrases be more formal, like the ones you would write for papers.

EXAMPLE   [1]<u>Although animals can't speak, they have several other forms of communication.</u> [2]Some animals communicate with sounds. [3]They use high-pitched cries to signal "move closer," or they growl to say "go away." [4]Animals also use smells to communicate. [5]Some beetles, for example, give off an odor when they want to greet a potential mate. [6]Body language is another way animals communicate. [7]To keep intruders away, geese puff up their feathers, making themselves look larger. [8]Similarly, cats make themselves look more imposing* by arching their backs and rapidly swinging their tails back and forth.

Paraphrase   Just because animals don't speak does not mean they can't communicate.

_____

EXPLANATION   As it should, the paraphrase alters the author's words without changing the meaning.

1. [1]It's been more than one hundred years since Mary Surratt was hanged for her role in the assassination of Abraham Lincoln. [2]Yet, even today, there are those who doubt Surratt's involvement in Lincoln's death. [3]There is, after all, no hard evidence linking her to the assassination. [4]Then, too, one of the three men executed with Surratt insisted on her innocence until his death. [5]Some people also believe the place of her execution, Fort McNair, is haunted by a ghost protesting her innocence. [6]Children report playing with a woman in black, and lights constantly flicker. [7]One man even claims to have heard a woman crying "I am innocent" on Lincoln's birthday.

Paraphrase   _____

_____

_____

*imposing: impressive.

2. [1]The financial and human costs of the Civil War were enormous. [2]Estimates for the total cost of the war exceed $20 billion. [3]This amount is five times the amount spent by the federal government from its creation to 1861. [4]The South, which bore the brunt,* borrowed over $2 billion and lost much more than that in damages and destruction. [5]In southern war zones, houses, crops, barns, and bridges were destroyed. [6]Factories were looted by Union troops, who also put two-thirds of the South's railroad system out of service. [7]The human toll, too, was huge. [8]In a nation of only 31 million people, the total number of military casualties on both sides was over 1 million. [9]About 360,000 Union soldiers died from battle wounds or disease, and another 275,175 were wounded. [10]An estimated 260,000 Confederate soldiers were killed, and almost as many were wounded. (Adapted from Norton et al., *A People and a Nation*, pp. 422–23.)

Paraphrase

_____

_____

3. [1]In 1964, researchers Robert Rosenthal and Lenore Jacobson administered an intelligence test to the entire student body of an elementary school in the San Francisco area. [2]Teachers in the school were then told that the test had identified children who were about to take a major leap in their ability to learn. [3]These children were labeled "bloomers." [4]In point of fact, however, the children had been chosen at random.* [5]They had not shown any particular signs of improvement. [6]Yet when the test was administered again in 1965 and 1966, the so-called bloomers showed larger educational gains than the other children in the study. [7]The research conducted by Rosenthal and Jacobson—which later appeared as a book titled *Pygmalion in the Classroom*—suggested to many that teacher expectation plays a major role in student performance.

Paraphrase

_____

_____

_____

_____

*brunt: burden.
*at random: without plan.

4. ¹In both body and spirit, President Lyndon Baines Johnson was a big man. ²Having clawed his way to the height of political power, he didn't believe in limitations. ³Johnson believed he could wheedle,* bully, or charm anyone into doing just about anything. ⁴For a good many years, he seemed to be right. ⁵A political force in Washington, Johnson got what Johnson wanted. ⁶Yet in the end, even the great wheeler and dealer Lyndon Baines Johnson met his match when confronted by the awesome power of television. ⁷Feeling himself a poor country boy lacking in sophistication, Johnson was afraid of acting natural before a TV audience. ⁸According to journalist David Halberstam, Johnson always tried "to play someone else—Kennedy, Roosevelt, Churchill, almost anyone but Lyndon Johnson." ⁹And the public generally didn't buy his performance. ¹⁰When public sentiment turned against the war in Vietnam, Johnson tried to defend his policies on television. ¹¹But it was a disaster. ¹²He seemed nervous and insincere. ¹³Over time, Johnson made fewer and fewer appearances on TV.

Paraphrase _____

_____

_____

---

*wheedle: persuade by charm or flattery.

ROUNDING UP THE KEYS

Here is a list of all the reading keys introduced in the chapter. Use them to review for the test on page 171. If a particular reading key doesn't make sense on its own, go back to the page where it appeared and review the section preceding it.

○—ⱳ **READING KEY: Topic Sentences in Third Place**

◆ Transitional words such as *but* and *however*, which indicate a shift in the author's point of view, are like red flags when they appear in sentences that open paragraphs. They are the author's way of saying, Now I'm getting to the real point of the passage. (p. 139)

○—ⱳ **READING KEY: Topic Sentences Closer to the Middle**

◆ If a general sentence in the middle of a paragraph is further developed by almost all the more specific sentences that follow, it's likely to be the topic sentence. (p. 143)

○—ⱳ **READING KEY: Transitional Sentences**

◆ There are times when an entire sentence can function as a transition. (p. 148)

○—ⱳ **READING KEY: Topic Sentences at the End**

◆ If the final sentence in a paragraph is general and the rest are more specific, that final sentence is likely to be the topic sentence. (p. 149)

○—ⱳ **READING KEYS: Paraphrasing**

◆ To remember more of what you read *and* to test your understanding, make paraphrasing a regular habit. (p. 158)
◆ Paraphrasing forces you to really dig into a text and determine an author's meaning. That kind of close attention improves comprehension and wards off forgetting. (p. 161)

Ten More Words for Your Textbook Vocabulary

1. **legitimate:** legal, respected, in good standing

   The prince was a *legitimate* successor to the throne; nevertheless, his subjects preferred his stepbrother, who had no legal right to be king.

2. **perseverance:** the ability to stick to a task; refusing to give up easily

   Hard work, long hours, and *perseverance*, the simple refusal to give up, had taken the young woman to the top of her profession.

3. **successive:** one after the other

   Before Lyndon Johnson became president in 1963, four *successive* Democratic administrations had tried to pass legislation guaranteeing medical coverage.

4. **inadvertently:** unintentionally, done without any conscious purpose in mind

   Some critics suggest that IBM, the computer company, *inadvertently* developed a culture that discouraged risk taking.

5. **inclusion:** acceptance or addition of

   Some of the early unions were reluctant to accept the *inclusion* of women and minorities.

6. **comprehensive:** broad, wide-ranging

   In the late nineteenth century, city leaders who were impatient with small, piece-by-piece reforms began demanding *comprehensive* solutions to urban poverty.

7. **fiscal:** relating to government spending

   Founding father Alexander Hamilton believed that the United States needed a central bank if the country were to ever have a sound *fiscal* policy.

8. **entrepreneurial:** willingness to take risks in business

The British were quick to criticize the American colonies for their refusal of British rule, but even the British had to admire the country's *entrepreneurial* spirit.

9. **allegedly:** supposedly, suspected but lacking in hard evidence

When President Woodrow Wilson was so ill he had become a shadow of his former self, his wife Edith *allegedly* took over his duties.

10. **incentive:** motive or reward for doing something

Many educators believe that students perform better when their *incentive* for achievement is internal—a sense of accomplishment—rather than external—money.

◆ **EXERCISE 7   Building an Academic Vocabulary**

DIRECTIONS   Fill in the blanks with one of the words listed below.

incentives   successive   legitimate inclusion   entrepreneurial
perseverance comprehensive fiscal   inadvertently allegedly

1. After a string of _____ victories in the primaries, Barack Obama's candidacy no longer seemed to be a long-shot.

2. J. Edgar Hoover, the former director of the FBI, _____ kept a secret file on every important public official.

3. Good managers provide their employees with strong _____ to do good work.

4. It was obvious that a(n) _____ overhaul of the tax code would take a year or more.

5. The _____ of reporters at the conference made everyone less willing to speak freely.

6. If the World Bank lends money to a financially troubled country, it expects to dictate the country's _____ policy.

7. Bill Bowerman and Phil Knight, the co-founders of Nike, are perfect examples of the _____ spirit at work.

8. The researcher _____ reversed the number of no responses and significantly changed the outcome of the interviews.

9. In studying those who achieve great success in life, researchers found that _____ was just as important as talent.

10. No _____ lawyer would betray the confidence of his or her client.

DIGGING DEEPER   **Family Ties**

Looking Ahead   Here's another reading on what were once called Siamese twins (the accepted term is now *conjoined twins*). This reading describes Chang and Eng, the two brothers from whom the term *Siamese twins* was derived. As you read, look for the topic sentences and main ideas in paragraphs. In addition, look for a sentence that sums up the entire reading.

1   Chang and Eng, the twin boys who gave rise to the term *Siamese twins*, were born in what is now Thailand on May 11, 1811. At birth, their bodies were tightly connected by a band of cartilage that united them at the breastbone. Initially, at least, that unbreakable link seemed to spell their doom. Considered an omen of misfortune, the boys were ordered put to death. But at the last minute, the king of Siam intervened, taking pity on them and sparing their lives.

2   When the boys were 18, a Scottish trader paid their parents a small sum of money and got permission to take them on tour in a circus act. Billed as the "Siamese Double Boys," Chang and Eng were the prize exhibition in a tour of Britain and the United States. Aware, however, that they were being exploited, the twins left the show to go out on their own.

3   In 1839, they applied for U.S. citizenship and set out to become farmers in North Carolina. In the mid-forties, Chang and Eng married a pair of sisters, Adelaide and Sally Yates. They also took for themselves a very American name. They called themselves Bunker. Accepted and even admired by many members of the community, the Bunker brothers developed a special "double-chop" method for felling the trees on their land. Their method, uniquely adapted to their own physical requirement, caught on and is still in use today.

4   Like the "double-chop" method they created, the brothers themselves have not been forgotten. Between them they fathered twenty-one children, and to this day, the descendants of those children meet for regular re-unions. Unfortunately, the publication of a book, *Chang and Eng*, by writer Darin Strauss in 2000 brought heated controversy to what were once happy family get-togethers. Told from Eng's point of view, the novel suggests that Eng at least dreamed of being free and separate from his brother.

5   Although some of Chang and Eng's descendants thought Strauss's novel a great tribute, others loathed the picture it painted. When the author, on a book-signing tour, visited White Plains, North Carolina, home of the Bunkers

and scene of the reunions, the controversy only deepened. Betty Bunker Blackmon bought nine copies of *Chang and Eng* and asked the author to sign every single one. Tanya Rees, however, a great-great-granddaughter of Eng, was furious. From her perspective, Strauss had "cheapened" her family history.

6   Aware that some family members were not happy with his portrayal of their ancestors, Strauss attended the 2000 Bunker family reunion. He brought with him a peace offering in the form of fried chicken. What Strauss didn't bring were any copies of his book. Yet, to his surprise and delight, a number of family members showed up with their own copies, all of which he graciously autographed.

7   It's generally agreed that Strauss truly healed the family's wounds when he was called on to make a speech. Thanking the Bunker descendants for their hospitality, Strauss explained that he had never meant to cheapen or sensationalize their family history. On the contrary, his intent had been to do Chang and Eng justice. In his words, they were "two of the most heroic people in American history." When the author finished speaking, he received a round of applause. Strauss had apparently won over even those who had initially hated the book and its attendant publicity. At the reunion's end, the Bunker family was once again united, secure in the belief that their famous ancestors had been accorded the respect they deserved.

Sharpening Your Skills

DIRECTIONS   Answer the following questions by filling in the blanks or circling the letter of the correct response.

1. What is the main idea of the entire reading?
    a. Chang and Eng were remarkable people who let no obstacle stand in their way, and, to this day, there are tributes to them in White Plains, North Carolina, where they settled.
    b. The descendants of Chang and Eng are understandably proud of their ancestors.
    c. A novel about the conjoined twins Chang and Eng temporarily disrupted what had once been happy family reunions.
    d. The term "Siamese twins" originated with the brothers Chang and Eng, who were born in 1811.

2. How would you paraphrase the topic sentence in paragraph 5?

_____

_____

3. How would you paraphrase the topic sentence in paragraph 7?

_____

_____

4. What would be a good synonym for the word *omen* in paragraph 1?

_____

5. In paragraph 7, what transition introduces a reversal in the writer's train of thought?

_____

WWW

INTERNET RESOURCE For additional practice with topic sentences, go to the self-study quizzes accompanying *Reading Keys* at www.cengage.com/devenglish/Flemming/rk3e. See also *Reading Keys* Additional Material and Online Practice at laflemm.com.

▶ **TEST 1**   **Reviewing the Key Points**

DIRECTIONS   Answer the following questions by filling in the blanks or circling the letter of the correct response.

1. Transitional words like ＿＿＿＿＿＿ and ＿＿＿＿＿＿ are red flags when they appear at the beginning of sentences that open a paragraph. They signal that a topic sentence is on its way.

2. The topic sentence has to be
   a. the most interesting sentence in the paragraph.
   b. the longest sentence in the paragraph.
   c. the most general sentence in the paragraph.
   d. the first sentence in the paragraph.

3. If the topic sentence comes in the middle of a paragraph, the first few sentences are usually equally ＿＿＿＿＿＿ and lead to a more ＿＿＿＿＿＿ sentence.

4. When topic sentences come at the end, writers usually pile ＿＿＿＿＿＿ upon example until readers are ready for the ＿＿＿＿＿＿ conclusion.

5. The key rule of paraphrasing is to
   a. keep the paraphrase shorter than the original.
   b. modify the author's words as little as possible.
   c. change the wording without altering the meaning.
   d. paraphrase only when you don't understand what an author is saying.

To correct your test, turn to page 553. If one or more of your answers is incorrect, re-read the Rounding Up the Keys section of the chapter to find out where your mistakes might be.

▶ **TEST 2**   **Recognizing Topic Sentences**

DIRECTIONS   Identify the topic sentence by filling in the blank with the appropriate number.

1. ¹Cats were so loved and respected in ancient Egypt that Egyptian laws protected cats from mistreatment. ²Like their human owners, dead cats were often embalmed in the finest linen and placed in chests of gold and precious stones. ³In India, early Sanskrit† writings describe cats who were so beloved they were treated like miniature gods. ⁴Around 500 B.C. in China, the philosopher Confucius is said to have always kept his favorite cat nearby. ⁵Going Confucius one better, the prophet Muhammad sometimes preached with a cat in his arms. ⁶Around 600 A.D., the Japanese kept cats to protect their sacred manuscripts. ⁷The cats that did their jobs well were especially cherished. ⁸But even those not in charge of manuscripts were admired because of their mousing abilities. ⁹Given its long history, it seems that the affectionate bond between cats and their owners is hardly a modern phenomenon.

Sentence _____ is the topic sentence.

2. ¹Ever since George Washington, presidents have claimed the right to withhold information from Congress. ²The president's right to withhold information is known as *executive privilege*. ³Presidents who use executive privilege usually insist on the need to keep government papers secret. ⁴Critics charge, however, that executive privilege can be used to hide questionable behavior. ⁵The most serious challenge to executive privilege came in 1973. ⁶That was the year a federal court ruled that President Richard Nixon had to turn over secret tape recordings he had made of conversations held in his office. ⁷President Nixon refused, and the case went to the Supreme Court. ⁸In July 1974, the Court ruled against the president.

Sentence _____ is the topic sentence.

3. ¹In June 1955, the quiz show known as *The $64,000 Question* made its debut on CBS. ²Within a month, the ratings were sky high.

---

†Sanskrit: the classic literary language of India.

[3]It was the top-rated show on television, drawing a weekly audience of close to fifty million viewers. [4]The show's popularity was not lost on competing networks, which were anxious to field a hit as well. [5]Less than a year later, NBC launched a quiz show called *Twenty One*. [6]Wildly popular at first, *Twenty One* eventually put an end to the public's love affair with big-money quiz shows. [7]Dan Enright, *Twenty One*'s producer, had decided that the show needed to be more suspenseful. [8]Unlike the contestants on *The $64,000 Question*, who were experts in one particular field, those on *Twenty One* had to be knowledgeable in more than a hundred different areas. [9]Unfortunately, Enright's idea posed a problem. [10]Contestants could rarely answer a string of questions from so many different fields. [11]Enright solved the problem by supplying some of the contestants with answers. [12]When one of the *Twenty One* contestants, Herb Stempel, blew the whistle on the rigged quiz show, the rest of the popular game shows quickly fell under the shadow of suspicion.

Sentence _____ is the topic sentence.

4. [1]On the night of July 28, 1976, Tangshan, China, was hit by an earthquake. [2]Although other earthquakes have registered higher on the Richter scale than the one in Tangshan, no other earthquake in modern history has caused such widespread death and devastation. [3]Even the atomic bombs that were dropped on Japan during World War II did not do as much damage. [4]Although the official death toll for the Tangshan earthquake is 242,419, that number is only a guess because many bodies went unrecovered. [5]Some claim that as many as 800,000 people died as a result of the earthquake. [6]In addition, more than 350,000 people were hurt. [7]Nearly half of them were seriously injured. [8]Almost all of the city's buildings were reduced to rubble. [9]One hundred of Tangshan's major bridges fell to the ground. [10]In at least 7,000 cases, entire families were completely wiped out, and some 4,000 children lost both parents. [11]As a result of the earthquake, the Chinese government instituted strict building codes that featured earthquake-safe materials and structures.

Sentence _____ is the topic sentence.

5. [1]Computer engineers classify threats to a company's computer security into four categories. [2]Two categories come from within the company itself. [3]One of them, an "internal hostile" threat, is posed by an angry employee who has access to information and uses that knowledge to do some damage. [4]The other, "internal nonhostile," is posed by an employee who forgets or fails to follow procedures designed to protect the company's computer system. [5]The two other categories of threat come from outside the company. [6]One of them, "external hostile," describes corporate spies who gain access to a company's computer system to steal or destroy information. [7]The final category, "external nonhostile," refers to computer hackers, who try to break into a company's system just to show they can do it.

Sentence _____ is the topic sentence.

▶ **TEST 3**   **Recognizing Topic Sentences**

DIRECTIONS   Identify the topic sentence by filling in the blank with the appropriate number.

1. ¹Every spring, Americans must grapple with one of our country's biggest problems: the tax code. ²Now a mind-boggling 60,000 pages long, this collection of rules has grown so complex that U.S. citizens must annually waste 6.2 million hours and $203.4 billion just to complete their tax returns. ³Even worse, ever-expanding tax laws are killing jobs by forcing employers to factor the impact of new tax laws into their every hiring decision. ⁴Ironically, even tax cuts don't help. ⁵Two major cuts in 2001 and 2003 only made the code *more* complicated. ⁶Like the South's rampant kudzu vine, the tax code continues to spread, strangling and choking everything in its path. ⁷Clearly, the only way to solve this problem is to go to the root. ⁸Congress must scrap the current tax code and create a new one from scratch. ⁹This time, the tax code should be based on a flat rate. ¹⁰A single low rate for everyone would eliminate the need for complicated deductions and loopholes. ¹¹It would be fairer and easier to understand. ¹²Even more important, it would free taxpayers from an outrageously wasteful system while stimulating America's economy. (Source of statistics: Dick Armey, "Scrap the Tax Code," *USA Today*, November 16, 2004, p. 10A.)

    Sentence _____ is the topic sentence.

2. ¹Ancient Egyptian wall paintings show pictures of soldiers marching to war with dogs by their side. ²Likewise, Persian historians write that guard dogs were used to alert soldiers to Greek invaders. ³During the Napoleonic Wars of the nineteenth century, a dog named Moustache was celebrated for his exceptional bravery. ⁴When an enemy tried to steal the French flag, Moustache bit him so hard he ran away. ⁵During World War I, a British canine called Stubby received a medal for capturing a German spy. ⁶A little more than two decades later, in World War II, at least ten thousand dogs served in the U.S. military's Canine Corps. ⁷The dogs worked as sentries, delivered messages, and were crucial to search and rescue efforts. ⁸No wonder so many military museums include memorials celebrating canine heroism.

    Sentence _____ is the topic sentence.

3. ¹Within small groups, there appear to be two kinds of leaders. ²**Instrumental leaders** are concerned with reaching goals and trying to keep the group on track. ³They are likely to say things like "I think we are getting sidetracked" or "Shouldn't we get back to work now?" ⁴**Expressive leaders** are more concerned with members of the group. ⁵They try to make sure that the individual members are happy and satisfied. ⁶Instead of emphasizing goals, these leaders are more likely to focus on members' feelings with comments like "Is everybody happy with that decision?" (Adapted from Thio, *Sociology*, p. 147.)

Sentence _____ is the topic sentence.

4. ¹It's often claimed that some people think better on their feet. ²As it turns out, at least one experiment suggests that most people do think better while standing. ³At UCLA, a researcher flashed commands on a computer screen. ⁴Then he timed the responses of people in various age groups. ⁵He found that all of the respondents answered faster when they stood up, improving by 5 to 20 percent. ⁶This result seemed to intensify with age. ⁷The older the person, the faster the response, as long as it was made while standing up.

Sentence _____ is the topic sentence.

5. ¹Pol Pot, the dictator who ruled Cambodia from 1976 to 1979, is believed to have been born on May 19, 1928, in the village of Prek Shaur. ²In interviews, Pol Pot claimed to be the son of a peasant and to have spent six years in a monastery. ³According to records, he became a communist in 1946, and by the early 1970s he had become a power in the party. ⁴Although there is nothing particularly unusual about Pol Pot's early history, his brief dictatorship turned out to be brutal and bloody almost beyond belief. ⁵At Pol Pot's orders, anyone known to disagree with the government was executed. ⁶To ensure that intellectuals would make no trouble for his regime, Pol Pot had anyone who spoke French† killed. ⁷Then he launched a campaign against those he considered outsiders. ⁸At his order, hundreds of thousands of Muslims, Chinese, Vietnamese, and Thais

---

†Speaking French, the language of Cambodia's former rulers, was an indication of higher status and better education.

were tortured and killed. [9]Estimates of how many people died vary. [10]Some say a million; others say two million. [11]No one will ever know for sure.

Sentence _____ is the topic sentence.

▶ **TEST 4**   **Recognizing Topic Sentences**

DIRECTIONS   Identify the topic sentence by filling in the blank with the appropriate number.

1. ¹In Palm Harbor, Florida, the five members of the Brandon family crawl over their lawn on their hands and knees. ²Their mission is to search for and destroy any weed they find among their precious blades of grass. ³When a weed dares to invade Andy Anderson's nearly perfect lawn in Greenville, South Carolina, Andy uses needle-nose pliers to hold the intruder upright. ⁴Then his wife, Carolyn, dabs its leaves with a cotton swab dipped in weed killer. ⁵Terry Meuret of Riverside, Ohio, cleans his lawn by washing it with ammonia and liquid soap. ⁶He also feeds the lawn stale beer. ⁷His wife says that, at their house, driving, parking, or walking on the grass after a heavy rain are terrible crimes. ⁸Greg Haworth of Oklahoma City vacuums his lawn to pick up debris after a rain. ⁹In Galloway, New Jersey, Frank Rudisill dyes green any brown patches that appear on his grass. ¹⁰Clearly, some people are fanatics about their quest for the perfect lawn. (Source of examples: Steve Bender, "Turf Love," *Southern Living*, August 2001, pp. 86–89.)

   Sentence _____ is the topic sentence.

2. ¹Isaac Asimov was one of the most productive authors who ever lived. ²Born in 1920, he started to write at the age of 11 and sold his first story at the age of 18. ³He contributed many stories, including the *I, Robot* collection, to science fiction magazines in the 1940s and 1950s. ⁴During the 1950s, he also wrote several science fiction novels. ⁵After the Soviet Union launched *Sputnik*, the first satellite, into outer space, Americans became concerned about the general lack of scientific knowledge. ⁶Echoing that concern, Asimov increased his output of nonfiction on popular science topics and gained a reputation as a "Great Explainer" of science. ⁷In addition, over the next three decades he wrote and published columns, essays, humorous poetry, autobiographies, memoirs, guides to the Bible and Shakespeare, histories, mysteries, and books for young readers. ⁸By the time he died in 1992 at the age of 72, he had written almost 500 books. ⁹Asimov himself wrote, "What I *want* to be remembered for is no one book, or no dozen books.... My total corpus for

quantity, quality, and *variety* can be duplicated by no one else. [10]That is what I want to be remembered for." (Source of quotation: "Isaac Asimov," Wikipedia, en.wikipedia.org/wiki/Isaac_Asimov.)

Sentence _____ is the topic sentence.

3. [1]Studies show that prolonged stress may damage memory. [2]When experiencing severe, chronic stress, for example, a chaotic work environment, an overload of responsibilities, or the death or illness of a loved one—the brain releases a hormone called cortisol. [3]Cortisol triggers the body's fight-or-flight response, which increases the heart rate and causes adrenaline to pump throughout the body. [4]Too much cortisol seems to interfere with cells in the hippocampus, the part of the brain responsible for practical, everyday memory. [5]When the cells of the hippocampus are damaged, an individual has more difficulty recalling even basic information, like a friend's telephone number. [6]Not surprisingly, people who do not handle stress well seem to be more likely to show significant memory loss with age.

Sentence _____ is the topic sentence.

4. [1]Supreme Court Justice Sonia Sotomayor was born to Puerto Rican parents in 1954. [2]Growing up in a public housing project in the South Bronx, a borough of New York City, Sotomayor knew early on that life was a serious business. [3]Her father had only a third-grade education, didn't speak English, and worked in a factory. [4]Her mother was a practical nurse. [5]Both parents worked hard to make ends meet. [6]At the age of eight, young Sonia was diagnosed with diabetes, and, a year later, her father died, leaving her mother alone to raise Sonia and her younger brother. [7]Always a bookish child, Sotomayor turned to books for comfort, a choice that probably helped her become the valedictorian of her class at Cardinal Spellman High School. [8]She went on to win a scholarship to Princeton University, where she graduated with high honors and followed up that triumph by entering Yale Law School. [9]After spending five years as an assistant district attorney in Manhattan, she entered private practice in 1984, specializing in international corporate law. [10]In 2009, Sonia Sotomayor was named to the Supreme Court, becoming the first Hispanic to wear the robes of a Supreme Court justice.

[11]Skeptics might scoff at the idea of the American Dream with its poor person makes good story line, but the life of Sonia Sotomayor proves the American dream can, sometimes, become that reality.

Sentence _____ is the topic sentence.

5. [1]The fast-growing southern weed call *kudzu* has both plusses and minuses, but the drawbacks far outweigh the advantages. [2]On the one hand, the lush, fragrant vine is useful for shading porches from the hot sun. [3]It can also be a food source for both animals and humans. [4]Sheep and goats eat kudzu; some southerners enjoy eating deep-fried kudzu leaves and making jelly and syrup from the blossoms. [5]Kudzu vines can also be woven into hats and baskets. [6]Unfortunately, those benefits are outweighed by the plant's growth rate. [7]Growing almost a foot per day during the summer months, kudzu quickly climbs utility poles. [8]Consequently, it interferes with electric service. [9]Kudzu also strangles and kills trees. [10]It grows so fast and thick that it can quickly overwhelm everything in its path. [11]Yet cutting the plant back does not destroy it, and it's difficult to get rid of permanently because its roots grow deep. [12]Some herbicides kill kudzu, but they are expensive and time consuming to apply.

Sentence _____ is the topic sentence.

▶ **TEST 5**   **Recognizing Topic Sentences**

DIRECTIONS   Identify the topic sentence by filling in the blank with the appropriate number.

1. ¹Some adventurous scuba divers are drawn to the beauty and mystery of underwater caves. ²However, cave diving is extremely dangerous. ³In fact, it is considered the world's most hazardous sport. ⁴Diving in dark caverns, divers can easily become disoriented* because of limited visibility. ⁵They can also quickly lose their way in a confusing network of tunnels. ⁶Many divers have lost their lives because they took a wrong turn and couldn't find their way out of a cave before using up their air supply. ⁷In Florida alone, more than 350 people have drowned in underwater caves.

    Sentence _____ is the topic sentence.

2. ¹Brilliant, ambitious, and determined, the nineteenth-century social reformer Frances Wright desperately wanted to improve the world. ²But unfortunately, Wright's decision to found an experimental community where she could put her good intentions into practice ended in failure. ³In 1825, Wright founded a community called Nashoba, near Memphis, Tennessee. ⁴Ideally Nashoba was to be a place where black slaves could go to school while working to purchase their freedom. ⁵Yet, dedicated as the participants were, Wright and Nashoba were plagued by bad luck. ⁶Illness and debt haunted the community. ⁷Foul weather was constant. ⁸By 1830, Wright had relinquished her dream, and Nashoba became just a memory.

    Sentence _____ is the topic sentence.

3. ¹Sandra Day O'Connor, the U.S. Supreme Court's first female justice, certainly sided with the Court's other conservative members on key decisions throughout her twenty-four years on the bench. ²For example, she voted with them in 2000 to stop ballot recounts requested by presidential candidate Al Gore and declare Republican candidate George W. Bush the winner of the election. ³However, as a moderate conservative, she was a key "swing voter" who sometimes

---

*disoriented: confused.

sided with the Court's liberal justices. [4]In 1989, for instance, she refused to join with the four members of the Court who were ready to reverse the 1973 decision giving women the constitutional right to have an abortion. [5]Then, in 1992, she was part of the five-justice majority that reaffirmed the 1973 ruling. [6]Although she usually sided with conservatives about the death penalty, her writings and speeches expressed her anxiety about whether that form of punishment was being fairly administered. [7]Thus, she was said to have been an enormously powerful justice who held down the Supreme Court's center for almost a quarter century. (Source of information: Associated Press, "Sandra Day O'Connor Leaving Supreme Court," CNN.com, July 1, 2005, www.cnn.com/2005/LAW/07/01/oconnor.resigns.ap/.)

Sentence _____ is the topic sentence.

4. [1]A jury of twelve men believed Lizzie Borden did not murder her father and stepmother in 1892. [2]Of course, there's always a chance that the jury made a mistake. [3]In fact, evidence the jury did not get to hear suggests that Lizzie Borden was actually guilty of the double murder. [4]Lizzie did not like her stepmother, Abby Borden. [5]She was also unhappy about her father's gift of property to Abby's family. [6]The day her parents were hacked to death with an ax, Lizzie was at home. [7]After the murders, Lizzie was discovered burning a dress in the kitchen stove. [8]A hatchet that seems to have been the murder weapon was found in the barn. [9]In addition, Lizzie's answers to the district attorney's questions were inconsistent and aroused suspicion. [10]The jury, however, did not get to hear her testimony. [11]At the end of her sensational trial, Lizzie was acquitted. [12]But to the townspeople, the acquittal meant nothing. [13]For the rest of her life Lizzie Borden was shunned by her former friends and neighbors.

Sentence _____ is the topic sentence.

5. [1]To be truly effective, a reward system for employees must meet several requirements. [2]First, it should allow people to satisfy basic needs for food and shelter. [3]Second, it should provide financial rewards equal to those in other companies. [4]Third, the financial rewards must be distributed among all employees equally and fairly. [5]An effective reward system must also recognize that different people have different needs and desires. [6]Some people feel rewarded if they

make more money. [7]Others consider increased leisure time a desirable reward. [8]Then there are those who think praise and recognition are the best rewards.

Sentence _____ is the topic sentence.

▶ **TEST 6**   **Paraphrasing**

DIRECTIONS   Underline the topic sentence. Then paraphrase the topic sentence in the blank provided.

1. ¹Consumed by his hatred of the U.S. government, Timothy McVeigh bombed a federal building and took the lives of innocent fellow citizens. ²On April 15, 1995, the 26-year-old ex-soldier rented a Ryder truck in Kansas. ³On April 16, he and his accomplice, Terry Nichols, drove to Oklahoma City to leave McVeigh's getaway car. ⁴On April 18, the two men filled the back of the truck with 7,000 pounds of explosives. ⁵McVeigh then drove back to Oklahoma and spent the night in the cab of the truck. ⁶He woke at dawn on April 19, 1995, and headed toward Oklahoma City, arriving at about 8:50 a.m. ⁷When he reached downtown, he pulled over and lit a five-minute fuse. ⁸Continuing on toward his target, he lit a two-minute fuse. ⁹He then parked the Ryder truck in front of the Alfred P. Murrah Federal Building, got out, locked the truck, and walked away. ¹⁰At 9:02 a.m., the bomb exploded, rocking every building in the downtown area. ¹¹The whole front of the Murrah Building was blown off, and 168 people, including 19 children, were killed. ¹²By 9:10 a.m., McVeigh was exiting the city in his getaway car. ¹³By 11:00 a.m., however, he was in jail. ¹⁴An alert state trooper had arrested him for driving without a license tag and unlawfully carrying a weapon. ¹⁵Just two days later, on April 21, FBI agents figured out that McVeigh was the bomber. ¹⁶They went to his jail cell to charge him with the crime.

Paraphrase   _____

    _____

2. ¹In *I Love Lucy*, the long-running and popular television sitcom that featured his wife, Lucille Ball, Desi Arnaz played a hot-tempered Cuban musician with a strong accent. ²Although Ball was definitely the star of their TV show, while Arnaz played second banana, in real life Desi Arnaz was the first major Latino multitalent on television. ³Arnaz didn't just star in the show, he produced it. ⁴During the show's run, he pioneered a three-camera technique for filming comedy. ⁵That technique is still in use today. ⁶Because Arnaz was smart enough to

maintain ownership of the filmed series, he made a fortune from the reruns. [7]Arnaz then used his millions to oversee the development of several other memorable series. [8]Among them were the long-running *Lou Grant*, *The Untouchables*, and *Star Trek*.

Paraphrase   _____

                         _____

3. [1]Nowadays getting the flu is unpleasant, but it's not usually deadly.[†] [2]However, in 1918, the opposite was true; the influenza pandemic was one of the worst disasters in world history. [3]The 1918 flu seems to have made its first appearance some time in March of that same year, when soldiers on an army base came down with influenza. [4]At the time, however, the outbreak seemed mild. [5]Next, the virus turned up in Europe. [6]This time the outbreak was deadly. [7]By the end of spring, the flu had spread to almost every inhabited portion of the world. [8]As fall approached, the strain was becoming deadlier by the minute, and the death rate kept growing. [9]At the end of the year, the flu had killed thirty million people worldwide. [10]Although research on the rare flu strain continues to this day, scientists still do not know why it was so virulent, or infectious.

Paraphrase   _____

                         _____

4. [1]In busy emergency rooms and battleground hospitals, medical professionals are forced to use a system called *triage* to classify patients. [2]This entails examining patients and grouping them into one of three categories. [3]The first category includes those who will not survive even if they receive treatment. [4]These patients are given only pain relief. [5]Members of the second group have a higher chance of survival if immediate treatment is given. [6]This group is assigned the highest priority, particularly when resources are limited. [7]The third category includes those who will survive even without treatment. [8]These people are given the lowest priority.

[†]Exceptions to this general rule are the elderly and those with already damaged immune systems.

⁹However, doctors and nurses do reexamine patients periodically to check for changes in their status.

Paraphrase

_____

_____

5. ¹Tornadoes, the most violent of storms, have less total energy than some other storms. ²However, the strength of the tornado's winds gives the storm its enormous destructive power. ³The high-speed winds of a tornado can push in the walls of a house and lift off its roof. ⁴A tornado can even mangle steel structures. ⁵Characterized by a whirling, funnel-shaped cloud that hangs from a dark cloud mass, the tornado is commonly referred to as a twister. ⁶Tornadoes are classified using the Fujita Tornado Scale, or F-Scale. ⁷The F-Scale has six separate categories, ranging from 0 to 5. ⁸At F0, the tornado winds have speeds of 20–72 miles per hour. ⁹They are capable of smashing chimneys, breaking branches off trees, and tearing down signs. ¹⁰At F5, the winds can be as high as 300 miles per hour. ¹¹They are strong enough to lift houses from their foundations and carry them a considerable distance.

Paraphrase

_____

_____

▶ **TEST 7** **Developing Your Textbook Vocabulary**

DIRECTIONS   Fill in the blanks with one of the words listed below.

> entrepreneurial inadvertently successive   comprehensive fiscal
> inclusion   incentive   perseverance legitimate   allegedly

1. A series of _____ defeats had left the Democrats in despair until Barack Obama energized the party.

2. Wages are not the only _____ that can improve employee performance; the chance of promotion also has a positive effect.

3. A(n) _____ conservative is someone who believes government spending should be kept to a minimum.

4. The _____ of a clause decreasing health benefits further inflamed the union representatives.

5. When gold was found in the Black Hills of South Dakota, the Indians' _____ claims to the land were simply ignored.

6. Because the new regulations covered only a small portion of banking activity, critics of the president's new economic plan said the changes weren't _____ enough.

7. Special Olympians show amazing _____ in pursuing their sport; they will not give up no matter what challenges they face.

8. After the restaurant owner _____ revealed that his store had been cited for serious health violations, his customers disappeared.

9. _____, the virus had entered the country through the arrival of exotic birds from Indonesia, but it wasn't clear if this was a proven theory or a rumor.

10. The creators of Facebook have both technological and _____ skills.

Working Together: Topic Sentences and Supporting Details

5

> ## IN THIS CHAPTER, YOU WILL LEARN
>
> - how supporting details make topic sentences clear and convincing.
> - how you can tell the difference between major and minor details.
> - how to outline, summarize, or diagram what you read.

As you already know, general sentences usually need to be accompanied by specific ones. There's no better illustration of this principle than the relationship between topic sentences and supporting details. Without supporting details, topic sentences could easily cause confusion. Because they are so general, topic sentences can usually be understood in different ways. It's the job of supporting details to eliminate meanings the writer never intended.

The Function of Supporting Details

JOHN: Honestly, raising a child is difficult.

DAVID: I know exactly what you mean. You can't do what you want anymore; you're tied down all the time. Once you have a child, your life is over.

JOHN: I didn't mean that at all. I just meant it's difficult to make decisions for another human being. I'm always nervous about making the wrong one.

Note the communication problem between these two people. John makes a general statement about raising children. In response, David assumes he understands what John has in mind. But, in fact, he hasn't understood John's message at all. To make David see what he means, John provides specific details.

This kind of confusion is not restricted to conversation. It can also occur between writers and their audiences. The writer has an idea in mind and communicates it in writing. But readers may take away a completely different message, one the writer never intended.

Fortunately, most writers—particularly writers of textbooks—are aware of this potential problem and try to prevent it. Because they know that most general statements are open to misinterpretation, or misunderstanding, they are careful to include supporting details.

Supporting Details Clarify, Explain, and Convince

By means of **supporting details**, writers anticipate and answer questions readers might have about a main idea. Writers use supporting details to supply the reasons, dates, examples, statistics, facts, studies, and so on that make main ideas both clear and convincing. For an illustration of what supporting details contribute to a paragraph, take a good look at this topic sentence:

In the eighteenth century, few American poets achieved any lasting fame; Phillis Wheatley, however, was an astonishing exception.

After reading this topic sentence, you certainly know the author's point. However, you might not know who Phillis Wheatley was or what she wrote. For that information, you need the supporting details that follow that topic sentence. Here they are:

Topic Sentence

Supporting Details

In the eighteenth century, few American poets achieved any lasting fame; Phillis Wheatley, however, was an astonishing exception. A slave in a Massachusetts household, Wheatley was taught to read and write by her owners. By the age of 13, she was writing religious poems. When the Wheatley family traveled to England, the Wheatleys took Phillis with them and encouraged her to read her poems at public gatherings. The response was so enthusiastic that word of the girl's talent got back to the colonies. By the time she returned home, Phillis Wheatley was famous.

Supplied with the appropriate supporting details, you are now more likely to understand and accept the main idea of the paragraph. Against all odds, Phillis Wheatley did not suffer the fate of most eighteenth-century American poets. She became famous.

READING KEYS

◆ Supporting details supply the reasons, illustrations, facts, figures, and studies that make the main idea clear and convincing to readers.

◆ Supporting details are the author's way of guiding readers to the appropriate meaning. They are the author's way of saying to readers, "I mean this and not that."

◆ The form of supporting details varies. Details can range in form from reasons to statistics. The main idea is what causes supporting details to vary. When the main idea changes, so do the details that develop it.

IDIOM ALERT: Unsung hero

An *unsung hero* is a person who has done great or important work but has never been recognized for his or her contributions. Here's an example: "Although his wife, Lucille Ball, got most of the credit for their successful show, *I Love Lucy*, Desi Arnaz, Ball's Cuban-born husband, was the unsung hero behind the show's phenomenal success."

◆ **EXERCISE 1**   **Matching Topic Sentences to Supporting Details**

DIRECTIONS   Read each topic sentence. Then circle the letters of the two sentences that qualify as supporting details.

EXAMPLE

Topic Sentence Talking to a therapist online has some definite advantages.

Supporting Details (a.) If you can't see the therapist, you are likely to be less self-conscious.

     b. Online therapy is becoming increasingly popular.

     c. Online, the therapist can't read the patient's body language.

    (d.) Patients are more willing to speak freely when they talk to a therapist online.

EXPLANATION   The key word in the above topic sentence is *advantages*. A reader is bound to ask, "What are those definite advantages?" Sentences *a* and *d* provide answers to that question.

Topic Sentence **1.** Mammals are warm-blooded animals classified according to a number of different characteristics.

Supporting Details

    a. There are more than 4,000 species of mammals.

    b. Mammals always have hair and a middle ear formed by three small bones.

    c. A number of mammals are on the Red List of endangered species.

    d. In mammals, the lower jaw consists of only two bones.

Topic Sentence **2.** A growing number of men are having cosmetic surgery to hold on to their youth.

Supporting Details

    a. In an even more disturbing trend, teenage girls as young as 13 are begging their parents for cosmetic surgery.

    b. In the past, cosmetic surgery has been considered the province* of women.

    c. Disturbed by fat accumulating on their chests, men are resorting to surgery to get rid of it.

    d. Many men, nervous about being seen as too old on the job market, are having the bags under their eyes removed.

Topic Sentence **3.** To this day, Fred Shuttlesworth remains an unsung hero of the civil rights movement.

Supporting Details

    a. No matter what happened, Fred Shuttlesworth was always convinced that he was doing God's work.

    b. The Ku Klux Klan tried to stop Shuttlesworth's organizing activities by bombing his house, but he refused to give in.

    c. Although the intrepid Shuttlesworth was active in every aspect of the civil rights movement, the media preferred to focus on the bravery of Martin Luther King Jr., whose eloquence made him so quotable.

    d. Diane McWhorter's book *Carry Me Home*, an account of both her Alabama childhood and the civil rights movement, won a Pulitzer Prize.

---

*province: territory, area.

Topic Sentence 4. Every year, thousands of Tibetan children flee their homeland in a desperate attempt to escape Chinese rule.[†]

Supporting Details
    a. Very often, the children are sent on their journey by parents who want their sons and daughters to be Tibetan rather than Chinese.

    b. For fifteen years, photographer Nancy Jo Johnson has used photographs to publicize the plight of the Tibetans.

    c. Today, Tibet has been completely transformed, and little remains of the pre-1950 Tibetan culture.

    d. The fleeing children cross the Himalaya Mountains hoping to reach India or Nepal, where they can stay in special villages established just for them.

◆ EXERCISE 2   Matching Topic Sentences to Supporting Details

DIRECTIONS   Read each set of three supporting details. Then look over the two topic sentences that follow. Circle the number of the topic sentence that is explained by the three supporting details.

EXAMPLE

Supporting Details
    a. At one time, many therapists believed that anorexia nervosa, also called the starvation disease, was a form of rebellion.

    b. However, other therapists argued that anorexia was a way of avoiding adulthood.

    c. Researchers are now finding evidence that the disease may be caused by a chemical imbalance in the brain.

Topic Sentence

1. Some victims of anorexia nervosa—unnecessary or irrational dieting—seek out psychiatric treatment; however, they more often try to hide their disease.

2. Although no one really knows what causes anorexia nervosa—unnecessary or irrational dieting—several theories have been put forward.

[†]Chinese rule: The Chinese invaded Tibet in 1950, drove out the Dalai Lama (Tibet's religious leader), and took control of the country.

EXPLANATION   Each supporting detail introduces a theory about what causes anorexia nervosa. Because the second topic sentence tells us there are several different theories about what causes the disease, it's the better choice.

Supporting Details 1. a. Some people worry that friends will envy them if they become successful.

b. Others are afraid that success will make them stand out in a crowd.

c. Then there are those who simply fear the hard work necessary to maintain a high level of achievement.

Topic Sentence

1. In our society, far too many people are successful but unhappy workaholics.

2. A surprising number of men and women are afraid of being successful.

Supporting Details 2. a. People with claustrophobia, or fear of enclosed spaces, get anxious on elevators.

b. People suffering from agoraphobia, the fear of open spaces, are unlikely to leave home.

c. People with zoophobia, or fear of animals, are unlikely to own pets.

Topic Sentence

1. Phobias are irrational fears that persist even when there is no real danger.

2. Social phobia is the fear of situations in which one might be observed, judged, or embarrassed.

Supporting Details 3. a. About 95 percent of all adults use the left side of the brain for speaking and writing.

b. The left side of the brain is also superior at doing math.

c. The right side, however, excels at recognizing patterns, faces, and melodies.

Topic Sentence

> 1. The left side of the brain controls the right side of the body.
>
> 2. The two sides of the brain perform different activities.

Supporting Details

4. a. People interested in dating often ask their friends if they know anyone who is available.

 b. Some people look for dates in online newspapers and magazines.

 c. Others prefer to use dating services that, for a fee, guarantee a perfect match.

Topic Sentence

> 1. Nowadays, there are a number of ways for people to get a date.
>
> 2. American-style dating is all but unknown in Europe.

⚿ READING KEY

 ◆ If the supporting details don't fit what you think is the topic sentence, you probably need to look for another topic sentence.

VOCABULARY EXTRA

From your context and your knowledge of word parts (*ir* means "not"), you probably figured out that *irrational* (p. 194) means "not based on reason." If you are adding that word to your list of words to study, make sure you also add the antonym, *rational*, meaning "reasonable." You should also add the word *rationalize*, which frequently refers to a type of behavior that falls between the two poles of reason and unreason. Here's an example: "She tried to *rationalize* her rudeness by telling her friends she was under stress." Used in this context, *rationalize* means to offer a reason that appears logical but is really self-serving. To remember all three words, learn them together and create sample sentences that reflect their meanings.

Major and Minor Details

Until now, we've talked only about supporting details. However, there are actually two kinds of supporting details: major and minor.

Major Details

Major details lead directly back to the idea expressed in the topic sentence. Major details pin down general words or phrases introduced in the topic sentence. In the absence of supporting details, it's precisely the most general words that can lead readers astray. Supporting details prevent that from happening.

To illustrate, here's a topic sentence set free from the larger context of a paragraph: Unwanted noise, especially if it persists over time, can cause problems.

Spotting the general word, *problems*, readers are free to interpret the word in different ways. They might assume the problems have to do with anything from angry neighbors to hearing loss. To be sure readers get the intended meaning, the author of this topic sentence was careful. He supplied three more-specific major details. Notice how the details pinpoint precisely the "problems" the author had in mind:

> [1]Unwanted noise, especially if it persists over time, can cause problems. [2]Research suggests, for example, that continued exposure to noise in the workplace can contribute to heart disease and ulcers. [3]In addition, people who live in noisy areas have been found to have higher blood pressure than those who live in quieter surroundings. [4]Moreover, people continually exposed to high noise levels, whether at home or in the workplace, report a high degree of conflict in their lives. (Adapted from Rubin, *Psychology*, p. 105.)

In this paragraph, sentences 2, 3, and 4 are major supporting details. Each detail identifies one of the "problems" mentioned in the topic sentence. By using supporting details, the author avoids being misunderstood.

Minor Details

Minor supporting details are even more specific than major ones. They appear in the paragraph for three reasons: (1) Minor details further explain major ones, (2) they repeat key points for emphasis, and (3) they add colorful tidbits of information to stimulate reader interest.

Fleshing out major details is the most important function of minor details. Look, for example, at the following paragraph. Note the italicized minor details. Each adds to the major detail that precedes it.

> [1]Unwanted noise, especially if it persists over time, can cause problems. [2]Research suggests, for example, that continued exposure to

noise in the workplace can contribute to heart disease and ulcers. [3]*It's not surprising, then, that factory workers who spend eight hours a day surrounded by noisy machinery are likely to have heart and stomach problems.* [4]In addition, people who live in noisy areas have been found to have higher blood pressure than those who live in quieter surroundings. [5]*It's been shown, for example, that among those living near airports, train tracks, or interstate highways, high blood pressure is a common problem.* [6]Moreover, people continually exposed to high noise levels, whether at home or in the workplace, report a high degree of conflict in their lives. [7]*They tend to argue more readily with family members and coworkers.* (Adapted from Rubin, *Psychology,* p. 105.)

O═╗ READING KEYS

◆ Major details pin down general words and phrases introduced in the topic sentence.

◆ Minor details have three functions: (1) They make major details more specific, (2) they provide emphasis, and (3) they add color. The first function is the most important.

Evaluating Minor Details

Although major details are essential for clarifying topic sentences, don't assume that minor details have no importance. In fact, when you take notes on a paragraph, you should always *evaluate the minor details.* That is, you should decide how necessary minor details are to your understanding of the paragraph.

For example, in the paragraph about noise, you might want to remember that people who live and work in noisy areas tend to argue with family members and coworkers. True, this is a minor detail. But without it, the major detail—that persistent noise seems to cause conflict—remains unclear. That's because the word *conflict* is extremely general. Over time, you might forget what kind of conflict the author had in mind unless you mentally connected the major detail to the more specific minor one.

O═╗ READING KEY

◆ Minor details that make major ones more specific are worthy of your attention.

◆ EXERCISE 3   Identifying Major and Minor Details

DIRECTIONS   Each paragraph is followed by a partially completed diagram. Complete the diagrams by filling in the remaining boxes with the appropriate sentence numbers.

EXAMPLE   [1]Most people are unaware of two interesting facts about the Declaration of Independence. [2]First, although the document is dated July 4, 1776, the day of our current annual celebration, the actual document was not created or signed on that day. [3]The final draft was approved and sent to the printer on July 4, but most of the men who signed it did not do so until August 2. [4]A second interesting fact is that the document's author, Thomas Jefferson, may have meant for the Declaration to be recited aloud. [5]His handwritten draft included marks to indicate pauses and stresses that an orator would need as he read the document aloud to an audience.

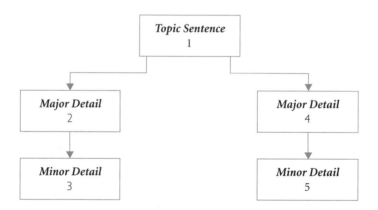

EXPLANATION   The topic sentence introduces the general phrase "two interesting facts about the Declaration of Independence." As you would expect, the major details identify those facts. The minor details provide more information about each of the two facts.

1. [1]Few would deny the energy and originality of rap music, but even diehard fans admit that the world of rappers has been plagued by violence. [2]Some of rap music's biggest superstars have been gunned down in their prime. [3]For example, Tupac Shakur was shot to death in 1996 at age 25; the Notorious B.I.G. was murdered in 1997 at

age 24; and Jam Master Jay, DJ for the popular group Run-DMC, was shot to death in his recording studio in 2002. [4]Many less well-known rappers—including Mr. Cee, Malcolm Howard, MC Big L, MC Ant, Q-Don, Yusef Afloat Muhammad, and Bruce Mayfield—have also been murdered since 1990. [5]In 2001, for instance, rapper Lloyd "Mooseman" Roberts was killed in a drive-by shooting, and rapper Tonnie Sheppard was stabbed to death. [6]People associated with rappers, too, have become victims of violence. [7]Since 2003, the former bodyguard of rap star Sean "Diddy" Combs, a federal prosecutor involved in the drug trial of rapper Deon Lionnel Smith, and the promoter of rapper Kanyva have all been gunned down.

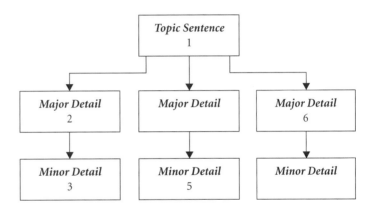

2. [1]The Soap and Detergent Association describes women in terms of five different attitudes toward cleaning. [2]One group is the *Mop Passers*. [3]These women—11 percent—like their homes to be clean, but they don't spend much time cleaning, and a dirty house does not embarrass them. [4]The next group is the *Strugglers*. [5]Twenty-one percent of women don't view housework as an important part of their lives and find it difficult to keep their homes neat. [6]*Dirt Dodgers* are a third group. [7]These women, 18 percent of all females, usually avoid cleaning and are generally dissatisfied with their homes' level of cleanliness. [8]Twenty-four percent of women, however, are *Mess Busters*. [9]They take pride in keeping their homes clean, and a neat environment gives them a sense of personal satisfaction. [10]The final category is called the *Clean Extremes*. [11]This group, 26 percent of women, cannot relax unless their houses are spotless, and many would rather clean house than do anything else.

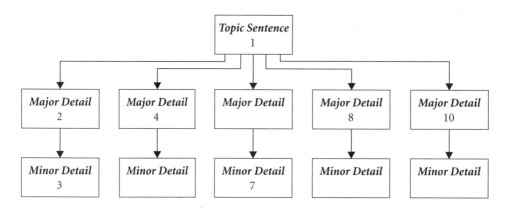

◦⫞ READING KEY

◆ Don't be fooled by the name. *Minor* details may or may not be important. It depends on what they contribute to the major details.

> **IDIOM ALERT: Take the initiative**
>
> When someone *takes the initiative*, he or she is the first one to begin a task or plan of action—for example, to quote tennis champion Chris Evert, "You've got to *take the initiative* and play 'your' game. In a decisive set, confidence is the difference."

◆ EXERCISE 4 Recognizing Major and Minor Details

DIRECTIONS Read each paragraph. Then fill in the diagrams with the appropriate numbers.

1. [1]The invention of air conditioning had a big impact on the southern way of life. [2]First, the availability of cool, dehumidified air altered southern architecture. [3]Before air conditioning, Southerners built homes with wide, shady porches; afterward, porches became far less common. [4]Second, air conditioning decreased the amount of social interaction among people. [5]Once air conditioning arrived, people stayed inside their houses, where they were cooler but more isolated from their neighbors. [6]Third, air conditioning changed summer leisure-time activities. [7]Prior to the arrival of air conditioning, people

flocked to beaches and pools and avoided hot, enclosed spaces; however, with air conditioning in place, people could go to concerts, films, and plays without fear of sweltering.

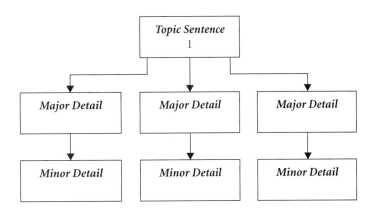

2. [1]For more than a decade, several state governments have been taking the initiative in an attempt to combat rising divorce rates. [2]In 1998, Florida, for instance, decided to make marriage a course of study for teenagers. [3]Thus, marriage education and relationship training officially became part of the curriculum in Florida's public schools, where teenagers learned, for instance, how to resolve disagreements with a partner. [4]Similarly, Arkansas has tried using education to reduce divorce rates. [5]Under the state's "community marriage" policy, clergy members voluntarily agree to marry only those couples who have completed a premarital education course. [6]Louisiana, like Arkansas, has made "covenant marriage" a legal alternative to traditional marriage agreements. [7]Couples who agree to a covenant marriage have a more difficult time finding grounds for divorce. [8]Accepted grounds for divorce in a covenant marriage are usually restricted to circumstances where one of the partners has been abusive, committed a felony, or engaged in adultery. [9]Oklahoma is yet another state trying to combat divorce. [10]The state spent millions of dollars on its Marriage Initiative program, which provides support for secular* and religious premarital education.

---

*secular: nonreligious.

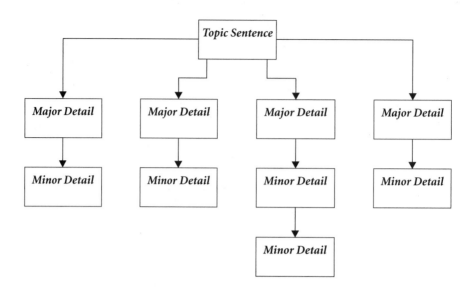

 ## Clues to Major Details in Topic Sentences

When you are trying to distinguish between major and minor details, it helps if the topic sentence includes a plural word like the following:

advantages	factors	reasons
attitudes	forms	roles
categories	functions	similarities
causes	goals	stages
characteristics	groups	steps
classes	kinds	symptoms
clues	methods	types
decisions	patterns	varieties
differences	points	ways

Words like *forms, factors,* and *advantages* announce to readers that the major details will identify each individual *form, factor,* or *advantage.* Look, for example, at the following paragraph from Chapter 4. Note how each major detail narrows the meaning for that more general word *forms.*

[1]Although animals can't speak, they have other forms of communication. [2]Some animals communicate with sounds. [3]They use high-pitched cries to signal "move closer," or they growl to say "go away."

[4]Animals also use smells to communicate. [5]Some beetles, for example, give off an odor when they want to greet a potential mate. [6]Body language is another way animals communicate. [7]To keep intruders away, geese puff up their feathers, making themselves look larger. [8]Similarly, cats make themselves look more imposing by arching their backs and rapidly swinging their tails back and forth.

In this passage, the major details—sentences 2, 4, and 6—all identify the forms of communication the author had in mind.

Number Clues

Identifying major details is even easier when a number is named in the topic sentence. Take, for example, the following paragraph:

[1]A group can be defined as two or more people who work together to achieve a goal. [2]However, for a group to function effectively, three elements need to be present. [3]Although there is no fixed limit on the size of a group, it shouldn't get too large. [4]A group that gets too large stops working as a unit. [5]Then, too, members must have the chance to meet regularly, so they can learn to know one another as individuals. [6]Group members must share a common purpose. [7]For example, individual workers might become a group in an effort to change company policy. [8]Similarly, managers might unite to develop a new product. (Adapted from Van Fleet, *Contemporary Management*, p. 383.)

In this case, the plural word *elements* in the topic sentence is accompanied by the number three. That number is an announcement to the alert reader: If you don't end up with *three* major details, you are missing something.

⊶ READING KEYS

- ◆ Check the topic sentence for broad, general words like *forms*, *groups*, *causes*, and *advantages*. These words are clues to major details.
- ◆ Be alert as well to numbers in the topic sentence that tell you how many major details are present.

◆ EXERCISE 5   Recognizing Clues to Major Details

DIRECTIONS   Read each paragraph. Then circle the word or phrase in the topic sentence that can help you locate major details. In the blank lines that follow, number and paraphrase all the major details in the paragraph.

EXAMPLE ¹There are (two chief causes) of wildlife destruction. ²First is human invasion. ³When loggers cut forests or contractors drain marshes, animals lose their homes and their food supply. ⁴For instance, environmentalists are worried that northern spotted owls may not survive if the forests where the owls roost continue to disappear. ⁵The second cause of wildlife destruction is uncontrolled hunting or fishing. ⁶The passenger pigeon and the heath hen have both been hunted into extinction.* ⁷The American bison almost disappeared for the same reason.

Major Details   1. People invade the wilderness.

2. Hunting and fishing without controls

EXPLANATION   In the topic sentence, the phrase "two chief causes of wildlife destruction" tells us that each cause is a major detail. Sentences 2 and 5 each introduce a different cause of wildlife destruction.

1.   ¹No one knows exactly what causes insomnia. ²It seems, in fact, that people suffer from insomnia for different reasons. ³Some people can't sleep because they take their daytime worries to bed with them. ⁴Consequently, they toss and turn. ⁵Depression is another common reason. ⁶Those suffering from the disease usually find it hard to sleep. ⁷Then, too, people with irregular schedules are frequently plagued by insomnia. ⁸Pilots and nurses, for instance, often suffer from bouts of sleeplessness.

Major Details

2.   ¹Researcher Ernest Hilgard has described several changes that frequently take place in people under hypnosis. ²Under hypnosis, a person's attention becomes totally focused. ³Instructed, for instance, to listen only to a particular voice, the hypnotized subject seems not to hear other voices in the room. ⁴Hypnotized subjects tend to

*extinction: disappearance from the earth.

believe whatever the hypnotist says. [5]If told, for instance, that a puppy is sitting on the table in front of her, the hypnotized subject may begin playing with an imaginary dog. [6]A good hypnotist can also change someone's behavior. [7]Under hypnosis, a shy young man can become lively and outgoing. [8]Or an outgoing young woman can become withdrawn under the influence of hynosis.

Major Details

    _____

    _____

    _____

    _____

3. [1]Across the country, enthusiasm for the death penalty seems to be fading. [2]Actually many people now believe that a life sentence without parole has three definite advantages over the death penalty. [3]First, a life sentence without parole protects society without taking human life. [4]Second, it eliminates the lengthy court appeals that result from a death sentence. [5]Finally, it ensures that criminals really pay for their crimes by staying in jail. [6]With parole allowed, a life sentence can be as short as fifteen years. [7]However, a life sentence without parole means just that. [8]It lasts a lifetime.

Major Details

    _____

    _____

    _____

    _____

    _____

4. [1]Power is certainly the basis of leadership. [2]Most people agree, however, that there are five different types of power . [3]*Legitimate power* is created by and within an organization. [4]A manager, for example, can tell employees what to do and expect to be obeyed. [5]The second type of power is *reward power*—the power to give and withhold rewards. [6]In most organizations, those in upper-level management have reward power. [7]*Coercive* power* relies on force and threats to make people obey. [8]In some military and prison settings, coercion is

---

*coercive: applying force or punishment to control behavior.

the chief source of power. [9]*Expert power* is based on knowledge and experience. [10]The scientist who astonishes his colleagues with his knowledge has expert power. [11]The fifth type of power is *referent power*, based on personality and style. [12]If, for example, a teenager dresses like his or her favorite rock star, that rock star has referent power over the teenager. (Adapted from Van Fleet, *Contemporary Management*, pp. 328–29.)

Major Details

 _____

 _____

 _____

 _____

 _____

5. [1]Each year, thousands of Americans, mostly men,[†] use a marriage service to find a foreign-born spouse. [2]Why do they look overseas for a mate? [3]Actually, there are several reasons why men are drawn to the idea of looking abroad for a wife. [4]Almost half of those looking for foreign-born wives have already failed with an American spouse and hope to do better with a foreign one. [5]Then, too, some believe that the screening process provided by the matchmaking service will effectively weed out bad choices. [6]These mate seekers believe they increase their odds of finding the right wife if somebody else eliminates all the wrong possibilities. [7]While the men themselves might be taken in by a pretty face, they assume the professional matchmaker will not be so easily won over. [8]At least a quarter of the men seeking wives overseas also claim that American women are not willing to play the appropriate wifely role. [9]In the eyes of these men, American women are too independent and not inclined to obey their husbands. [10]Thus, some men seek wives abroad in the hope that women from other countries where feminism is not an issue will be more obedient. [11]It's also true that a number of men are looking both at home and overseas. [12]Their goal is simply to enlarge their pool of choices.

Major Details

 _____

 _____

[†]Yes, some women do use a service to find a foreign-born spouse. But in general, it is mainly men who look overseas for a wife.

_____

_____

_____

_____

 ## Topic Sentences, Transitions, and Major Details

In addition to numbers and plural words in topic sentences, textbook authors, in particular, use transitions to help readers identify major details. For example, the topic sentence in the following paragraph announces that the authors are going to identify the "three general categories" of franchising agreements.

To make sure that readers recognize the individual categories, the authors introduce each new one with what's called an **addition** or **continuation transition**. Addition transitions are words or phrases that say, "Here's another idea that continues the train of thought begun in the previous sentence." These transitions, italicized in the following paragraph, tell readers that the authors have finished describing one category and are starting to describe another.

¹Franchising* agreements fall into three general categories. ²*In the first type* of agreement, a manufacturer authorizes, or legally allows, a number of retail stores to sell a certain brand-name item. ³Thus, franchising is common in sales of cars, trucks, farm equipment, paint, and petroleum. ⁴*In the second type* of franchising agreement, a producer allows distributors to sell a given product to retailers.* ⁵This arrangement is common in the soft-drink industry. ⁶Most national manufacturers of soft-drink syrups—Coca Cola, Dr. Pepper, PepsiCo, Seven-Up, Royal Crown—use this type of franchising agreement. ⁷*In yet a third form* of franchising, a franchiser supplies brand names, techniques, or other services, instead of a complete product. ⁸Although the franchiser may provide a variety of services, its main role is the careful development and control of marketing strategies. ⁹This approach to franchising, which is the most typical today, is used by Holiday Inn, Howard Johnson, AAMCO Transmissions, McDonald's, Dairy Queen,

_____

*franchising: authorizing someone to sell a company's goods and services.
*retailers: people who sell goods directly to consumers.

Avis, Hertz, KFC, and H&R Block, to name just a few. (Adapted from Pride, Hughes, and Kapoor, *Business*, p. 126.)

The authors use three different examples to illustrate the topic sentence: "Franchising agreements fall into three general categories." To make sure that readers know where one category leaves off and another begins, the authors separate the major details with transitional phrases that signal addition.

Transitions Signaling Addition ◆		
Above all	For instance	Moreover
Adding to that	For one thing	Plus
Another	It's also true that . . .	Similarly
Besides	Like	Then, too
Finally	Likewise	Yet another
First, second, third		

○━╥ **READING KEYS**

◆ Textbook authors, in particular, like to use transitions to separate supporting details.

◆ Transitions signaling addition are commonly used to introduce major details.

◆ **EXERCISE 6** **Using Topic Sentences and Transitions to Identify Major Details**

DIRECTIONS Underline the topic sentence and circle the transitions introducing major details. Then paraphrase the major details according to the order in which they appear.

EXAMPLE ¹People in groups typically go through a period of growth and development. ²<u>Although there is no exact pattern for everyone, most groups follow four general stages.</u> ³The (first) step is called *forming*. ⁴During this stage, members come together to talk about a common purpose. ⁵In the (second), or *storming*, stage, conflicts emerge. ⁶The members may begin to argue. ⁷At this point, some members may even talk openly about leaving the group. ⁸During the (third), or *norming*, stage, people either accept the group or leave it. ⁹(Finally), the group enters the *performing* stage. ¹⁰This is the point at which members actively begin working toward common goals. (Adapted from Van Fleet, *Contemporary Management*, p. 387.)

Major Detail 1   "Forming" is the first stage.

Major Detail 2   In the "storming" stage, there are arguments and conflict.

Major Detail 3   During the "norming" stage, people accept or leave the group.

Major Detail 4   In the "performing" stage, members work toward common goals.

EXPLANATION   In the context of the paragraph, *first, second, third,* and *finally* are all transitions indicating addition. With the help of these transitions, it's easy to identify the four major details in the paragraph.

1. [1]Although animals signal danger in a variety of ways, many rely primarily on their tails to communicate the presence of a threat. [2]The white-tailed deer, for instance, raises its highly visible white tail as a warning. [3]If deer are contentedly grazing, and one of them lifts its white tail, they will all disappear in a flash. [4]Like deer, beavers also use their tails to signal danger. [5]They will slap the water with a loud smack if a threat approaches. [6]Similarly, geese and pigeons ruffle or fan out their tails when angry or fearful.

Major Detail 1   _____

Major Detail 2   _____

Major Detail 3   _____

2. [1]Positive thinking—the belief in our own self-worth and the worth of others—is essential. [2]But, as we all know, it's sometimes hard to think positive thoughts and easy to think negative ones. [3]There are, however, concrete* steps we can all take to develop a positive frame of

---

*concrete: real, physically doable or observable.

mind. [4]First, actively seek out good news: [5]If you're talking to friends or chatting with strangers, encourage them to talk about situations in which they emerge as heroes or winners. [6]The conversation will make them feel great and probably raise your spirits as well. [7]Second, always keep in mind that very few important goals can be achieved over-night. [8]If you're still far away from achieving an objective, remind yourself that this is normal, and keep taking things one step at a time. [9]Third and last, make a list of positive statements that you can recite whenever negative thoughts come to mind. [10]Anytime you feel that you're not capable of achieving the goals you've set for yourself, it helps to say something like "I know I can do this; all I need is time."

Major Detail 1   _____

_____

Major Detail 2   _____

_____

Major Detail 3   _____

_____

Paragraphs and Note-Taking

Now that you have the basic elements of the paragraph—main ideas, sup-porting details, and transitions—you are ready to think more about a topic introduced in Chapter 1, **note-taking**. There are several different ways to take notes, depending on (1) the type of text you are reading and (2) your personal preference. This chapter explains three of the most pop-ular methods: outlining, summarizing, and mapping (or diagramming).

Outlines

When you take notes on paragraphs using the outline format, the out-line you create for your personal use is somewhat different from the formal outlines you may have learned about in composition courses. When you outline a text for later test reviews, you can, if you choose, use all numbers instead of letters. You can also combine sentences with phrases, if you wish, rather than using one *or* the other. The kinds of symbols you use are strictly up to you.

Note-Taking Requirements

Outlining for note-taking has only three requirements: (1) the relationships between the items in your outline have to be obvious at a glance; (2) the sentences and phrases in the outline need to be paraphrased, not copied from the text; and (3) the sentences or phrases in your outline need to be complete, so they are meaningful after time has gone by. In other words, there's no point in using a shorthand code that you yourself can't understand after three weeks have passed.

For an example of a good outline, read the following paragraph. Then study the accompanying outline:

> Gossip actually serves three important purposes: networking, enhancing one's image, and forming social alliances. Networking is a way of gathering information about other people in a social hierarchy.* Knowing about the other people within a social structure gives individuals a better understanding of their own position within it and helps them attain a higher ranking. The second function of gossip is to suggest that the person in possession of the gossip is someone of importance. Those in possession of up-to-date gossip appear to be closely connected to people who are professionally or socially powerful. Forming useful alliances is the third purpose of gossip. People sometimes offer up gossip in order to be looked upon favorably by those higher on the social or professional ladder.

Main Idea ⟶ **Three Important Purposes of Gossip**

Supporting Details ⟶ **1.** Networking: gathering info about others in social hierarchy

Benefit: people have an understanding of their function in group

2. Indicates personal importance: person who knows the gossip is considered important to the group

Benefit: those with gossip seem well connected

3. Creates alliances

Benefit: people exchange gossip as way of climbing professional ladder

You can see from the outline how the major details fill out the "purposes" of gossip introduced in the paragraph's topic sentence. This is precisely what an outline should do. Outlines should clarify the relationships between the main idea and supporting details.

It's important to point out that in this paragraph the minor details are significant and add crucial information to the major details. Thus, they

---

*hierarchy: order from higher to lower.

appear in the outline. However, minor details aren't always so crucial. Therefore, you need to be selective about including minor details in your notes.

Outline Pointers ◆	1. Indent and label to show relationships between the main idea and details.
	2. Paraphrase rather than copying verbatim, or word for word.
	3. Abbreviate carefully so that the meaning does not disappear with the words eliminated.
	4. Be selective about which major and minor details you need to include and which you don't.

Summaries

Outlines are good for detailed textbooks that have a lot of specifics. Summaries, however, work well with texts that are less detailed. Summaries are particularly good for more-general writing, especially when the author gives an **opinion**, or personal point of view, and then follows it with reasons or examples designed to convince, as in the following example:

> When parents read aloud to their young children, the children benefit in two important ways. First, story time promotes bonding between parents and their children. Snuggling with mom or dad while enjoying a good story gives children the physical affection they crave. Second, reading aloud to children enlarges both their vocabulary and their imagination. New words are more meaningful because they are introduced in the context of a story. Plus children imagine the plot as they hear it read to them and they get into the habit of visualizing words.

Reduced to summary form, this paragraph could be much abbreviated. A good summary would explain the two reasons why reading aloud to children is beneficial. But because the explanations are fairly self-explanatory, minor details can be eliminated.

Sample Summary

> Children benefit in two ways when parents read aloud. First, story time gives kids the opportunity to bond through cuddling up to the parent reading. Second, kids learn the words in the stories and give their imagination a workout by visualizing the plot.

Don't assume, though, from this example that every summary you write has to include all the major details and none of the minor details.

The summary has to identify the main idea. But the number of major and minor details can vary. The number of details you include depends on the main idea being explained.

Pointers on Summary Writing ◆	1. Open with the main idea.
	2. Be selective about your choice of supporting details. Use only what you need in order to clarify or prove the main idea.
	3. Use addition and reversal transitions to clarify relationships.

Diagrams

In this chapter, exercises 3 and 4 gave you examples of one way to diagram the ideas in paragraphs. There are, however, some other possibilities to consider. For example, if the paragraph does not emphasize how events are ordered in real time, consider making a concept map like the one following this paragraph.

Concept maps put the main idea in the center of the page. The details appear as spokes, or lines, connected to the main idea.

Brainstorming is a method of generating creative solutions to problems. Although it can be done alone, brainstorming works best in a group. To be really effective, the process of brainstorming has to follow four rules. First, group members should clearly state and agree on the problem to be solved. Second, members should say whatever comes to mind, even if an idea doesn't seem appropriate. In brainstorming, the quantity of ideas is more important than the quality. Third, no one should criticize or comment on the ideas expressed. Fourth, after several solutions have been identified, members of the group should agree on which solutions they want to discuss first. At this stage, none of the possible solutions should be abandoned, not even those that seem silly.

Concept Map

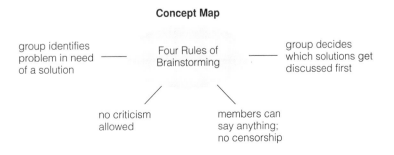

Flow Charts

If the order of events in a paragraph is significant, then consider the diagram below. Called a **flow chart**, the diagram highlights the flow, or sequence, of events.

> Some sociologists think relationships progress through a series of stages. Bernard Murstein, for instance, identifies three stages. In the *stimulus stage*, attraction is sparked by external attributes such as appearance. Next comes the *value stage* in which attachment is based on similarity of values and beliefs. Then after an attachment is formed, the relationship progresses to the *role stage* in which commitment is based on the performance of such roles as husband and wife. (Adapted from Brehm, Kassim, and Fein, *Social Psychology*, p. 329.)

Flow Chart

Bernard Murstein believes that relationships go through three stages.

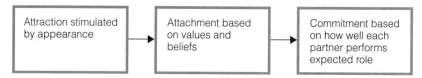

Attraction stimulated by appearance → Attachment based on values and beliefs → Commitment based on how well each partner performs expected role

◆ EXERCISE 7 Knowing What Counts in Notes

DIRECTIONS   Circle the appropriate letter to answer the questions that follow.

EXAMPLE   [1]Psychologists often classify self-esteem as two types: *earned self-esteem* and *global* self-esteem*. [2]A person acquires earned self-esteem when he or she successfully accomplishes a certain task. [3]For example, if a student gets an A on a test, he or she will feel a sense of earned self-esteem. [4]Global self-esteem does not arise from any one particular achievement. [5]It is an overall positive view of oneself regardless of abilities or accomplishments.

1. What kind of detail is sentence 3?

   a. major

   (b.) minor

---

*global: total, related to the larger world.

2. Should sentence 3 be paraphrased and appear in notes on the paragraph?

a. yes

(b.) no

Why or why not? <u>Common sense could provide an answer.</u>

3. What kind of sentence is sentence 5?

a. major

(b.) minor

4. Should sentence 5 be paraphrased and appear in notes on the paragraph?

(a.) yes

b. no

Why or why not? <u>The minor detail is essential to a definition of "global</u>

<u>self-esteem."</u>

5. Which outline would be more useful for future reviews?

(a.) Psychologists think self-esteem can be divided into two kinds.

    1. earned self-esteem comes with achievement

    2. global self-esteem not based on tasks completed

       a. based on a positive view of oneself

b. Psychologists often classify self-esteem into two types: earned and global.

    1. A person develops earned self-esteem if he or she successfully completes a certain task.

       a. getting an A on an exam

    2. Global self-esteem is not based on achievement.

       a. It's an overall sense of oneself as being gifted.

EXPLANATION Outline *a* is the better outline. It paraphrases instead of copying the text. The relationships are clearer in outline *a*. It also doesn't include any unnecessary information. Outline *b* distorts the original meaning and includes unnecessary details.

1. ¹All over the country, police departments use sophisticated computer technology to do their jobs. ²But some police agencies have found that a more ancient means, the horse, offers several advantages even in today's modern times. ³First, police officers on horseback have a height advantage. ⁴They can see more of what's going on around them than an officer on foot. ⁵Second, horses are effective for crowd control. ⁶The physical presence of a horse is intimidating. ⁷As a result, agitated* crowds, such as those engaging in protest demonstrations, are less likely to try to injure a mounted officer. ⁸Furthermore, people often develop affection for a police horse they encounter regularly. ⁹This fondness for the animal can lead to greater respect and admiration for the officer who rides it.

1. What kind of detail is sentence 3?

   a. major

   b. minor

2. Should sentence 3 be paraphrased and appear in notes on the paragraph?

   a. yes

   b. no

   Why or why not? _____

   _____

3. What kind of detail is sentence 4?

   a. major

   b. minor

4. Should sentence 4 be paraphrased and appear in notes on the paragraph?

   a. yes

   b. no

   Why or why not? _____

   _____

———————————

*agitated: excited, stirred up.

5. Fill in the circles in the concept map.

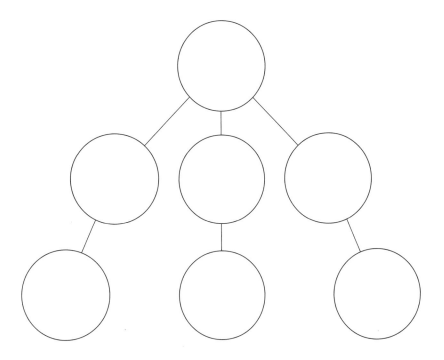

2. [1]Milk has been criticized for being filled with additives and bad for people with digestive problems. [2]However, for most people, milk's health benefits still outweigh any possible risks. [3]For one thing, milk is a convenient source of calcium. [4]People of all ages need calcium to build and maintain bone mass. [5]Also, milk contains several essential nutrients, such as vitamin D, potassium, and magnesium. [6]Studies show that a diet that includes fruits, vegetables, and dairy products— including milk—can even help lower blood pressure. [7]Furthermore, some research indicates that milk may lower the risk of colon cancer.

1. What kind of detail is sentence 4?

    a. major

    b. minor

2. Should sentence 4 be paraphrased and added to notes on the paragraph?

    a. yes

    b. no

Why or why not? _____

_____

3. What kind of detail is sentence 5?

a. major

b. minor

4. Should sentence 5 be paraphrased and added to notes on the paragraph?

a. yes

b. no

Why or why not? _____

_____

5. Which summary best fulfills the pointers identified on page 213?

a. Milk has a long history of being criticized for various reasons, but it's clear that milk has numerous benefits. It's a convenient source of calcium, which builds bones and muscles. It also provides other nutrients like vitamin D, potassium, and magnesium. Milk can help lower blood pressure and reduce the risk of colon cancer.

b. Drinking milk offers numerous benefits. It provides the body with calcium, which keeps bones strong. Milk also provides the body with necessary nutrients such as vitamin D, potassium, and magnesium. It may even help control blood pressure and reduce the risk of colon cancer.

c. Milk is a convenient source of calcium and other nutrients. It also lowers blood pressure and decreases the risk of cancer.

3. ¹Hospitals are finding different ways to increase infant security in order to prevent the kidnapping of babies. ²For example, more guards now patrol hospital halls and conduct periodic* safety drills to keep all personnel alert. ³Also, hospitals are requiring babies to wear sophisticated identification bracelets. ⁴These bracelets automatically alert an electronic security system if they are removed or

_____

*periodic: regular but unscheduled.

taken beyond the baby's assigned unit. [5]In addition, more hospitals are including the mother's thumbprint and the baby's footprint in medical records. [6]Finally, many hospitals no longer release birth announcements to the local media.

1. What kind of detail is sentence 3?
   a. major
   b. minor

2. Should sentence 3 be paraphrased and added to notes on the paragraph?
   a. yes
   b. no

   Why or why not? _____

   _____

3. What kind of detail is sentence 4?
   a. major
   b. minor

4. Should sentence 4 be paraphrased and added to notes on the paragraph?
   a. yes
   b. no

   Why or why not? _____

   _____

5. Fill in the blanks left in the informal outline.

Main Idea _____

_____

Supporting Details

1. _____

2. _____

3. _____

4. _____

4. [1]In 1996, with the birth of Dolly, the first cloned sheep, *cloning*, the creation of genetically identical animals, became a reality. [2]The process used to create Dolly, called *somatic cell nuclear transfer* (SCNT), starts with an unfertilized egg called an *oocyte*. [3]Scientists remove the oocyte nucleus, which contains the egg's genetic, or hereditary, instructions. [4]Then a *somatic cell*—somatic cells come from any part of the body except sperm and eggs—from the animal to be cloned is cultured in an incubator and injected under the outer layer or coating of the unfertilized oocyte. [5]Next, a mild electrical impulse is used to encourage fusion between the oocyte and the injected cell. [6]If fusion is successful, the newly created, fused cell behaves as if it were a fertilized egg and produces an embryo. [7]The embryo is then placed in the uterus of the surrogate mother. [8]If embryo development proceeds normally, the cloned animal is born. (Source of sequence: www.enotalone.com/article/8929.html.)

1. What kind of detail is sentence 3?

　a. major

　b. minor

2. Should sentence 3 be paraphrased and added to notes on the paragraph?

　a. yes

　b. no

　Why or why not? _____

　_____

3. What kind of detail is sentence 4?

　a. major

　b. minor

4. Should sentence 4 be paraphrased and added to notes on the paragraph?

　a. yes

　b. no

　Why or why not? _____

　_____

5. Complete the flow chart to explain the process of cloning.

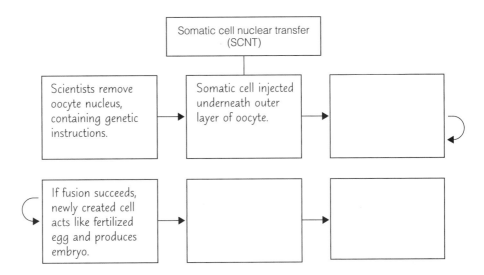

ROUNDING UP THE KEYS

Here is a list of all the reading keys introduced in the chapter. Use them to review for the test on page 230. If a particular reading key doesn't make sense on its own, go back to the page where it appeared and review the section preceding it.

READING KEYS: The Function of Supporting Details

◆ Supporting details supply the reasons, illustrations, facts, figures, and studies that make the main idea clear and convincing to readers. (p. 191)

◆ Supporting details are the author's way of guiding readers to the appropriate meaning. They are the author's way of saying to readers, "I mean this and not that." (p. 191)

◆ The form of supporting details varies. Details can range in form from reasons to statistics. The main idea is what causes supporting details to vary. When the main idea changes, so do the details that develop it. (p. 191)

◆ If the supporting details don't fit what you think is the topic sentence, you probably need to look for another topic sentence. (p. 195)

READING KEYS: Major and Minor Details

◆ Major details pin down general words and phrases introduced in the topic sentence. (p. 197)

◆ Minor details have three functions: (1) They make major details more specific, (2) they provide emphasis, and (3) they add color. The first function is the most important. (p. 197)

READING KEYS: Evaluating Minor Details

◆ Minor details that make major ones more specific are worthy of your attention. (p. 197)

◆ Don't be fooled by the name. *Minor* details may or may not be important. It depends on what they contribute to the major details. (p. 200)

READING KEYS: Clues to Major Details in Topic Sentences

◆ Check the topic sentence for broad, general words like *forms*, *groups*, *causes*, and *advantages*. These words are clues to major details. (p. 203)

◆ Be alert as well to numbers in the topic sentence that tell you how many major details are present. (p. 203)

READING KEYS: Topic Sentences, Transitions, and Major Details

◆ Textbook authors, in particular, like to use transitions to separate supporting details. (p. 208)
◆ Transitions signaling addition are commonly used to introduce major details. (p. 208)

Ten More Words for Your Textbook Vocabulary

1. **momentum:** strength or force gained as events unfold

   Any presidential candidate who wins a string of primaries has *momentum* on his or her side.

2. **sustain:** maintain; keep going; experience

   After his successful speech in Chicago, presidential candidate William Jennings Bryan tried to *sustain* the momentum inspired by the convention. (Adapted from Boyer et al., *The Enduring Vision*, p. 615.)

3. **divergent:** different, various

   Trade associations, which represent entire industries, have widely *divergent* interests, ranging from government regulation of food and drugs to the regulation of the import of beef from Argentina. (Gitelson, Dudley, and Dubnick, *American Government*, p. 213.)

4. **subordinates:** those subject to the control of a higher authority; secondary in rank

   The former Secretary of Defense was famous for treating his *subordinates* with contempt.

5. **delegate:** (*v.*) to assign work or roles to others; (*n.*) person representing some group

   The primary reason managers *delegate* is to get more work done. (Griffin, *Management*, p. 341.)

6. **inception:** beginning, start

   One reason for the company's success since its *inception* was the presence of truly top-rate management.

7. **deprive:** to take away; to keep from possessing

   The war, which lasted for six years, *deprived* them of their right to a childhood.

8. **extensive:** widespread

   Poverty in poor countries is more severe and more *extensive* than in the United States. (Adapted from Macionis, *Sociology*, p. 296.)

9. **foster:** stimulate, encourage

   A leader can strengthen a group by his or her ability to *foster* responsibility among group members.

10. **coherent:** connected, unified

    A leadership approach is defined as a *coherent*, explicit style of management, not a personal style.

◆ **EXERCISE 8**   **Building an Academic Vocabulary**

DIRECTIONS   Fill in the blanks with one of the words listed below.

foster	delegate	coherent	momentum	sustaining
inception	deprived	extensive	divergent	subordinates

1. After scoring three goals in a row, the underdog team had the
   _____ to win.

2. From its _____, the National Organization for Women has focused on discrimination against women in the workplace.

3. In the United Nations, members are inclined to differ because they come from so many _____ countries.

4. The president's ability to _____ responsibility is said to be one of his strengths.

5. The commissioner's _____ resented the rude tone he used when interrupting.

6. In the hopes of _____ the rebellion, the chief called on neighboring tribes to join in the uprising.

7. The discussion, meant to calm troubled waters, only served to _____ anger on both sides.

8. If the opposition offers a clear and _____ plan, agreement is possible.

9. The early colonists felt _____ of their rights and decided to throw off British rule.

10. The damage from the fire was more _____ than was originally thought.

DIGGING DEEPER   **Killer Waves**

Looking Ahead   Here's a topic you've already read about, those killer waves called *tsunamis*. Read to discover the main idea and to locate the supporting details *essential* to explaining it.

1   A tsunami, from the Japanese words *tsu* ("harbor") and *nami* ("wave"), is a series of large waves that smash into coastal areas. The most destructive tsunamis are generated by violent underwater disturbances like earthquakes. During an earthquake, two of the plates that make up the earth's crust move past each other. If this occurs on the ocean floor, a vast amount of water is displaced. The resulting waves move outward from the source event in all directions. These waves can travel great distances from the earthquake's point of origin without losing much speed or energy until they reach land.

2   Unfortunately, when the massive waves hit land, they usually cause horrific destruction. The explosive impact of a great wall of water slamming into shore instantly kills or severely injures those unlucky enough to be nearby. Others are pummeled with floating debris or sucked into the sea as the water recedes. As a result, the death toll can be significant. Buildings, too, are either destroyed or damaged by the force of the impact, the flooding, or wreckage being thrown about by the swirling current. Afterward, survivors often face a catastrophic lack of basic necessities, such as clean water, food, clothing, shelter, electricity, and medical care.

3   Because tsunamis can be so devastating, it is imperative that every country bordering an ocean maintain a good tsunami warning system. In the Pacific Ocean region, for example, hundreds of stations scan for undersea earthquakes capable of causing a tsunami. Also, underwater detectors register changes in water pressure and then relay the information to buoys on the ocean's surface. These buoys transmit the information to satellites. Scientists get the information from satellites and then warn the public using sirens, notices to government officials, and media broadcasts.

4   Although no huge tsunamis in the Pacific have occurred since this warning system was established, it has already successfully detected and informed coastal inhabitants about smaller ones. For example, Japan's meteorological* agency notified residents of the island of Hokkaido of a tsunami in 1993. Although 239 people died when the waves hit, many people were able to flee to higher ground and save their lives.

*meteorological: related to weather forecasting.

5   However, the 2004 tsunami in the Indian Ocean demonstrated the kind of tragedy that can occur when an effective warning system is not in place. Scientists at the Pacific Tsunami Warning Center in Hawaii knew an earthquake had occurred off the coast of Indonesia on December 26, 2004. However, because no sensors or buoys were in place in the Indian Ocean, they were unable to confirm the presence of a tsunami there. Although the scientists still tried to inform countries in the area about the potential danger, these countries were not part of the warning system because proper communication channels had not yet been established. Consequently, the tsunami hit the people of Indonesia, Thailand, India, and Sri Lanka with no warning. More than 200,000 were killed, and many populated areas were flattened.

6   It's certainly true that tsunamis move fast and often don't allow enough time for an adequate warning. However, had a proper warning system been in place in the Indian Ocean in 2004, thousands of people could have reached higher ground in time and would have been spared. In this era of instant global communications, it is absolutely inexcusable that so many were caught by surprise. While we cannot prevent tsunamis, we *can* reduce the magnitude of such natural disasters by using our ability to communicate with one another. (Sources of statistics: "NOAA and the Indian Ocean Tsunami," *NOAA News Online*, December 29, 2004, www.noaanews.noaa. gov/stories2004/s2358.html; Bennett Richardson, "New Push for Tsunami-Alert System," *The Christian Science Monitor*, December 29, 2004, www. csmonitor.com/2004/1229/p01s03-woap.htm.)

Sharpening Your Skills

DIRECTIONS   Answer the following questions by filling in the blanks or circling the letter of the correct response.

1. Based on the context, how would you define the word *pummeled* in paragraph 2?

    _____

2. Based on the context, how would you define the word *imperative* in paragraph 3?

    _____

3. What is the main idea of the entire reading?

   a. Tsunamis are violent and destructive forces of nature.

   b. Tsunami warning systems are essential for countries that border oceans.

   c. The lack of any warning system in the Indian Ocean is a direct result of governmental incompetence.

   d. The 2004 tsunami in the Indian Ocean hit Indonesia particularly hard.

4. Which of the following is a major detail?

   a. Although no huge tsunamis in the Pacific have occurred since this warning system was established, it has already successfully detected and informed coastal inhabitants about smaller ones (paragraph 4).

   b. For example, Japan's meteorological agency notified residents of the island of Hokkaido of a tsunami in 1993 (paragraph 4).

   c. More than 200,000 were killed, and many populated areas were flattened (paragraph 5).

5. Which of the following is a minor detail?

   a. Although 239 people died when the waves hit, many people were able to flee to higher ground and save their lives (paragraph 4).

   b. However, the 2004 tsunami in the Indian Ocean demonstrated the kind of tragedy that can occur when an effective warning system is not in place (paragraph 5).

INTERNET RESOURCE For more practice with topic sentences and supporting details, go to www.cengage.com/devenglish/flemming/rk3e.

▶ TEST 1   **Reviewing the Key Points**

DIRECTIONS   Answer the following questions by filling in the blanks or circling the correct response.

1. General statements are open to _____.
    For that reason, writers and speakers are careful to include
    _____.

2. *T* or *F.* Supporting detail sentences are more general than introductory or topic sentences.

3. Major supporting details supply the reasons, examples, dates, and so on that _____.

4. The content of the supporting details depends on _____.

5. *T* or *F.* Major details are more specific than minor ones.

6. Minor supporting details have three functions. Those functions are

    1. _____

    2. _____

    3. _____

7. The most important function of a minor detail is to _____
    _____.

8. *T* or *F.* Minor details may or may not be important enough to be included in your notes.

9. Two examples of words that offer clues to major details are
    _____.

10. Supporting details are the author's way of saying to readers

_____.

> To correct your test, turn to page 553. If one or more of your answers is incorrect, re-read the Rounding Up the Keys section of the chapter to find out where your mistakes might be.

▶ **TEST 2**   **Recognizing Supporting Details**

> **DIRECTIONS**   Read each topic sentence. Then circle the letters of the two sentences that qualify as supporting details.

Topic Sentence 1. Newborns have definite preferences.

Supporting Details
- a. Newborns prefer moving objects to still ones.
- b. Some research suggests that infants may actually remember sounds heard in the womb.
- c. As they get older, infants sleep less during the day.
- d. Babies only a day or two old appear to like high-pitched "baby" talk more than a normal adult voice.

Topic Sentence 2. In Brazil, family ties are extremely important.

Supporting Details
- a. In Brazil, children often choose to live at home until they are married.
- b. When Brazilian children grow up and leave home to marry, they often establish their new home close by.
- c. For Brazilians, personal relations are an important part of doing business.
- d. Brazilians are more likely than Americans to greet one another with a kiss on the cheek.

Topic Sentence 3. For ancient Greek and Roman males, the presence or absence of a beard was highly significant.

Supporting Details
- a. The Roman male prized his beard as a symbol of masculinity.
- b. Throughout history, hair has been considered a sexual symbol.
- c. In the story of Samson and Delilah, Samson loses his physical strength when Delilah cuts his hair.
- d. The Greeks shaved daily because being beardless was considered a sign of beauty.

Topic Sentence 4. Although there hasn't been a case of smallpox in years, the virus still exists.

Supporting Details
- a. A test tube containing the virus is in a Moscow laboratory.
- b. Like the flu virus of 1918, the smallpox virus could do unimaginable harm if it were let loose on the world.

    c. A second dose of the virus is in Atlanta at the Centers for Disease Control and Prevention.

    d. Some people believe the smallpox virus should be destroyed.

Topic Sentence **5.** Over the years, the German population has grown extremely diverse, or varied.

Supporting Details a. The wall dividing Germany into two countries, East and West, was erected in 1961.

    b. When East and West Germany[†] became one country in 1991, the non-German population increased dramatically.

    c. At the end of the Cold War, a substantial number of immigrants from the Soviet Union arrived in Germany.

    d. Throughout history, Germany has rarely been united.

[†]Divided into East and West Germany after World War II, Germany became one country again in 1991.

▶ **TEST 3**   **Recognizing Supporting Details**

DIRECTIONS   Circle the letters of the three details that could support the topic sentence.

Topic Sentence 1. Frogs are disappearing from the face of the earth.

Supporting Details

a. Many frogs are dying from a waterborne fungus called chytrid.

b. Frogs and toads belong to the class of animals called amphibians.

c. One researcher, desperate to save Panama's frogs from being attacked by the chytrid fungus, housed those that were still healthy in a luxury hotel.

d. Frogs are one of Panama's national symbols.

e. In some locations, frogs multiply in great numbers and are considered a major nuisance.

f. Frogs are also disappearing because their habitats are being destroyed by humans.

Topic Sentence 2. President Lyndon Baines Johnson didn't just talk about the Great Society; he tried to build it through legislation.

Supporting Details

a. Johnson was an insecure man who was worried about how he would be viewed compared to his predecessor, the glamorous John F. Kennedy.

b. Johnson used all of his mastery of congressional rules to get Congress to pass important civil rights legislation.

c. Thanks to Lyndon Baines Johnson, people over sixty-five have medical insurance.

d. Johnson proposed legislation increasing funding for both education and the arts.

e. The Vietnam War eventually drove Lyndon Baines Johnson from office.

f. When Johnson arrived in the Oval Office, no one expected him to care about civil rights in the way that his predecessor had, but Johnson surprised those who doubted him.

Topic Sentence 3. Unions have tried, unsuccessfully, to organize Walmart employees.

Supporting Details

a. Walmart was founded by Sam Walton and is a family-owned business.

b. At one point, the Teamsters tried to organize Walmart but failed after the company launched a publicity campaign, focusing on allegedly illegal Teamster activities.

c. A number of women have filed lawsuits against Walmart, claiming that the company's hiring practices discriminate against females.

d. The United Food and Commercial Workers union tried to organize Walmart employees after the chain started selling groceries.

e. In 2005, Walmart agreed to pay $11 million to settle allegations that it had failed to pay overtime to janitors, many of whom worked seven nights a week.

f. When the United Food and Commercial Workers union won the right to organize Walmart butchers, Walmart defeated union efforts by ordering cut meat from suppliers outside the company.

Topic Sentence **4.** Eleanor Roosevelt, wife of President Franklin Delano Roosevelt, played an active role in her husband's administration.

Supporting Details

a. Eleanor Roosevelt was a personal hero of former New York senator and former first lady Hillary Clinton.

b. Eleanor Roosevelt, in an attempt to shape presidential policy, made it a point to introduce her husband to reformers and social activists.

c. Eleanor Roosevelt traveled so much during her husband's administration that a newspaper headline once announced "Mrs. Roosevelt Spent Night at White House."

d. A passionate supporter of women's rights, Eleanor Roosevelt ensured that women were appointed to public office in her husband's administration.

e. Eleanor Roosevelt played a key role in launching the Public Works Administration, which provided jobs for the unemployed.

f. Eleanor Roosevelt had many admirers, but there were just as many who detested her and complained about her unelected role in the administration.

Topic Sentence **5.** Good leaders seem to have several traits in common.

Supporting Details

a. One of the key characteristics researchers have noted is that good leaders have a high level of self-confidence.

b. Good leaders are also able to inspire faith in their right to take charge.

c. Good leaders are able to balance their sense of confidence with a healthy dose of humility.

d. Personality traits are observable both within and outside the work situation.

e. There is a difference between being in a position of power and being a leader.

f. The traits of a good leader can vary depending on the culture.

▶ **TEST 4** **Taking Notes on Paragraphs**

DIRECTIONS Complete the notes following each paragraph.

1. Abraham Maslow, an American psychologist whose best-known works were published in the 1960s and 1970s, developed a theory of motivation based on what he called a "hierarchy of needs." At the most basic level are physiological needs, the things we require to survive, like food, water, clothing, shelter, and sleep. At the next level are safety needs, the things we require for physical and emotional safety. Safety needs may be satisfied through job security, health insurance, pension plans, and safe working and living conditions. Next are social needs, the human requirements for love, affection, and a sense of belonging. At the next to last level are esteem needs, the desire for respect and recognition from others. At the top of the hierarchy are our self-actualization needs, the longing to grow and develop and become all we are capable of being. (Adapted from Pride, Hughes, and Kapoor, *Business*, pp. 306–7.)

Main Idea   According to Abraham Maslow, human needs are organized into a hierarchy that can help explain motivation.

Supporting Details   _____

_____

_____

_____

_____

_____

_____

_____

_____

_____

2. While humor has the potential to make us feel good, it can also be used as a form of attack. Men who make fun of feminists, for

example, are typically voicing some measure of hostility. Similarly, jokes at the expense of gay people express the tensions and anxiety surrounding rigid notions of sexual roles. Around the world, conflict and hostility among ethnic groups is expressed by means of jokes. In this kind of negative humor, an ethnic group is portrayed as too stupid to master even the most basic skills, such as screwing in a light bulb. Minorities also like to use humor to attack those in power. Women, for instance, frequently make jokes about the inability of men to understand even the most obvious emotions. Similarly, African-Americans joke about white people in ways that make them look awkward and uptight.

Main Idea   Humor can hurt.

Supporting Details   _____

_____

_____

_____

_____

_____

_____

_____

_____

▶ **TEST 5**   **Understanding Major and Minor Details**

DIRECTIONS   Answer the questions following each paragraph by circling the letter of the correct response.

1. ¹After achieving their independence in the eighteenth century, Americans didn't have much time to think about entertainment. ²But as cities began to expand in the nineteenth century, three branches of show business emerged and flourished: theatrical drama, musical comedy, and vaudeville. ³Focusing on the Wild West and the Old South, theatrical dramas made other parts of the country come alive for those who had never set foot outside their home state. ⁴Cowboys and outlaws like Buffalo Bill, Davy Crockett, and Jesse James had a particular appeal for city audiences and were often the stars of these dramas. ⁵Along with theatrical dramas, musical comedies arrived on the scene to entertain audiences with songs, jokes, and dance. ⁶In 1866, *The Black Domino / Between You and Me and the Post* made its debut in New York City and became the first theatrical performance to publicly call itself "a musical comedy." ⁷Playing alongside dramas and musicals were vaudeville shows. ⁸Vaudeville featured a variety of different acts, ranging from jugglers to song-and-dance routines and comedic skits, or scenes. ⁹In vaudeville, there was something for everybody.

1. Which sentence is the topic sentence?
    a. sentence 1
    b. sentence 2
    c. sentence 3

2. Sentence 4 is
    a. a major detail.
    b. a minor detail.

3. Sentence 6 is
    a. a major detail.
    b. a minor detail.

4. In this paragraph, identifying the major details is aided by
    a. a word or words in the topic sentence.
    b. addition transitions.
    c. both the topic sentence and addition transitions.

2. ¹Importing or exporting (or both) is usually the first type of international business in which a firm gets involved. ²Exporting, or making the product in the firm's domestic marketplace and selling it in another country, can involve both merchandise and services. ³Importing is bringing a good, service, or financing into the home country from abroad. ⁴For example, automobiles (Mazda, Ford, Volkswagen, Mercedes-Benz, and Ferrari) and stereo equipment (Sony, Bang & Olufsen, Sanyo) are routinely exported by their manufacturers to other countries. ⁵Likewise, many wine distributors buy products from vineyards in France, Italy, and/or California and import them into their own countries for resale. (Adapted from Griffin, *Management*, p. 135.)

1. Which sentence is the topic sentence?
   a. sentence 1
   b. sentence 2
   c. sentence 6

2. Sentence 3 is
   a. a major detail.
   b. a minor detail.

3. Sentence 4 is
   a. a major detail.
   b. a minor detail.

4. In this paragraph, identifying the major details is aided by
   a. a word or words in the topic sentence.
   b. addition transitions.
   c. both the topic sentence and addition transitions.

3. ¹Creative leaders, like creative workers of all types, are different in many ways from their less creative counterparts. ²They are devoted to their fields and enjoy intellectual stimulation. ³They also challenge the status quo, and this leads them to seek improvements in what already exists. ⁴For example, someone questioned why listening to music on the go needed to involve a device as big as a CD player, and the result was the MP3 player. ⁵Above all, creative people are mentally flexible and can see past the traditional ways of doing things. (DuBrin, *Leadership*, p. 324.)

1. Which sentence is the topic sentence?

   a. sentence 1

   b. sentence 2

   c. sentence 3

2. Sentence 3 is

   a. a major detail.

   b. a minor detail.

3. Sentence 4 is

   a. a major detail.

   b. a minor detail.

4. In this paragraph, identifying the major details is aided by

   a. a word or words in the topic sentence.

   b. addition transitions.

   c. both the topic sentence and addition transitions.

4. ¹Purchasing power is created by income. ²However, as every taxpayer knows, not all income is available for spending. ³For this reason, marketers consider income in three different ways. ⁴*Personal income* is the income an individual receives from all sources, less the Social Security taxes the individual must pay. ⁵*Disposable income* is personal income less all additional personal taxes. ⁶These taxes include income, estate, gift, and property taxes levied by local, state, and federal governments. ⁷About 3 percent of all disposable income is saved. ⁸*Discretionary income* is disposable income less savings and expenditures on food, clothing, and housing. ⁹Discretionary income is of particular interest to marketers because consumers have the most choice in spending it. ¹⁰Consumers use their discretionary income to purchase items ranging from automobiles and vacations to movies and pet food. (Pride, Hughes, and Kapoor, *Business*, p. 373.)

1. Which sentence is the topic sentence?

   a. sentence 1

   b. sentence 3

   c. sentence 6

2. Sentence 4 is
   a. a major detail.
   b. a minor detail.

3. Sentence 6 is
   a. a major detail.
   b. a minor detail.

4. In this paragraph, identifying the major details is aided by
   a. a word or words in the topic sentence.
   b. addition transitions.
   c. both the topic sentence and addition transitions.

5. [1]With the arrival of the twentieth century, Americans developed new patterns of everyday life. [2]One important change involved the use of time, and people were increasingly able to split their day into distinct time compartments: work, family, and leisure. [3]For many people, work on the job shrank as mechanization and higher productivity enabled employers to shorten the workweek for many industrial laborers from six days to five and a half. [4]At home, wives still worked long hours cooking and cleaning, but machines eased some of their tasks, and they were able to spend more time with their families. [5]In white-collar households, breadwinners started working a forty-hour week, enjoyed a full weekend off, and received annual vacations as a standard job benefit.

   1. Which sentence is the topic sentence?
      a. sentence 1
      b. sentence 2
      c. sentence 6

   2. Sentence 3 is
      a. a major detail.
      b. a minor detail.

   3. Sentence 4 is
      a. a major detail.
      b. a minor detail.

4. In this paragraph, identifying the major details is aided by
   a. a word or words in the topic sentence.
   b. addition transitions.
   c. both the topic sentence and addition transitions.

▶ **TEST 6** **Recognizing Major and Minor Details**

DIRECTIONS Fill in the blank boxes with the appropriate major and minor details. Keep in mind that you might not be able to fill in every box. *Note*: Use partial sentences whenever the sentences are too long to fit easily into the boxes.

1. ¹When you clean out your attic, don't throw out what looks like a piece of junk until you determine its potential as a collectible antique. ²For one thing, what appear to be old pieces of junk may actually be valuable treasures. ³For example, more and more collectors are interested in buying old record albums. ⁴Things that evoke powerful, nostalgic* memories are also in demand. ⁵Old radios, toys, and bottles that remind people of the "good old days" can be worth a lot of money. ⁶Anything that's unique to its era, or time, could be valuable, too. ⁷Furniture or decorative items in the style of the 1920s and 1930s, for instance, are popular with collectors. ⁸Finally, older handmade items could be treasures as well. ⁹Pottery and hand-hooked rugs are two examples of crafts that people want to add to their collections.

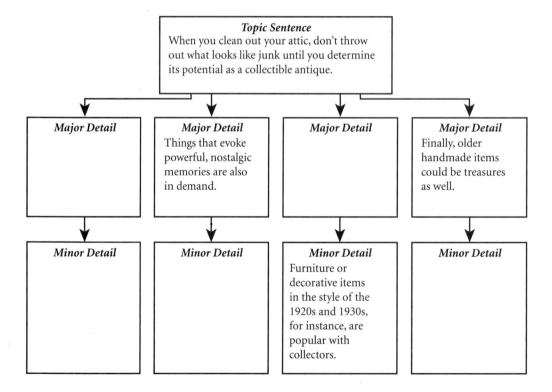

| **Topic Sentence** |
| When you clean out your attic, don't throw out what looks like junk until you determine its potential as a collectible antique. |

| **Major Detail** | **Major Detail** Things that evoke powerful, nostalgic memories are also in demand. | **Major Detail** | **Major Detail** Finally, older handmade items could be treasures as well. |

| **Minor Detail** | **Minor Detail** | **Minor Detail** Furniture or decorative items in the style of the 1920s and 1930s, for instance, are popular with collectors. | **Minor Detail** |

*nostalgic: longing for people or things of the past.

2. [1]The twentieth century has been labeled the Plastic Age, and for good reason. [2]In 1909, New York chemist Leo Baekeland introduced Bakelite, the world's first synthetic plastic. [3]Bakelite was a durable substance that could be molded into almost anything; by the 1930s, manufacturers were producing 90,000 tons of it every year. [4]During World War II, shortages of natural resources increased the demand for plastics even more. [5]The result was vinyl, a rubber substitute that provided soldiers with tents and boots. [6]After the war, plastic synthetics used for military purposes were adapted for everyday life. [7]The nylon in parachutes, for example, was turned into ladies' stockings. [8]By 1979, the United States was producing more plastic than steel. [9]Today, plastic is replacing the metal in buildings and machines, and almost all electronic data is stored on plastic.

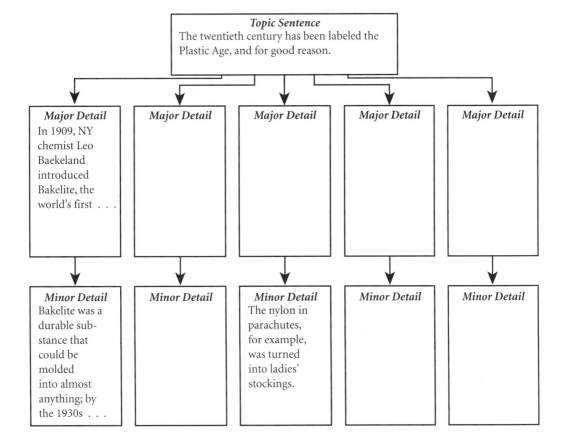

Topic Sentence
The twentieth century has been labeled the Plastic Age, and for good reason.

Major Detail
In 1909, NY chemist Leo Baekeland introduced Bakelite, the world's first . . .

Major Detail

Major Detail

Major Detail

Major Detail

Minor Detail
Bakelite was a durable substance that could be molded into almost anything; by the 1930s . . .

Minor Detail

Minor Detail
The nylon in parachutes, for example, was turned into ladies' stockings.

Minor Detail

Minor Detail

▶ **TEST 7**   **Writing Summaries**

DIRECTIONS   Circle the letter of the better summary.

1. At one time, kids in public schools memorized poems. Yes, that's right—memorized. Although memorizing has somehow become a dirty word in many educational circles, it used to be an essential part of elementary and high school training, and for good reason. Children committed poems and entire speeches to memory, and, without realizing it, they expanded their vocabulary to include the words they had learned by heart. They also developed a sophisticated sense of how words can produce different rhythms and emotional effects. Memorizing great poems and speeches also gave children some very sophisticated examples of sentence syntax, or word order. This may be one reason why letters written during the Civil War, even by lowly foot soldiers, reveal such writerly sophistication. The letter writers had memorized, already as children, some of the finest examples of English prose.

   a. Children lost out when schools stopped asking them to memorize great speeches and poems. Memorizing famous examples of poetry and prose boosted children's vocabulary. It also made them familiar with the kinds of music and feelings words can produce. The practice of asking children to memorize poems and speeches in elementary and high school may be one reason why the letters of Civil War soldiers were sophisticated in style and syntax.

   b. Civil War soldiers generally wrote very sophisticated letters to their families and friends back home. The style was so sophisticated that those who came after have wondered how soldiers, with relatively little education, could write with such skill. The reason has now been identified. In the nineteenth century, memorizing poems was part of the school curriculum, and children in all grades were exposed to good writing. Having been exposed to good writing, they took pains to make their own writing imitate what they had memorized. Memorization in schools was abandoned in the twentieth century, making the teaching of writing much harder.

2. In 1997, the Food and Drug Administration (FDA) relaxed its rules on advertising prescription drugs, allowing pharmaceutical companies to advertise their drugs in magazines and on television. This

change enabled the pharmaceutical industry to market its products directly to consumers. Prior to this time, the industry's ads were directed only to doctors. There is no doubt that this change has caused serious problems. First, there is evidence that advertising is responsible for 10 to 25 percent of the recent increase in prescription drug spending. Second, these increases in spending on prescriptions put additional demands on insurance companies, which pass on the costs to consumers in the form of higher premiums. A study by the nonprofit National Institute for Health Care Management suggested that the "advertisements might be persuading consumers to push for newer, costlier medicines when less expensive drugs would work just as well." For example, one health care executive noted that, for most people, "Celebrex is no more effective than Tylenol or ibuprofen that you can buy at the drugstore for pennies a day to treat arthritis pain. But it's much more expensive." (Adapted from Leslie, *Mass Communication Ethics,* p. 192.)

a. Since 1997, the FDA has allowed drug companies to market drugs directly to the consumer. This has been a disaster for all parties concerned. Patients march into their doctors' offices and ask for drugs they have seen on television. They are upset if they don't get them. And if they do get what they ask for, they might not really need the drug prescribed. Celebrex, for instance, is believed to be no more effective than Tylenol. It just costs a lot more, and people believe if it's more expensive, it's better. In addition, pharmaceutical companies feel free to overcharge for these drugs because they know people want them. The FDA should reverse this ruling before it does more damage.

b. Since 1997, the FDA has allowed drug companies to market drugs directly to consumers through magazine and television advertising. That change in FDA policy has caused problems. There has been, for instance, a noticeable increase in the amount of money spent on prescription drugs. Faced with larger prescription bills to cover, insurance companies have passed the increases on to consumers in the form of higher insurance premiums. Also, a study by the National Institute of Health Care Management suggests that the ads encourage people to take pricey drugs, which might not be any more beneficial than much cheaper medications. Celebrex, for instance, may be no better than Tylenol.

▶ **TEST 8**   **Developing Your Textbook Vocabulary**

DIRECTIONS   Fill in the blanks with one of the words listed below.

coherent	sustain	deprived	inception	divergent
subordinates	momentum	delegating	foster	extensive

1. At its _____ in 1868, the Elks Lodge was meant to be for men only, but as times changed, so did the club's rules, and the Elks now allow women to join.

2. After the health care legislation was submitted for approval, there were immediate demands for _____ changes.

3. The principal often complained about his heavy workload, but, to some degree, the problem was of his own making: He was incapable of _____ responsibility.

4. For years the manager of the bank had treated her _____ with contempt; thus, they were delighted to hear she had been fired.

5. The new president was trying hard to respond to so many _____ opinions; it was becoming harder and harder to construct a policy that would satisfy all of them.

6. The union leader was working around the clock to _____ enthusiasm for the strike, but people were clearly becoming discouraged.

7. In some parts of the country, the movement for windmill-driven energy seemed to be gaining _____.

8. The teacher knew how to _____ a desire to learn, and his students loved him for it.

9. The young reporter had real talent, but she needed to make her writing a little more _____ if she was going to sell her articles to a news service.

10. _____ of his visiting privileges, the prisoner became enraged and began tearing the room apart.

Drawing Inferences About Implied Main Ideas

6

IN THIS CHAPTER, YOU WILL LEARN

- how inferences are part of everyday life.
- how to infer implied main ideas in paragraphs lacking topic sentences.
- how to evaluate the inferences you draw.

Drawing inferences is not restricted to reading. We do it all the time. We take what we know and draw inferences about things left unsaid. Imagine, for example, that your best friend came in from a blind date looking utterly miserable. Without a word spoken, you knew that the date didn't go well. In other words, you drew an inference using the evidence at hand—in this case, the unhappy expression, the slumping shoulders, and the heavy silence. As this chapter shows, when you read you sometimes do much the same thing. Based on the clues supplied by the author, you fill in the gaps left in the text.

 ## Inferring Main Ideas

Inferring main ideas in reading relies on the same kind of thinking you would use to interpret a friend's mood or get a chuckle from a cartoon. First you look at the evidence supplied by the author, that is, the statements in the passage. Then based on what the author says, you infer a main idea that is implied, or suggested, but never explicitly, or directly, stated. For an illustration, read the following paragraph. There's no stated topic sentence. However, you can infer one based on what's actually stated.

> Over the last ten years, speed limits on America's roads and highways have increased by as much as a third. Yet many motorists are still speeding. The question is, Why? For some people, the right to speed is practically a civil rights issue. Because they believe that speed limits exist so that city and state governments can collect money, they consider speed limits to be an unnecessary interference with their right to drive as fast as they please. A second group of speeders acknowledges that speeding is dangerous. However, these drivers feel that at certain times they have a justifiable reason to speed. For instance, they are late for work or for a doctor's appointment and firmly believe that their lateness is a satisfactory excuse. A small minority of speeders seem to do it simply for the excitement it provides. Young males make up the majority of this group. These young men get a thrill out of driving at high speeds, often with friends who also consider speeding cool. In addition to the thrillseekers, there are, after all, the speeders who think they don't run a serious risk of punishment, so why not ignore speed limits. The odds are in their favor. These drivers know that there aren't enough police officials on the road to ticket all speeding vehicles. They also know that most police officials do not stop anyone who exceeds the limit by only ten or fifteen miles. In 2002, for example, only 7 percent of ticketed speeders were exceeding the limit by ten miles or less. The rest were exceeding the limit by twenty, thirty, even forty miles.

In this example, there is no one sentence that can generally cover all the specific points made in the passage. However, you can infer one, like "People speed for different reasons" or "There are several reasons why drivers exceed the speed limit." This implied main idea does what a stated topic sentence would do: It generally sums up all the specific details included in the paragraph.

Inferring Main Ideas
◆

To infer the implied main idea, you need to do the following:

1. Read all of the specific statements, not just the ones that open the paragraphs.
2. Think of a general statement that could sum up the specifics as effectively as any stated topic sentence.

3. Check to see that none of the sentences in the passage contradicts your general statement.

4. Ask yourself which specific statements support the main idea you inferred. If none do, you need to draw another inference.

READING KEYS

◆ No matter what the context—everyday life or textbook assignment— drawing inferences requires you to look at the existing evidence and figure out what it suggests about the person, situation, or passage.

◆ Your implied main idea should never be contradicted by the author's actual statements.

◆ The main idea inferred by readers should sum up a paragraph as effectively as a topic sentence.

VOCABULARY EXTRA

Many people confuse the words *infer* and *imply*. But, in fact, they have different meanings. They are *not* interchangeable. Authors or speakers *imply* by setting forth the evidence for a suggested but unstated conclusion. Readers and listeners then *infer* the author's or speaker's implied conclusion. In other words, only readers and listeners infer, whereas only authors or speakers imply.

IDIOM ALERT: Small world

The idiom *small world* is used to suggest that people are more connected and more likely to know one another than is commonly expected or assumed. "When David found out that his new girlfriend had just met his previous one at the gym, he muttered 'small world' and tried to change the subject."

◆ EXERCISE 1   Identifying the Implied Main Idea

DIRECTIONS   Circle the appropriate letter to identify the implied main idea.

EXAMPLE   "Nessie" is the mysterious aquatic, dinosaur-like creature who reportedly lives in Scotland's cold Ness *loch,* or lake. On the other side of the Atlantic, in the United States, both Lake Erie and Lake Champlain are said to contain at least one large creature who, like the Loch Ness monster, has a small head, long neck, humped back, and flippers. Witnesses claim to have spotted similar serpent-like creatures in Sweden's Lake Storsjön and Norway's Lake Seljordsvatnet. Canada's Lake Memphremagog and Turkey's Lake Van, too, allegedly house mysterious underwater monsters. Sightings, however, are rare, and several scientific expeditions have failed to produce proof of these creatures' existence. Nonetheless, camera-toting tourists flock to all of these lakes. The visitors hope to catch a glimpse of what some believe could be the last living dinosaurs.

Implied Main Idea

a. Numerous eyewitnesses have proven that the Loch Ness monster really does exist.

b. Although there's no real proof that dinosaurs have survived to this day, people around the world continue to believe in their existence.

c. It's generally believed that, in time, proof of the Loch Ness monster's existence will surface.

EXPLANATION   Answer *a* is incorrect. The Loch Ness monster is not even the topic of the paragraph, let alone the main idea. Answer *c* makes no sense because nothing in the paragraph describes what might happen in the future. Only answer *b* could effectively summarize the paragraph.

1. Was England's Stonehenge, the five-thousand-year-old ring of massive stones, constructed by prehistoric people to serve as a giant calendar? Well, if you stand in the center of the circle on the evenings of the summer or winter solstice (the longest and shortest days of the year), you can watch the sun set directly in line with the large stone that marks the entrance to Stonehenge. This alignment* seems intentional, as if Stonehenge's builders wanted to determine the solstices.† Identifying these events would have allowed them to predict and note changes in the seasons. The positions of other stones within

---

*alignment: arrangement in a straight line.
†solstices: events that occur twice each year when the Earth's axis is inclined toward or away from the sun.

Stonehenge's inner circle mark the lunar* cycle (29.5 days) and allow for the measure of months and years.

Implied Main Idea

a. The mystery of Stonehenge is unlikely to be solved anytime soon.

b. Stonehenge is a massive ring of stones in England that was built thousands of years ago.

c. The position of the massive stones that make up Stonehenge suggests it might have been used as a calendar.

2. In 1937, Amelia Earhart was trying to make history by flying around the world in a small plane. However, she and Fred Noonan, her navigator, suddenly disappeared over the Pacific Ocean in July of that year. They were never heard from again. One theory is that their plane ran out of fuel and crashed into the ocean. Another claims that the Japanese captured and executed the two aviators, believing them to be spies. Still another theory suggests that their plane crashed on a remote island, where cannibals killed and ate them. Some people have even speculated that Earhart and Noonan disappeared because they were lovers and wanted to live together.

Implied Main Idea

a. Despite still keen interest, the mystery of Amelia Earhart's disappearance will never be solved.

b. Several different theories have been offered to explain Amelia Earhart's disappearance.

c. Most people believe that Amelia Earhart's plane crashed over the ocean.

3. In the 1960s and 1970s, mothers believed that their babies could sleep well only in complete silence. Today, however, pediatricians advise parents to help their babies learn to sleep with background noise. Thirty to forty years ago, doctors told mothers to lay babies face down to sleep, so they would not choke on vomit or mucus. Nowadays, doctors say babies should sleep on their backs to lower the risk of suffocating. Decades ago, mothers gave their babies cereal beginning at six weeks. These days, pediatricians counsel parents to withhold solid food until the child is 4 to 6 months old. Moms of the 1960s and 1970s also believed that wheeled baby walkers helped their children learn to walk. Now, though, doctors say that walkers actually hinder

———————————
*lunar: having to do with the moon.

babies' walking. Decades ago, mothers bathed their infants daily. Today's doctors say babies need baths only about twice a week.

Implied Main Idea

a. Today's baby-care advice contradicts most of the baby-care advice of thirty to forty years ago.

b. Even with advice from experienced pediatricians, raising a child is undoubtedly the toughest job there is.

c. Everything doctors told mothers about baby care thirty years ago has been proven wrong.

4. In 1967, Yale psychologist Stanley Milgram gave a group of Midwesterners the name and address of a person they didn't know. Then he instructed them to try to send a letter to that person by passing it only through friends. The group members gave their letters to their friends, who, in turn, passed them on to their friends. On average, Milgram discovered, a letter passed through only five people before it reached its destination. This led him to conclude that everyone in the world is connected by just "six degrees of separation." Milgram's result was also described as the "small world phenomenon." However, in the years since, Milgram's experiment has not been successfully repeated despite several attempts. Also, another psychologist, Judith Kleinfeld of the University of Alaska Fairbanks, found flaws in Milgram's methods. Her study of the original research revealed that Milgram recruited especially sociable people rather than a random sampling of individuals. Kleinfeld also discovered that fewer than a third of Milgram's letters ever arrived at their destination.

Implied Main Idea

a. The notion that everyone is connected by "six degrees of separation" may be more myth than reality.

b. Although Milgram's experiments have not been successfully repeated, many people still believe that his results were correct.

c. We are all much closer than we realize.

Effective and Ineffective Inferences

To be a skillful reader, you often have to infer the author's main idea. It follows, then, that effective inferences should keep you on the same track as the author, whereas ineffective inferences will do the opposite. Ineffective inferences send you in a direction the author never intended.

They inhibit the reader's ability to understand the author's message and stir up confusion between writer and reader.

To illustrate the difference between effective and ineffective inferences, read the following paragraph. Then look over the implied main ideas that follow. Put a check mark next to the implied main idea that matches the author's train of thought. Put an *X* next to the one that would send the reader in the wrong direction.

> In the nineteenth century, African-American Henry Blair helped revolutionize the practice of farming. Blair invented a corn planter in 1834 and a cotton planter in 1836. Later that century, another African-American, Sarah Boone, aided housewives all over the country by inventing the ironing board. She patented* her design in 1892. Writers past and present can thank African-American W. B. Purvis, who patented the fountain pen in 1890. They also should be grateful to J. L. Love, who invented the pencil sharpener in 1897. Another nineteenth-century African-American who made life easier and safer was Virgie Ammons, who invented the fireplace damper. Among other nineteenth-century inventions credited to African-Americans were the lawn mower, the folding bed, and the golf tee.

Inference 1   In the nineteenth century, African-Americans were responsible for a number of inventions essential to both work and play. _____

Inference 2   Although African-Americans were responsible for many inventions that improved daily work and leisure, they were seldom given credit for their contributions. _____

If you put a check in the first blank and an *X* in the second, then you know how effective and ineffective inferences differ. The first inference is supported by the author's words. That support comes from the African-Americans' inventions cited by the author.

The second inference, however, relies far too heavily on the reader's personal opinion. Look for specific references to how the contributions of African-Americans were ignored, and you won't find any. As soon as you can't find an example, reason, study, story, or fact that supports the main idea you infer, you need to rethink it.

---

*patented: gained legal ownership or right to distribute; received official document conferring to an inventor, for a term of years, the exclusive right to make, use, or sell his or her invention.

○━╖ READING KEY

◆ Effective inferences keep writers and readers on the same track. Ineffective inferences send writers and readers in different directions.

Avoiding a Communication Breakdown

When you read the second inference on page 256, you might have thought to yourself, so what if the inference is not based on the author's words? If the author didn't make that point, she should have. What's the problem? The problem is this: With the wrong inference, reader and writer can end up miles apart in their thinking, with the reader completely missing the writer's point and wasting time in pursuit of the wrong message or meaning. To illustrate, let's look at that first paragraph again, along with the one that follows it:

> In the nineteenth century, African-American Henry Blair helped revolutionize the practice of farming. Blair invented a corn planter in 1834 and a cotton planter in 1836. Later that century, another African-American, Sarah Boone, aided housewives all over the country by inventing the ironing board. She patented her design in 1892. Writers past and present can thank African-American W. B. Purvis, who patented the fountain pen in 1890. They also should be grateful to J. L. Love, who invented the pencil sharpener in 1897. Another nineteenth-century African-American who made life easier and safer was Virgie Ammons, who invented the fireplace damper. Among other nineteenth-century inventions credited to African-Americans were the lawn mower, the folding bed, and the golf tee.
>
> Throughout the first half of the twentieth century, African-Americans vastly improved the daily life of most Americans. Other useful inventions included the coin changer, the folding chair, and the stainless steel scouring pad, to name a few. However, in the early 1920s, the contributions of African-Americans became more cultural than functional. The clearest evidence for this claim can be found in the world of music. If W. C. Handy is widely acknowledged as the father of the blues, then Louis Armstrong is, without doubt, the all-time king of jazz. To this day, no one disputes the power of his influence. Then, too, the Harlem Renaissance[†] fanned out way beyond Harlem's borders. Writers like Zora Neale Hurston, Langston Hughes, and Jean Toomer

---

[†]Harlem Renaissance: period in the 1920s when Harlem was the center of an artistic explosion.

may have intended to explore, analyze, and celebrate black culture. Yet that racial focus didn't stop white writers like Sherwood Anderson and Allen Tate from reading and being influenced by black writers.

Readers guided by inference 1 on page 256 would move smoothly from the first paragraph to the second. They would correctly predict that the writer was going to discuss other inventions or innovations by African-Americans, and they would be right.

Readers guided by inference 2, however, would be expecting instances of African-Americans' contributions that were ignored. These readers would not be prepared for the writer's actual train of thought. In time, of course, they would probably get back on track. However, that would be time wasted, and it is wasted time that whittles away both motivation and concentration. Anytime the main idea you infer doesn't match the author's words, don't spend time trying to force a fit. Instead, revise the main idea you inferred.

Effective Inferences

- are solidly based on the author's actual words.
- never let the reader's ideas about a topic overshadow the author's.
- are never contradicted by the author's statements.

Ineffective Inferences

- have little connection to the author's actual statements.
- rely more heavily on the reader's ideas than on the author's.
- are likely to be contradicted by what the author says in the reading.

O▬ READING KEY

◆ To be effective, the main ideas you infer should be based on the author's words rather than your personal opinions.

◆ EXERCISE 2   Identifying the Implied Main Idea

DIRECTIONS   Circle the appropriate letter to identify the most effective inference.

EXAMPLE   For $14.99, a busy or an unimaginative man can buy a list of romantic marriage proposal ideas from an Internet company called Will You Marry Me? Or, he can surf the Internet for sites that offer free romance tips. He can also buy any number of books that describe unique and creative scenarios for a proposal. If he needs help with planning a memorable setting for a proposal, he can even hire a romance "specialist." The specialist will help him dream up and then engineer the special event. For example, *Will You Marry Me?* offers personalized services for $180 and up. Other companies that put together events such as weddings and parties can also be hired to create a romantic environment for popping the question.

Implied Main Idea (a.) Several sources of ideas exist for romantically challenged men who want to propose marriage.

    b. Women are better at proposing marriage than men; they don't need a romance "specialist."

    c. Men are unimaginative when it comes to romance.

    d. Men rely a good deal more on the Internet for finding romance than women do.

EXPLANATION   The focus here is on men and how they go about dealing with romance. Nothing is said about women, making *b* incorrect. Statement *c* may or may not be true, but there's no evidence that the author shares this opinion. Because nothing in the passage contrasts men with women, *d* is clearly not the right answer, making *a* the best implied main idea.

1. When he was riding in his motorcade, George W. Bush, the 43rd president of the United States, was referred to as "the package." At other times, he was known as POTUS, which stands for President of the United States. His wife was called FLOTUS, or First Lady of the United States. In Washington, the White House was called the "18 acres" or the "crown." The Capitol was the "punchbowl." The "blue goose" was a big presidential lectern.* The "football" was a black bag of national security information carried by a military aide, and the members of the media who followed the president around in public were known as the "pool."

Implied Main Idea   a. George W. Bush's staff used code names to protect the president from the threat of assassination attempts.

    b. President George W. Bush's staff used made-up names for the people, places, and things they encountered.

    c. For the staff of George W. Bush, secrecy was a top priority.

    d. All presidents rely on code names for staff members.

*lectern: a stand that serves as a support for notes.

2. Most people know that lack of sleep causes irritability and increases the risk of accidents while driving. However, researchers are finding evidence that long-term lack of sleep also weakens the body's immune system. Inadequate sleep may also be contributing to America's rising rates of diabetes and obesity. There is even new evidence that too little sleep may increase the risk of breast cancer and, perhaps, of other cancers, too. Furthermore, chronic lack of sleep affects metabolism and the secretion of hormones, producing striking changes that resemble advanced aging. Cheating on sleep for just a few nights apparently harms brain cells, too.

Implied Main Idea

   a. People who don't get enough sleep are likely to develop breast cancer.

   b. Chronic insomnia is a symptom of many different illnesses, including diabetes.

   c. New research suggests that adequate sleep is essential to good health.

   d. Inadequate amounts of sleep can speed the process of aging.

3. Today's trendy teenager probably owns a miniskirt, a style first popularized in the 1960s. She's likely to wear jeans embroidered with bright designs similar to the ones that hippies wore. Her wardrobe probably also includes 1960s-inspired tie-dyed and fringed clothing. She may also wear beaded accessories such as jewelry, belts, and handbags. No doubt she will own a pair of hip-hugger bellbottoms, a pant style that was all the rage in the 1970s. Her closet will probably contain platform shoes or boots and at least one pair of clogs. These two styles of footwear were popular in the disco era.

Implied Main Idea

   a. Teenagers dress in whatever clothing will annoy their parents most.

   b. Today's teenagers have little or no fashion sense, so they look to the past for inspiration.

   c. In a gesture of rebellion, today's teenagers have embraced fashion from the 1960s.

   d. Today's fashions incorporate styles popular in the 1960s and 1970s.

4. Some readers have accused author J. K. Rowling, author of the Harry Potter novels, of relying too heavily on worn-out stereotypes. And it's

true that Harry, like many heroes before him, is an abused but lovable underdog who triumphs because he is a good person. It's also true that evil villains, like Harry's archenemy Voldemort, turn up in lots of adventure tales. So, too, do figures like Professor Dumbledore, Harry's wise and fatherly mentor. Yet, however similar Rowling's characters are to standard characters in other stories, there is a difference. Rowling is a talented writer with the gift of imagination. She supplies all of her characters, even the most conventional, with the kind of ingenious details that makes them both memorable and new.

Implied Main Idea

a. The Harry Potter novels are based on stock characters that appear in many other adventure stories.

b. Critics who claim J. K. Rowling relies on stereotypes are wrong.

c. J. K. Rowling knows that kids generally root for an underdog.

d. J. K. Rowling shot to fame with the Harry Potter novels.

READING KEY

◆ If you infer a main idea but can't find support for it in the passage, you need to rethink your main idea.

VOCABULARY EXTRA

The paragraph on page 259 mentioned the nicknames POTUS and FLOTUS. POTUS comes from the initials for *President of the United States*, FLOTUS from the initials for *First Lady of the United States*. Words created from initials of other words are called *acronyms*. Other examples of acronyms are NASCAR, NATO, and scuba. Do you know the original words from which these acronyms were derived? If not, turn to your dictionary or go to www.acronymfinder.com.

◆ EXERCISE 3   Identifying the Implied Main Idea

DIRECTIONS   Circle the appropriate letter to identify the implied main idea.

EXAMPLE   Although chocolate does contain sugar, caffeine, and saturated fat—none of which is particularly good for you—studies show that it's also rich in *antioxidants*. Antioxidants are chemical compounds that protect cells in the body. They also appear to raise the good cholesterol that breaks down artery-blocking substances. In addition, antioxidants block the bad cholesterol that clogs arteries. They also can prevent blood clots that cause heart attacks and strokes. Antioxidants release chemicals that relax blood vessels. This helps prevent high blood pressure. The good news about chocolate is sure to cause rejoicing among devoted chocolate lovers. Chocolate fans have long wanted an excuse to consume their favorite sweet. And now, as long as they do it in moderation, they've got it.

Implied Main Idea a. There's really nothing wrong with eating large amounts of chocolate on a regular basis.

(b.) Eating chocolate may have its drawbacks, but it also has some health benefits.

c. Foods rich in antioxidants are essential to a healthy diet.

d. Everyone with high blood pressure should eat more chocolate.

EXPLANATION   Because the first sentence of the paragraph points out that chocolate contains some ingredients that are not good for us, answer *a* can't qualify as a good inference. Answer *c* won't work because the paragraph is not about foods, it's about *one* food—chocolate. Answer *d* focuses just on blood pressure whereas the paragraph is more general than that. That leaves *b* as the implied main idea that best fits the author's words. It not only acknowledges chocolate's drawbacks but also recognizes its benefits.

1. Is stuttering purely psychological, or is it caused by physical factors? Scientists know that the left hemisphere, or half, of the brain is responsible for speech. Yet studies show that a stutterer's right hemisphere is quite active during speech. What this suggests is that the right side of the brain may be interfering with the left side's ability to produce words. One study also revealed that the area of the brain responsible for hearing is inactive in stutterers. This inability to hear his or her own speech may either cause or contribute to the stutterer's problem. Other researchers believe that the cause of stuttering can be found in the genes. Based on an analysis of human DNA,[†] these scientists claim that stuttering is an inherited disorder.

[†]DNA: the genetic information carried in cells.

Implied Main Idea

    a. Scientists have identified some physical factors that could explain the causes of stuttering.

    b. It's clear that psychological factors play a key role in causing stuttering.

    c. Stuttering appears to be an inherited disorder passed on from parent to child.

    d. The inability to hear one's own speech plays a key role in stuttering.

2. Can background music affect our attitudes toward a product? To answer that question, researchers at Carlsbad Marketing organized a study. Subjects in the study were shown slides of light blue or beige pens. At the same time that they looked at the pens, they heard either pleasant or unpleasant music. Later the subjects were told to choose one of the pens as a gift. The majority of the subjects chose the pen they had looked at while they were listening to pleasant background music. Oddly enough, most of the subjects weren't aware of how the music had affected their choice. Most said they did not know why they chose one pen over the other.

Implied Main Idea

    a. There's no real proof that consumers are affected by background music.

    b. People buy more when they are listening to pleasant background music.

    c. Background music in stores interferes with one's ability to make rational choices.

    d. There is some evidence that background music affects what consumers buy.

3. To many of us, the public schools' adoption of zero-tolerance policies for weapons, drugs, and violence is a source of jokes. What else can you do but laugh when, for example, a grown-up claims lemon drops bought in a health food store are a dangerous drug or that a key chain in the form of a gun can be a deadly weapon? It's kind of funny, right? Well, maybe. But, before laughing too hard, you might also want to consider some of the consequences of the zero-tolerance policy. Since public schools have adopted zero-tolerance policies, a first-grader in Youngstown, Ohio, got suspended from school for ten days. From his perspective, he was taking a plastic knife home from

the school cafeteria to show his mother he knew how to butter his own bread. To the authorities, however, he was brandishing a weapon. At Dry Creek Elementary School in Centennial, Colorado, seven fourth-grade boys were pointing "finger guns" at one another as kids have done for decades in the name of play. But the principal thought otherwise and required them to serve one week's detention. At LaSalle Middle School in Greeley, Colorado, one boy ended up enrolled in an anger management program with kids who had actually been convicted of crimes. According to school authorities, he belonged there because he had brought a "firearm facsimile" to school. The facsimile was a two-and-one-half-inch laser pointer, which has been popular with the younger set for over a decade. Such incidents are numerous and, if nothing else, they are making kids lose respect for adults who take zero tolerance so seriously they abandon their common sense.

Implied Main Idea

a. In schools in the West, the policy of zero tolerance has been taken much too far.

b. Girls are never punished under zero-tolerance guidelines.

c. Examples of school authorities rigidly enforcing zero-tolerance policies may seem funny, but the consequences suggest they are no laughing matter.

d. If parents spoke up more, school authorities would be fearful of rigidly enforcing zero-tolerance policies in ways that defy all common sense.

4. In 1975, the prominent biologist John Cairns wrote that "during the last 150 years, the Western world has virtually eliminated death due to infectious disease." At the time, Cairns's assessment did not seem overly optimistic. After all, by 1882 incidents of tuberculosis had been steadily declining thanks to a better understanding of the disease and how to treat it. In 1928, the Scottish physician Alexander Fleming had discovered the antibiotic penicillin. With penicillin available for treatment, formerly deadly infections like pneumonia, tetanus, gangrene, and scarlet fever were no longer terrifying threats to human life. Polio had been defeated through the development of the Salk vaccine in 1952. Measles, once among the top ten causes of death, had lost its power to kill thanks to a vaccine that became available in 1963, and smallpox was close to being wiped out. With a combination of vaccines and antibiotics, a host of other illnesses,

such as diphtheria, typhoid, and influenza, were no longer among the leading causes of death. No wonder, then, that so many experts were optimistic. They did not yet know that a deadly plague called AIDS was going to ravage parts of the globe. Nor did they have any idea that diphtheria would re-emerge as a major killer of adults in the former Soviet Union. No one suspected that tuberculosis was going to make a comeback with nearly eight million new cases being reported in 1991. The optimistic experts of the 1970s probably never dreamed that yellow fever, thought to be a disease solely for the history books, would also return to parts of Africa, increasing from a few hundred cases in the late 1940s to 200,000 cases per year today. (Source of information: www.vaccinationnews.com/DailyNews/May2001.)

Implied Main Idea

a. Medical experts often make optimistic predictions that are proven to be wrong.

b. When AIDS first came to public notice, few realized that the disease was going to turn into a deadly epidemic that threatened people all over the globe.

c. The initial optimism of medical experts in the 1970s has proven to be unfounded.

d. Medical care in the former Soviet Union is so poor that even diphtheria has made a comeback and re-emerged as a major killer of adults.

♦ **EXERCISE 4**   **Identifying the Implied Main Idea**

DIRECTIONS   Circle the appropriate letter to identify the implied main idea.

1. Although they are always pictured in the same dreary colors, the Pilgrims who settled Plymouth Colony in 1620 did not wear only black and white. Women, for instance, wore red, green, blue, and violet. In fact, records from that period indicate that even the men wore colorful capes. Although the Pilgrims are always shown wearing buckles on their shoes, hats, and belts, buckles were not popular until later in the seventeenth century. Also, there's no indication that the Pilgrims ever landed at Plymouth Rock in Massachusetts, despite the stone marker there indicating that they did. And they certainly did not graciously lay out a big feast and invite their Native

American friends. Whatever food was shared in the Pilgrims' early version of Thanksgiving—probably turkey, pumpkin, and squash—was provided by or supplied with the aid of the local Native Americans. From the beginning, they were the ones who generously kept the Pilgrims from starving.

Implied Main Idea

a. The Pilgrims did not wear the clothing popularly associated with them.

b. Many popular beliefs about the early Pilgrims are inaccurate.

c. The Pilgrims actually loved colorful clothing.

d. The local Native Americans did a good deal more for the Pilgrims than the Pilgrims did in return.

2. What is the most effective cure for a *phobia*—an intense, unreasonable fear not grounded in any experience? Exposure therapy has certainly had some success. With this form of therapy, a person with, say, a fear of cats would start treatment by looking at pictures of cats. Then he would be exposed to a toy cat. Next he might watch a cat video. Step by step, he would work toward being near a cat without feeling any fear. Other people suffering from phobias have overcome them with what's called virtual reality therapy. Computer software programs simulate, or imitate, actual exposure to the feared thing or experience. Through repeated computerized experiences, the phobic patient learns not to be afraid. For example, a person who fears flying might take several simulated flights. Through this process, she would conquer her terror. Phobias are also treated with a variety of medications. Some sufferers have found, for example, that the drug Paxil helps them control their fear of social situations.

Implied Main Idea

a. Phobias can be treated in at least three different ways.

b. Exposure therapy is the best way to treat a phobia.

c. Fear of cats is the most common phobia.

d. Virtual reality therapy is the clear winner when it comes to curing phobias.

3. Chimpanzee and human DNA differ by only 1 percent. A chimpanzee's blood composition and immune system are also strikingly similar to those of humans. Similarly, the anatomy of a chimpanzee's brain and central nervous system is also much like a human's. It's

also true that chimpanzees have demonstrated the capacity to reason, in ways similar to humans.

Chimps can make decisions, show cooperative behavior, and use tools. Furthermore, some chimpanzees have been taught to communicate through American Sign Language (ASL). They also exhibit many nonverbal human behaviors, including hugging, kissing, back patting, and tickling. Like people, chimpanzees feel and express emotions such as happiness, sadness, and fear. They form relationships with one another, too, just as humans do. Special emotional bonds between chimpanzee mothers and their babies, and between siblings, last the animals' whole lives.

Implied Main Idea

    a. Although many similarities exist between chimpanzees and humans, this does not mean that chimps deserve human rights.

    b. Chimpanzees and human beings share a striking number of mental and physical traits.

    c. The chimpanzee's immune system is similar to that of humans.

    d. Chimpanzees have the same range of emotions as humans do; they also express their emotions in ways similar to humans.

4. Psychics are people who supposedly have supernatural powers the rest of us do not possess. Thus, psychics claim to contact the dead, read minds, tell the future, even make inanimate objects move. But before you pay hard-earned money to have your fortune told by a psychic, you might want to ask yourself a few pointed questions. For example, why don't psychics display their powers nationwide by performing truly amazing feats? If they can foretell the future, why don't they predict who is going to win a multimillion-dollar lottery prize? If they know what will happen years from now, what about coming up with at least a few hints about how to cure cancer? James Randi, who has made a career of testing the powers of psychics, may have the answer to these and similar questions. Randi claims that when psychics have their powers tested under controlled conditions, such as a laboratory setting where they are under observation, they constantly fail. They can't make spirits appear or read anyone else's mind except their own. What's the reason for the failure? The psychics say that laboratories don't offer the right atmosphere for their work. The failure rate of psychics tested by Randi may be one of the reasons why famed psychic

Sylvia Brown hasn't yet fulfilled her promise to let him test her psychic abilities. (Sources of information: www.randi.org; Carroll, *The Skeptic's Dictionary*, p. 307.)

Implied Main Idea

a. Psychics have supernatural powers.

b. James Randi has spent years exposing the tricks of psychics.

c. Sylvia Brown will probably be the psychic who proves Randi wrong.

d. Psychics don't really possess supernatural powers; they are frauds.

CLASS ACTION

Quips, or clever, witty remarks, often require you to draw inferences. For instance, what was comedian Jay Leno implying when he quipped, "Here's something to think about: How come you never see a headline like 'Psychic Wins Lottery'?"

◆ **EXERCISE 5**   **Identifying the Implied Main Idea**

DIRECTIONS   Circle the appropriate letter to identify the implied main idea.

1. Born in 1858 to one of New York City's wealthiest families, Theodore Roosevelt was a happy, expressive child who seemed to have inherited his father's extraordinary enthusiasm for life. Writing of his father later in life, Roosevelt himself noted, "I never knew anyone who got greater joy out of living than did my father." By the time he reached Harvard University, Teddy, as young Roosevelt was now called, was a popular young man, and his classmates all recalled him as energetic and ambitious. Teddy Roosevelt was seen as a fast-moving, fast-talking young man, who was expected to go far. As it turned out, those expectations were right. In 1881, Roosevelt was elected to the New York State Assembly, and from that point on, he never slowed down. By 1901, he was serving as vice president of the United States when William McKinley was assassinated. At the age of 42, Roosevelt became the youngest man to ever hold the office of president. Once again, his joyous enthusiasm impressed itself on those who met him. As one reporter wrote, "The President goes from one to

another . . . always speaking with great animation, gesturing freely, and in fact talking with his whole being . . . a hundred times a day the President will laugh and when he laughs he does it with the same energy with which he talks." (Source of information: Jamison, *Exuberance*, p. 10.)

Implied Main Idea

a. Theodore Roosevelt was highly ambitious, and nothing got in the way of his ambition.

b. Throughout his remarkable life and career, Theodore Roosevelt never lost the energy and enthusiasm with which he had been born.

c. Born to wealth and privilege, Theodore Roosevelt was energetic and enthusiastic, but then again, who would not be in his situation.

d. Theodore Roosevelt was loved by just about everyone who ever met him.

2. Leadership brings with it enormous responsibility. It also exposes one to blame when things go wrong. Given those twin burdens, the question is, Why would anyone want to be a leader? First, some people like to be leaders because the role offers them access to special information. Organizational and institutional leaders know what's going to happen before anyone else. Second, when things go well, the leader usually gets the credit, and praise is always an appealing reward. But people who aspire to be leaders are also inclined to think they can do a better job than anyone else. An instructor, for instance, may want to become department chair to bring about what he or she considers necessary reforms. Acceptance is yet another motive for leadership. People who don't feel personally successful sometimes convince themselves that becoming a leader in their profession will win them the approval of others. Finally, some people want to become leaders because they like the idea of gaining public recognition. Becoming the president of a company or, for that matter, of the PTA all but guarantees public notice.

Implied Main Idea

a. Leadership carries with it so many burdens that it's a wonder anyone wants to be a leader.

b. The desire for public recognition is the primary reason people aspire to leadership positions.

c. People in leadership positions are often professional successes but personal failures.

d. People wish to become leaders for a number of different reasons.

3. As most people know, there is now a writing section on the SAT, which students take to apply to colleges and universities. Students get twenty-five minutes to write an essay on an assigned theme, such as "Is creativity needed more than ever in the world today?" What most people want to know—particularly those taking the exam—is what counts toward a good score? Well, one answer is vocabulary. Writers who use at least a few sophisticated words tend to get higher scores. Coherence also gets high grades. Essays in which the ideas seem connected and flow gracefully from one to the next do well. So far, good handwriting doesn't seem to earn any extra points, whereas original thinking does. One student wrote a three-paragraph essay that was slightly illegible. Yet scorers considered it worth the eyestrain. Rich in original insight and packed with unexpected allusions,* the essay earned the top score among the first batch of SAT tests. (Source of information: Ramin Setoodeh, "What's Your Score?" *Newsweek*, April 4, 2005, p. 9.)

Implied Main Idea

a. Students taking the SAT are nervous about the new writing section.

b. Grading the writing section of the SAT is an almost impossible job.

c. Getting a high score on the writing section of the SAT depends on several factors.

d. Students who want to do well on the writing section of the SAT should work on coherence, an important factor that scorers look for in the essays.

4. Today, spectators of the Olympic Games enjoy the events in comfort and style. But ancient Greek sports fans had to travel to Olympia on foot or by mule across rugged mountains in the blistering summer heat. Even the 150-mile hike from Athens usually took two weeks. When the exhausted travelers finally trudged into the arena, they found almost no facilities. Athletes bunked in spartan barracks. The

---

*allusions: references to real or fictional people, places, and events, used to make a point—e.g., When it came to housekeeping, no one was ever going to confuse my mother with Martha Stewart.

only inn was reserved for aristocrats. The 80,000 other spectators had no choice but to turn the surrounding fields into an unsanitary campground, using riverbeds for bathrooms and heaping their garbage in stinking piles. The ancient Olympic Stadium had no seats and no shade, so the sweaty throng had to stand in the blazing sun to watch the events. Water was scarce, and fans would regularly pass out from dehydration* and heatstroke. At the end of the five-day festival, spectators who couldn't bear the idea of walking home faced yet another indignity. They were forced to linger for days at the smelly site while trying to arrange a ride home with greedy mule drivers. (Source of information: Tony Perrottet, "In the Grip of Hercules," *Condé Nast Traveler*, April 2004, pp. 163, 222–23.)

Implied Main Idea

a. Attending the ancient Olympic Games was unpleasant but worth the effort.

b. For most spectators, attending the ancient Olympic Games was a grueling ordeal.

c. Facilities at the ancient Olympic Games were sorely lacking.

d. Although spectators at the ancient Olympic Games were not royally treated, they still attended in droves.

◆ **EXERCISE 6**   **Inferring the Implied Main Idea**

DIRECTIONS   Read each paragraph. Then write the implied main idea in the blanks.

EXAMPLE   In 1792, Duke Ferdinand of Brunswick had his coffin built with a window. He also included an air hole and a lid that could be opened from the inside. In 1868, New Jersey inventor Franz Vester patented a coffin that included a hollow passageway to the ground's surface. The passageway contained a ladder so that a person buried prematurely could climb out of the grave. Dozens of other coffins invented around this time included signaling devices such as flags and bells. A person who awoke from a coma to find himself buried alive could pull a cord to operate these devices and attract the attention of passersby. Another coffin, invented by a German named Herr Gutsmuth, included a speaking tube. A person mistakenly declared dead could use the tube to yell for help.

---

*dehydration: suffering from lack of fluids.

Implied Main Idea <u>In past times, people were afraid of being buried alive.</u>

_____

EXPLANATION   Because the paragraph offers several examples of people in earlier times who tried to make sure they were not buried alive, we can safely draw this inference.

1. Chemistry has played an important role in the processing of foods. Foods are chemically treated so that they remain fresh and free of harmful toxins for a longer period of time. Industrial chemists are hard at work researching ways to alleviate the world's food shortage. Thousands of drugs to treat disease have been discovered by applying medical knowledge in the chemical and pharmaceutical industries. Just a few of the chemically based products we use are plastics, cleansing agents, paper products, textiles, hardware, machinery, building materials, dyes and inks, fertilizers, and paints. (Adapted from Sherman et al., _Basic Concepts of Chemistry_, p. 8.)

Implied Main Idea

_____

2. If you want to avoid the flu without getting a shot, stay away from crowds during flu season. Flu viruses are easily carried by coughs and sneezes as well as by hand-to-hand contact, so washing your hands frequently is important. And if you smoke, stop. Smokers are more likely than nonsmokers to get serious viral infections. Taking vitamin and mineral supplements during flu season can also help fight off the flu, so plan on increasing your intake of vitamin C, vitamin A, and zinc. In addition to taking vitamin supplements, eat a lot of garlic, broccoli, and cauliflower. Those vegetables contain natural antibiotics that can protect you against disease.

Implied Main Idea

_____

3. Describing his adventures in America, Captain John Smith, the founder of the Jamestown colony, claimed that Pocahontas, a Native

American girl, saved him from execution at the hands of her people. However, John Smith didn't tell anyone this tale until after Pocahontas and her father, the two primary witnesses, were dead. Captain Smith published three different volumes describing his experiences in the Virginia colony. However, he did not publish his account of Pocahontas's rescue until fifteen years after it supposedly happened. In the meantime, Smith had undoubtedly heard other similar stories. For instance, a Spanish soldier named Juan Ortiz claimed to have been saved in 1529 by an Indian girl in Florida. When Captain Smith finally did start telling his own tale, he changed the details every time he told it. In addition, he told other stories of being rescued from danger by foreign maidens. For example, he claimed to have been captured by the Turks, who took him to their capital of Constantinople.[†] There, Smith said, the ruler's wife fell in love with him and helped him escape to freedom.

Implied Main Idea _____

_____

4. In the seventeenth century, the King James, or English, version of the Bible began to be mass-produced on a new printing press. Suddenly, ordinary men and women had access to Scriptures[†] in their own tongue. Scholars believe that this version of the Bible actually helped shape the English language itself. For example, it gave us many new words now in common use. The words *scapegoat*, *beautiful*, *nowadays*, and *peacemaker* were all coined by seventeenth-century Bible translators. Those same translators also gave our language numerous sayings such as "sour grapes" and "like a lamb to the slaughter." The King James Bible may also have contributed to the birth of democratic government. People who could read the Bible for themselves were less inclined to be ruled by others.

Implied Main Idea _____

_____

[†]Scriptures: sacred writings of the Bible.
[†]Constantinople is now called Istanbul.

Allusions and Inferences

The word *allusions*—references to people, events, and places that writers (and speakers) use to make or clarify a point—was defined on page 270. What wasn't mentioned on that page, however, is that allusions also test your ability to draw inferences.

For instance, note how the following allusion tells you that the author's mother liked to give people advice: "My mother was the neighborhood Dr. Phil. There wasn't a problem she didn't have a solution for." The allusion to Dr. Phil, television's most famous therapist, tells readers that the author's mother liked giving advice.

However, to draw inferences based on allusions, you have to understand the allusion itself. Dr. Phil is a well-known public figure. Thus, it wasn't hard to draw the right inference based on the author's allusion. But not all allusions are so obvious. For example, what do you think the author implies in the following sentence alluding to the Montagues and Capulets? "Although cooperation may have been the order of the day twenty years ago, today's Republicans and Democrats are the Montagues and Capulets of Congress." Exactly what the author is trying to say here might remain somewhat vague unless you have read William Shakespeare's *Romeo and Juliet* and know that the Montagues and the Capulets are feuding families. Thus, the allusion suggests that the Republicans and Democrats have lost the ability to cooperate and are intent on endless quarreling.

The message here is simple: Don't think of allusions as pretty decorations in a sentence. They are often essential to an author's meaning. Thus, it pays for you to enlarge the store of allusions you know on sight. A number of paperback reference books deal with allusions, and it's worth your while to purchase one to study in your spare moments. However, you can also use a search engine to look up allusions on the Web. Look up one or two a night and copy them into a notebook. Then review them on a regular basis.

◆ **EXERCISE 7**   **Understanding Allusions**

DIRECTIONS   Each question first defines an allusion and then uses it in a sentence. Circle the appropriate letter to identify the inference readers should draw from the allusion.

Allusion **EXAMPLE** *Waiting for Godot* by Samuel Beckett is a play about two tramps, Vladimir and Estragon, who wait for a man called Godot. Each day a boy comes to tell them Godot will be there tomorrow, but, as the play ends, Vladimir and Estragon are still waiting.

Sentence Waiting for the judge to arrive, I felt like a character in Beckett's *Waiting for Godot*, and messages from the bailiff that the judge was on her way did little to cheer me up.

Inference The allusion suggests that

    a. the person waiting is fearful the judge will be stern and harsh.

    b. the person waiting is convinced he will be convicted of a crime.

    (c.) the person waiting doesn't believe the judge will ever show up.

EXPLANATION Because Beckett's play is famously about an endless wait, references to it immediately suggest that, for some, the wait never ends.

Allusion 1. *Cyrano de Bergerac* is a play written in the nineteenth century by Edmond Rostand. Cyrano was burdened with an enormous nose that made him unwilling to pursue Roxanne, the woman he loved. Instead, he wrote love letters for his handsome rival so that Roxanne could be happy with a more suitable lover, one with a handsome face and a gift for words. Allusions to Cyrano usually play on his large nose or his speaking gifts used in service to someone other than himself.

Sentence Tongue-tied in Emily's presence, the young man hoped his more eloquent sister could be persuaded to play Cyrano and express her brother's feelings.

Inference The allusion suggests that

    a. the young man's sister will befriend Emily.

    b. the young man's sister will encourage Emily to make the first move.

    c. the young man's sister will express to Emily what her brother cannot say.

Allusion 2. In Shakespeare's play *Macbeth*, Lady Macbeth is plagued by ambition and, at first, it is she who incites her husband to commit murder.

Sentence   "Mrs. Clinton likely played First Lady Macbeth, though she had said she did not, in the stupid decision to fire the White House travel staff." (Tom Teeper of Cox News Service, *Kansas City Star*, January 14, 1996.)[†]

Inference   The allusion suggests that

a. The White House travel staff was known to be incompetent, but its members were well-connected.

b. During her stay in the White House, Mrs. Clinton often played the role of efficiency expert.

c. Mrs. Clinton was behind her husband's misguided decision to fire the White House travel staff.

[†]The sample sentence comes from the Merriam-Webster *Dictionary of Allusions*, edited by Elizabeth Webber and Mike Feinsilber. The book belongs on every college student's bookshelf.

ROUNDING UP THE KEYS

Here is a list of all the reading keys introduced in the chapter. Use them to review for the test on page 284. If a particular reading key doesn't make sense on its own, go back to the page where it appeared and review the section preceding it.

READING KEYS: Inferring Main Ideas

- No matter what the context—everyday life or textbook assignment—drawing inferences requires you to look at the existing evidence and figure out what it suggests about the person, situation, or passage. (p. 252)
- Your implied main idea should never be contradicted by the author's actual statements. (p. 252)
- The main idea inferred by readers should sum up a paragraph as effectively as a topic sentence. (p. 252)

READING KEYS: Effective and Ineffective Inferences

- Effective inferences keep writers and readers on the same track. Ineffective inferences send writers and readers in different directions. (p. 257)
- To be effective, the main ideas you infer should be based on the author's words rather than your personal opinions. (p. 258)
- If you infer a main idea but can't find support for it in the passage, you need to rethink your main idea. (p. 261)

Ten More Words for Your Textbook Vocabulary

1. **commerce:** an exchange of goods, especially on a large scale

   The war had interrupted *commerce* between the two countries, and on both sides of the conflict people felt the lack of ordinary necessities.

2. **commodities:** products that are traded or sold

   On the stock market, *commodities* like oil and gas were reaching new highs, and only the very wealthy were unconcerned.

3. **patriarch:** the male head or leader of a family, group, or tribe

   In her grandmother's day, men were more like proud *patriarchs* than husbands, but thankfully her grandmother's way of life was gone; she and her husband were equals.

4. **idealize:** to think of as perfection

   As small children, we often *idealize* our parents; as teenagers, we do exactly the opposite.

5. **deplete:** to destroy or empty out

   Historians suspect that the city's residents were forced to *deplete* the nearby forests in order to get firewood. (Adapted from Bulliet et al., *The Earth and Its Peoples*, p. 383.)

6. **convert:** to change or transform from one thing into another

   In the fifteenth century, the cathedral was *converted* into a mosque.

7. **ritual:** an established procedure or ceremony

   In some cultures, boys entering puberty endure painful *rituals* before they are allowed to be called men.

8. **garb:** clothing or dress

   Although European travelers commented on the veiling of women in sixteenth-century Iran, paintings indicate that ordinary female *garb* consisted of a long dress and a head scarf.

9. **receptive:** responsive or open to

   American psychology was not always *receptive* to the study of thinking or cognition. (Nevid, *Psychology: Concepts and Applications*, p. 424.)

10. **saturate:** to soak through; to completely fill or absorb

    The directions from the campaign office were to *saturate* the area with materials promoting and explaining the candidate's position.

◆ **EXERCISE 8**   **Building an Academic Vocabulary**

DIRECTIONS   Fill in the blanks with one of the words listed below.

receptive	depleted	idealize	garb	saturated
ritual	converting	commerce	patriarch	commodity

1. Many scientists suspect that the hippocampus, a structure of the brain, plays an important role in _____ a short-term memory into a long-term one. (Adapted from Nevid, *Psychology: Concepts and Applications*, p. 245.)

2. After the tankers collided and sank, the shoreline was _____ with oil and the wildlife began dying.

3. The lawyer argued that his client should get a light sentence because of his age, but the judge was not _____ to the idea.

4. The birds engaged in an elaborate mating _____ that required the male to pursue the female for days on end, all the while flapping his wings and chirping enthusiastically.

5. The pastor's clerical _____ discouraged the other four members from telling any off-color jokes.

6. If the forest is not better protected, much of the vegetation will be completely _____ in a matter of months.

7. The girl's parents wanted to forgive her for running away, but the grandfather, who was still the family _____, refused to allow her return.

8. More than one company has gone bankrupt trying to figure out how to make money from online _____.

9. For many years, vanilla was the island's most well-known export _____.

10. The further we get away from our childhood, the more inclined we are to _____ it.

DIGGING DEEPER Are Employers Making a Mistake Banning Facebook from the Workplace?

Looking Ahead Like paragraphs, longer readings can imply rather than state the main idea. What overall main idea about the entire reading is implied in this essay about accessing social-networking sites while at work?

1   A growing number of employers are making the decision to block employee access to social-networking sites such as Facebook and MySpace. Many of these employers are convinced that productivity suffers when employees can "log on for just a quick look" at their favorite site. Businesses that monitor their employees' use of the Web—and there are many that do—have discovered that even employees with the best intentions don't realize how much time they are wasting. As one Information Technology (IT) consultant puts it, "Facebook in particular is a rat's nest of status updates, social applications, and conversational opportunities, and can suck in well-meaning employees who suddenly forget how long a lunch break is supposed to be." Because employees lured into browsing Facebook or MySpace do tend to forget time, more than half of all employers now block employee access to social networks and feel fully justified in doing so. Social-networking sites are time wasters, after all, and of no value for the employer, or so employers tend to think. Not surprisingly, not everyone agrees.

2   Although many employees who use social-networking sites such as Facebook and MySpace acknowledge that employers have the legal right to block access to these sites, they insist that employers are making a mistake by doing so. In fact, they claim that blocking the use of social-networking sites is counterproductive because employees will get angry if they can't log on to Facebook during their lunch hour. The result will be a disgruntled workforce, and unhappy workers aren't likely to be productive workers. Even more to the point, many young employees say they won't work for a company that blocks social-networking sites, leaving companies with a shrinking pool of employees to choose from.

3   Supporters of Facebook in the workplace also agree that social-networking sites are an effective way of making new contacts, who might then purchase or support a company's products and services. This argument was significantly bolstered by the Red Cross's 2007 decision to use Facebook to raise money for disaster relief. The Red Cross, like many private companies, had initially blocked their employees from gaining access to social-networking sites. However, it removed the blocking software in

order to enter a contest run by the Western Union Foundation. Winning the contest required voters to identify the most effective disaster-relief organization, and the Red Cross created a Facebook page to solicit the votes of Facebook members. Numerous Facebook members responded, earning the Red Cross a $50,000 donation from Western Union.

4   The Red Cross's experience is certainly one piece of evidence to suggest that employers might be missing the point when it comes to using social-networking sites in the workplace. But there's more. A recent Australian study indicates that employees who use social-networking sites at work are more rather than less productive. Researchers at Australia's University of Melbourne found that "people who do surf the Internet for fun at work—within a reasonable limit of less than 20% of their total time in their office—are more productive by about 9% than those who don't." Accessing a social-networking site, if the time is limited, seemed to function as a break that allowed employees to return to their tasks feeling refreshed and alert. While only time will tell if the results of this study are confirmed, it does suggest that employers might want to think twice before blocking access to social-networking sites. (Sources of quotations: www.itexpertmag.com/security/controlling-anti-social-networking-a-guide-to-blocking-employees-access-to-facebook-myspace-and-more; www.readwriteweb.com/archives/shocking_news_scientists_say_workplace_social_netw.php.)

Sharpening Your Skills

DIRECTIONS   Answer the following questions by filling in the blanks or circling the letter of the correct response.

1. What's the implied main idea of the reading?
    a. Employers have every right to ban social-networking sites from the workplace.
    b. More research needs to be done before any serious claims can be made about the benefits of allowing access to social-networking sites in the workplace.
    c. The Red Cross's experience with Facebook illustrates how useful social networks can be in the workplace.
    d. Some evidence suggests that employers might be making a mistake by blocking access to social-networking sites in the workplace.

2. In paragraph 2, the topic sentence is
   a. the first sentence.
   b. the second sentence.
   c. the third sentence.

3. Based on the context, how would you define the word *disgruntled* in paragraph 2: "The result will be a *disgruntled* workforce, and unhappy workers aren't likely to be productive workers."

   _____

   What kind of context clue did you use to get an approximate meaning?
   a. contrast
   b. restatement
   c. example

4. The study done at the University of Melbourne is used to prove that
   a. social-networking sites in the workplace are a huge waste of time.
   b. social-networking sites in the workplace might benefit employers more than they realize.
   c. access to social-networking sites in the workplace is likely to double employee productivity.

INTERNET RESOURCE For additional practice with inference, go to the ACE Tests accompanying *Reading Keys* at www.cengage.com/devenglish/Flemming/rk3e. See also *Reading Keys*, Additional Material and Online Practice at laflemm.com.

▶**TEST 1**   **Reviewing the Key Points**

   DIRECTIONS   Answer the following questions by filling in the blanks or circling the correct response.

   1. *T* or *F*. Drawing inferences is only essential to the act of reading.

   2. When you draw a reading inference, you need to first _____ _____; then you need to _____ _____.

   3. *T* or *F*. You should be able to infer the implied main idea after you've read only one or two sentences of a paragraph.

   4. The main idea inferred by readers should sum up the paragraph as effectively as _____.

   5. The wrong inferences can lead to _____ between reader and writer.

   6. An effective inference is solidly based on _____ _____.

   7. To draw an effective inference, readers can't let their ideas about a topic _____.

   8. *T* or *F*. If the author's train of thought doesn't fit your inference, it's a good idea to re-read the material until the author's ideas and your inference seem to fit.

   9. If the main idea you inferred doesn't match the author's words, that's a good sign _____.

   10. The main idea implied by the reader should never _____.

To correct your test, turn to page 553. If one or more of your answers is incorrect, re-read the Rounding Up the Keys section of the chapter to find out where your mistakes might be.

▶ **TEST 2**   **Identifying the Implied Main Idea**

DIRECTIONS   Circle the appropriate letter to identify the implied main idea.

1. According to a recent study in the journal *Pediatrics*, 91 percent of parents believe that a fever is harmful to their children. About 89 percent of them give their kids fever reducers like acetaminophen and ibuprofen before their temperature reaches 102 degrees. However, the American Academy of Pediatrics says that many illness-causing microbes cannot reproduce in the higher temperatures caused by a fever. A fever also stimulates a child's immune system, causing it to increase production of disease-fighting white blood cells. Therefore, fever helps the child's body battle the infection and may actually reduce the length and severity of a cold or flu. Furthermore, a 2004 study published in the *Journal of Allergy and Clinical Immunology* found that infants who have a fever during their first year of life are less likely than children who don't have a fever to develop allergies later in childhood. (Source of information: Avery Hurt, "Friendly Fevers," *Better Homes & Gardens*, November 2004, pp. 272–75.)

Implied Main Idea   a. Most parents believe that fevers are harmful to children.

b. Fevers help prevent allergies in children.

c. Contrary to popular belief, fevers can be beneficial.

d. When children are sick, parents should try to induce a fever.

2. More than ten years ago, scientists at Auburn University created a healthier, low-fat hamburger. This burger contained only 5 percent fat, but it tasted as good as, if not better than, a burger with 20 percent fat. When the researchers conducted blind taste-test studies, they discovered that people actually liked the taste of the leaner burger more than that of the higher-fat version. Not long after, McDonald's created the McLean Deluxe, a lower-fat burger. Four years after introducing it, however, the company removed it from the menu. Customers didn't want the burger because it was billed as the healthy choice. People just assumed it would not taste as good as a regular hamburger and didn't select it.

Implied Main Idea   a. It's impossible to create low-fat food that tastes good, and fast-food companies should abandon the effort.

b. McDonald's almost went into bankruptcy after adding low-fat foods to its menu.

c. Low-fat foods taste better than foods high in fat.

d. People incorrectly assume that foods labeled "low fat" will not taste as good as higher-fat foods.

3. Every year, the number of deaths due to motor vehicle fatalities ranges somewhere between 40,000 and 45,000 people. In comparison, the number of aircraft fatalities averages 169 per year over a five-year period, making the death rate about 0.3 per 100,000 people. Only about one in almost 1.6 million passengers dies in an airplane crash, even though every day more than three million people fly in a commercial aircraft. Thirty years ago, fatal air crashes occurred once for every 140 million miles flown. Today, however, a fatal accident occurs only once every 1.4 *billion* miles flown, reflecting a tenfold increase in safety. In contrast, the number of motor vehicle accidents tends to remain steady year after year. In fact, traffic accidents are the number one cause of death for people from 6 to 27 years old.

Implied Main Idea

a. Traffic accidents may well double in the next few years.

b. Flying is safer than ever before.

c. Air travel is safer than driving.

d. Airplane crashes are a thing of the past.

4. For centuries, Chinese families longed for a son who would grow up to be a source of protection and financial support, things it was assumed a girl could not provide. Thus, the Chinese *Book of Songs* (1000–700 B.C.) advised parents to dress a son "in fine clothes and give him jade to play." If a daughter was born, however, that same *Book of Songs* told parents to "let her sleep on the ground . . . and give broken tiles to play." More recently, when a Chinese government tried to limit population growth by enforcing a one-child-per-family law, girls were sometimes aborted or abandoned in the hope that the next child would be a much-desired boy. Now, however, the Chinese government has launched a "Girl Care Project," a program of slogans and bonuses designed to promote the importance of females and discourage families from aborting, neglecting, abandoning, or killing female babies. Currently, there are around 120 boys for every 100 girls, and the government is worried that as adults many men

won't be able to find a woman to marry if that gender imbalance is not corrected. There is also the worry that men who are unable to settle into a family life and have children will be more likely to engage in antisocial behavior. Already there are "bachelor villages" in China. The fear is that such villages will multiply if more isn't done to make girls a desirable addition to the family. (Source of quotations: www.msnbc.msn.com/id/5953508.)

Implied Main Idea

a. When the Communists took over the government in China, they brought with them a prejudice against females.

b. The Chinese believe that men are naturally more aggressive, and it is, therefore, dangerous to let too many men live together in one location as they are now doing in "bachelor villages."

c. Because a prejudice against females has produced a gender imbalance in China, the government has launched a program designed to eliminate that prejudice and encourage the birth of more girls.

d. Although the Chinese government has launched the "Girl Care Project" to correct the gender imbalance between males and females, there is little hope for the project's success.

▶ **TEST 3**   **Identifying the Implied Main Idea**

DIRECTIONS   Circle the appropriate letter to identify the implied main idea.

1. The guillotine is named for Joseph-Ignace Guillotin, a French physician who urged his government to adopt a humane method of execution. The sandwich is named after John Montagu, the fourth Earl of Sandwich, who became famous in the eighteenth century for eating that food while he gambled. The word *mesmerize* comes from Friedrich Anton Mesmer, a German physician who treated disease with animal magnetism, an early form of hypnotism. The leotard is named after Jules Leotard, a nineteenth-century French aerialist who wore a stretchy, one-piece garment. The volt was named in honor of Count Alessandro Volta, an Italian scientist who experimented with batteries and electric current. William Lynch was a vigilante from Virginia. He is responsible for the word *lynch*, which describes mob execution of a person by hanging.

Implied Main Idea

   a. The French have made numerous contributions to the English language.

   b. Many common words are *eponyms*, or words named after people.

   c. The Italians have contributed many words to the vocabulary of science.

   d. Most words in the English language are derived from people's names.

2. Certain breeds of dogs are by nature predisposed to be mean. The pit bull and the Rottweiler, for instance, have been selectively bred to be aggressive and threatening. However, not all dogs bred to be mean really are. It's also true that some nonviolent breeds can occasionally be extremely aggressive. Usually that's because owners deliberately set out to make their dogs aggressive by playing roughly with them or by praising them when they growl at people or other animals. Abused or neglected dogs, too, can exhibit particularly aggressive behavior. Furthermore, two or more otherwise friendly dogs can fuel each other's aggressive tendencies.

Implied Main Idea

    a. Dog owners who do not control their pets' aggressive behavior should face legal penalties.

    b. Mean behavior in a dog can be the result of different factors.

    c. Mean behavior in a dog is always caused by cruelty and abuse.

    d. Most aggressive dogs were bred to be that way.

3. Harry Houdini, whose given name was Erich Weiss, was born in Budapest, Hungary, in 1874. When he was a child, his family immigrated to the United States. They were extremely poor, so Erich and his siblings worked to help support the family. Beginning at age 8, Erich sold newspapers, shined shoes, and cut fabric in a tie factory. Desperate to keep himself and his family from starving, Erich took any available job. As a teenager, though, he had a stroke of good fortune. He discovered his talent for magic and illusion. He read books about magicians and learned to perform card tricks and escape from handcuffs. At this point, Erich Weiss changed his name to Harry Houdini, after famous magician Robert Houdini. The newly named magician then began performing in amusement parks, in beer halls, in museums, and at fairs. Soon he was known worldwide. Throughout his career, Houdini demonstrated a remarkable ability to free himself from any restraint, including straitjackets, prison cells, and coffins. One of his most renowned tricks was the escape from the dangerous "Chinese Water Torture Cell."[†] The public couldn't get enough of this particular stunt and begged to see it again and again. Houdini died in 1926 of peritonitis[*] caused by a ruptured appendix when a young man punched him in the stomach.

Implied Main Idea

    a. At the height of his career, Houdini felt trapped by his own success because the public always wanted to see the same magic trick.

    b. Erich Weiss never forgot his humble beginnings, even after he became the world-famous magician Harry Houdini.

    c. Harry Houdini rose from humble beginnings to become a world-famous magician and escape artist.

    d. Houdini never forgot his humble beginnings, and he was haunted by the fear of being poor.

[†]Chinese Water Torture Cell: Houdini was placed in water in a cell six feet tall and one foot wide. His body would be wrapped in chains, and he would be suspended upside down. Nevertheless, he always managed to escape.
[*]peritonitis: inflammation of the membrane lining the abdominal cavity.

4. No one can say for sure when the first pro-ana site appeared on the Web. Although some claim that the first one surfaced around 1998, others insist that 2001 saw the first appearance of a pro-anorexia site. And no, your eyes haven't deceived you. That is the prefix *pro*, meaning "in favor of," appearing right before the word *anorexia*. There are actually hundreds of websites that offer support for anorexia, also known as the wasting or starvation disease. In addition to tips on how to hide the disease from those who would try to cure it, these sites provide pep talks designed to make victims of anorexia feel like they are healthy rather than suffering from a serious disease. In fact, some sites vigorously castigate those who seek treatment for the disease instead of celebrating it as a positive life choice. Although many people, particularly young women, die from this ghastly disease, you would never know it from the pro-ana sites, which make it sound like a lifestyle choice, similar to vegetarianism or Buddhism.

Implied Main Idea

a. The first appearance of a pro-ana site is still a matter of debate.

b. Pro-ana sites offer dangerous advice and should be sharply criticized.

c. Pro-ana sites make it clear that anorexia is a matter of personal choice.

d. Pro-ana sites arose in reaction to the media criticism of anorexia victims.

▶ **TEST 4**   **Identifying the Implied Main Idea**

DIRECTIONS   Circle the appropriate letter to identify the implied main idea.

1. Women who wear high-heeled shoes can end up with deformed feet. High heels compress the toes and prevent them from functioning as shock absorbers during walking. A condition called hammer toes, or permanently claw-shaped toes, can be the end result. Wearing high heels can also cause neuroma, a painful pinching of the nerves of the feet. Women who wear high heels are also more likely to suffer from ingrown toenails, corns, and bunions. High-heeled shoes also force the knees to rotate more than normal because the toes are locked into place. This additional stress can lead to serious knee problems and even low back pain. Women in high heels are at greater risk of tripping or literally falling off their shoes. They can sprain an ankle or suffer other harm when they fall.

Implied Main Idea

   a. Wearing high-heeled shoes is a bad idea for a number of reasons.

   b. Women who wear high heels are at a disadvantage in situations where they might have to run.

   c. Women know that high-heeled shoes are bad for them but for some strange reason wear heels anyway.

   d. Women are often victims of their vanity.

2. In 1973, at the height of the women's liberation movement, fast-talking tennis star Bobby Riggs defeated the top female tennis player, Margaret Court, and declared himself the champion of women's tennis. He taunted female athletes and claimed that they belonged in the home, not on the courts and playing fields of sports. Then tennis pro Billie Jean King agreed to play Bobby Riggs in a match that was promoted as the "Battle of the Sexes." On September 20, 1973, they played in the Houston Astrodome before an estimated television audience of 50 million people. Before the match, Bobby Riggs made a grand entrance into the stadium in a carriage pulled by women. Billie Jean King responded by presenting him with a live pig, a symbol of his male chauvinism. During the game, Riggs played hard, but King overwhelmed him with her speed, her strength, and her agility. She also outplayed and outcompeted him.

When she won the match, women in the audience were jumping up and down with glee. For them, the game was about a lot more than tennis.

Implied Main Idea

a. Had Bobby Riggs been in his prime—he was 55 at the time of the match—he would have won.

b. Bobby Riggs might have beaten Billie Jean King if he had not underestimated her abilities.

c. Billie Jean King became a tennis legend because of her victory over Bobby Riggs.

d. For some, the 1973 tennis match between Bobby Riggs and Billie Jean King symbolized women's battle to overcome sexism.

3. The Robomower was created to mow your lawn while you sit in a lawn chair and watch. Similarly the Roomba vacuum by iRobot allows for automated vacuuming, so that you are free to do other things. iRobot also builds robots that perform minesweeping and information gathering for the military and reconnaissance* for the police. The same company produces robots that can patrol your house while you're out of town. The machine, which can even climb stairs, allows you to view the rooms of your home through the Internet. Another company, called RedZone Robotics, has developed machines that will investigate a contaminated nuclear reactor or clean an oil tank. The Nursebot, a rolling robot that helps busy health care professionals keep an eye on patients, became available in 2010. Robots also help scientists gather information in places like volcanoes and outer space.

Implied Main Idea

a. If people get any lazier, they will need robots to help them stay awake.

b. Researchers keep building new robots, but the public mistrusts the notion of robots replacing human workers.

c. Robots can now perform a wide range of tasks that were once done by humans.

d. Women are the ones most likely to benefit from the newly designed robots.

*reconnaissance: inspection of an area to gather military information.

4. Mohandas Gandhi, influential leader and political reformer of India, said that his schooldays were the most miserable of his life. Nobel Prize–winning novelist Thomas Mann considered school dull. Albert Einstein, who is acknowledged as one of the greatest scientific thinkers of all time, was a dreamy child who struggled in school. His parents even feared that he might be mentally retarded. As a boy, Winston Churchill, prime minister of Britain during World War II, was placed in classes for slow children. Famed inventor Thomas Edison went to public school for only three months. He didn't seem very bright, so his teacher told his parents not to waste time trying to educate him.

Implied Main Idea

a. The really brilliant never do well in school.

b. People who achieve great things in life are not necessarily high achievers in school.

c. Most schools don't do enough to encourage creativity in students.

d. Brilliant men often have a hard time in school; the opposite is true for brilliant women.

▶ **TEST 5**   **Inferring the Implied Main Idea**

DIRECTIONS   Read each paragraph. Then write the implied main idea in the blanks.

1. In Saudi Arabia, women cannot appear in public unless they are covered from head to toe in loose black scarves and robes. The Saudis interpret Islam, their religion, to mean that all women should be shielded from view. Women are also not allowed to drive. When they ride in a car, they must sit in the back seat. They cannot travel without male consent, either. A wife has to obtain a permission slip from her husband before she can check into a hotel or leave the country. Women are not allowed to work or study alongside men. Their Islamic religion also forbids them from entering cemeteries because their mourning might distract men.

Implied Main Idea   _____

_____

2. In the year 1 A.D., Roman citizens did not consider children to be fully human until they walked or talked. If five other people agreed that an infant was sickly, parents could legally abandon the child to die. Lawbreakers in Roman society could be fed to hungry beasts such as lions or tigers. Crowds at these gory "spectacles" would cheer while carnivorous animals tore condemned criminals into pieces. For entertainment, Romans enjoyed watching gladiators fight one another to the death. They also flocked to violent chariot races, delighting in wrecks that produced a tangle of screaming horses and bloody drivers.

Implied Main Idea   _____

_____

3. In 1864, a thousand immigrants traveled the Bozeman Trail, a route from the Oregon Trail through Wyoming to Montana. Throughout that year, angry Native American warriors harassed the white settlers building on their land. In 1865, after the Civil War ended, the U.S. Army turned its attention to what was thought to be a pesky little

problem with the Indians out West. The government closed the Bozeman Trail to civilians. General Patrick E. Connor and a thousand soldiers were sent to settle the Indian troubles once and for all. Despite Connor's proud boasts of what the troops would accomplish, the expedition was a disaster. His men alternately froze and starved. The single Arapaho village Connor did manage to find and destroy had been, prior to his attack, friendly.

Implied Main Idea   _____

_____

4. Many American kids participate in a lot of extracurricular activities. They play sports and musical instruments, join clubs and organizations, and take lessons and extra classes. Some children thrive in a nonstop whirlwind of after-school activities. These kids like the opportunities to explore their interests, discover their talents, and develop their abilities. They find a constant schedule of activities essential preparation for the competitive world of college admissions. Their involvement and accomplishments give them an edge over other students. Other children, however, cannot handle the stress of juggling many obligations. This stress can cause burnout, anxiety, or even physical illness. Sometimes these kids turn to drugs or alcohol to cope with their sense of being overloaded. Years of rushing from one event to the next can overwhelm some kids. In response, they quit everything. Refusing to keep up a hectic pace, they may not engage in any activities at all.

Implied Main Idea   _____

_____

▶ **TEST 6**   **Developing Your Textbook Vocabulary**

DIRECTIONS   Fill in the blanks with one of the words listed below.

convert	commodities	garb	saturated	rituals
receptive	patriarch	commerce	depleted	idealized

1. He was supposed to be the wise _____ of the family flock, but most people close to the family knew that in all important decisions, he turned to his wife for advice.

2. Once the stores of food were _____, the Arctic explorers stranded on the ice had no choice but to eat their sled dogs.

3. The presidential candidate was hoping to _____ vague promises of support into firm commitments for contributions.

4. When the young woman said that she wanted to get married in city hall because she detested the _____ associated with marriage, her mother turned pale and gripped the back of the kitchen chair.

5. The younger brother _____ the older one; everything the older brother did the younger brother imitated.

6. Dressed in full military _____, the soldiers saluted their fallen comrades.

7. The governor was not _____ to the idea of using the federal funds to extend unemployment benefits.

8. The rain _____ the dry earth just in time to save the harvest.

9. Once the war was over, _____ between the two countries was renewed to the benefit of both.

10. In a time of scarcity, _____ like oil, coal, and wheat were being bought and sold at a dizzying pace, and someone somewhere was making an enormous profit.

Recognizing Patterns of Organization

7

> **IN THIS CHAPTER, YOU WILL LEARN**
>
> - how to recognize common organizational patterns authors use to explain relationships.
> - how to identify the key points in each pattern.
> - how to recognize clues to the presence of each pattern.
> - how to match your notes to the pattern.

Chapter 7 focuses on six common methods of organization writers are likely to use in order to make their ideas understandable to readers. Although not all paragraphs reveal one **primary**, or central, pattern, many do. Readers who can recognize the pattern underlying an author's statements automatically know what's essential to the paragraph or reading. They know, in other words, what to look for, what to remember, and what to record in their notes.

Time Order

Two different patterns rely heavily on **time order**, or the actual order of events as they happen or happened in real time. One pattern is called *process*. The other is *sequence of dates and events*.

Process

Writers use a **process** pattern of organization to explain step by step how something functions, develops, or occurs. In the process pattern, the order of information is extremely important. The author *must* put the event that happened first in real time at the beginning of the paragraph. The event that happened last *must* go at the end. You are most likely to find the process pattern in science, business, or psychology textbooks. Look for it whenever you see topic sentences such as "There are three different steps in jury selection" or "People who survive a tragic accident usually go through four stages of emotional recovery."

For an illustration of the process pattern, read the following paragraph. Note how the author explains, step by step, how a tree decays.

Topic Sentence [1]Researchers have identified four general stages in the decay of a tree. [2]*In the first stage*, the wood is firm and solid, but the tree is beginning to show signs of decay. [3]Few new leaves or shoots are present, and the branches may sag. [4]*In the second stage*, the bark begins to soften, and the branches continue to sag. [5]*By the third stage*, the tree loses bark, and branches fall to the ground. [6]*Finally*, the tree becomes a soft, powdery mound.

Typical for the process pattern, the topic sentence in the sample paragraph does little more than sum up the number of steps in the process. The topic sentence does, however, point the way to the major details. The topic sentence tells us that each major detail describes a new stage or step. Note, too, how the italicized transitional phrases separate each step. The transitions make the individual stages easier to recognize.

⊶ **READING KEY**
   ♦ Writers use the process pattern to explain how something functions, develops, or occurs.

Clues to the Pattern

In the paragraph about decaying trees, the first clue to the pattern is the subject matter. That topic—the decaying of trees—is a process. This immediately suggests the author is going to explain step and step how that process takes place.

The topic sentence is the second clue. It confirms the author's intention to describe "four general stages" in a larger process or whole.

Anytime a plural word like *steps, stages, series, phases,* or *sequence* appears in a topic sentence, you can rightly expect the paragraph to follow a process pattern of development.

The italicized transitions in the sample paragraph provide an additional clue. Writers often use these words and phrases to guide readers through a series of events, steps, or stages. Like the transitions in the sample paragraph, the words and phrases in the following box also suggest that the process pattern is at work. This is particularly true if several such words or phrases appear in a paragraph.

Transitions to Watch For ◆	after	finally	next
	after a while	first	now
	afterward	following this step	once
	as a result	in a few days	second
	at the end	in the end	then
	at this point	in the final stage	third
	at this stage	(step, phase)	throughout
	during this	in the first stage	within days
	stage (phase)	(step, phase)	within minutes

⊶ **READING KEYS**

◆ If the topic itself is a process and most of the sentences in the passage describe individual stages or steps, you are most likely dealing with the process pattern.

◆ If the topic sentence includes words like *steps, stages,* or *phases,* you are probably dealing with a process pattern.

◆ In the process pattern, the topic sentence often announces the type and number of major details.

What's Important

What do you absolutely have to learn from a piece of writing using the process pattern? To begin, you need to get a solid grasp of the process being described. You also need to know exactly how many steps or stages are involved and what each one entails, or requires. Then, too, you need to know the order in which the steps occur.

O⌐ READING KEY

◆ When dealing with the process pattern, make sure you can identify the process described and list each step in the right order.

Using Flow Charts

Passages that outline a process lend themselves particularly well to flow charts, which indicate the sequence of steps and the content of each step. Flow charts are excellent devices for recording information in process paragraphs because they provide a visual image of the sequence described. Here's a flow chart for the passage on tree decay:

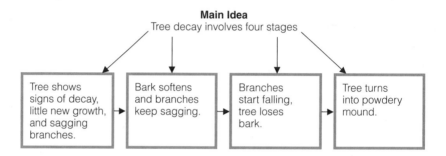

Main Idea
Tree decay involves four stages

| Tree shows signs of decay, little new growth, and sagging branches. | Bark softens and branches keep sagging. | Branches start falling, tree loses bark. | Tree turns into powdery mound. |

Outlining the Steps

As you probably know, people have different learning styles. Some people learn better from lectures, others from reading. The same is true for note-taking. Thus, you may prefer to take notes by outlining. Notes based on an informal outline† of a process paragraph would look something like this:

Main Idea Tree decay involves four general stages.

Support *Step 1*: Signs of decay and sagging branches with few new leaves or shoots
Step 2: Softening bark
Step 3: Falling branches
Step 4: Tree becomes a powdery mound

To determine which note-taking method works better for you, try them both. Use one method for at least a week. Then try the other for the same

---

†Informal outlines do not follow any rules about how symbols, such as a, b, 1, and 2, are used; in an informal outline, indenting to show relationships is the key factor.

amount of time. You'll know soon enough which method makes the material clearer and easier for you to remember.

◆ **EXERCISE 1**   **Understanding the Process Pattern**

DIRECTIONS   Read each paragraph. Then fill in the blanks and circle the transitional clues to the process pattern of organization.

EXAMPLE   Rain and warm weather stimulate the growth of seeds. When water enters a seed, the seed leaves get wet and start to swell. (Then) the seed cover splits, allowing the root to grow out of the seed. (Next,) the root grows downward and absorbs water. (Finally,) the plant grows up out of the ground, where it is exposed to sunshine. (Adapted from Tanzer, *Biology and Human Progress*, p. 313.)

Process   <u>the growth of seeds</u>

Transitional Clues   <u>3</u>

EXPLANATION   In this paragraph, the steps all describe the growth of seeds. That's the process under discussion. As the transitions show, the process described—the growth of seeds—includes three steps.

1. Fireflies do not give off electric light. Rather, fireflies produce light by means of a chemical reaction. That reaction is stimulated by the firefly's need to attract a mate. To create the tiny flashes of light that will draw potential mates, the firefly first sucks in air through tiny breathing tubes. The oxygen in the air then reacts with chemicals in the firefly's abdomen. The chemicals produce a glow, making light shine through the insect's skin.

Process   _____

Transitional Clues   _____

2. How does an airplane rise into the air? An airplane's lift into the air occurs when the plane's wings create differences in the pressure of moving air. First, air flows over the top of the wings. It sticks to the curved surface and is pulled downward. Next, the air that is bent downward pulls on the air above it, creating a low-pressure zone.

Newton's[†] third law of motion says every action causes an opposite reaction. That's why the low-pressure zone on top of the wings then creates a high-pressure zone underneath the wings. In the end, this upward force on the wings causes them to lift into the air. In other words, the wings push the air down, so the air pushes the wings up.

Process _____

Transitional Clues _____

◆ EXERCISE 2   Understanding the Process Pattern

DIRECTIONS   Identify the process. Then list the stages or steps involved according to their order in time.

EXAMPLE   The first step in growing bean sprouts is to purchase some tiny green mung beans from a health food store. Next, line the bottom of a pot with pebbles and place a layer of beans over the pebbles. Then put enough water over the beans to wet them thoroughly. Cover them with a damp cloth and place the pot in a warm spot. Once the beans are in a warm spot, they must be rinsed daily with fresh water. In seven or eight days, they should sprout. The sprouts can be used in salads or on cooked vegetables.

Process _____

Steps 1. Purchase tiny mung beans.

2. Line bottom of pan with pebbles.

3. Place layer of beans over pebbles.

4. Wet beans thoroughly with water.

5. Cover beans with damp cloth.

6. Put in warm spot.

7. Rinse daily with fresh water.

8. In seven or eight days, beans will sprout.

_____

[†]Isaac Newton (1642–1727): English mathematician, scientist, and philosopher who developed, among other things, the theory of gravitation.

EXPLANATION   There is no topic sentence in this paragraph. However, we can infer a main idea that sums up the paragraph: "Growing bean sprouts involves several simple steps." The process then is "growing bean sprouts," and the main idea is less important than the individual steps involved in that process. Those steps are the essential elements in the paragraph and must appear in the correct order.

1. Moths pass through four distinct stages of development: egg, larva, pupa, and adult. The process begins when the female lays her eggs. Within a few days, the eggs hatch and the larvae appear. During this stage, the eggs and larvae are often eaten by birds and other insects. In the pupa stage, wings begin to form and reproductive organs begin to develop. At this point many larvae spin cocoons for protection. In the final stage, the insects leave the cocoons. Within minutes, they expand their wings and are ready to fly. (Adapted from Curtis, *The Second Nature of Things*, p. 156.)

Process

Stages

_____

_____

_____

_____

_____

_____

_____

2. States generally use a three-step procedure to choose juries in court trials. First, a state or county compiles a list of people eligible for jury duty. Usually, they search voter registration or driver's license records for prospects who are at least 18 and who have no felony* convictions. Second, local officials randomly select a group of potential jurors. Each of these prospects receives a summons to appear at court for jury duty on a certain date. Third, lawyers interview people in the jury pool and decide whether to choose them for a particular trial.

_____

*felony: a serious crime, such as murder, rape, or burglary.

Process   _____

Steps   _____

           _____

           _____

           _____

           _____

VOCABULARY EXTRA

Felony is the word for a serious crime. A person who commits a serious crime is a *felon*. The opposite of a *felony* is a *misdemeanor*. Although few people know it, there is a word for someone who commits a misdemeanor. That word is *misdemeanant*. But the word is used so infrequently that the only time you'll use it might well be in a game of Scrabble.

Sequence of Dates and Events

The time order pattern described in this section, **sequence of dates and events**, is closely related to the process pattern outlined on pages 299–303. However, the sequence of dates and events pattern isn't used to explain how something functions or works. Instead, the pattern is used to (1) trace a series of dates and events considered remarkable or unusual; (2) make some general point about an event, a career, or a life; or (3) describe the events leading up to or following a significant historical happening. Here are two examples:

Example 1   Between 1993 and 2001, the United States became intimately acquainted with the horrors of terrorism. On February 16, 1993, the first terrorist attack on U.S. soil took place when a truck bomb exploded at the World Trade Center in New York City. On April 19, 1995, a homemade bomb exploded outside the Murrah Federal Office Building in Oklahoma City, killing 168 people. On November 13, 1995, a bomb left in a van parked at U.S. military headquarters in Riyadh, Saudi Arabia, exploded and killed seven people. On June 25, 1996, a truck bomb exploded at U.S. military headquarters in Dhahran, Saudi Arabia, killing nineteen Americans. On August 7, 1998, two more truck bombs exploded at U.S. embassies in East Africa, killing 258 and injuring over five thousand. On October 12, 2000, a small boat laden with explosives blew up alongside the navy ship USS *Cole*, killing seventeen U.S. sailors. And finally, on September 11, 2001, the World Trade Center was destroyed and the Pentagon damaged when terrorists hijacked four airliners and succeeded in using three of the planes as weapons. The death toll in this attack rose into the thousands. (Source of information: Susan Page, "A Decade of Terrorism," *USA Today*, November 12, 2001, p. 9A.)

Example 2   Grammy Award–winning trumpet player Arturo Sandoval gave up his native country, Cuba, for his family and his music. In the 1960s, Sandoval studied classical trumpet at the Cuban National School of Arts. It was there that he discovered both a talent and a passion for jazz. Throughout the 1970s and 1980s, Sandoval toured the world, recording albums and performing in jazz ensembles. From 1982 to 1990, he was voted Cuba's best instrumentalist. The Cuban government even allowed him to leave the country. However, it also forced him to pledge his loyalty to the Communist Party and would not allow Sandoval's wife and children to travel with him. In 1990, during a tour with the United Nations Orchestra, the musician finally persuaded the Cuban government to let his family join him in Rome. While there, he appealed to the American government for political asylum,* and then–Vice President Dan Quayle helped Sandoval resettle in Miami, Florida. Between 1994 and 1997, Sandoval struggled to become a U.S. citizen. But his attempts were denied because of his previous membership in Cuba's Communist Party. Sandoval persisted, and in 1998 he was finally granted U.S. citizenship.

Clues to the Pattern

Several dates and events all presented in the order in which they occurred are obvious clues to this pattern. But so, too, is a topic sentence like the one in the paragraph on terrorism. When the topic sentence announces that a particular era, or period of time, was significant in some way, a sequence of dates and events is likely to follow. It's also true that the sequence of dates and events pattern is likely to include transitions like those listed in the following box, where the blanks represent specific dates.

---

*asylum: a place offering legal protection from harm.

Words and Phrases That Signal the Sequence of Dates and Events Pattern ◆	After the _____ century[†]
	At a later date
	Before the _____ century
	Between _____
	   and _____
	By the year _____
	From _____ to _____
		Then in _____
		On _____
		In the days (weeks, months)
		   following _____
		By the _____ century
		In the years since
		Until _____

READING KEYS

◆ Dates and events introduced in the order in which they occurred in real time are a surefire clue to the sequence of dates and events pattern.

◆ Passages or readings using this pattern are likely to focus on three kinds of topics: (1) a particular segment of time, considered unusual or extraordinary; (2) a person's life or career; or (3) the events leading up to or following a significant historical event.

What's Important

The dates and events are obviously an important element of this pattern. But so is the *order* in which they occurred. Thus, you shouldn't neglect dates that are implied rather than stated. For example, if the passage contains a phrase like "Twenty years after the end of World War II," you need to figure out that the author is talking about 1965. Jot down that date in the margin or make it a point to remember it because, implied or not, the date is likely to be important.

Ask yourself if any statements lacking in dates contribute to the author's main idea. Those that do deserve your attention. In other words, don't focus only on sentences including dates. There may be other supporting details that are also essential to the main idea.

Timelines

Flow charts can help you visualize the steps in a process. Timelines can do the same for dates and events. Like flow charts, timelines are easy to

---

[†]Normally, blanks would be filled by numbers or dates.

create. They also offer you a visual image of the dates and events you are trying to anchor in memory.

To make a timeline, draw a straight vertical line. Then create ruler-like breaks in the line, so you can separate each date and event. Here to illustrate is a timeline based on the paragraph from pages 306–7.

Main Idea In the years between 1993 and 2001, the U.S. learned the meaning of terrorism.

2/16/93	Truck bomb explodes at World Trade Center.
4/19/95	Bomb explodes outside Oklahoma's Murrah Federal Office Building and kills 168.
11/13/95	Bomb explodes at Riyadh military headquarters and kills 7.
6/25/96	Truck bomb explodes at military headquarters in Dhahran, Saudi Arabia, killing 19.
8/7/98	Two more truck bombs kill 258 and injure over 5,000 at U. S. embassies in East Africa.
10/12/2000	Explosive-filled boat blows up alongside the USS *Cole* and kills 17.
9/11/2001	The World Trade Center is destroyed and Pentagon damaged by terrorists.

When you are reading paragraphs or chapter sections that deal with a series of dates and events, try using timelines to chart the dates and events mentioned.

O⌐ᴍ READING KEY

◆ The dates and events that give this pattern its name are always significant. However, don't automatically ignore the supporting details that lack dates. Evaluate them to see if they contribute anything to the main idea.

VOCABULARY EXTRA

The word *asylum* (p. 307) has an important synonym you should also learn. That synonym is *sanctuary*. Although both *asylum* and *sanctuary* offer a place of safety, *asylum* suggests legal safety. Thus, people who seek political asylum hope to gain the legal right to stay in a place where they are safe from harm. The word *sanctuary* suggests a place that is sacred and, therefore, protected. For example, "The political refugees sought *sanctuary* in the church because they knew the soldiers would respect its sacred ground."

> ## IDIOM ALERT 1: Heyday
>
> *Heyday* refers to a period in the past when someone was at the height of his or her powers. It can also describe the best years of some institution, theory, or group. Here's an example: "In his *heyday*, Brazilian soccer player Pele had no peer; he was unquestionably the single, best soccer player in the world."
>
> ## IDIOM ALERT 2: Getting a second wind
>
> Runners often talk about *getting a second wind* after feeling that they are close to exhaustion. They use this expression to indicate a renewed sense of energy. However, people feeling that they have exhausted their energy to complete some project can talk about getting a second wind in order to indicate that their spirits and abilities have revived. Here's an example: "Midway through her speech, the lecturer seemed bored by her own topic. But when an audience member posed an interesting question about the relationship between self-confidence and achievement, the speaker seemed to *get a second wind* and once again seemed engaged and enthusiastic."

◆ EXERCISE 3   Understanding a Sequence of Dates and Events

DIRECTIONS   Read each paragraph. Then create timelines for the supporting details that flesh out the main idea.

EXAMPLE   Rumors that Coney Island was dying have been around for years, but supporters of the Brooklyn amusement park are worried that the park may really be breathing its last. In its heyday in the late 1800s, Coney Island was the playground of the rich. By 1910, however, the racetrack and the expensive hotels had closed down. The wealthy had found other, more fashionable playgrounds to visit. Coney Island only got its second wind in the 1920s after a new subway line connected New York City to Coney Island. For more than twenty years, until the end of World War II, a visit to Coney Island became an exciting event for hordes of people. By the 1960s, though, attendance was so low that fifty acres of the resort were demolished and replaced by high-rise apartments. In 2001, it looked like Coney Island might be saved again when New York's mayor promised $30 million worth of improvements designed to lure fun seekers back to the island. There was even hope that Coney Island might be the site of the Olympics. But when that plan did not material-ize, in 2006 the owner of the park sold it to real estate developers, who quickly began evicting the original tenants. While the name Coney Island might survive, the new park probably will be a very different place from the old.

Main Idea The Coney Island of old may well be disappearing.

Timeline	1800s	playground for the wealthy
	1910	wealthy leave; hotels shut down
	1920–1945	new subway lines bring crowds
	1960s	fifty acres of Coney Island demolished; high rises built
	2001	mayor of New York promises $30 million for improvements that might bring fun seekers back
	2006	Coney Island sold to developers who start evictions

EXPLANATION As it should, the timeline for this passage records dates and events. These dates and events support the idea that Coney Island may not survive the latest threat to its existence.

1. Since their introduction in the late nineteenth century, skyscrapers have been climbing higher and higher. In 1885, the first skyscraper, the 9-story Home Insurance Building, was erected in Chicago. New York's first skyscraper, the 11-story Tower Building, was built in 1888. New York's 50-story Metropolitan Life Insurance Tower was completed in 1909. It held the title of the world's tallest build-ing until 1913, when the Woolworth Building bested it by 10 sto-ries. In the 1920s and 1930s, a building boom resulted in the construction of many famous skyscrapers, including New York's 77-story Chrysler Building and the 102-story Empire State Build-ing. For forty-two years, from 1931 until 1973, the Empire State Building held the record as the world's tallest building until the dedication of the World Trade Center in 1973. By 1998 the record was broken by the Petronas Towers in Kuala Lumpur, Malaysia, and then came the 1,670-foot, 101-story Taipei 101 Tower in Taiwan in 2004. If construction is completed, the tallest building will scrape the sky at 2,684 feet. That building is the Burj Dubai, located in the United Arab Emirates.

Main Idea   Skyscrapers seem to get taller and taller with the passage of time.

Timeline[†]

(blank timeline)

2. The eighteenth-century Danish explorer Vitus Bering (1681–1741) is credited with proving that Asia and North America are separate continents. In the early 1700s, when much of the world was still unknown, the Russians decided to find out if Siberia was connected to the North American continent. Because Bering had served in the Russian navy, he was selected to lead an expedition* that set out in 1725 to answer precisely that question. Three years later, in 1728, he sailed through what was later named the Bering Strait, proving that Asia and North America were two separate continents. Its goal accomplished, the expedition returned to Russia in 1730. Bering, however, set out again in 1733 on a quest to map the northern Siberian coast. In 1741, his ship wrecked on the shore of a deserted island. Bering died on the island in December of that same year.

Main Idea   The Danish explorer Vitus Bering proved that Asia and North America were two different continents.

[†]The ranking shown here is based on http://architecture.about.com/library/bltall.htm. Rankings differ depending on what's counted; for instance, flagpoles may or may not be factored in.
*expedition: a journey undertaken by a group for a specific purpose.

Timeline _____

CLASS ACTION

Bering Strait and *Bering Sea* are both examples of *eponyms*, words derived, or taken from, the names of people. Here now is a list of twenty-three eponyms. Pick one and search out its origin. Be ready to explain both definition and origin at the next class session.

bedlam	valentine
bloomers	tantalize
boycott	Luddite
cardigan	mackintosh
chauvinism	Mae West
galvanize	Herculean
maverick	dunce
maudlin	graham crackers
Ponzi scheme	sadism
quisling	masochism
spoonerism	Heimlich maneuver
tawdry	

Word origins can often be found in a good desk dictionary, like the *American Heritage,* or online at www.members.tripod.com/foxdreamer. If that Web page has disappeared, type *eponyms* into your search engine box.

Simple Listing

How the supporting details were ordered was important in the first two patterns introduced in this chapter. However, order is not always a significant element in patterns of organization. In the **simple listing** pattern, supporting details can be switched around without disturbing paragraph meaning. Compare, for instance, the order in these two paragraphs, both of which make the same point: The symptoms accompanying migraine headaches are extremely varied.

Paragraph 1   Migraine headaches are accompanied by a number of different symptoms, and sufferers don't necessarily share the same experience. For some migraine victims, the first sign is something called an "aura." This occurs when the actual headache is preceded by flashing lights, spots, wavy lines, or a pins-and-needles sensation in the hands, arms, or face. Many migraine sufferers, however, don't experience an aura. Instead, they experience nausea or vomiting at the same time that their head starts to throb. Then again, some victims don't get an upset stomach. Instead they get a sudden sensitivity to light or noise. For some, becoming abruptly sensitive to smells is a sign that a migraine is on the way.

Paragraph 2   Migraine headaches are accompanied by a number of different symptoms, and sufferers don't necessarily share the same experience. Some migraine sufferers get an upset stomach, and their pounding headache is accompanied by nausea or vomiting. Others, however, have no sign of stomach discomfort. Instead, their migraines are accompanied by a sudden sensitivity to light, noise, even smell. Some migraine sufferers also experience a warning called an "aura," right before the headache hits. The aura can take the form of flashing lights, spots, wavy lines, or a pins-and-needles feeling in the hands, arms, or face.

Both paragraphs make the same point. But they don't both order the material in the same way because the content doesn't require it. With the simple listing pattern, the order is created by the writer because the order itself is not central to paragraph meaning.

⊶ READING KEY

◆ In the simple listing pattern, the author can choose the order of details. The order is not part of the content as it is with process or sequence of dates and events patterns.

Clues to the Pattern

The biggest clue to the pattern is a plural word that does not imply any particular order in time. Topic sentences that tell readers about a number of characteristics, studies, symptoms, or problems associated with the topic are a strong clue that you are dealing with the simple listing pattern.

Another clue is the ease with which the reader can switch the supporting details around, even if that means turning the first supporting detail into the last. If changing the order is easy to do, and the paragraph is still readable, then the paragraph is very likely to be simple listing.

○━╖ READING KEY

◆ The biggest clue to the simple listing pattern is a topic sentence that includes a plural word like *characteristics*, *symptoms*, *studies*, etc.

What's Important

With the simple listing pattern, a plural word in the topic sentence usually tells readers what to look for. Imagine, for instance, that this was a topic sentence: "Sleep serves several functions." The key word here is *functions*. It tells readers to look for each *function* mentioned in the paragraph. After reading the paragraph, readers should be able to explain the different functions of sleep.

○━╖ READING KEY

◆ In the simple listing pattern, a plural word in the topic sentence usually tells readers what they need to know.

Concept Maps

If the paragraph offers a relatively simple list without much detail, a concept map can be a very effective note-taking device. For an illustration, read this paragraph and then look at the notes that follow:

> In the English language, money, like sex, is often associated with the presence or absence of dirt. Not surprisingly, several common idioms link the two together. "Money laundering," for example, refers to making illegally earned money look as if it had been gotten by legal

means—for example, "Convicted for being involved in a money-laundering scheme, the immigration officer got a long jail sentence." "To grub" is to dig for roots and bugs in the dirt as pigs are known to do. However, when humans are called "moneygrubbers," it means they think of nothing else except money and getting more of it. "He was getting old and he was not proud of the moneygrubbing existence he had led." If some person or group takes all of a person's money, that person is said to be "cleaned out," as in "This year my tax bill really cleaned me out." Not surprisingly, when people have a huge amount of money, we say that they are "filthy rich." Donald Trump, for example, would, currently at least, be considered filthy rich.

To learn these idioms, you could make a concept map like the following:

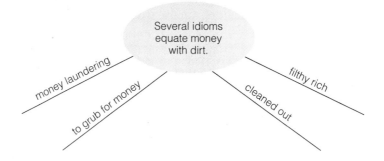

Outlines

If a paragraph using simple listing has a lot of detail, you might want to consider making an outline, which gives you more leeway for including specifics. Look, for example, at the following paragraph and outline:

During World War I, when the U.S. was at war with Germany, German-Americans became the subject of numerous attacks and insults. One Iowa politician charged that "90 percent of all the men and women who teach the German language are traitors." German books vanished from libraries. Some towns with German names changed them to sound more American. On menus, foods with a German origin or sound such as "sauerkraut" and "hamburger" had their names changed to "liberty cabbage" and "liberty sandwich." Some orchestras banned the playing of all German music. But if these incidents sound mainly silly, what happened to the German-American Robert Prager was not. Prager, a coal miner, was wrapped in a flag and hanged for the crime of being German-born. When the men who hanged him were brought to trial, they were acquitted and praised for patriotic loyalty.

In this case, the plural words that should focus your notes are *attacks* and *insults*. But because not all of the attacks and insults can be described in a brief phrase or sentence, an outline might be the better choice.

Main Idea While America was at war with Germany during World War I, everything German came under attack.

Supporting Details 1. German language teachers accused of being traitors and German books banished from libraries.

2. German food taken off menus and German music removed from orchestra programs.

3. German-American Robert Prager was lynched.

   a. men who hanged Prager acquitted

   b. Prager's "crime" was being German-born

◆ **EXERCISE 4**   **Understanding the Simple Listing Pattern**

DIRECTIONS   Read each paragraph. Although the paragraphs are similar, not all of them are simple listing. In the blank at the end, write an *S* if the pattern is simple listing and a *T* if the order of events or steps is a crucial part of the content.

EXAMPLE   Managers are important to most business ventures. There are, however, a number of different management functions. *Marketing managers*, for instance, are responsible for pricing, promoting, and distributing a company's products and services. *Operations managers* are responsible for seeing to it that the goods and services produced by the organization are created. *Finance managers* are responsible for managing the financial assets of the organization. They oversee accounting systems and investments, while providing information about the company's financial health. *Human resource managers* are in charge of hiring the right kind of people for the company. They also design compensation and evaluation programs. *Administrative managers* are the most general among the group. They oversee a number of different activities that can include some functions from all areas of the company. (Adapted from Pride, Hughes, and Kapoor, *Business*, p. 26.)   <u>S</u>

EXPLANATION S is correct because the various areas in management could be put in any order the writer chose. Nothing in the paragraph suggests that order in time plays any role in the organization of the supporting details.

1. Polar bears are amazing creatures with a number of striking features. Although they are most often pictured with white fur, a polar bear's coat can vary from pure white to creamy yellow, even light brown, depending on the season. Polar bears are the largest land carnivores, or meat-eaters, and the biggest recorded polar bear weighed over 2,000 pounds, with a length of twelve feet long. Polar bears have huge paws, which are large even in comparison to their large body size. The paws of a polar bear have to be big because the bear's paws function like snowshoes, spreading out the bear's weight as it moves over icy snow. Although polar bears are often used in commercials for soft drinks, ski wear, and toilet paper, they are not cuddly and playful as they appear to be in the ads. For polar bears, humans are on the menu, and the bears should be approached with caution. Better still, humans would do well to keep a distance between themselves and the bears. _____

2. Frederick W. Taylor was an industrial engineer interested in something called "scientific management." The goal of scientific management was to find a system that would maximize employee output. Taylor believed, as many did who came after him, that scientific management depended on a sequence of three steps. First, the manager had to study different jobs and identify the skills and talents each one required. Next, the manager had to select and train the workers who appeared to have these particular abilities. Third, the manager had to monitor those he had picked to make sure they were performing their tasks in the most efficient manner. Throughout this process, it was the manager's, rather than the workers', job to make all planning and organizing decisions. _____

3. Many Americans suffer from sleep apnea, a condition in which the sleeper suddenly has difficulty breathing and wakes up throughout the night. Not all sleep apnea, however, is the same; there are three different kinds. Obstructive sleep apnea (OSA), the most common form of apnea, is typically caused by a breathing obstruction that prevents the flow of air into the nose and mouth. No one knows what

causes the obstruction, which occurs in the region of the throat's soft palate. One theory is that the muscles around the soft palate collapse during sleep and close off the air passage. Typically afflicted by this form of apnea are those who are extremely overweight. Central sleep apnea (CSA) is more rare. It happens when there is a delay in the brain signal that orders the body to breathe. Such delays can be brought about by disease, but they can also be caused by an injury involving the brainstem—for instance, a stroke, brain tumor, chronic respiratory disease, or even a brain infection. Complex sleep apnea refers to the combination of the two other forms of sleep apnea, namely obstructive sleep apnea and central sleep apnea. _____

4. Old wives' tales are unverified, or unproven, claims that have somehow survived for generations. The notion, for instance, that a mother bird will reject her children if they have been touched by a human is completely false. Birds don't have a strong enough sense of smell to tell if the birds in their nest have been touched by human hands. Also misguided is the idea that the full moon causes mad or criminal behavior. There is absolutely no evidence to justify this old wives' tale. Downright dangerous is the idea that eating the leaves of poison ivy will render your skin immune to the rash caused by its leaves. What will happen is that the lining of your throat will develop the rash you would have gotten from touching the leaves with your hands. And don't be afraid to bring flowers to a sick person. Cut flowers in the room do not suck the oxygen out of the air. That's just another old wives' tale. _____

◇ Definition

Paragraphs based on the **definition** pattern usually begin with the word or term being defined. Often authors use boldface type or italics to make the word or phrase stand out. Then they give the definition and follow it with an example or two. Sometimes authors also explain how the term being defined differs from a similar or a related term. Look, for example, at the following paragraph:

Topic Sentence

Examples

A **bonus** is a payment made in addition to wages, salary, or commissions.* Bonuses are considered extra rewards for an outstanding job

---

*commissions: percentages of profits.

performance. Kollmorgen Corporation of Stamford, Connecticut, for example, rewards its workers for increasing the company's growth. Bonuses may also mark a special occasion like Christmas or Thanksgiving. Elm City Industries of New York always gives bonuses at Christmas. Bonuses, however, are not considered part of wages. Thus employers may, if they wish, choose not to give them. (Adapted from Pride, Hughes, and Kapoor, *Business*, p. 268.)

Clues to the Pattern

Paragraphs using this pattern contain two essential elements: the definition of a key term and at least one example of the definition. Often, there's also a sentence or two explaining how the term differs from other similar terms, how it's been misunderstood, or when it first came to be used.

⊙▭ READING KEYS
- ◆ Textbook writers using the definition pattern often put the key term in boldface and follow it with a brief definition. Frequently, there's also an example or two illustrating the term being defined.
- ◆ The definition pattern may also explain how a word came into being, how it differs from related terms, or how the word has been misapplied or misused.

What's Important

The three essential elements of this pattern are (1) the term being defined, (2) the definition, and (3) at least one example used for illustration. However, if an author gives you the history of the word, contrasts it with another term, or explains how it's been misused, you should pay attention. That information might turn up as a test question like "How do bonuses differ from regular wages?"

Concept Maps and Definitions

To pull out and highlight key elements in a definition passage, consider using a concept map. Start by placing the word and definition in the middle of the page and circling both. Then you can attach to the circle everything important in the paragraph. Look, for example, at the following passage and the accompanying concept map.

> **Litigation** is an adversarial kind of communication in which a dispute is settled by a judge, who decides who is lying. Litigation is usually conducted by lawyers who call witnesses and question them to reveal information. Litigants must follow a prescribed set of rules that have been established by law and interpreted by the person in charge, usually a judge. (Adapted from Berko, Wolvin, and Wolvin, *Communicating,* p. 198.)

What your concept map for a definition paragraph looks like depends a lot on the content of the passage. The only thing typical of concept maps in general is that the term and its meaning appear in the middle because they are the most important thing in the pattern.

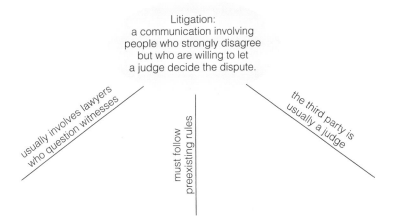

◆ EXERCISE 5   **Understanding the Definition Pattern**

DIRECTIONS   Read each paragraph. Then answer the questions that follow.

EXAMPLE   **Agoraphobia** is a strong fear of being separated from a safe place or person and left without means of escape from a difficult or dangerous situation. People who suffer from agoraphobia are often terrified of leaving their homes. In Western cultures, agoraphobia occurs more often among women. In fact, many women who suffer from agoraphobia are completely homebound by the time they seek help. However, in India, where homebound women are not considered unusual, agoraphobics are more likely to be men. Among all phobias, agoraphobia is the one most likely to be treated. People are more willing to seek help for agoraphobia because it so thoroughly disrupts their everyday life. (Adapted from Bernstein and Nash, *Essentials of Psychology*, p. 421.)

1. What term is defined in the paragraph?

   agoraphobia

2. In your own words, what's the definition of that term?

   Agoraphobia is a strong fear of being cut off from safety and left

   alone to face a dangerous situation.

3. If the author uses an example to illustrate the definition, describe that example in your own words.

   People with agoraphobia can be afraid to leave the safety of

   their homes.

4. Does the author do any of the following?

   a. Explain how the term defined differs from or resembles a related term? _no_

   b. Describe the origin of the word defined? _no_

   c. Explain how the word has been misused? _no_

EXPLANATION   The use of boldface type to highlight *agoraphobia* is a strong clue to the definition pattern. And, as usual, the definition follows right after the first mention of the term.

1. **Psychonomics** is a new buzzword in the consumer products industry. A branch of psychology, psychonomics is concerned with the relationship between the human mind and objects. Manufacturers have found that understanding how people mentally interact with a product can help designers incorporate features that will make it easier and more enjoyable to use. In other words, psychonomics helps match a product's design to the way consumers think and behave. For example, designers created a wireless Web TV keyboard because they knew people wanted to be able to use it while relaxing on the couch. Products such as office equipment, furniture, electronics, and housewares are all being designed with psychonomics in mind.

1. What term is defined in the paragraph?

   _____

2. In your own words, what's the definition of that term?

   _____

   _____

3. If the author uses an example to illustrate the definition, describe that example in your own words.

   _____

   _____

4. Does the author do any of the following?
   a. Explain how the term defined differs from or resembles a related term? _____
   b. Describe the origin of the word defined? _____
   c. Explain how it's been misused? _____

2. **Rip currents** are a familiar but misunderstood beach hazard. Also known as riptides and undertows, a rip current is actually a narrow stream of water created by the return of waves thrown onto the beach. As the water retreats from the shore, it forms channels that extend into the ocean for hundreds of yards. Within these channels, which are about ten to thirty feet wide, water can move at up to five miles per hour. The bigger the wave, the stronger the current. Contrary to popular belief, these powerful currents don't pull people underwater. However, they often do drag swimmers into deep water, where they can drown. Rip currents kill 100–200 Americans each year and require lifeguards to rescue 20,000 more.

1. What term is defined in the paragraph?

   _____

2. In your own words, what's the definition of that term?

   _____

   _____

3. If the author uses an example to illustrate the definition, describe that example in your own words.

_____

_____

4. Does the author do any of the following?

    a. Explain how the term defined differs from or resembles a related term? _____

    b. Describe the origin of the word defined? _____

    c. Explain how the word has been misused? _____

◆ **EXERCISE 6**   **Taking Notes on the Definition Pattern**

> **DIRECTIONS**   Read each paragraph and complete the accompanying maps. _Note_: You may have to add new lines, or spokes.
>
> **EXAMPLE**   In **arbitration**, a third party is brought in to settle a dispute. The third party hears evidence and makes a decision on how the conflict will be resolved. Both parties have previously agreed that they will abide by the decision. This is a common technique that is used when negotiation has failed. (Adapted from Berko, Wolvin, and Wolvin, _Communicating_, p. 198.)

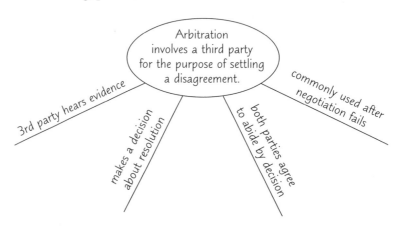

1. The **communication channel** is the medium, or mode, through which messages pass. It's a kind of bridge connecting source and receiver. Communication rarely takes place over one channel. Two, three, or four channels are often used simultaneously. For example, in face-to-face interaction, you not only speak but you also gesture. At times, one or more channels may be damaged. For example, in the

case of the blind, the visual channel is impaired, so adjustments have to be made. (Adapted from DeVito, *The Interpersonal Communication Book*, p. 16.)

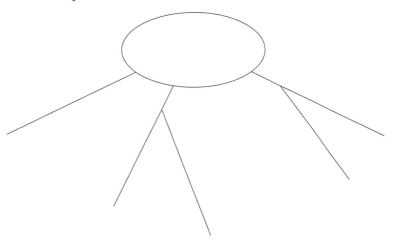

2. *Phishing* is a computer term for the act of tricking people into revealing information like passwords and credit card numbers. People who "phish" set up seemingly legitimate websites and e-mail addresses. Then they send out e-mail messages that request information for some official purpose. In this way, online scam artists "fish" for details they can use for criminal activities. For example, in the first phishing attacks in the mid-1990s, con artists posing as AOL staff members sent messages to potential victims to ask them to "verify your account" or "confirm billing information." Once victims replied and sent back their AOL passwords, the con artist could use the accounts for illegal purposes. (Source of information: "Phishing," Wikipedia, http: //en.wikipedia.org/wiki/phishing.)

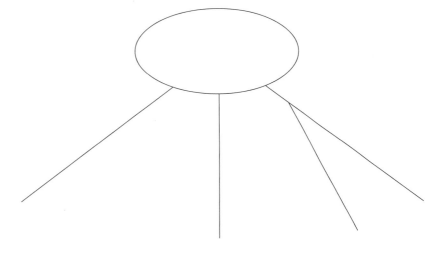

> **CLASS ACTION**
>
> What kinds of definitions can you come up with for seemingly impossible-to-define terms like *love*, *marriage*, *friendship*, *grief*, and *betrayal*? Yes, you'll certainly find dictionary definitions for these words, but most people have their own personal ones as well. That's what's being asked for here.

Cause and Effect

The **cause and effect** pattern turns up just about everywhere. It explains how one thing, idea, or event leads to or produces another. History, science, sociology—these are all subjects that rely heavily on cause and effect. Cause and effect relationships are also evident in daily life. If you have ever explained why you bought a used car, changed jobs, or chose a particular physician, you are familiar with the cause and effect pattern. In these three cases, the choices are effects, while your reasons for making them are causes.

Here now is the topic sentence of the following passage. Which part of the sentence describes the cause and which part the effect?

> Perhaps not enough has been said about home schooling's disadvantages.

Did you decide that "home schooling" was the cause and "disadvantages" referred to the effects? If you did, you were right on the money. Look now at the paragraph in its entirety:

> A great deal has been said and written about the advantages of home schooling for students. But perhaps not enough has been said about home schooling's disadvantages. The first and most obvious disadvantage of home schooling is that local schools lose per-pupil funding from the state. Even worse, parents who have lost faith in their schools do not support increases in property taxes, which are an important source of funds for a school's operating budget. Another disadvantage has to do with quality. Parents who home school their kids tend to be committed,* affluent,* and articulate.* When these parents

---

*committed: dedicated.
*affluent: well-off.
*articulate: well-spoken.

withdraw their voices, talents, and involvement, public schools suffer, and their overall quality deteriorates a little more.

In this paragraph, the supporting details specify the disadvantages (or effects) that can result from home schooling. Yet, as you probably suspected, the cause and effect pattern does not always focus mainly on effects. It can also spotlight causes. Here's an example:

Topic Sentence

<u>Shyness has several causes.</u> Unfamiliar social situations are probably the most common cause. For example, a person who isn't shy with friends may become clumsy and awkward with strangers. Meeting someone higher in status is another cause of shyness. Students, for instance, often become tongue-tied in the presence of their professors. Then, too, being the focus of attention can cause shyness, even in people who normally feel comfortable in social situations.

As the topic sentence suggests, the supporting details in this paragraph focus on the causes of shyness. In this case, each major detail introduces a different situation or setting that causes shyness.

⌐ READING KEYS

- ◆ Paragraphs relying on the cause and effect pattern explain how one event led to or produced another.
- ◆ The cause and effect pattern may focus on causes, effects, or a mix of both.

Clues to the Pattern

Often the topic sentence of a paragraph will tell you to expect a cause and effect pattern of organization. This is certainly true for the previous two paragraphs. It's also true of these topic sentences:

1. Some situations are likely to create stress in almost anyone.
2. The war had a terrible effect on the children.
3. Researchers have identified several causes of insomnia.

As soon as a topic sentence tells you that one situation, idea, or event led to or produced another, you should start looking for causes and effects.

Transitions That Signal Cause and Effect ♦	as a result because consequently for this reason	hence in response to in the final outcome	thanks to therefore thus

Cause and effect paragraphs are also likely to contain one or more of the following verbs, or action words.

Verbs That Signal Cause and Effect ♦	affect bring about cause change contribute create determine	generate increase inspire instigate introduce lead to make happen	produce reduce result in set off stimulate trigger

O─┐ READING KEYS

♦ Verbs like *generate*, *increase*, *determine*, and *produce* are clues to the cause and effect pattern, as are transitions like *therefore*, *thus*, and *consequently*.

♦ The strongest clue to the cause and effect pattern is a topic sentence that says one event led to or produced another.

What's Important

Make sure you have a clear understanding of the general cause and effect relationship described in the topic sentence. For example, in the two sample paragraphs on pages 326–27, you need to understand that home schooling has disadvantages in addition to advantages and that shyness has more than one cause. When you have a clear understanding of the general cause and effect relationship described, it's easier to remember the specific causes and effects mentioned in the reading.

Diagramming Cause and Effect

Outlining cause and effect passages may well become your note-taking format of choice. However, consider using cause and effect diagrams to supplement or even replace your outlines. Diagrams like the following are effective because they help you visualize the relationship between cause and effect.

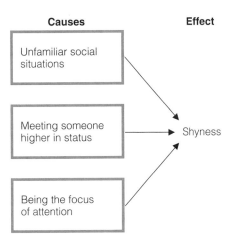

Diagrams like this next one are especially useful if you need to sort out a cycle of causes and effects, where an effect becomes the cause of yet another effect.

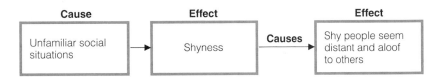

◆ **EXERCISE 7**   **Understanding the Definition Pattern**

DIRECTIONS   Read each paragraph, making sure to look closely at the underlined topic sentence. Then answer the questions that follow. *Note*: You can refer to the boxes on page 328 for help if necessary.

EXAMPLE   [1]For years, the highest number of what doctors call "repeated motion injuries" occurred among workers in meat factories who chopped meat from dawn to dusk. [2]However, the arrival of computers in business changed all that; now office workers also suffer from repeated motion injuries. [3]Backache, neckache, and eyestrain are among the most common complaints. [4]Numb fingers and wrist pain are also common, so much so that surgery may be necessary. [5]According to the doctors who treat these complaints, the human arm wasn't designed to be in the same position for hours on end. [6]If it is, pain can be the unpleasant result.

1. Fill in the boxes to identify the cause and effect relationship described in the topic sentence.

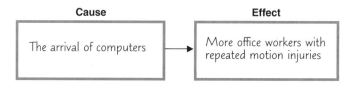

Cause		Effect
The arrival of computers	→	More office workers with repeated motion injuries

2. Do any verbs suggest the cause and effect pattern? _yes_

   If so, identify the verb or verbs. _changed_

3. Do transitions suggest the cause and effect pattern? _no_

   If so, what are they? _____

EXPLANATION   The topic of the paragraph is "repeated motion injuries." This is the subject repeatedly referred to. The topic sentence tells us that the arrival of computers in business caused office workers to join the ranks of those suffering from repeated motion injuries. The verb *changed* signals the cause and effect pattern. However, there are no transition clues.

1. [1]Several studies indicate that laughter produces some positive side effects. [2]It appears, in fact, that laughter can increase creativity. [3]In one study, two groups of college students were asked to take a problem-solving test. [4]One group watched several television comedies before taking the test. [5]The other group watched more serious dramas and newscasts. [6]Test results showed that the students who laughed at the television comedies came up with better solutions. [7]Studies of teachers, nurses, and computer programmers have arrived at similar conclusions.

   1. Fill in the boxes to identify the cause and effect relationship described in the topic sentence.

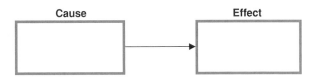

| Cause | | Effect |

2. Do any verbs suggest the cause and effect pattern? _____

If so, what are they? _____

3. Do any transitions suggest the cause and effect pattern? _____

If so, what are they? _____

2. [1]As late as 1950, only 7 percent of American women dyed their hair. [2]The current figure is about 75 percent. [3]The question is, What brought about this change? [4]The answer is fairly straightforward. [5]Thanks to Clairol, women changed their attitude toward coloring their hair. [6]In the 1950s, Clairol, a company that makes hair dye, launched a nationwide campaign. [7]The campaign featured the slogan "Does she or doesn't she? [8]Only her hairdresser knows for sure." [9]The ads also included an attractive woman accompanied by a child. [10]The ads, with their emphasis on motherhood, were meant to suggest that even respectable women dyed their hair. [11]Clairol's ad campaign was a spectacular success. [12]As a result, sales of Clairol's products increased dramatically. [13]By the 1960s, almost 70 percent of American women colored their hair.

1. Fill in the boxes to identify the cause and effect relationship described in the topic sentence.

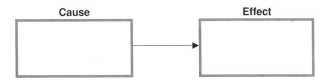

| Cause | | Effect |

2. Do any verbs suggest the cause and effect pattern? _____

If so, what are they? _____

3. Do any transitions suggest the cause and effect pattern? _____

If so, what are they? _____

Comparison and Contrast

In our daily lives, we frequently compare and contrast two objects, people, or events. When we **compare**, we look for similarities: "The twins both like contact sports." When we **contrast**, we look for differences: "However, one twin is a computer geek, while the other has a hard time using a DVD player."

As you might expect, comparison and contrast thinking is not limited to casual conversation. Writers also compare and contrast. In the following paragraph, for example, the author compares and contrasts two different religions, Islam and Christianity.

Comparison and Contrast

The world religions of Christianity and Islam share some similarities, but they also differ in significant ways. Both worship one deity, or god. Both believe Jerusalem to be a holy city, and both teach that one's fate after death is decided on a day of judgment. The two religions, however, differ when it comes to their central teacher or prophet. For Christians, that figure is Jesus. For Muslims, as the followers of Islam are called, that figure is Muhammad. Christianity and Islam also revere different sacred works. The sacred text at the center of Christianity is the Bible, whereas the Koran is the holy book of Islam. For Christians, the appropriate place of worship is a cathedral or church. Muslims worship in a masjid, or mosque. A mosque is architecturally quite different from a Christian church.

Although the above passage mentions similarities as well as differences, writers who use this pattern may focus on one or the other. Here, for example, is a paragraph that features similarities:

Comparison

Baseball greats Jackie Robinson and Hank Greenberg had much in common. Both, for example, endured insults and abuse from fans and other players. Upon becoming the first African-American Major League baseball player in 1947, Jackie Robinson suffered racist attacks so hateful that he came close to having a nervous breakdown. The Jewish Hank Greenberg, who became a legend while playing for the Detroit Tigers, had similar experiences. He was the target of anti-Semitic slurs so mean that he vowed to physically retaliate* against those who tormented him. Yet the abuse the two men endured forged a friendship between them, and each man identified with and admired the other. Robinson was deeply moved by Greenberg's support of him.

---

*retaliate: respond in kind.

Greenberg, for his part, wrote in his autobiography that Robinson was a "special person." Both stars continued to fight racism and anti-Semitism even after they stopped playing baseball. Greenberg worked as the general manager of the Cleveland Indians, a team that hired a significant number of African-American players. Robinson not only contributed to the desegregation of baseball, but he also worked hard to raise funds for other civil rights causes.

Look now at a paragraph that focuses on differences:

Contrast Psychologist Carl Rogers drew a distinction between noxious and nourishing people. *On the one hand*, noxious people criticize and find fault with just about everything. Not surprisingly, these people are difficult to be around. More important, *however*, is that with time, it's easy to believe that their criticism is justified. When that happens, our self-esteem is likely to diminish. Nourishing people, *on the other hand*, are positive. They're optimists. They reward, stroke, and make us feel good about ourselves. With time, it's easy to believe their compliments, and as a result we are likely to have more self-esteem. (Adapted from De-Vito, *The Interpersonal Communication Book*, p. 70.)

⊙—ᔕ **READING KEY**

 ◆ Paragraphs based on the comparison and contrast pattern may mention both similarities and differences. However, they can also focus solely on one or the other.

Clues to the Pattern

The most obvious clue to comparison and contrast is the presence of two different topics. This pattern is also likely to include a topic sentence that practically shouts to readers: "This pattern is comparison and contrast." Consider as examples the three topic sentences you have already encountered.

1. The world religions of Christianity and Islam share some similarities, but they also differ in significant ways.

2. Baseball greats Jackie Robinson and Hank Greenberg had much in common.

3. Psychologist Carl Rogers drew a distinction between noxious and nourishing people.

Topic sentences like the above come close to announcing to readers the presence of a comparison and/or a contrast. Topic sentences like the one that follows are a bit more subtle. However, they send the same message: The comparison and contrast pattern organizes this paragraph.

> Technophiles* don't like to admit it, but the old manual typewriters have some definite advantages over computer word processing.

Writers who tell you that one topic is better or worse, more effective or less effective, than another frequently use a series of comparisons and contrasts to make their point.

Additional clues to the pattern are transitions like the ones listed in the following two boxes.

Transitions That Signal Similarities or Comparison ◆	along the same lines also by the same token in like fashion in like manner	in much the same way or manner in the same vein just like similarly likewise

Transitions That Signal Reversal or Contrast ◆	actually but despite these differences however in contrast	in reality instead of just the opposite nevertheless nonetheless on the contrary	on the one hand on the other hand rather unlike whereas yet

○━ **READING KEY**

◆ The topic sentence is often a dead giveaway to the comparison and contrast pattern. So, too, are transitions such as *likewise, similarly, in contrast,* and *on the contrary.*

What's Important

You definitely need to know exactly what two topics are under discussion. You also need to decide if the author has focused on both

---

*technophiles: lovers of technology.

similarities and differences or has favored one over the other. Make sure, too, that you have a clear grasp of the main idea developed by the similarities and differences. Don't assume that the similarities and differences are an end in themselves. They are not. They're there to support a larger point. Your job is to figure out what that point is.

If there are minor details that clarify similarities or differences, be sure to evaluate them. Would you understand the difference or similarity without the additional example or tidbit of information offered in the minor detail? If the answer is yes, then you don't need to store that bit of information in memory or record it in your notes. But if the difference or similarity is clear to you only if you connect it to, say, an example, then that example is a minor detail you need to remember.

Comparison and Contrast Diagrams

The comparison and contrast pattern readily lends itself to a note-taking format that highlights similarities and differences. When you encounter the comparison and contrast pattern in your reading, consider making a diagram like the following:

Main Idea The psychologist Carl Rogers made a distinction between noxious and nourishing people.

⊶ **READING KEY**

♦ Transitions like *similarly* and *in contrast* can signal the presence of the comparison and contrast pattern. So, too, can verbs such as *differ*, *contrast*, and *resemble*.

♦ **EXERCISE 8**   **Understanding the Comparison and Contrast Pattern**

DIRECTIONS   Read each paragraph. Then circle the correct letter and fill in the blanks to answer the questions that follow.

EXAMPLE   In general, Americans and Spaniards have very different responses to a bullfight. When Americans watch a bullfight, they usually wonder why the matador would want to risk his life. Spaniards, in contrast, imagine the excitement of controlling the bull and displaying courage in the face of death. Few Americans see beauty in the matador's movements. Spanish spectators, however, are trained to understand and appreciate his every twist and turn. They cheer the matador who executes his movements gracefully and skillfully. They just as quickly boo the one who lacks the appropriate grace and training. Most American spectators are just the opposite. They focus more on the bull than the matador. Outnumbered by the matador and his banderilleros, or assistants, the bull is often pitied by American spectators. This attitude usually tries the patience of Spanish spectators.

1. This paragraph
   a. compares two topics.
   (b.) contrasts two topics.
   c. compares and contrasts two topics.

2. What two topics are compared and/or contrasted?

   Topic 1: _Americans at a bullfight_

   Topic 2: _Spaniards at a bullfight_

3. What is the main idea of the paragraph?
   a. Few Americans understand why bullfighting is so popular in Spain.
   b. It's impossible for people to overcome their cultural differences.
   (c.) Americans and Spaniards often react quite differently to a bullfight.
   d. The Spaniards don't see bullfighting as a sport; it's an art.

4. List any similarities mentioned.

List any differences mentioned.

(1) Americans don't understand why the matador takes the risk, while Spaniards appreciate the matador's control. (2) Americans don't see the beauty, while Spaniards understand and judge each movement. (3) Americans focus more on the bull than on the matador.

5. Do any transitions suggest the use of a comparison and contrast pattern? _yes_

If so, what are they? in contrast; however; Most American spectators are just the opposite

EXPLANATION   The differences mentioned in this paragraph are specific examples of the topic sentence: "In general, Americans and Spaniards have very different responses to a bullfight." No similarities are mentioned. The transitions *in contrast* and *however* are clues to this pattern. Another clue is the phrase "different responses" in the topic sentence.

1. Outwardly, sleepwalking and sleeptalking seem to be different sleep disturbances. Sleepwalkers are capable of walking down stairs or, for that matter, out of doors, all the while remaining fast asleep. Sleeptalkers, in contrast, stay still, but they effortlessly carry on long conversations. To be sure, little of what they say makes any sense. Yet despite the differences, there are some similarities between the two sleep disturbances. During their waking hours, neither sleepwalkers nor sleeptalkers remember what happened the night before. Also, both disturbances appear to be hereditary, or to run in families.

    1. This paragraph

        a. compares two topics.

        b. contrasts two topics.

        c. compares and contrasts two topics.

2. What two topics are compared and/or contrasted?

Topic 1: _____

Topic 2: _____

3. What is the main idea of the paragraph?

    a. Sleepwalking is dangerous because the sleepwalker can walk outside while still fast asleep.

    b. Many people suffer from sleep disturbances that interfere with daily life.

    c. Sleepwalking and sleeptalking appear to be very different sleep disturbances, but they actually share some similarities.

    d. Sleepwalking and sleeptalking are both hereditary.

4. List any similarities mentioned.

_____

_____

_____

List any differences mentioned.

_____

_____

_____

5. Do any transitions suggest the use of a comparison and contrast pattern? _____

If so, what are they? _____

_____

2. During robotic surgery, a human surgeon operates a robot that repairs damage to the patient's body. *Robosurgery*, as the procedure has come to be known, has improved upon conventional surgery in several ways. First, robosurgery is almost bloodless. Conventional surgery often requires patients to get blood transfusions due to blood loss. In robosurgery, however, the robot's instruments and cameras enter the patient's body through tiny incisions, causing far less trauma to the body and reducing the need for transfusions. Second, robotic surgeons can do things human surgeons can't. For example, the use of robots eliminates any trembling in fingers. Also, robots can work with precision on a scale barely visible to the human eye. Finally, robosurgery results in far fewer post-operative complications. Cardiac bypass patients, for instance, who were operated on with the help of robots spent an average of only two to eight days in the hospital. In comparison, conventional bypass patients stayed an average of six to eight days.

1. This paragraph
   a. compares two topics.
   b. contrasts two topics.
   c. compares and contrasts two topics.

2. What two topics are compared and/or contrasted?

   Topic 1: _____

   Topic 2: _____

3. What is the main idea of the paragraph?
   a. Robots are becoming common in all fields of medical care.
   b. Human surgeons can do things robots could never master.
   c. Robosurgery has dramatically shortened hospital stays.
   d. Robosurgery has some advantages over the more traditional surgical procedures.

4. List any similarities mentioned.

   _____

   _____

   _____

   List any differences mentioned.

   _____

   _____

   _____

   _____

5. Do any transitions suggest the use of a comparison and contrast pattern? _____

If so, what are they? _____

_____

 # Classification

Writers who use the **classification** pattern divide a larger group into smaller categories. Then they define and describe each category, as the author of the following passage has done:

> Burns can be classified according to their causes. **Thermal** burns are those caused by flames or extreme heat. Such heat can result from fire, steam, hot liquid, or a hot object. **Light** burns are caused by light sources or by ultraviolet light from the sun. **Radiation** burns are those produced by nuclear sources such as bombs. **Electrical** burns are caused by electrical current and lightning. **Chemical** burns, as their name suggests, are caused by corrosive* chemical substances that contact the skin.

Here the general topic is "burns." The topic sentence tells readers that burns can be classified, or broken down, into smaller, more specific categories, based on their causes.

Classification and Simple Listing

Classification and simple listing are similar in that the real order of events in time plays no role in how supporting details are organized. The key difference between the two patterns is usually found in the topic sentence. Classification topic sentences announce that some larger group can be categorized into smaller subgroups, which account for *all* members of the larger group: "Our society recognizes five kinds of power."

Simple listing, in contrast, does not suggest that the paragraph takes into account all members of some larger group. In other words, there could be other individual people, events, or experiences left unaccounted for, as in the following example: "A number of Supreme Court decisions have changed our society in dramatic and profound

*corrosive: gradually and steadily destructive.

ways." This topic sentence does not suggest that the paragraph will take into account *all* Supreme Court decisions that have profoundly influenced society. Instead, it will take into account some of them, based on the author's sense of their significance. Keep this difference in mind when asked to identify patterns of organization in the tests that end this chapter.

⊶ READING KEY

◆ Writers using the classification pattern identify, describe, and often name the smaller subgroups that make up a larger whole.

Clues to the Pattern

Next to the sequence of dates and events, the classification pattern is probably the easiest to recognize. This is a good thing because classification is a very common textbook pattern in subjects such as biology and business. Especially in textbooks, the pattern almost always begins with a topic sentence identifying the larger group being subdivided and the number of categories created—for instance, "There are five categories of power," "Managers use three types of interviews when seeking employees," and "Low-cost housing can be divided into four different groups."

Often, the topic sentence identifies the method used to create the categories. Frequently, but not always, writers will use boldface to emphasize the individual categories. One thing, however, is constant: Authors always give the characteristic of each subgroup.

What's Important

Once you spot this pattern, make sure you know exactly what larger group is being subdivided. Get a clear grasp, too, of how many subgroups there are. You should be able to describe each one. If names are included, you need to know them as well.

Classification Charts

Once you know you are working with a classification pattern, consider making a chart to illustrate the number of categories and characteristics of each. Many students find that "charting" the categories makes the subgroups of the classification clearer and more memorable. Here's an example to get you started.

Burns can be classified according to their causes.

Thermal Burns	Light Burns	Radiation Burns	Electrical Burns	Chemical Burns
caused by flames or other extreme heat	caused by light sources or sunlight	produced by nuclear sources like bombs	caused by electrical current and lightning	caused by corrosive chemicals

⚷ READING KEYS

◆ Classification is one of the easiest patterns to spot because the topic sentence usually announces that a large group can be divided into smaller subgroups.

◆ Classification topic sentences frequently identify the method used to create the categories.

◆ Classification paragraphs always describe each category mentioned in the topic sentence.

◆ EXERCISE 9 Understanding the Classification Pattern

DIRECTIONS Read each paragraph. Then answer the questions that follow.

EXAMPLE Prisons are classified into three main types, according to their security level. The most restrictive type is the close-security prison. Close-security prisons usually consist of single cells. Each cell has its own sink and toilet. Inmates' movements are severely limited and supervised by the prison staff. The entire facility is surrounded by a double fence that is watched or patrolled by armed guards. In some cases, inmates are confined to their cells twenty-three hours a day. The second type of prison is referred to as a medium-security facility. In medium-security prisons, inmates can leave their cells a little more. But they are housed in secure dormitories. Armed guards usually watch over a double fence surrounding the prison. Minimum-security prisons are the third type. Inmates assigned to this kind of facility pose the least safety threat. Thus, they are housed in dormitories patrolled by corrections officers. A single fence encloses the facility. The fence is not patrolled by armed guards. Many inmates of minimum-security prisons leave the grounds on a regular basis during the day to participate in work programs. They return to prison at night.

1. What larger group is divided into smaller subgroups or categories?

prisons

2. How many subgroups are mentioned? 3

3. Name and describe each subgroup.

1. Close-security prisons consist of single cells. Prisoners are closely watched.

   Their movements are limited; some inmates stay in their cells 23 hours a day.

2. Medium-security prisons give prisoners more freedom of movement, but

   prisoners are watched over by armed guards who patrol a double fence.

3. Minimum-security prisons house the least dangerous prisoners. Inmates

   live in dormitories controlled by corrections officers. Although a single

   fence surrounds the prison, there are no armed guards. Many inmates

   leave the grounds for work.

EXPLANATION   Notes on this paragraph should describe the three main types of prisons mentioned in the topic sentence.

1. Shopping centers come in three different types. One is the neighborhood shopping center, which serves customers who usually live within a two- or three-mile radius.* This type usually contains a grocery store, drugstore, gas station, and one or more fast-food restaurants. The community shopping center draws its customers from a much wider area. It usually includes one or two department stores and specialty stores that sell products not available in neighborhood shopping centers. The third type is the regional shopping center. This shopping center, usually called a "mall," generally targets at least 150,000 customers. It contains large department stores and many specialty stores, along with restaurants and movie theaters.

1. What larger group is divided into smaller subgroups or categories? _____

2. How many subgroups are mentioned? _____

---

*radius: a bounded range of activity or influence.

3. Name and describe each subgroup. If no names are included, just describe each separate category.

_____

_____

_____

_____

_____

_____

_____

_____

_____

2. The airspace over the United States is classified as one of five different types. Class A airspace is the area from 18,000 to 60,000 feet above sea level. All pilots entering this airspace must fly according to instrument flight rules and obtain clearance from air traffic control. Class B airspace covers the area from the surface to 10,000 feet up. It surrounds the busiest metropolitan airports, such as those in Chicago and Los Angeles. A pilot must have approval from air traffic control to enter this airspace. Class C airspace surrounds other airports, such as the Anchorage International Airport in Alaska. It covers the space up to 4,000 feet, encircling the airport for a five- to ten-mile radius. Pilots must receive permission from air traffic control to enter it. Class D airspace, which rises 2,500 feet above the surface, applies to airports with control towers that are not surrounded by class B or class C airspace. Pilots must have two-way radio communication with the airport's control tower to enter this space. The last category is class E. This category includes all other airspace not classified as A, B, C, or D. It also surrounds all airports that do not have control towers.

1. What larger group is divided into smaller subgroups or categories? _____

2. How many subgroups are mentioned? _____

3. Name and describe each subgroup. If no names are included, just describe each separate category.

_____

_____

_____

_____

_____

_____

_____

_____

_____

ROUNDING UP THE KEYS

Here is a list of all the reading keys introduced in the chapter. Use them to review for the test on page 354. If a particular reading key doesn't make sense on its own, go back to the page where it appeared and review the section preceding it.

READING KEYS: Time Order—Process

◆ Writers use the process pattern to explain how something functions, develops, or occurs. (p. 300)

◆ If the topic itself is a process and most of the sentences in the passage describe individual stages or steps, you are most likely dealing with the process pattern. (p. 301)

◆ If the topic sentence includes words like *steps*, *stages*, or *phases*, you are probably dealing with a process pattern. (p. 301)

◆ In the process pattern, the topic sentence often announces the type and number of major details. (p. 301)

◆ When dealing with the process pattern, make sure you can identify the process described and list each step in the right order. (p. 302)

READING KEYS: Time Order—Sequence of Dates and Events

◆ Dates and events introduced in the order in which they occurred in real time are a surefire clue to the sequence of dates and events pattern. (p. 308)

◆ Passages or readings using this pattern are likely to focus on three kinds of topics: (1) a particular segment of time, considered unusual or extraordinary; (2) a person's life or career; or (3) the events leading up to or following a significant historical event. (p. 308)

◆ The dates and events that give this pattern its name are always significant. However, don't automatically ignore the supporting details that lack dates. Evaluate them to see if they contribute anything to the main idea. (p. 309)

READING KEYS: Simple Listing

◆ In the simple listing pattern, the author can choose the order of details. The order is not part of the content as it is with process or sequence of dates and events patterns. (p. 314)

◆ The biggest clue to the simple listing pattern is a topic sentence that includes a plural word like *characteristics*, *symptoms*, *studies*, etc. (p. 315)

◆ In the simple listing pattern, a plural word in the topic sentence usually tells readers what they need to know. (p. 315)

READING KEYS: Definition

◆ Textbook writers using the definition pattern often put the key term in boldface and follow it with a brief definition. Frequently, there's also an example or two illustrating the term being defined. (p. 320)

◆ The definition pattern may also explain how a word came into being, how it differs from related terms, or how the word has been misapplied or misused. (p. 320)

READING KEYS: Cause and Effect

◆ Paragraphs relying on the cause and effect pattern explain how one event led to or produced another. (p. 327)

◆ The cause and effect pattern may focus on causes, effects, or a mix of both. (p. 327)

◆ Verbs like *generate, increase, determine*, and *produce* are clues to the cause and effect pattern, as are transitions like *therefore, thus*, and *consequently*. (p. 328)

◆ The strongest clue to the cause and effect pattern is a topic sentence that says one event led to or produced another. (p. 328)

READING KEYS: Comparison and Contrast

◆ Paragraphs based on the comparison and contrast pattern may mention both similarities and differences. However, they can also focus solely on one or the other. (p. 333)

◆ The topic sentence is often a dead giveaway to the comparison and contrast pattern. So, too, are transitions such as *likewise, similarly, in contrast*, and *on the contrary*. (p. 334)

◆ Transitions like *similarly* and *in contrast* can signal the presence of the comparison and contrast pattern. So, too, can verbs such as *differ, contrast*, and *resemble*. (p. 336)

READING KEYS: Classification

◆ Writers using the classification pattern identify, describe, and often name the smaller subgroups that make up a larger whole. (p. 341)

◆ Classification is one of the easiest patterns to spot because the topic sentence usually announces that a large group can be divided into smaller subgroups. (p. 342)

◆ Classification topic sentences frequently identify the method used to create the categories. (p. 342)

◆ Classification paragraphs always describe each category mentioned in the topic sentence. (p. 342)

Ten More Words for Your Textbook Vocabulary

1. **accelerate:** speed up

   The momentum for a change in the civil rights laws *accelerated* in the 1950s as African-Americans mounted protests against racism.

2. **conformity:** tendency to follow or imitate the behavior of others

   When social psychologists talk of *conformity*, they specifically refer to the tendency of people to change their perceptions, opinions, and behavior in ways that are consistent with group norms. (Brehm, Kassim, and Fein, *Social Psychology*, p. 230.)

3. **precedent:** pattern or example that influences similar events

   The Supreme Court set a *precedent* when it argued for limiting free speech only in the face of immediate danger.

4. **contemporaries:** people living in the same time period

   In the eighteenth century, New Englanders lived longer and raised larger families than their *contemporaries* in England. (Adapted from Boyer et al., *The Enduring Vision*, p. 65.)

5. **predominate:** rule, overshadow

   Throughout the novel, an antiwar theme *predominates*; thus the ending is a surprise.

6. **hypothesis:** theory not yet proved by evidence

   Their *hypothesis* is that the language we have at our disposal affects what we are capable of thinking about.

7. **facilitated:** made easier

   Communicating with others is *facilitated* if we understand not only our own attitudes, beliefs, and values but also the attitudes, beliefs, and values of the people with whom we share relationships. (Adapted from Gamble and Gamble, *Contacts*, p. 307.)

8. **ironic:** meaning the opposite of what is expressed; the opposite of what was expected occurring

It's *ironic* that a man who said he didn't like dogs now has three of them.

9. **assumption:** belief

The jurors' mistaken *assumption* was that eyewitness testimony could be trusted.

10. **incidence:** frequency

The *incidence* of sexually transmitted diseases is on the rise among the elderly.

◆ EXERCISE 10 Building an Academic Vocabulary

DIRECTIONS   Fill in the blanks with one of the words listed below.

incidence	predominately	conformity	facilitating	precedent
assumption	accelerated	hypothesis	ironically	contemporary

1. When Bill Clinton went on television late night talk shows during his campaign, he set a(n) _____ for those candidates who came after him.

2. It's a rare teenager who will go against the group and strike out on his or her own; _____ is simply part of being a teenager.

3. In the run-up to the Iraq war in 2003, the population was _____ pro-war.

4. The government's refusal to acknowledge the course of the disease only _____ its spread.

5. When Alfred Wegener first put forth his _____ that, at one time, the continents had been joined together, he was laughed

at and called a lunatic. But with the passage of time, Wegener was proven correct.

6. A(n) _____ of painter Salvador Dalí and filmmaker Luis Buñuel, the great Spanish poet Federico García Lorca was brutally murdered because he championed democracy in a time of dictatorship.

7. The usual _____ is that fingerprint evidence can't lie, but as evidence, fingerprints are coming under increasing attack.

8. To call attention to the terrible starvation the Irish were enduring, the poet and essayist Jonathan Swift wrote an article called "A Modest Proposal," in which he argued _____ that the Irish, since they had nothing to eat, should consider eating their young. When the British and Irish alike took him seriously, Swift was furious.

9. The journalist was supposed to be _____ the discussion between the two candidates, but they paid no attention to him whatsoever.

10. When the _____ of swine flu began to mount, people began to panic.

DIGGING **The Origins of Cinco de Mayo**
DEEPER

Looking Ahead The patterns of organization described in this chapter aren't limited to paragraphs. They can and do appear in longer readings as well. As you read the selection that follows, try to identify the different patterns used to organize the content.

1   At one time, the holiday known as Cinco de Mayo (May 5) was celebrated primarily in Mexico. It was also celebrated in U.S. cities with a large Mexican population. Recently, however, American businesses, aware of the market possibilities, have begun to promote the holiday more heavily than ever before. As a result, many people now celebrate Cinco de Mayo without quite knowing why. Yet the story behind the holiday is a proud one and deserves to be told.

2   By 1821, Mexico had finally gained independence from Spain; yet the country was not allowed to enjoy peace after throwing off the Spanish yoke. Instead, there were political takeovers and wars, including the Mexican-American War (1846–1848) and the Mexican civil war (1858–1861). During this chaotic* period, the Mexican government accumulated a number of debts to Spain, England, and France. All three countries began demanding payment. France, however, decided to use the debts as an excuse to expand its empire.

3   In 1862, France invaded the Gulf of Mexico and marched toward Mexico City. Along the way, French troops encountered some strong resistance. The Battle of Puebla on the fifth of May left French forces stunned and in retreat. Led by General Ignacio Zaragoza Seguin, a small, poorly armed band of Mexican soldiers defeated a well-outfitted French army of more than 6,500 soldiers. The Mexican victory in the Battle of Puebla is remembered to this day in the celebration known as Cinco de Mayo.

4   Unfortunately, Mexico's triumph was short lived. Upon hearing of the Puebla defeat, the French emperor immediately sent 30,000 more troops to Mexico. A year later, in 1863, the French army took over Mexico City. The emperor's nephew, Archduke Maximilian of Austria, was installed as the ruler of all Mexico. However, Maximilian had no popular support. Less than three years later, he was executed by the leaders of Mexico's revolution, and the French were driven out of the country. To this day, many historians insist that it was the Mexican triumph on Cinco de Mayo that fueled the fight against Maximilian and France. The Mexican population—soldiers and civilians alike—was convinced that since a miraculous victory had happened once, it could happen again.

---

*chaotic: confusing, unsettling.

Sharpening Your Skills

DIRECTIONS Answer the following questions by filling in the blanks or circling the letter of the correct response.

1. Overall, what three patterns organize the reading?
   a. time order, definition, cause and effect
   b. definition, classification, comparison and contrast
   c. cause and effect, simple listing, time order
   d. definition, comparison and contrast, time order

2. What's the main idea of paragraph 2?

   _____

   _____

3. What's the main idea of paragraph 3?

   _____

   _____

4. What's the main idea of paragraph 4?

   _____

   _____

5. What's the main idea of the entire reading?

   _____

   _____

6. What type of transition opens paragraphs 1 to 3?

   _____

7. What type of transition opens paragraph 4?

   _____

8. The first sentence of paragraph 4 is

   a. an introductory sentence.

   b. a topic sentence.

   c. a transitional sentence.

9. Which of the following is a major supporting detail?

   a. Recently, however, American businesses, aware of the market possibilities, have begun to promote the holiday more heavily than ever before (paragraph 1).

   b. In 1862, France invaded the Gulf of Mexico and marched toward Mexico City (paragraph 3).

10. In paragraph 1 the claim that at one time Cinco de Mayo was celebrated mainly in Mexico is a

    a. major detail.

    b. minor detail.

INTERNET RESOURCE For additional practice with patterns, go to the ACE Tests accompanying *Reading Keys* at www.cengage.com/devenglish/Flemming/rk3e.

▶ **TEST 1**   **Reviewing the Key Points**

DIRECTIONS   Answer the following questions by filling in the blanks or circling the letter of the correct response.

1. In the process pattern, the individual steps are really important, but so is _____.

2. If the topic sentence uses words like _____, you are probably dealing with a process pattern.

3. If the topic sentence announces that a particular era, or period of time, was significant in some way, a _____ pattern is likely to follow.

4. With the simple listing pattern, the _____ of the supporting details is determined by the _____ rather than by the _____.

5. The definition pattern usually opens with _____ _____.

6. The cause and effect pattern explains how _____ _____.

7. Which of the following is *not* a typical cause and effect verb?
   a. generate
   b. introduce
   c. determine
   d. celebrate

8. Which of the following transitions does *not* signal the comparison and contrast pattern?
   a. consequently
   b. whereas
   c. likewise
   d. however

9. Why is the classification pattern easy to spot?

   _____

   _____

10. In the classification pattern, the topic sentence often identifies

   _____.

> To correct your test, turn to page 554. If one or more of your answers is incorrect, re-read the Rounding Up the Keys section of the chapter to find out where your mistakes might be.

▶ **TEST 2**   **Recognizing Patterns and Topic Sentences**

DIRECTIONS   Read each topic sentence. Then circle the letter of the pattern suggested by the topic sentence.

1. German and English grammar differ a great deal.
    a. simple listing
    b. definition
    c. cause and effect
    d. comparison and contrast

2. Different cultures have different rituals for expressing grief.
    a. time order
    b. definition
    c. cause and effect
    d. simple listing

3. In the simplest of terms, an earthquake is a trembling of the ground.
    a. time order
    b. definition
    c. cause and effect
    d. comparison and contrast

4. In superficial ways, movies and television are alike, but as mass media they differ enormously.
    a. time order
    b. definition
    c. cause and effect
    d. comparison and contrast

5. Becoming addicted to alcohol is a slow, step-by-step process.
    a. time order
    b. definition
    c. cause and effect
    d. simple listing

6. The philosopher John Locke had a powerful effect on America's rebellion against England.
   a. simple listing
   b. definition
   c. cause and effect
   d. comparison and contrast

7. Most people have three categories of friends, and the categories seldom overlap.
   a. definition
   b. cause and effect
   c. comparison and contrast
   d. classification

8. The history of television goes back a good deal longer than many people realize.
   a. time order
   b. definition
   c. simple listing
   d. comparison and contrast

9. Thinking about the United States before and after September 11, 2001, is like pondering the fate of two different countries.
   a. definition
   b. cause and effect
   c. comparison and contrast
   d. classification

10. There are three main non-volcanic types of mountains.
    a. definition
    b. cause and effect
    c. comparison and contrast
    d. classification

▶ **TEST 3** **Recognizing Patterns of Organization**

DIRECTIONS   Circle the appropriate letter to identify the primary pattern in each paragraph. Circle all clues to the pattern you select.

1. Eponyms are words derived from the names of people and places, both the real and the fictional. The word *sandwich*, for instance, originated with the Earl of Sandwich, who liked to gamble so much, he didn't have time to eat. Anxious not to miss a moment away from the gaming tables, he ordered that a piece of meat between two pieces of bread be brought to his chair; thus, the sandwich was born. Similarly, the cardigan sweater is named for the seventh Earl of Cardigan, who liked to sport collarless sweaters with buttons down the front. The word *echo* is yet another example of an eponym. It originated with the story of Echo, a figure from Greek mythology, who used constant chatter to distract Hera, the Queen of the Heavens, from her husband's flirtations. When Hera figured out what was going on, she punished Echo by taking away her powers of speech and making her repeat the words of others. Even *forsythia*, the yellow flowers announcing the coming of spring, were named for a person. They were named for William Forsyth, the eighteenth-century superintendent of the British Royal Gardens, who introduced the flowers to Great Britain.

    a. simple listing

    b. definition

    c. cause and effect

    d. classification

2. Wildly energetic singer La Lupe was once considered the Queen of Latin Song, but she died poor and forgotten. In 1962, she moved from Cuba to New York, where she soon became famous as a soloist. During the 1960s and 1970s, she sold millions of records, performed in Carnegie Hall, and appeared on several television shows. In 1965 and 1966, New York's Latin press named her Singer of the Year. La Lupe fascinated her fans with her frenzied behavior on stage. Flinging her body around the stage, she threw her wigs, shoes, clothing, and jewelry into the audience. In the 1980s, however, misfortune struck. Her husband became mentally ill; she suffered a back injury; and bad business deals ruined her financially. By the late 1980s, the Queen of Latin Song was living on welfare and had spent time in

homeless shelters. In the last few years of her life, she recorded only a few pieces of Christian music. La Lupe died in 1992 at age 53.

a. time order
b. comparison and contrast
c. classification
d. cause and effect

3. People seeking to overcome problems with alcohol can either get help from Alcoholics Anonymous or take part in the Moderation Management treatment program. The two programs share a similar format, but their numbers, target group, guidelines, and level of acceptance differ. Both programs consist of free instructional meetings for participants. However, Moderation Management offers chapters in only fourteen states. Alcoholics Anonymous programs can be found all over the country. Alcoholics Anonymous is available to all problem drinkers, regardless of the severity of their disease. In contrast, the Moderation Management program is designed for mild to moderate problem drinkers only. The two programs' guidelines differ, too. Alcoholics Anonymous stresses that problem drinkers must refrain from drinking all alcohol. Moderation Management, however, sets a weekly quota of drinks for participants. Men are limited to fourteen drinks a week, and women are limited to nine. Finally, the two programs' level of acceptance differs significantly. Alcoholics Anonymous, an established program begun in 1935, is widely accepted and rarely criticized. The newer Moderation Management program, created in 1994, has its critics. They charge that its methods do not permit alcoholics to recover from their disease.

a. time order
b. simple listing
c. definition
d. comparison and contrast

4. If your country were to institute a draft, men could still apply to the Selective Service System for an exemption.* The Selective Service System classifies men who are exempt according to their particular circumstances or beliefs. One category of exemptions includes

*exemption: being freed from something required.

those who serve as religious clergy. Another category applies to individuals who need a hardship deferment.* Someone in this group must prove that military service would cause difficulties for his family, perhaps because he is the sole supporter or caregiver. A third category is that of the conscientious objector. This group includes people who oppose military training or service because of their moral or religious beliefs. One subcategory of conscientious objectors opposes only training or service requiring the use of arms. These men can fulfill their service obligation in a noncombat position. The other subcategory of conscientious objectors opposes all military positions, both combatant and noncombatant. If approved for exemption, these individuals usually still serve by being placed in jobs that help national interests. Yet another group of men who sometimes qualify for exemption includes aliens* or those who are citizens of two countries at the same time.

a. definition

b. cause and effect

c. comparison and contrast

d. classification

5. A **hospice** is a special program for the terminally ill. Hospices may be housed in medical centers, but they can also exist on their own. Hospice care neither hastens nor postpones death. Simply put, the goal of hospice is to improve the quality of life for those who are dying. A trained staff, supportive volunteers, pleasant surroundings, and a sense of community all help patients cope with anxiety about death. Relatives and friends, even pets, are all allowed to visit a hospice resident at any time. Patients at a hospice make their own decisions about medical treatment and the use of drugs. If they wish, they can reject both. But they can also receive drugs for pain control if they choose. Within the hospice setting, life goes on for the dying.

a. time order

b. simple listing

c. definition

d. cause and effect

---

*deferment: official postponement of military service.
*aliens: citizens of another country.

▶ **TEST 4**   **Recognizing Patterns of Organization**

DIRECTIONS   Circle the appropriate letter to identify the primary pattern in each paragraph.

1. Hetty Howland Green, who was known as the "Witch of Wall Street," devoted her life to money. In 1834, Hetty was born to a wealthy family who, nevertheless, lived a simple life. In 1865, Hetty inherited $10 million when both her father and an aunt died. Two years later, Hetty married Edward Green, but she and her husband agreed to keep their finances separate. For almost fifty years until her death, Hetty built her fortune by investing in railroad stocks, government bonds, and mortgage loans. At the same time, she earned the *Guinness Book of World Records* title of "World's Most Miserly Woman." Hetty lived in poor housing, dressed in shabby clothes, ate cheap food, and got medical care at free charity clinics. By 1900, when the average family income was $500 a year, Hetty Green's income was $7 million a year. When she died in 1916 at age 81, her estate was worth more than $100 million. Nonetheless, her name had become a synonym for *miser*.

   a. time order

   b. simple listing

   c. definition

   d. cause and effect

   e. comparison and contrast

   f. classification

2. A *prayer labyrinth** is an ancient aid for meditation, but it's being revived by modern spiritual seekers. Unlike a maze—a network of pathways built with high boundaries such as walls or bushes—a labyrinth is laid out with stones, bricks, or paint, usually in a circular pattern that winds toward the center. To use the labyrinth, one simply walks along the path, concentrating on thoughts and prayers. This is how prayer labyrinths were used by some North American peoples such as the Hopi. European Christians also built them during the Middle Ages. Today, there are more than 650 labyrinths in the United States alone, many of them at Episcopal or Catholic parishes.

---

*labyrinth: a complicated structure of interconnected passages.

a. time order

b. simple listing

c. definition

d. cause and effect

e. comparison and contrast

f. classification

3. Schools have implemented several strategies to combat the problem of bullying among students. The most successful schools have begun by establishing firm anti-bullying policies. They have educated teachers, staff, students, and parents about bullying behaviors; as a result, everyone is able to recognize bullying when it occurs. In addition, the schools have established clear consequences for bullying behaviors and posted this information so that potential bullies will be aware of the risks involved. Schools successful at reducing bullying have also encouraged the reporting of bullying incidents. For example, some schools have set up a "bully hotline" or a "bully box," where people can submit information. Such reporting systems expose problems and identify situations that require the intervention of school officials. Finally, schools committed to getting rid of bullying behaviors have changed the environment in order to reduce opportunities for bullying. They have begun monitoring unsupervised areas like restrooms. They have also tried to reduce the amount of time students spend in less supervised areas. In addition, some schools have also taken steps to separate specific bullies from their victims. In most cases, these initiatives have led to a significant decrease in bullying incidents. (Source of information: Center for Problem-Oriented Policing, "Responses to the Problem of Bullying in Schools," www.popcenter .org/Problems/problem-bullying_p3.htm.)

a. time order

b. simple listing

c. definition

d. cause and effect

e. comparison and contrast

f. classification

4. The United States Coast Guard classifies personal flotation* devices (PFDs) into five different types. Type I PFDs are offshore life jackets that are either inflatable or made of buoyant* material. Preferred in all situations, this type is absolutely necessary in remote or rough waters. The type I jacket tends to be bulky. However, it's the best type of flotation device for nonswimmers or for someone who is unconscious. That's because it keeps a person turned face-up. Type II PFDs are also inflatable or made of buoyant materials. These life vests are less bulky than type I PFDs. The type II PFD is appropriate for calm or near-shore waters where there's a good chance of a speedy rescue. Type III PFDs are flotation aids of various styles of vests and jackets. They do not prevent the wearer from going face-down in the water, though. Thus they are best for general boating activities in waters where rescue will be quick. Type IV PFDs are throwable devices, such as floating rings and cushions, that a person can hold onto until rescue. They should be used only in calm water with heavy boat traffic where help is always nearby. Type V PFDs are made for special conditions or activities. They are not intended for general use. This class of PFDs includes canoe and kayak vests, boardsailing vests, and work vests for commercial vessels, among others.

   a. time order
   b. simple listing
   c. definition
   d. cause and effect
   e. comparison and contrast
   f. classification

5. Boxing is a brutal and violent sport; nonetheless, many women are still willing to climb into the ring. Some of them participate because of the financial rewards. Not only do female boxers make money for each fight, but the most successful of them also earn money for endorsing commercial products. Other women, like female boxer Laila Ali, are more interested in becoming famous and want to be as well-known as celebrities. Still others thirst for respect and equality. They want to prove that women, far from being the weaker sex, can be as tough as men. And some simply like the excitement of participating in the

---

*flotation: floating.
*buoyant: capable of floating.

sport. As boxer Trina Ortegon put it, "I've never done anything else that's given me such an adrenaline rush."

a. time order
b. simple listing
c. definition
d. cause and effect
e. comparison and contrast
f. classification

▶ **TEST 5**   **Recognizing Patterns of Organization**

DIRECTIONS   Circle the appropriate letter to identify the primary pattern in each paragraph.

1. Among the various ways corporations can distribute authority, decentralized and centralized organization stand out as two particularly popular and very different methods. With decentralized organization, management tries to spread authority across various levels of the organization. Coca-Cola is a good example of this type of organization. In the past, for instance, all decisions, even those affecting Coke abroad, had to be approved by its Atlanta, Georgia, office. Because this method of decision making cost a good deal of time, Coca-Cola has now decentralized authority and allowed local executives around the world to make decisions. A centralized organization, in contrast, does not even attempt to distribute authority among the various organizational levels. On the contrary, centralized organizations work hard to keep authority restricted to the upper levels of management. Many large companies are based on a centralized method of organization, where decision making stays at the highest level of management and decisions are then passed down to the lower levels. K-Mart Corporation and McDonald's are examples of centralized organization.

    a. time order
    b. simple listing
    c. definition
    d. cause and effect
    e. comparison and contrast
    f. classification

2. Progressive muscle relaxation is a technique for relieving stress. The technique goes like this. Once or twice a day, lie down on a soft surface. Then start squeezing and releasing the muscles of each body part. Begin with the right hand. Make a fist and give a good, firm squeeze for three to five seconds. Then go completely limp for ten to twenty seconds. Focus on how the muscles in the hand feel during a state of relaxation. Next, squeeze and release the muscles of the right arm. Repeat this process with the left hand and arm. Move on to the shoulders, shrugging them toward the ears. Then squeeze the jaw and facial muscles. Continue by moving down the body, concentrating on the

chest muscles, the abdominal and back muscles, and then the hips and buttocks. Finally, squeeze and release the muscles down each leg, from the thighs to the calves to the feet. With each session, you'll gain more awareness of muscle tension and how to relieve it.

a. time order

b. simple listing

c. definition

d. cause and effect

e. comparison and contrast

f. classification

3. Bred for their ability to do work for their human owners, working dogs can be divided into four basic categories. *Search and rescue dogs* are used to locate people who are missing, lost, or dead. They are essential to rescue efforts after earthquakes, tornados, or avalanches, but they also track criminals on the run and locate human remains. As their name implies, *police dogs* are used by the police force to keep watch over suspects found at the scene of a crime. They also help in the detection of bombs, explosives, and firearms. Police dogs used in the detection of drugs are specially trained to pick up the scent of narcotics on people and objects. *Assistance and service dogs* help physically or mentally disabled persons in their everyday activities. The most commonly known assistance and service dogs are those used to guide people who are partially sighted or blind. In this category are also dogs trained to hit buttons or push wheelchairs in emergency situations. Unlike assistance and service dogs, *therapy dogs* do not necessarily perform any specific tasks. Their main role is to be a comforting presence. These dogs are used to help specific patient populations such as the aged, ailing children, and those with severe phobias, or fears that have no basis in reality.

a. time order

b. simple listing

c. definition

d. cause and effect

e. comparison and contrast

f. classification

4. There are many theories about the functions of sleep. For example, there is a theory that the major function of sleep is to conserve our energy. Another suggestion is that as the hunger mechanism is suppressed during sleep, we sleep in order to conserve food supplies. That means that sleep is a protective mechanism developed early in human evolution. Another theory is that because we are the weakest in the time of darkness, sleep forces us to withdraw from the world and renders us less likely to become a tasty meal for nocturnal animals. Some sleep researchers argue that sleep gives the brain a chance to reorganize and store the information gathered during the day. Apart from those theories, there is still also the common belief that sleep helps the body recover lost energy.

a. time order
b. simple listing
c. definition
d. cause and effect
e. comparison and contrast
f. classification

▶ **TEST 6** **Recognizing Patterns of Organization**

DIRECTIONS Circle the appropriate letter to identify the primary pattern in each paragraph.

1. When the famous civil rights activist Rosa Parks died in November 2005, she was mourned across the nation. Parks had helped ignite the civil rights movement in December 1955 when she refused to give up her bus seat to a white rider. Parks insisted that she would rather go to jail than be treated with such contempt, and her stubborn refusal encouraged civil rights supporters, black and white, to rally to her cause. Most important, her arrest resulted in a 381-day boycott of the bus system by the black community in Montgomery, Alabama. Not surprisingly, Rosa Parks's heroic action is reported in almost every history book, and it is usually assumed that she was the first black person to take such a stand. But in fact, she was not. In March 1955, fifteen-year-old Claudette Colvin[†] had taken the very same stand, but her act of rebellion has only recently been celebrated. In March 1955, Colvin was told by the driver of her bus that she and her three friends had to give up their seats. The three friends did as they were told. Colvin refused. Unlike Parks, Colvin had had no training in passive resistance and no involvement in the civil rights movement. All she had were her defiance and her courage. Although they did not look like much when she was arrested and taken to jail, they proved to be powerful weapons. With three other women who had been similarly treated, Colvin went to court with future Supreme Court Justice Thurgood Marshall representing the four women. Their legal action resulted in a 1956 Supreme Court ruling, which labeled the segregated bus system unconstitutional. Perhaps because of her age, Colvin's contribution was generally ignored until December 2005 when the Smithsonian opened a traveling exhibit dedicated to honoring Claudette Colvin and other unsung heroes of the civil rights movement.

   a. time order
   b. simple listing
   c. definition
   d. cause and effect
   e. comparison and contrast
   f. classification

[†]Claudette Colvin is now a retiree living in the Bronx, a borough of New York City.

2. By the 1890s, class conflict was evident in practically every area of city life, from mealtime manners to popular entertainment and recreation. As new immigrants flooded the tenements and spilled out into neighborhood streets, it became impossible for native-born Americans to ignore the newcomers' strange religious and social customs. In addition to ethnic differences, there were also class differences. Often poor and from peasant or working-class backgrounds, the immigrants from southern and eastern Europe took unskilled jobs and worked for low wages. The slums and tenements in which they lived had high rates of disease. Middle- and upper-class Americans often responded by moving to fashionable avenues or suburbs and by treating the new arrivals as if they were inferior. (Boyer et al., *The Enduring Vision*, p. 592.)

   a. time order

   b. simple listing

   c. definition

   d. cause and effect

   e. comparison and contrast

   f. classification

3. The late, great paintings of Jackson Pollock and Mark Rothko could not be more different. Pollock's are nervous, edgy webs of lines that seem ready to careen off the canvas at any moment, while Rothko's are smooth, peaceful slabs of color that suggest, as the artist meant them to, a world of quiet and calm. However, the two men, considered by many to be among America's greatest artists, did have one thing in common: Fame seemed to bring them nothing but misery. The more famous they became, the more self-destructive they grew. When a *Life* magazine article brought Pollock to the public's attention, he became, almost overnight, the art world's first big superstar. A brawling drunk, Pollock was a tough guy who could make great art, and his fans were fascinated by the seeming contradiction. Painfully embarrassed by his success, which he both craved and shunned, Pollock started drinking around the clock. In 1956, only an hour away from his home, he wrapped his car around a tree and died instantly. Rothko became famous more slowly, but success took the same toll. The more people recognized his work, the more the shy, overweight Rothko over-ate and swallowed pills washed down with alcohol. In 1970, at the height of his fame, Rothko slashed the veins in his arms and bled to death in his studio.

    a. time order

    b. simple listing

    c. definition

    d. cause and effect

    e. comparison and contrast

    f. classification

4. In the nineteenth century, the word *family* was generally applied to heterosexual parents and their children. But times have changed and the word *family* is now applied to many different kinds of relationships. In addition to the traditional nuclear family, consisting of two heterosexual parents and their children, there are *single-parent families* in which only the mother or father is present. There are also *integrated families* in which the parents or the children come from different races. The word *families*, as in *single-parent families*, is now also used to describe same- or different-sex couples who live together without being married and do or, for that matter, do not, raise children. The term *boomerang families* has arrived on the scene to describe families with adult children living at home. Like boomerangs, the children leave but come back to where they started. It's also becoming common to hear about *commuter families*, where one or more members of the family commutes to a work location and stays there for an extended period of time before returning home.

    a. time order

    b. simple listing

    c. definition

    d. cause and effect

    e. comparison and contrast

    f. classification

5. Conflict can be categorized according to three kinds of intensity. For instance, those involved in low-intensity conflict do not usually seek to destroy one another; instead, they interact in a way that helps resolve the conflict. Where to go for dinner, for example, would be classified as a low-intensity conflict. In a medium-intensity conflict, winning, rather than compromise, concludes the conflict. Competing with a friend to be captain of a sports team is an example of a medium-intensity conflict. In a high-intensity conflict, the goal is to

seriously wound or destroy the other person or party. An angry divorce or a war are examples of a high-intensity conflict. (Adapted from Gamble and Gamble, *Contacts*, p. 325.)

a. time order
b. simple listing
c. definition
d. cause and effect
e. comparison and contrast
f. classification

▶ **TEST 7**   **Developing Your Textbook Vocabulary**

DIRECTIONS   Fill in the blanks with one of the words listed below.

precedents	contemporaries	accelerate	predominates	facilitated
ironic	hypothesis	incidence	assumption	conformity

1. The underlying _____ of the argument was that people are naturally selfish and interested solely in their own well-being; given that the audience consisted of human rights workers, who constantly risked their lives for others, it's not surprising that the audience did not agree.

2. Japan is a society that encourages _____, and following the rules of the group is considered praiseworthy while striking out on one's own is not.

3. Given the _____ of car accidents that occur while drivers are talking on the cell phone, every state should ban the use of cell phones while driving.

4. The truck driver meant to slam on the brake, but he was so groggy from lack of sleep, his foot hit the gas pedal, causing the truck to _____ instead of slowing down.

5. When lawyers go to trial to argue a case, they need to be well-informed about past _____ if they are going to properly defend their clients.

6. The notion that the brain learns while the body is asleep is still a(n) _____, but evidence supporting the theory continues to mount.

7. How _____ that it took a tragic illness to bring the husband and wife together; when things were going well, they were barely talking to one another.

8. Jackson Pollock and his _____ were the first American artists to make European critics sit up and take notice.

9. Arrogance is the attitude that _____ among the very rich.

10. What _____ the company's failure was management's refusal to consider that long-term planning might be more important than short-term profits.

Mixing and Matching Patterns

8

> **IN THIS CHAPTER, YOU WILL LEARN**
>
> ● why writers often combine patterns.
>
> ● which patterns are most likely to appear together.
>
> ● why combining patterns is practically essential in longer readings.

At this point, you can identify the six patterns of organization often used by writers. Now let's take that knowledge a step further to work more on longer readings that mix, or combine, patterns.

 ## Pure versus Mixed Patterns

Whether a writer uses a pattern of organization in its pure form or mixes it with others depends on one thing: the main idea. Imagine, for instance, that you're writing a paragraph for a health class. You've been assigned to describe the different types of vegetarians. The main idea could be expressed in a topic sentence like this: "There are four different types of vegetarians." As that topic sentence suggests, the supporting details will fall neatly into a straightforward classification pattern. Take a look:

> There are four different kinds of vegetarians. **Semi-vegetarians** don't eat red meat. They do, however, consume fish, chicken, egg, milk, and cheese. **Lacto-ovo-vegetarians** will consume eggs, milk, and cheese, but they won't eat fish or chicken. **Lacto-vegetarians** will drink milk

and eat cheese, but they don't eat eggs or any animal meat. **Vegans** eat no animal flesh or products at all. They eat only fruits, grains, and vegetables.

There's no need for mixing patterns in this paragraph. The main idea can be fully explained through classification.

Now consider the main idea expressed in this topic sentence: "According to economists, there are four different types of unemployment, each with its own specific cause." Do you think that main idea could be developed solely by the classification pattern? You're right: It couldn't. This time around, the author's main idea requires two patterns: classification *and* cause and effect.

According to economists, there are four different types of unemployment, each with its own specific cause. The first type of unemployment is **seasonal**. Workers in certain industries—such as agriculture, resorts, and retail—are subject to fluctuating demands for their services because of peak and off-peak times in these industries. This type of unemployment is regular, predictable, and relatively short-term. The second type of unemployment is referred to as **frictional**. It is caused by school and college graduates seeking jobs for the first time and by workers changing jobs. These people usually remain unemployed for just a short time while they seek a position. A third type of unemployment is **structural**, caused, for example, by the use of new machinery, such as robots, that can perform simple repetitive tasks. Workers displaced by structural changes often experience long-term unemployment while seeking a job that matches their skills and salary expectations. The last type of unemployment is **cyclical**. This kind is produced by the overall business cycle. Cyclical unemployment increases in recessions;* it decreases during growth periods.

In this case, the main idea has two essential parts. It tells us that (1) there are four different types of unemployment, and (2) each of those types has its own cause. Because of its content, the main idea needs the support of two patterns rather than one.

O—ᴛ READING KEY

◆ The main idea determines the patterns a writer will use. It follows, then, that the main idea is also the best clue to the patterns present in the reading.

---

*recessions: periods of economic downturn.

IDIOM ALERT 1: Take a shine to

This idiom means to have or show a quick liking for, as in "The king *took a shine to* the actress, and his admiration gave her instant respectability despite the rumors about her past."

IDIOM ALERT 2: Short shrift

In the Middle Ages, *short shrift* was a brief penance given to a person condemned to death so that the individual could be forgiven for his or her sins. Over time, though, being given *short shrift* came to mean "being given little or no attention," as in the following sentence: "The superintendent was given a list of teacher grievances, but he typically gave it *short shrift.*"

VOCABULARY EXTRA

The word *frictional* on page 375 offers a good example of the way words can take on very specialized meanings when used in an academic context. The most common meaning for *frictional* is "relating to the rubbing of one object or surface against another." But that meaning changes dramatically in the context of discussions about unemployment, where *frictional* refers to job changing.

◆ EXERCISE 1   Recognizing Patterns in Paragraphs

DIRECTIONS   Read each passage. Then indicate the pattern or patterns present by circling the appropriate letters. *Note*: Keep in mind that the main idea is the best clue to the pattern or patterns an author will use.

EXAMPLE   One way to classify burns is by their degree of severity. **First-degree burns** are those that affect only the outer layer of skin. They are the most common and least serious type of burn. Although they are red and painful, they do not produce blisters. First-degree burns usually heal on their own in two to five days and leave no scars. A **second-degree burn** occurs when the first layer of skin is burned through, and the second layer is damaged as well. These burns are red, produce blisters, and are very painful. However, they usually heal within three weeks and leave little scarring. The worst type of burn is a **third-degree burn**. This kind of burn damages all of the skin's layers. If the skin's nerve endings are not destroyed, these burns cause a great deal of pain. As third-degree burns heal, they create thick scars. Skin grafting is sometimes necessary to correct the damage.

a. time order

b. simple listing

c. definition

d. cause and effect

e. comparison and contrast

f. classification

EXPLANATION   This paragraph creates categories by referring to the degree of burn severity. Because the severity of a burn is also the effect, the writer needs two patterns: classification *and* cause and effect, with both patterns being equally important. The author also needs the definition pattern to define each kind of burn.

1. By all indications, crows are very, very smart creatures. They are also quite sociable. There are, in fact, numerous reports of crows making regular visits to people they have taken a shine to. However, whatever charms crows may possess, history records numerous superstitions related to crows. Most of those superstitions suggest that crows, unlike bluebirds who are consistently associated with good tidings, bring bad luck. In early New England, for instance, it was believed that two crows flying together was a sign of bad events to come. In Europe, it was thought that crows that remained quiet were plotting with the devil. The French even had a saying that evil priests would, after death, turn into crows. The Greeks said "Go to the crows" in the same way we might say "Go to the devil." In parts of England, people used to carry an onion to ward off crows in much the same way people in horror movies carry garlic to keep away vampires. Perhaps the biggest indication of how crows were viewed comes from the superstition that a dead crow in the road brought good luck.

   a. time order

   b. simple listing

    c. definition

    d. cause and effect

    e. comparison and contrast

    f. classification

2. A computerized pool-monitoring system called *Poseidon* is helping lifeguards save people from drowning. The system works like this: First, cameras are installed in the walls of the pool. The cameras monitor the bottom of the pool and transmit images to a computer. The computer then analyzes these images for signs of swimmers in trouble. When it sees images of objects that are sinking or have sunk, it sends a signal to a waterproof pager worn by the lifeguard. The pager alerts the lifeguard to possible trouble. He or she can then dive in to help the victim. To be sure, lifeguards already save many people from drowning. The purpose of the Poseidon system is to increase the speed of those rescues, thereby saving more swimmers from potential harm. Poseidon's supporters also believe it will prevent the severe brain damage that can occur when a swimmer is deprived of oxygen for too long.

    a. time order

    b. simple listing

    c. definition

    d. cause and effect

    e. comparison and contrast

    f. classification

3. In October 2001, efforts began to raise the nuclear submarine *Kursk* from the bottom of the sea. On August 12, 2000, the *Kursk*, one of the Russian navy's most advanced warships, was engaging in naval exercises in the Barents Sea. At least two of its torpedoes mysteriously exploded. The next day, the submarine was located on the sea floor, 377 feet below the surface. For nine days, rescue divers tried to dock with the submarine, but a damaged hatch prevented them from getting inside. On August 21, divers finally opened an inner hatch and found the cabin flooded. The same day, the Russian navy announced that the *Kursk*'s entire crew—118 men—was dead. On October 9, 2001, portions of the 18,000-

ton wreck were finally pulled from the sea. Then, divers spent three months drilling holes in the submarine and sawing off its front compartment, which might have contained unexploded torpedoes. Next, a barge on the ocean's surface lowered into each hole a special plug attached to a cable. When that was done, twenty-six lifting jacks aboard the barge slowly pulled in small sections of cable at a time. Finally, these jacks lifted sections of the sub from the sea's bottom and pulled them to dry dock for examination.

a. time order

b. simple listing

c. definition

d. cause and effect

e. comparison and contrast

f. classification

4. Two famed cult* novels among teenagers, J. D. Salinger's *The Catcher in the Rye* (1951) and Sylvia Plath's *The Bell Jar* (1963), share a number of similarities, including an almost uncanny* aptitude* for reaching each new generation of young readers. Both contain similar main characters—highly intelligent but extremely unhappy young people. Salinger's character, Holden Caulfield, is a cynical* and self-destructive teenager who feels alienated* from society. Plath's heroine, Esther Greenwood, is a college student who, like Holden, feels depressed and confused about what's expected of her. Not surprisingly, *The Bell Jar*'s first reviewers declared Esther to be Holden's female counterpart. However, there is a notable difference. Esther experiences a complete breakdown, goes insane, and ends up in a mental institution. Holden, in contrast, manages to function in a world he generally despises. Yet, despite those differences, the novels do develop similar themes. They each focus on youthful characters responding to societal pressure and to their own

*cult: a group of persons sharing an artistic or intellectual interest; also, an excessive devotion to a person or an idea.
*uncanny: weird.
*aptitude: natural ability.
*cynical: suspicious and critical of people's motives.
*alienated: cut off; separated from.

developing sexuality. As a result, both books have been read by several generations of adolescents.[†]

a. time order

b. simple listing

c. definition

d. cause and effect

e. comparison and contrast

f. classification

5. For the last one hundred years, advertisers have both shaped and reflected American society's ideas about femininity. In the postindustrial revolution era of the 1890s through 1920, advertisements were filled with pictures of beautiful, devoted mothers. They all, of course, bought products that made their homes comfortable, attractive, and safe. The decade of the 1920s, however, was known as the Jazz Age. Women in ads from that time openly longed for glamour, youth, and sex appeal. In the meantime, homemakers were given short shrift. They quietly disappeared from the world of advertisements. By the 1930s, while America was in the grip of the Depression, advertisers were telling women they should be stylish. In effect, the message was, "Looking good can defeat financial hardship." After America's entry into World War II in 1941, women were needed in the workplace. As a result, ads featured women like Rosie the Riveter.[†] The point was that women were needed to serve their country. With the war over, women in the 1950s were encouraged to be guardians of the family. Many advertisements once again celebrated the woman as homemaker. But the 1960s and 1970s brought political change into the lives of women. Quick to respond to a cultural shift, ads from these decades portrayed women using beauty and household products in order to discover their identity. By the 1980s and 1990s, the women in advertisements were decidedly feminist: confident, career-oriented, and successful. But, as always, they remained beautiful.

[†]A 2009 *New York Times* article, "Get a Life, Holden Caulfield," says that the current generation of high school students does not empathize with Holden. They think he needs anti-depressants.

[†]Rosie the Riveter: a popular figure in a World War II campaign designed to encourage women to become factory workers.

a. time order

b. simple listing

c. definition

d. cause and effect

e. comparison and contrast

f. classification

VOCABULARY EXTRA

Although we now use the word *cynic* to describe someone who mistrusts the motives of others, the original Cynics (there's another eponym for you) were Greek philosophers who believed that striving for virtue was the essential goal in life. Unfortunately, in their pursuit of virtue, Cynics often pointed out the faults of others. Thus, the word came to mean "suspicious and critical of others."

Combining Patterns in Longer Readings

If paragraphs need to combine patterns, so, too, do longer readings. In fact, while paragraphs frequently rely on a single pattern, longer readings seldom do. Thus, it makes sense for readers to be on the lookout for two or more patterns when a reading extends beyond a single paragraph. Read the selection that follows.

Look closely at the stated main idea, which in longer readings is called the **thesis statement**, because the main idea may require several sentences. As you read, try to identify the patterns used to clarify and explain the main idea.

It Pays to Imitate Mother Nature

Thesis Statement 1 Biomimicry comes from *bios*, meaning "life," and *mimesis*, meaning "to imitate." It is a new science that studies nature for ways to answer the needs of humans. According to author and biomimicry expert Janine Benyus, nature has already invented many processes and products far superior to what humans have created. Benyus says that "animals, plants, and microbes are the consummate* engineers. They have found what works, what is appropriate, and, most important, what *lasts* here on Earth." Two examples

---

*consummate: perfect, best.

of biomimicry are the airplane and the telephone. The Wright brothers studied birds to learn how they fly. Inventor Alexander Graham Bell replicated the human tongue and eardrum to create his original telephone speaker and receiver.

2   Another famous example of biomimicry is Velcro. One summer day in 1948, Swiss inventor George de Mestral took his dog for a nature hike. They both returned from the hike covered in burrs. De Mestral studied one of the burrs under his microscope and discovered it was covered with tiny hooks. The hooks grabbed the loops in the fabric of the clothing and stuck. From studying the burrs, De Mestral got the idea to develop a hook and loop fastener made of nylon. He called it Velcro, a combination of the words *velour* and *crochet*. In 1955, he patented his design. Today, of course, Velcro is a multimillion-dollar company.

3   Yet another example of a product conceived through biomimicry is a house paint called Lotusan. This paint mimics the self-cleaning properties of the lotus flower's leaves. German botanist Dr. Wilhelm Barthlott discovered this process when he noticed that a lotus leaf is covered with tiny points. When a speck of dirt lands on the leaf, it perches atop those points. Then, as water flows over the leaf, it easily picks up the dirt and carries it away. Lotusan is guaranteed to stay clean for five years without washing.

4   In the world of biomimicry, a current major goal is to recreate spider silk. This substance is five times as strong as steel, yet still light and elastic. Researchers are studying how spiders spin silk. So far, they know only that spiders first eat and digest insects for protein. Glands in the spider's body then add water to the proteins to create a wet solution. When the spider squirts this wet solution through a tiny opening, the soluble* proteins turn into an insoluble fiber, a strand of silk. This last step of the process is the secret scientists hope to be able to unlock and duplicate. (Sources of examples: Jim Robbins, "Engineers Ask Nature for Design Advice," *New York Times*, December 11, 2001, p. 24; "Biomimicry Explained: A Conversation with Janine Benyus," www.biomimicry.net/faq.html; J. Madeleine Nash, "Science: Copying What Comes Naturally," *Time*, March 8, 1993, p. 58.)

The main idea here is expressed in the first two sentences of the reading, which make up the thesis statement. We can paraphrase that thesis statement like this: "Scientists use biomimicry to create new products modeled on the natural world." If you look over the remaining paragraphs in the reading, you'll see the author uses four different

---

*soluble: capable of being dissolved.

organizational patterns to make that point: (1) simple listing to identify the products mimicking the natural world, (2) definition to explain what biomimicry is, (3) sequence of dates and events to describe its development, and (4) process to describe how spiders spin silk.

⊙━ᴨ READING KEYS

♦ When a reading extends beyond a paragraph, expect a combination of patterns rather than a single one.

♦ In longer readings, the sentence or sentences expressing the main idea are called the *thesis statement*.

Patterns and the Implied Main Idea

In the next reading, the main idea is implied: "Started thousands of years ago by Greece's King Iphitos, the Olympic Games continue to this day; but although some similarities remain, the modern Olympics differ a good deal from the original." Notice now how the author uses three patterns—comparison and contrast, sequence of dates and events, and classification—to develop that point.

The Olympic Games: Past and Present

1   Around 824 B.C., Greece's King Iphitos began a movement to establish what became the Olympic Games. As a result of Iphitos' efforts, the first Olympic Games were held in 776 B.C. in Greece. Thereafter, they occurred every four years as a part of a religious festival, a period when all fighting and hostilities within the Greek world ceased. These ancient games continued for twelve consecutive centuries. In 394 A.D., they were abolished by the Byzantine emperor Theodosius.

2   In 1896, they were officially revived by avid* sportsman Pierre de Fredy, the baron de Coubertin, who believed that sports could bring together nations from all over and thereby encourage world peace. Coubertin organized a meeting in Paris in 1894. There, an international group of delegates planned the first modern Olympic Games. These games took place in Athens in 1896. Subsequent games have occurred every four years since, except for the years during World Wars I and II.

3   Until 1924, only the Olympic Summer Games existed. Not until 1924 did the first Olympic Winter Games take place in France. Before that, the figure skating and ice hockey competitions were part of the Summer Games.

---

*avid: enthusiastic.

Beginning in 1924, though, these sports joined others, such as skiing and bobsledding, to become the Winter Games. Now, Olympic sports are classified as either a summer or winter event. The Olympic Summer Games include, among others, sports such as baseball, basketball, boxing, diving, field hockey, gymnastics, soccer, and track and field. The Olympic Winter Games include alpine skiing, biathlon, bobsled, cross-country skiing, curling, figure skating, ice hockey, luge, Nordic combined, ski jumping, snowboarding, and speed skating.

4   Over time, the Winter Games have added many new sports that were not part of the original games. But the Summer Games, too, have expanded to include many more sports than were part of the ancient events. Like the original Olympic Games, the modern games include boxing, running, jumping, discus, and javelin. However, the modern games incorporate many newer sports, too. There are now thirty-seven major sport categories—from archery to yachting— and two hundred medal events for the Olympic Summer and Winter Games. Not surprisingly, the Games have grown from a one-day affair to one that lasts sixteen days each time it is held. Yet despite those changes, some important similarities between the ancient and modern games remain. For one thing, both the past and present games have inspired young athletes to strive to be the best in their sports. Also, both past and present games continue to draw many different nations together in the spirit of peaceful competition.

Once you recognize the patterns present in a reading, it's time to decide which of those patterns are essential to explaining the main idea. If you know that, you're in a much better position to decide what's essential information and what's not.

Deciding What's Important

In the Olympics reading, the comparison and contrast pattern is central to developing the author's main idea, which stresses differences and similarities between the Olympics past and present. Thus, it's important to know how the ancient and modern games are similar or different. However, the dates and events pattern is also important. After all, the main idea focuses on changes taking place over time. Therefore, the order of events over time is critical to understanding how the Olympics have changed or stayed the same.

The classification pattern introduced in paragraph 3 is probably the least significant pattern. It doesn't contribute all that much to the main idea. After all, it's possible to understand how the games developed and evolved without knowing exactly which activities are part of the Summer Games and which ones belong to the Winter Games. In fact, you can generally rely on common sense to figure out which activities make up the Summer Olympics and which ones the Winter Olympics.

Now, here's the point of the example: *The importance of a pattern depends on its relationship to the main idea.* Yes, one reading may consist of several patterns. But that doesn't mean that every element of each pattern carries equal weight. If a pattern is central to explaining the main idea, pay special attention to the information related to the pattern. If a pattern does not contribute much to the main idea, it doesn't deserve the same amount of attention.

To see a specific example of how the various patterns in a reading are not all equally significant, read the following selection. As you read, ask yourself these two questions: (1) What patterns of organization does the author use and (2) Which patterns are central to developing the main idea?

The Placebo Effect

1   The word *placebo* is a centuries-old term that is derived from the Latin phrase for "I shall please." The word entered medical terminology in the nineteenth century to describe a medicine or procedure administered to please or calm, rather than cure, a patient. There are two types of placebos: inert (or inactive) placebos and active placebos. Inert placebos do not cause any action within the body. Active placebos do have effects of some kind, but they are not specific to the disease for which they are given.

2   Placebos are used in clinical trials[†] designed to test the effectiveness of a particular treatment. In clinical trials, some participants in the study get real treatment, and some get a placebo. None of the participants knows what he or she is getting. In this way, researchers can test the benefits of a

Thesis Statement   drug or procedure. <u>Yet, astonishing as it may seem, some clinical trials have shown that patients who are given placebos—active or inert—often seem to improve.</u> For example, in one trial testing the worth of a specific surgical procedure, doctors anesthetized all the subjects. But in half of them, the physicians did no more than nick the skin. They performed no surgery, whereas they actually operated on the other half of the group. As it turns out, both groups claimed to feel better after "surgery."

3   In another study of two thousand heart attack patients suffering from irregular heartbeat, the death rate was cut in half for both those who took the real drug *and* those who took the placebo. Similarly, studies of

---

[†]clinical trials: studies of a drug or treatment that are based on direct observation.

pain-relief drugs have shown that some patients who take a placebo experience maximum relief one to two hours after treatment. In other words, they have exactly the same reaction as patients who actually received the real drug. In another study, 70 percent of depressed patients improved after a few weeks even when they received only a placebo. This phenomenon has come to be known as the *placebo effect*.

4   Why does this placebo effect occur? Researchers believe that expectations play a central role. People who expect to improve are more likely to do just that. Another cause of the placebo effect may well be the kind of medical care that patients receive while participating in a study. Just like patients who get the real drug, patients who take a placebo are immersed* in a healing environment. This environment includes caring, responsive doctors and nurses; regular examinations; and many opportunities to discuss their illness and courses of treatment. Some psychologists believe that this nurturing, or caring, atmosphere promotes recovery, regardless of whether treatments are real.

5   Therefore, researchers wonder if the use of placebos could eventually lead to reductions in the dosage of actual medications. In other words, a patient in pain might be first treated with a placebo. If it worked, the real medication would not be prescribed. Substituting placebos for actual medication could result in lower costs and fewer side effects for patients. Of course, the medical community must first resolve the ethical dilemma involved in the use of placebos. If doctors tell patients they are prescribing a placebo, the placebo effect is lost. If doctors tell patients that a placebo is real medicine, however, they are being dishonest. Despite these ethical questions, some scientists still believe that placebo treatments could benefit those who suffer from illnesses for which there is no other treatment. (Source of studies: Walter A. Brown, M.D., with Barbara Severs, "Placebos: Fooling the Body to Heal Itself," *USA Today Magazine*, July 1999, pp. 32–33.)

In this selection, the author needs three different patterns to develop the thesis statement. She clearly needs the definition pattern to make sure readers understand what a placebo is. However, cause and effect is the most essential pattern. That's because the message or main idea of the reading revolves around a cause and effect relationship: In clinical trials, placebos have appeared to offer (or cause) a medical benefit. There is also a comparison and contrast pattern in paragraph 1, where the author contrasts active and inert placebos. However, this pattern is the least

---

*immersed: completely covered or involved.

significant because the reading suggests that placebos of both types have shown some kind of healing property. The difference between active and inert placebos doesn't seem to play much of a role in that effect.

⊙━ᴍ READING KEYS

- ◆ Once you identify the patterns used in a reading, identify the elements of each one. Then decide how many of those elements are essential to the main idea. These are the ones to store in your memory or record in your notes.
- ◆ The importance of a pattern depends on its relationship to the main idea.

CLASS ACTION

Everyone writes down one idea that could be developed into an essay. Have a classmate collect and list all the ideas on the board. Then analyze each idea to decide which pattern or patterns might be appropriate given the main idea.

◆ EXERCISE 2   Recognizing Patterns in Longer Readings

DIRECTIONS   Read each selection and look closely at the underlined thesis statement. Then circle the letters of the patterns present. There might be two, three, or even four.

EXAMPLE

Saving Our Children

1 The fates of Adam Walsh and Amber Hagerman were tragically similar. Both were small children when they were kidnapped and murdered. In 1981, when Adam was 6 years old, a stranger abducted him from a department store in Florida. Sixteen days later, he was found dead, and his killer was not identified until 2008.[†] In 1996, 9-year-old Amber went out to ride her bicycle around her Texas neighborhood and vanished. Four days later, she, too, was found dead. The person who killed Amber was never brought to justice.

[†]According to Florida police, it wasn't new evidence that finally solved the case. It was a re-analysis of preexisting evidence. The loss of his son turned the boy's father, John, into an advocate of missing children. He co-founded the National Center for Missing and Exploited Children.

2   From these and other abductions, police learned that speed is essential in rescuing a kidnapped child. According to the Justice Department, three out of every four victims are killed within three hours of being taken. Consequently, parents, law enforcement officials, and organizations that advocate for children worked together to create two systems for responding quickly when a child is abducted. Code Adam, named after Adam Walsh, is a notice distributed throughout the building from which a child has disappeared. An Amber Alert is a notice to the general public about a kidnapped child. AMBER is not only the system's namesake but also an acronym for America's Missing Broadcast Emergency Response.

3   A Code Adam alert attempts to prevent an abduction from being completed in a public place like a store. If a parent or guardian reports a missing child to an employee or official on the premises, a five-step sequence is set in motion. The first step involves developing a detailed description of the missing child. Next, the person in charge uses the public address system to page everyone in the building, and announces a "Code Adam" followed by the child's description. This alert signals the building's employees to initiate the third step. Designated employees go to the building's exits and begin monitoring everyone who leaves. At the same time, most of the other employees begin searching the premises for a child resembling the description. If the child is not found within ten minutes, someone calls the police. The fourth step depends upon who is with the child when he or she is found. If the child is alone and unharmed, he or she is reunited with the parent or guardian. If the child is with someone other than the parent or guardian, employees try to prevent that person from leaving without putting themselves, other staff members, or customers in danger. In the fifth and final step, the incident is concluded by a "Code Adam cancelled" announcement on the public address system.

4   If the Code Adam fails or if the child is abducted from some place other than a building, police issue an Amber Alert, after confirming that the child has been abducted and hasn't run away. Next, they determine whether the child is in danger of being harmed or killed. Then, they produce descriptions of the child, the suspected abductor, and the suspect's vehicle. Finally, they distribute a notice to the public via television, radio, the Internet, and electronic highway signs. This notice includes details about the child's description and abduction location. The public is asked to immediately report any sighting of the child or abductor.

5   Both systems have successfully recovered many abducted children. According to the National Center for Missing and Exploited Children, the Amber Alert system has returned 137 victims to their families. The Code

Adam program, which is now in place in more than 30,000 stores across the country, has also foiled numerous child abductions in many states. (Sources of information: Aaron Larson, "Amber Alerts and Code Adam Alerts," ExpertLaw, August 2003, www.expertlaw.com/library/pubarticles/amber_alerts.html; Richard Willing, "Amber Alert Links Up to Web Today," *USA Today*, July 19, 2004, p. 1A.)

(a.) time order

b. simple listing

(c.) definition

(d.) cause and effect

(e.) comparison and contrast

f. classification

EXPLANATION   In this case, the author needs four different patterns to develop the main idea. The time order pattern is essential for telling the stories of Adam and Amber and for explaining how the two response systems work. The definition pattern is needed to clearly state what the terms *Code Adam* and *Amber Alert* mean. The cause and effect pattern is needed to explain why the two systems were created and, in the final paragraph, the results of implementing them. Comparison and contrast is important only to point out a few similarities between Adam and Amber, so it's the least important of the four patterns.

1. Kwanzaa

1   Kwanzaa is a nonreligious African-American celebration. It takes place from December 26 to January 1 each year. The name Kwanzaa comes from the Swahili phrase *matunda ya kwanza*, which means "first fruits." This festival originated in ancient Egypt and Nubia, when African people gathered to celebrate the harvest. Since then, the holiday has been observed by numerous African kingdoms and tribes, both large and small. In 1966, the celebration was introduced to America by civil rights activist Dr. Maulana Karenga, professor and chair of the Department of Black Studies at California State University at Long Beach. Since then, Kwanzaa has spread across the United States, becoming a mainstream African-American holiday tradition.

2   Dr. Karenga conceived of this celebration in the context of the Black Liberation Movement of the 1960s. He hoped it would encourage African-Americans to reconnect with their African heritage. He also hoped the

holiday would strengthen community and family ties. Dr. Karenga believed Kwanzaa celebrations would promote the values that encourage personal and professional achievement. For this reason, Kwanzaa rituals in America emphasize seven principles: unity, self-determination, collective work and responsibility, cooperative economics, purpose, creativity, and faith.

3   During the seven-day Kwanzaa celebration, participants devote one day to each of these seven principles. Observers, often wearing traditional African clothing, gather together each evening. They greet each other with the phrase *Habari gani,* which is Swahili for "What's new?" The answer is the Swahili word for the principle of the day. Then participants light one or more of seven candles in a special candelabra called a kinara. Each candle represents one of the seven principles. Next, participants discuss how that day's principle affects their lives. The ritual may also include the exchange of small gifts; a meal of traditional African foods; and musical performances, dances, or poetry readings. The evening ends with the participants calling out *Harambee* (Swahili for "let's all pull together") seven times. On the final night of the holiday, friends and relatives join in a feast called the *Karamu.*

4   The celebration of Kwanzaa continues to grow as more and more African-Americans seek to discover their heritage. Those who participate say they cherish the opportunity to remember and reflect upon their past and to set goals for their future. They like the celebration's emphasis on family and community, noting that the rituals leave them with a positive feeling of black pride. Kwanzaa is a cultural holiday, not a religious one, so most people observe it in addition to Christmas. However, Kwanzaa is also viewed by many in the black community as an antidote to the increasingly commercial Christmas season.

a. time order

b. simple listing

c. definition

d. cause and effect

e. comparison and contrast

f. classification

2. Unions and the Government

1   Unionization in state and local government developed and flourished in the 1960s and 1970s, some thirty years after the heyday of private-sector unionism. During the 1960s, the number of public-employee union members more than tripled. Why the sudden growth? In retrospect, several reasons are apparent.

2   First, the rise of unionism in government was spurred by the realization by state and local employees that they were underpaid and otherwise maltreated in comparison to their counterparts in the private sector who had progressed so well with unionization and collective bargaining. Second, the bureaucratic and impersonal nature of work in large government organizations encouraged unionization to preserve the dignity of the workers. A third reason for the rise of state and local unionism was the employees' lack of confidence in many civil service systems. Not only were pay and benefits inadequate, but grievance processes were controlled by management, employees had little or no say in setting personnel policies, and "merit" selection, promotion, and pay often were fraught with management favoritism. Fourth, public employees got caught up in the 1960s' fervor of social change. They saw other groups in American society winning concessions from government authorities and they decided to join in.

3   Perhaps most important, the growth of unions in government was promoted by a significant change in the legal environment of labor relations. The rights of public employees to join unions and bargain collectively with management were guaranteed by several U.S. Supreme Court rulings, state legislation, local ordinances, and various informal arrangements that became operative during the 1960s and 1970s. Wisconsin was the first state to permit collective bargaining for state workers, in 1959. Today, forty-two states specifically allow at least one category of state or local government employees to engage in collective bargaining. (Bowman and Kearney, *State and Local Government*, pp. 225–26.)

a. time order

b. simple listing

c. definition

d. cause and effect

e. comparison and contrast

f. classification

Common Combinations

There's no strict rule as to how organizational patterns combine. In fact, they can combine in any number of ways. However, some combinations are more likely to occur than others. If, for example, you encounter a reading organized around dates and events, check to see if the cause and effect pattern is also present. These two patterns are likely to appear together. For an example, look at the following reading. Note how the sequence of dates and events pattern combines with cause and effect to develop the underlined thesis statement.

The Legacy of P. T. Barnum

1 In the nineteenth century, Phineas Taylor (P. T.) Barnum made a name for himself as a showman while almost single-handedly transforming the taste of the American public—and not necessarily for the better.

2 Born in 1810, Barnum, the son of a wealthy businessman, launched his entertainment career when he was just 25. It was at that point that he took under his wing an elderly black woman named Joice Heth. Heth claimed to be 166 years old. She also claimed to have been George Washington's nurse. Whether or not Barnum believed her story, he billed her as a "living mummy" and made himself a small fortune.

3 After his success with Heth and similar attractions—like the three-foot-tall man Tom Thumb—Barnum bought his own museum in 1841. He packed it with oddities like the skeleton of a mermaid—probably a fish tail attached to a monkey's skeleton—and made the museum into a national attraction. And there were more successes to come. In 1881 Barnum joined James A. Bailey to form a three-ring traveling circus that became Barnum & Bailey's "Greatest Show on Earth."

4 Barnum died only ten years after launching the circus tour. But by that time he had changed the face of American entertainment. More than anyone else, P. T. Barnum had whetted* the public's appetite for the sensational. He had titillated* his audiences with bearded ladies, pretzel-limbed contortionists, and the conjoined twins Chang and Eng. Even when some of Barnum's so-called freaks of nature, like the gorilla-man dressed in a fur suit, turned out to be frauds, the public applauded and called for more.

In this reading, the sequence of dates and events pattern is necessary to trace some key events in Barnum's career. But the cause and effect pattern is also necessary because Barnum's successful career (the cause) powerfully influenced public taste (the effect).

As you might expect, the two patterns in the Barnum reading are not the only two that readily combine. Here are some other common combinations:

---

*whetted: stimulated.
*titillated: excited.

Patterns That Frequently Combine ◆	Time Order with Cause and Effect
	Time Order with Definition
	Cause and Effect with Simple Listing
	Cause and Effect with Comparison and Contrast
	Classification with Comparison and Contrast

Knowing that classification and comparison and contrast are likely to team up doesn't mean they always go hand in hand. Still, if you recognize the classification pattern, it's smart to be on the lookout for signs of comparison and contrast. The faster you recognize which patterns are present, the quicker you can make decisions about what's important and what's not.

READING KEY

◆ If you spot a pattern that commonly combines with another pattern, check to see if the other pattern is present. That way, you can speed up the process of deciding what's important.

ROUNDING UP THE KEYS

Here is a list of all the reading keys introduced in the chapter. Use them to review for the test on page 404. If a particular reading key doesn't make sense on its own, go back to the page where it appeared and review the section preceding it.

READING KEY: Pure versus Mixed Patterns

◆ The main idea determines the patterns a writer will use. It follows, then, that the main idea is also the best clue to the patterns present in the reading. (p. 375)

READING KEYS: Combining Patterns in Longer Readings

◆ When a reading extends beyond a paragraph, expect a combination of patterns rather than a single one. (p. 383)

◆ In longer readings, the sentence or sentences expressing the main idea are called the *thesis statement*. (p. 383)

READING KEYS: Deciding What's Important

◆ Once you identify the patterns used in a reading, identify the elements of each one. Then decide how many of those elements are essential to the main idea. These are the ones to store in your memory or record in your notes. (p. 387)

◆ The importance of a pattern depends on its relationship to the main idea. (p. 387)

READING KEY: Common Combinations

◆ If you spot a pattern that commonly combines with another pattern, check to see if the other pattern is present. That way, you can speed up the process of deciding what's important. (p. 393)

Ten More Words for Your Textbook Vocabulary

1. **fertile:** capable of producing or giving birth

   When homesteaders went west in 1862, they expected to find lush, *fertile* fields, but instead they found desert and rock.

2. **allocation:** to set apart or distribute for specific purposes

   The purpose of the meeting was to discuss the *allocation* of resources for the new hospital.

3. **symbiotic:** related in a mutually beneficial way

   A third factor in government labor relations is the *symbiotic* relationship that can develop between unions and elected officials. (Bowman and Kearney, *State and Local Government*, p. 228.)

4. **entail:** to require or impose

   Deciding the winner will *entail* a recount of the votes.

5. **paramount:** main, chief, primary

   The diplomat's *paramount* concern was to see to it that all parties in the negotiations felt responsible for the outcome.

6. **transient:** short lived; temporary

   Some psychological disorders are mild and *transient*; others are severe and chronic, lasting, in some cases, a lifetime.

7. **contention:** claim

   Many findings support the *contention* that rape has more to do with power, aggression, and violence than with sex. (Sue, Sue, and Sue, *Abnormal Psychology*, p. 318.)

8. **denigrate:** to speak in a negative or an insulting way

   People who suffer from depression are often inclined to *denigrate* their own accomplishments.

9. **denounce:** to condemn

   Once the revolution had begun, the king's former friends were quick to *denounce* him.

10. **injunction:** a command or court order

    The judge issued an *injunction*, which made it illegal for the strike to continue.

◆ EXERCISE 3 Building an Academic Vocabulary

DIRECTIONS   Fill in the blanks with one of the words listed below.

allocate	denigrate	paramount	injunctions	symbiotic
denounced	fertile	transient	entails	contention

1. Because the assistant chair had worked very hard on the revision of the company's mission, the other members of the group were not about to _____ her efforts.

2. The court expected its _____ to be obeyed without question.

3. After it was discovered that he had given the British secret information about America's military plans, Benedict Arnold was _____ as a traitor.

4. Britain's most famous prime minister, Winston Churchill, was prone to depression, and his good moods were all too _____.

5. In its controversial decision, the Supreme Court supported the _____ that voter fraud was a real problem rather than an imagined one.

6. Treating insomnia sometimes _____ the use of antidepressants.

7. Unfortunately, ignorance is often _____ ground for superstition.

8. The relationship between clownfish and sea anemones is a good example of a(n) _____ relationship: The clownfish protects the anemone from anemone-eating fish; the anemone, in turn, uses its sting to protect the clownfish from predators.

9. After the country was destroyed by war, the government had to carefully _____ its resources to combat shortages and maintain the economy.

10. Although he was thrilled to have an education at the military's expense, the boy's love of his country was the _____ reason for his enlistment.

The *Kursk*'s Tragic End

Looking Ahead The passage on pages 378–79 described the tragedy that befell the *Kursk*. This reading tells you more about the tragedy's causes and consequences.

1   On the morning of Saturday, August 12, 2000, the nuclear submarine *Kursk* was engaged in naval exercises deep in the Barents Sea just off the coast of Norway. Suddenly, at 11:28 a.m., the *Kursk* was ripped apart by two explosions that sent the ship plummeting even deeper into the Barents' murky waters. The commander of Russia's northern fleet, Admiral Vyacheslav Popov, knew immediately that there had been explosions in the area where the *Kursk* was located. Still, he did not investigate the ship's whereabouts. Instead, he put rescue vessels on immediate alert. Then, strangely, he waited more than eleven hours to dispatch them. During that time, Popov made no attempt to establish radio contact with the sunken sub. As a result, it took almost a full day for the submarine to be discovered lying at the bottom of the sea. Apparently following the admiral's example, navy spokespeople did not announce that a mishap had taken place until two days after the ship's sudden slide into the deep.

2   Normally, the bottom of the Barents is a dark and silent place. Yet, in the first few days after the *Kursk*'s descent, there were some hopeful sounds. Electronic listening devices used in the rescue effort picked up what seemed to be the *tap, tap, tap* of a hammer knocking on a pipe. Rescuers assumed that a sailor still alive on the sub was trying to make contact. A nearby vessel even claimed to have picked up the message "SOS . . . water." But by Wednesday, August 16, no more sounds came from the *Kursk*. It was only at this point that the Russian government asked Norway and Britain for help. Three days later, on August 19, a week after the ship went down, fully equipped rescue teams arrived from both countries. Tragically for the more than one hundred men trapped inside the doomed submarine, help had come too late.

3   In the first days following the tragedy, Russia's state-controlled televised news desperately tried to convince the families of those on board the *Kursk*, as well as the general public, that every possible rescue effort was being made. Yet, at the same time, newspaper journalists were boldly insisting that international help should have been requested immediately. Even worse, headlines like "Whose Honor Is Sinking in the Barents Sea?" suggested that the Russian government had refused to ask for help out of a misguided sense

of pride. If the government couldn't save the ship on its own, it may have been unwilling to make that admission to the world.

4   As a result of the newspaper coverage of the *Kursk*'s horrible plight, grief and outrage swept the country. Everyone wanted answers to the same two questions: Why had the *Kursk* dropped to the bottom of the Barents in the first place? Why hadn't the Russian government immediately asked for international help in the rescue attempt? The questions grew louder and angrier when it became obvious that both navy and government officials had been lying all along. Navy officials had claimed that radio communication had been established and that cables dropped from the surface were providing the ship with both electricity and oxygen. Neither claim was true. Russia's president, Vladimir Putin, who had been on vacation when the ship went down, insisted that everything that could be done was being done. Yet that was clearly not the case.

5   Even after the *Kursk* was fully lifted from the bottom of the Barents in 2001, both questions remained unanswered. Some experts believed fuel leaks aboard the *Kursk* ignited the explosions that sent crew members to their doom. Others pointed out that two of the soldiers in charge of the *Kursk*'s torpedoes were recent graduates of submarine courses. Thus, the explosions may have resulted from human error. One scenario suggested that crew members tried to expel a missile that failed to fire as expected. Instead, it remained inside its torpedo tube and exploded on board. That explosion then generated the second.

6   There's also more than one possible answer as to why the Russian government did not ask for help sooner. One explanation is that several important members of Russia's military were old-style cold warriors.[†] They might well have feared that bringing in outsiders could reveal state secrets to the West—the cardinal sin of cold-war thinking. Some Moscow analysts openly wondered if members of the old guard had kept the details of the disaster from President Putin himself. Otherwise, there is no satisfactory explanation as to why Putin first discussed the crisis some three days after the *Kursk* had sunk. Moreover, when Putin finally acknowledged the *Kursk*'s plight, he made a terrible mistake. He appeared on television looking tanned and relaxed. Wearing a white, open-necked golf shirt, he acted like a man still on vacation. This is hardly the image a president wants to convey when speaking to the public about a national tragedy. The suspicion is that Putin may not have been aware of how bad the situation

---

[†]cold warriors: During the 1950s, these were the people who believed that the United States and the Soviet Union were ready to go to war at any moment.

really was. Navy commanders may have kept him in the dark, just as they did the general public. Sadly, their secrecy seems to have only perpetuated a dangerous and potentially tragic situation.

7   In the fall of 2003, just three years after the *Kursk* tragedy, severe weather damaged another Russian nuclear submarine and sent it hurtling to the bottom of the Barents Sea. Rescuers who arrived on the scene were able to rescue one crew member. They found another one already dead and floating in the cold sea water. On the sea floor, seven crew members were trapped in the sub. Like the sailors on the *Kursk*, their rescue was impossible.

8   There was a difference, though; this time, officials spoke out about the causes of the tragedy. Russia's navy chief, Admiral Viktor Kravchenko, complained that during ship operations "all the imaginable safety rules were broken." Even the Russian defense minister, Sergei Ivanov, blamed those in charge for their "frivolous Russian reliance on chance, that everything will be okay."

9   For those who know anything about Russia's submarines, it's clear that everything is not okay. Russia's fleet of nuclear-powered submarines is in such disrepair that 126 of them lie in port. However, they can't be destroyed because the necessary funds aren't available for their demolition. Russian officials, however, do seem to have learned one lesson: When a potential tragedy threatens lives, call for help.

10   In 2005, a mini-submarine became trapped off Russia's coast and would have sunk without assistance. In response, Russian officials called for foreign assistance, and a British remote-controlled vehicle rescued all seven crew members. Although the outcome was a happy one, the Russian newspaper *Rossiyskaya Gazeta* asked a key question, "Where is the underwater technology the navy solemnly promised to get into shape after the *Kursk*?" So far at least, the paper and the public are still waiting for an answer.

Sharpening Your Skills

DIRECTIONS   Answer the following questions by filling in the blanks or circling the letter of the correct response.

1. What's the implied main idea of the entire reading?
   a. The *Kursk* tragedy was the result of human error, although the Russian government was slow to admit that fact.

b. The tragic fate of the *Kursk* and other Russian submarines suggests the Russian navy is in terrible shape, with more accidents likely to follow.

c. The tragedy of the *Kursk* proves what the world has known all along: The Russian navy is too poor to adequately equip and staff its ships.

d. Vladimir Putin's reputation will never recover from his mismanagement of the *Kursk* tragedy, and his days in office are numbered.

2. Overall, which two patterns organize the reading?

   a. comparison and contrast *and* classification

   b. process *and* comparison and contrast

   c. sequence of dates and events *and* cause and effect

   d. cause and effect *and* definition

3. Based on the context, how did you define the word *plummeting* in paragraph 1?

   _____

4. Based on the context, how did you define the word *mishap* in paragraph 1?

   _____

5. Use an online or a print dictionary to explain where the Barents Sea got its name.

   _____

   _____

6. Explain why Vladimir Putin's appearance (paragraph 6) was "hardly the image a president wants to convey when speaking to the public about a national tragedy."

   _____

   _____

   _____

7. In paragraph 3, the headline "Whose Honor Is Sinking in the Barents Sea?" is a supporting detail that illustrates what main idea?

a. Russian journalists boldly challenged the official version of events and suggested that the government had been at fault.

b. Like newspapers in the U.S., Russian papers were intent on stirring up interest in a potential government scandal.

c. Journalists everywhere like headlines that stir up controversy.

d. Russian journalists exposed the truth about the navy's substandard ships and equipment.

8. What pattern of organization is at work in paragraph 4?

a. comparison and contrast

b. cause and effect

c. time order

9. In your own words, what's the main idea of paragraph 5?

_____

_____

10. Beginning in paragraph 7, what point does the author imply about the tragedy that befell the *Kursk*?

_____

_____

_____

INTERNET RESOURCE For additional practice with patterns of organization, go to the ACE Tests accompanying *Reading Keys* at www .cengage.com./devenglish/Flemming/rk3e. For more practice with patterns, see also *Reading Keys*, Additional Material and Online Practice at laflemm.com.

▶ **TEST 1**   **Reviewing the Key Points**

DIRECTIONS   Answer the following questions by filling in the blanks or circling the correct response.

1. What determines the patterns a writer uses?

     _____

2. What is the reader's best clue to determining the pattern or patterns of organization used by the writer?

     _____

3. *T* or *F*. Single paragraphs are likely to combine patterns, but longer readings tend to rely on one pattern.

4. *T* or *F.* Some patterns are more likely to combine than others.

5. *T* or *F*. If a reading contains several patterns, all the patterns are equally important.

To correct your test, turn to page 554. If one or more of your answers is incorrect, re-read the Rounding Up the Keys section of the chapter to find out where your mistakes might be.

▶ **TEST 2**   **Recognizing Patterns in Paragraphs**

DIRECTIONS   Circle the appropriate letter or letters to identify the pattern or patterns of organization in each paragraph.

1. Most people know that lack of sleep causes irritability and increases the risk of accidents while driving. However, researchers are finding evidence that long-term lack of sleep also weakens the body's immune system. Inadequate sleep may also be contributing to America's rising rates of diabetes and obesity. There is even new evidence that too little sleep on a regular basis may increase the risk of breast cancer. Furthermore, chronic lack of sleep affects the metabolism and secretion of hormones, producing striking changes that resemble advanced aging. Cheating on sleep for just a few nights may even harm brain cells.

     a. time order

     b. simple listing

     c. definition

     d. cause and effect

2. The juvenile justice system has been evolving since the 1600s. Before the seventeenth century, society viewed children as miniature adults. Kids were held to the same standards of behavior as adults, so the justice system punished them as adults. In the seventeenth century, though, European church and community leaders managed to convince the rest of society that children were a distinct group, weaker and more innocent than adults. As a result, young offenders began to be judged against different, age-related standards. By the eighteenth century, English common law considered children under 14 to be incapable of having criminal intentions. Reflecting that belief, the first juvenile court was established in America in 1899. For the next hundred years, the juvenile justice system focused on reforming rather than punishing young offenders. Today, however, in the aftermath of numerous violent crimes committed by juveniles, many people are taking a harsher position. They want young lawbreakers referred to criminal courts and tried as adults.

     a. time order

     b. simple listing

c. cause and effect

d. classification

3. **Astrobiology** is a controversial new science that concerns the search for life in outer space. Astrobiologists study meteorites, which are fragments of rocks that have come from outer space. Researchers examine these rocks for evidence of life. For example, in 1996, excited NASA scientists found evidence of bacteria fossils in a meteorite that originated on Mars. The building blocks of protein—the basis of life—have been discovered in other meteorites. In addition to examining rocks that hit Earth, astrobiologists are also interested in sending orbiters or probes to other planets and moons to search for evidence that life exists elsewhere.

   a. simple listing

   b. definition

   c. cause and effect

   d. comparison and contrast

4. English explorer Captain Robert F. Scott tried with a team of four other men to be the first to reach the South Pole in Antarctica. Not only were Scott and his team beaten by another team, but they also lost their lives on their journey back to base camp. Scott's party reached the South Pole on January 17, 1912, only to find that Norwegian Roald Amundsen had arrived there a month before. Two days later, Scott and his companions headed for home. In early February, one of the men became ill because of malnutrition and injuries. He died on February 17. On March 17, another man, suffering from frostbite, also died. On March 20, the remaining three members of the team set up their final campsite just eleven miles from a depot containing food and heating oil. Tragically, a blizzard trapped the men in their tent. Scott, who was suffering from painful frostbite, recorded his final journal entry on March 29. Soon after, he and his two companions froze to death.

   a. time order

   b. simple listing

   c. definition

   d. cause and effect

5. Organizations use a variety of public relations tools to convey messages and construct an image. Written messages in the form of brochures, company magazines, annual reports, and news releases are one form of public relations tools. But spoken messages are important as well, and organizations rely on the spoken along with the written word to get their point across. They also use corporate-identity materials, such as business cards, logos, signs, and stationery. Event sponsorship is another public relations tool. It involves a company paying for all or part of a special event, such as a sports competition, concert, festival, or play. A good example of event sponsorship was Ben & Jerry's sponsorship of the "Pint for Pint" program that helped the Red Cross boost blood donations. Those who donated a pint of blood to the Red Cross got a free pint of ice cream. Increasingly, organizations are using the Internet for public relations through blogs and social-networking sites. (Adapted from Pride, Hughes, and Kapoor, *Business*, p. 485.)

a. simple listing

b. definition

c. cause and effect

d. classification

▶ **TEST 3**   **Recognizing Patterns in Paragraphs**

DIRECTIONS   Circle the appropriate letter or letters to identify the pattern or patterns of organization in each paragraph.

1. Many automotive experts claim that synthetic motor oil is better than natural petroleum oil. The most important differences between the two are related to vehicle performance, cost, and convenience. Synthetic oils increase an engine's performance and overall length of life because they are better than petroleum-based oils in several ways. Synthetic-based oils are better at protecting the engine from high temperatures. They flow more easily in cold temperatures, and they also prevent deposits from forming. In addition, synthetic oils reduce friction and wear more effectively than petroleum oils do. Also, the cost of synthetic oils is the same as or less than the cost of petroleum oil. Though a quart of synthetic oil can cost several dollars more than the same amount of petroleum oil, synthetic oil is changed much less often than petroleum oil. Generally, synthetic oils last two to three times longer than petroleum oils. For this reason, their longer life offsets their higher price. Furthermore, the reduced number of oil changes offered by synthetic oils results in greater convenience for car owners. Some oil manufacturers even suggest that the vehicle owner change synthetic oil every 25,000 miles, as opposed to every 3,000–5,000 miles for petroleum oils.

   a. simple listing
   b. definition
   c. cause and effect
   d. comparison and contrast
   e. time order

2. University of Virginia professor E. Mavis Hetherington has studied the effects of divorce on children. Her research has turned up some interesting similarities and differences between children of divorced parents and children with intact* families. According to Dr. Hetherington, only 10 percent of children from intact families appeared to have emotional problems. However, 25 percent of children with divorced parents experienced depression or antisocial behavior in school. Yet almost the same

---

*intact: complete, unbroken.

percentage of children in each group said they felt close to their biological mothers: Seventy percent of children in divorced families and 80 percent of children in intact families claimed to enjoy a good relationship with their moms. Perhaps most interesting, Dr. Hetherington found that a majority of children with divorced parents find divorce to be both acceptable and understandable. Seventy percent of young people with divorced parents said that divorce is acceptable, even if children are involved. In contrast, only 40 percent of children in intact families approved of divorce.

a. time order

b. simple listing

c. definition

d. cause and effect

e. comparison and contrast

3. **Electronic waste**, also known as "e-waste" and "e-trash," describes worn-out, broken, or obsolete computers, cell phones, videocassette recorders, and television sets that people throw out. Less than 10 percent of e-waste is recycled, so it now accounts for 1 percent of trash in the United States. As a result, it's becoming a problem for local governments all over the country. City and county officials are worried about the high cost of collecting and dumping e-waste in their crowded landfills. Already, California and Massachusetts have banned computer monitors from being dumped in the states' landfills and incinerators. Environmental groups, too, are concerned about the impact of e-waste. They fear that the lead, mercury, and other hazardous substances in electronic devices will leak into the soil and water. Overexposure to these toxins can cause serious health problems. For example, the lead that shields the user of an electronic device from radiation could seep into the groundwater. Lead poisoning can result in kidney, nervous system, and reproductive system damage.

a. time order

b. simple listing

c. definition

d. cause and effect

e. comparison and contrast

4. The two major branches, or types, of Islam are Sunni and Shia. Sunni Muslims account for 90 percent of Islam's followers. They accept the first three spiritual leaders who succeeded Muhammad, the religion's central prophet. This group believes community leaders should be chosen by election. The majority of Muslims in Egypt, Saudi Arabia, Syria, Jordan, Lebanon, Turkey, and Indonesia are Sunni Muslims. Also, most of America's African-American converts to Islam follow the Sunni traditions. Shiite Muslims account for about 10 percent of Muslims in the world today, mostly in Iran and Iraq. These Muslims accept only the fourth spiritual leader to follow Muhammad, rejecting his first three successors. Shiites believe their community leader is both a religious and a political authority, who can be appointed only by divine command. They tend to be more strict than Sunni Muslims in their religious practices. They are also more restrictive in their dietary rules and views on women.

   a. time order
   b. simple listing
   c. definition
   d. comparison and contrast
   e. classification

5. Fashion magazines love giving girls and women advice about beauty. They've been doing that since the mid-nineteenth century when the first beauty magazines were published. Unfortunately, much of that advice for cultivating beauty has ranged from silly to dangerous. Women were once told, for instance, that cutting their eyelashes would make them grow. In fact, cutting one's eyelashes only makes them short and stubby; it doesn't make them grow. As if that advice weren't bad enough, it was also suggested that women should put petroleum jelly on their lashes and then sprinkle coal dust over the lashes to make them appear darker and fuller. What that advice probably did was to give the women who followed it severe eye infections. In the past, women were also advised to take small doses of arsenic to whiten their skin. Although it's true that arsenic produces pale skin—considered desirable in the nineteenth century—it's also true that arsenic builds up in the body and can cause death. In the past, women were also told that a dark tan was both attractive and

good for the skin. Women who followed that advice ended up with leathery, lined skin if they were lucky, and with skin cancer if they weren't.

a. definition
b. simple listing
c. cause and effect
d. classification
e. comparison and contrast

▶ **TEST 4**   **Recognizing Patterns in Paragraphs**

DIRECTIONS   Circle the appropriate letter or letters to identify the pattern or patterns of organization in each paragraph.

1. An **antibiotic** is a chemical substance that destroys microorganisms in the body without harming the body itself. Produced by bacteria and fungi, antibiotics are now routinely used to treat a wide variety of illnesses. Discovered in 1928 by Alexander Fleming, penicillin was the first antibiotic. Then, in the early 1940s, researchers learned how to produce the antibiotic in commercial quantities to treat wounded World War II soldiers. In the 1950s and 1960s, scientists discovered many new classes of antibiotics and developed some of them for use against a broad range of microorganisms. Other antibiotics targeted specific kinds of bacteria. Unfortunately, far too many doctors and patients started turning to antibiotics for a quick cure. As a result, the medical community is now concerned about the growth of new drug-resistant bacteria. These bacteria no longer respond to the current crop of antibiotics. There are signs that existing antibiotics are proving less effective at treating serious diseases such as tuberculosis and strep infections.

   a. time order
   b. simple listing
   c. definition
   d. cause and effect
   e. comparison and contrast
   f. classification

2. In 1978, an underwater diver named Gerald Klein discovered the remains of a ship while diving in Biscayne National Park. Klein removed some items from the wreck, and, in 1979, he filed a claim with the district court in Florida, where the park is located. Believing that the items, dating back a century, were valuable, Klein asked to keep what he had taken or, at the very least, to receive a salvage award for his efforts. Salvage awards are monies paid for the rescue of property lost at sea, and the awards were created to encourage acts of rescue and salvage. To Klein, keeping the items or being rewarded for their discovery seemed the fair and obvious outcome for his efforts. Not so, said the district court in 1979 under the rule of Judge C. Clyde Atkins. As a result, Klein ended up appealing his case to the state of

Florida, where in 1985 he lost again. The judges, however, did not all agree, and they filed widely dissenting opinions. One judge found that because the United States was "the owner of the land on and/or in which the shipwreck is located, it owns the shipwreck." In his view, Klein had ignored legitimate property rights. Another argued that because Klein had removed the articles, which, it was assumed, would have been found eventually, he had actually done more harm than good, making it more difficult to trace the original ownership of both the ship and its contents. But another judge took a completely different position. He argued that the "plaintiff performed a highly valuable service simply by locating the shipwreck, and should be compensated accordingly." Unfortunately for Klein's estate—by 1985 Gerald Klein had died—this was a minority decision, and his widow was denied any claim to the ancient ship and its contents. (Source of case details: www.karlloren.com/healthinsurance/p12.htm; http://philtrupp.com/smith.htm.)

a. time order

b. simple listing

c. definition

d. cause and effect

e. comparison and contrast

f. classification

3. A growing number of Europeans and Americans who need serious medical care but cannot afford the price of it in their own country are traveling to India for medical treatment. Private Indian hospitals offer first-rate medical care at a price that foreign patients and well-off Indians can afford. Thus, when Ron Steeles of Alabama needed to have the mitral valve of his heart repaired, he flew halfway around the world to Bangalore, India, to have his surgery. After the mitral valve was repaired, Steeles recuperated quickly. The same is not true, however, for 150 Indian laborers who were ill during the same time Steeles was hospitalized. They died because the public hospitals where they were brought after drinking illegally brewed liquor could not provide adequate treatment. Many of the victims needed expensive medical equipment to help them breathe and keep the poison from overwhelming their system. The public hospitals, however, had neither the staff nor machines to keep the men alive. It's tragic but true that

India has a dual health care system: There's superb private care for those who can afford it and the bare minimum of treatment for those who cannot. (Source of information: Somini Sengupta, "Royal Care for Some of India's Patients, Neglect for Others," *New York Times*, June 1, 2008, p. 3.)

a. time order

b. simple listing

c. definition

d. cause and effect

e. comparison and contrast

f. classification

4. Having seen elephants only occasionally in a zoo or on a movie screen, most people don't realize how different Asian and African elephants really are. African elephants are the much bigger and heavier of the two. They are the ones with huge, floppy ears. Asian elephants, in comparison, have much smaller ears. They also have shorter tusks and smoother skin. The skin of the African elephant is wrinkled and thicker. In terms of personality, African elephants have been known to display a nasty temper while Asian ones are said to be more docile and trainable. The two animals also differ in their trunks. The African elephant has two finger-like pieces of skin at the end of its trunk. These two "fingers" help elephants pick up small objects, like peanuts, from the ground. Asian elephants have only one finger at the end of their trunks, not two. When it comes to the threat of extinction, it's the African elephant whose roamable habitat has been steadily reduced by the spread of farming and building and whose numbers have dramatically diminished in the last two decades.

a. time order

b. simple listing

c. definition

d. cause and effect

e. comparison and contrast

f. classification

5. Depending on how the skin has been broken or punctured, there are six different types of wounds: abrasions, incisions, lacerations,

punctures, avulsions, and amputations. With an abrasion, the top layer of the skin is rubbed or scraped off against a rough surface like a piece of rope or carpet. Because the wound from abrasion is large and open, the chance for infection is higher. Incisions are made by sharp instruments like knives, razors, or glass. Of the six wounds, incisions are the least likely to become infected because the blood flowing from an incision washes away bacteria-causing infection. Laceration wounds, such as those made by a dull knife, are jagged and deep and involve a good deal of tissue damage. This makes it likely for lacerations to be followed by an infection. Puncture wounds are also caused by objects that penetrate the body's tissue, but they leave a smaller surface opening. Puncture wounds are made by nails, needles, wire, and bullets, all of which are likely to carry bacteria that lead to infection. Avulsion wounds result when tissue is forcibly torn from the body, producing heavy bleeding. Avulsion wounds are typical of the wounds that occur in auto accidents. In some cases, it is possible to surgically reattach the torn tissue. With amputation wounds, entire limbs are accidentally torn from the body when, for instance, a finger or hand gets caught in a piece of machinery.

a. time order

b. simple listing

c. definition

d. cause and effect

e. comparison and contrast

f. classification

▶ **TEST 5**　　　**Recognizing Mixed Patterns in Longer Readings**

> **DIRECTIONS**　Circle the appropriate letter or letters to identify the pattern or patterns of organization in the following readings.

1. Norman Rockwell's Rising Reputation

1　For most of his professional career, painter and illustrator Norman Rockwell (1894–1978) was treated as something of a stepchild by the established art world. The public loved his portraits of small-town life. Art critics, however, considered Rockwell's work technically good but creatively worthless. For them, he was the "King of Kitsch."[†] In their eyes, Rockwell shamelessly tried to satisfy the public's desire to see the world through rose-colored glasses. Rockwell's critics claimed his work lacked the mystery and subtlety of great art. But in the end, Rockwell may have the last laugh. As is so often the case with artists despised during their lifetimes, a new generation of art critics has begun to reevaluate the work of Norman Rockwell.

2　Born in 1894, Rockwell showed a gift for drawing early on. By the age of 18, he was already supporting himself working as an illustrator. In 1916, when he was only 22 years old, Rockwell created his first cover for the weekly magazine *Saturday Evening Post*. He would go on to create a total of eight hundred covers for popular magazines. Of those eight hundred covers, more than three hundred were for the *Post*. Clearly hungry for Rockwell's vision of the world, people couldn't seem to get enough portrayals of happy families eagerly anticipating Thanksgiving turkey, kids paddling in swimming holes, or little girls contentedly cradling their dolls. As the United States and Europe slid into first an economic depression and then a brutal war, Norman Rockwell assured his public that the world was still a sane, safe, and fairly simple place.

3　It's not surprising, then, that Rockwell's work has often been compared to that of his contemporary, Walt Disney, the creator of Mickey Mouse and countless animated films. Disney was a big fan of Rockwell's. Judged by their work, both men seemed to have had a similar view of the world. While Rockwell painted what he described as "life as I would like it to be," Disney offered up a cartoon world where animated characters effortlessly survived every threat to health and happiness.

4　Naturally, Rockwell's link to Disney made him seem even more suspicious to members of the art world. Because of it, he was viewed as an entertainer rather than an artist. Probably for that reason, the Museum of Modern Art

---

†kitsch: corny and sentimental.

never once included Rockwell in exhibitions devoted to modern art. Respected museums generally didn't think Rockwell was fit to be seen alongside "real" artists.

5   Given his treatment at the hands of art critics, Rockwell might have been happy to learn that the current crop of critics does not necessarily share the old views. Biographer and art critic Laura Claridge, for example, insists that Rockwell has much in common with the great seventeenth-century Dutch painter Jan Vermeer (1632–1675). Claridge insists that Rockwell, like Vermeer, gave ordinary objects and settings a spiritual meaning. In Rockwell's paintings, families seated around the dinner table may have suggested more than life's simple pleasures. They represented a heroic determination to create a safe haven* in a world gone mad from hunger and war. Such interpretations may seem strained to those used to dismissing Rockwell as a popular hack. Nevertheless, these interpretations are more frequent than ever before. If the current trend persists, Norman Rockwell's work may finally end up hanging in the great museums of the world.

a. time order

b. simple listing

c. definition

d. cause and effect

e. comparison and contrast

f. classification

2. "Moonshine" Lives On

1 The manufacture of the strong country whiskey known as moonshine, hooch, and white lightning began in the Appalachian Mountains in the 1700s. Scots-Irish immigrants arriving in America brought with them their recipes for brewing sugar and yeast into a powerful drink. Unfortunately for those involved in moonshining, the United States began taxing liquor in 1781. To avoid having to pay these taxes, descendants of those original Scots-Irish settlers began making their spirits in secret after dark. From this nighttime necessity, the term *moonshining* was coined.

2   The practice of moonshining continued throughout the Civil War and beyond. It particularly thrived during the 1930s, when Prohibition[†] laws forbade the selling of alcohol. In the 1960s and 1970s, even legalized liquor

---

*haven: place of rest and safety.
[†]Prohibition: the period (1920–1933) when the 18th Amendment forbade the manufacture and sale of alcohol.

sales in southern cities did not put an end to the homebrews. On the contrary, even today, some southern towns—for example, New Prospect, South Carolina; and Dawsonville, Georgia—celebrate their moonshining heritage with annual festivals. Many Southerners still keep a bottle under the sink. At the same time, though, federal and state alcohol-control agents are cracking down on bootleg whiskey makers. In 2001, agents wrapped up Operation Lightning Strike, an eight-year series of raids that put twenty-seven major moonshiners out of business.

3   The government is persistent about eliminating moonshine for several reasons. First, moonshiners don't pay taxes. They wouldn't even consider it, and the U.S. government does not smile on tax evasion. Then, too, the large-scale manufacture of moonshine often leads to other crimes, such as money laundering.[†] In addition, bootleg whiskey can be a health hazard. Moonshiners have used old truck radiators as stills,[*] and some brewers get their water from creeks that cattle walk through. As a result, moonshine has sometimes been contaminated with dangerous toxins, such as radiator fluid and lye. The production process can also accidentally create wood alcohol, which can cause blindness if drunk.

4   Despite these health concerns, though, there has been a market for moonshine in both the South and the North for more than three hundred years. People like bootleg liquor because it's cheap. A gallon jug of home-brew is 50 percent alcohol, yet it costs only $20 to $30 per gallon. That's half the price of legal whiskey. Over the centuries, moonshine has also been one of the most valuable trading goods for poor rural Southerners. In an odd way, moonshine also enjoys a certain mystique.[*] Those who make it often consider themselves to be daredevil descendants of Robin Hood. They see themselves as unwilling to bow their heads to the rule of an unjust law. Furthermore, many people believe the illegal brew tastes better than commercial liquors.

a. time order

b. simple listing

c. definition

d. cause and effect

e. comparison and contrast

f. classification

[†]money laundering: using illegally earned money in a noncriminal enterprise so that the money appears to be legally earned.
[*]stills: apparatus for purifying liquids such as alcohol.
[*]mystique: mystery.

▶ **TEST 6** **Recognizing Mixed Patterns in Longer Readings**

> **DIRECTIONS** Circle the appropriate letter or letters to identify the pattern or patterns of organization in the following readings.

1. "Hybrids" Make Good Sense

1 The Toyota Prius and Honda Insight are gasoline-and-electric-powered cars called "hybrids." They work by getting power from both a gasoline engine and an electric motor. First, the car's batteries feed power to the electric motor. This motor gets the car moving. Then, when the car's speed reaches 15 miles per hour, the gasoline engine takes over. This engine begins sending power to a generator. In turn, the generator feeds power to the electric motor and the batteries. As the car continues to accelerate, the batteries send power to the electric motor, which increases the gasoline engine's performance. Finally, as the car slows down, the electric motor transfers energy from the spinning axles and uses it to recharge the batteries.

2 Relying on two sources of energy—gasoline and electricity—results in amazing fuel efficiency. In the city, both cars average 60 miles per gallon. Consequently, owners of these cars realize big savings at the gas pump. Someone who switched to a hybrid car from a small car like a Honda Civic would save about $500 a year on fuel. Someone who switched to a hybrid from a less fuel-efficient vehicle would save even more.

3 Because hybrid cars use so much less fuel than traditional cars, they could help reduce or even eliminate America's dependence on foreign oil. If everyone in this country drove a hybrid, we would need fewer barrels of oil per year. Hybrids would allow us to take care of our own energy needs. We would no longer have to buy fuel from other countries.

4 Hybrids also produce a third positive effect: They are much less damaging to the environment than traditional cars. They do not emit as many polluting gases. They also generate only half of the carbon dioxide released by other cars. Cars that produce less of that particular gas could help slow or even stop global warming. Given the benefits of hybrid cars, the public needs to pressure automakers into producing more of them at cheaper prices. If hybrids were more affordable, more people would buy them, and the whole world would reap the reward of cleaner air.

a. time order

b. simple listing

    c. definition

    d. cause and effect

    e. comparison and contrast

    f. classification

2. **The Sinking of the *Andrea Doria***

1   The *Andrea Doria*, named after one of Italy's great sea captains, was among the fastest ships in the world when she made her maiden voyage in January 1953. Just three and a half years later, though, she collided with the *Stockholm* and sank to the bottom of the sea.

2   The last voyage of the *Andrea Doria* began on July 17, 1956, in Genoa, Italy. After stops in Cannes, Naples, and Gibraltar, the ship headed out to sea on July 20 for what would have been her fifty-first crossing to New York City. She carried 1,134 passengers and 572 crew members. The voyage was routine until July 25. On that day, dense fog formed off the Massachusetts coast, so the captain reduced the ship's speed. At 9:30 p.m., the *Andrea Doria*'s crew noticed a blip on the radar screen. That blip was the *Stockholm*, a Swedish passenger liner that had left New York at 11:31 that morning. It was seventeen miles away, but the two ships were headed directly toward each other. Heeding the signal, the captain of the *Andrea Doria* ordered a change of course. Then, during the next hour and a half, the *Andrea Doria*'s crew continued to monitor the radar and make adjustments to their own course. Tragically, crew members misinterpreted the radar information. A little after 11:00 p.m., crews on each ship could see the other vessel's lights through binoculars. The *Andrea Doria*'s crew blew the foghorn, but the two captains' attempts to evade each other had actually resulted in a collision course. At 11:11 p.m., about fifty miles south of Nantucket Island, the *Stockholm* crashed into the side of the *Andrea Doria*.

3   The impact ripped open the *Andrea Doria*'s steel hull. A number of luxury cabins and a garage containing automobiles were demolished. The ship's fuel tanks were ruptured, and water began pouring in. The *Stockholm* reversed its engines and pulled back. But the *Andrea Doria*'s deep gash was a mortal wound. Within a minute, the ship began to lean as seawater continued to flood into the hole. Engineers aboard the *Andrea Doria* could find no way to stop the flooding, so the captain ordered the crew to begin loading passengers aboard lifeboats. He also sent out a distress signal. Several ships responded and began heading to the scene. The French passenger liner *Ile de France* and the freighter *Cape Ann* were the first two

ships to arrive, at about 2:00 a.m. Along with the *Stockholm*, these ships rescued about 1,600 of those aboard the *Andrea Doria*. Fifty-two people were killed in the collision. At 9:45 a.m. on July 26, the *Andrea Doria* capsized.* At 10:09 a.m., eleven hours after being hit, she was swallowed by the sea.

4   Today the *Andrea Doria* lies 230 feet below the ocean's surface, where she is a favorite destination of scuba divers. The first divers descended just one day after the ship sank. A month later, *Life* magazine sent a team of diver-photographers to bring back pictures and artifacts from the ship's watery grave. The dive is dangerous because the water is deep. Divers can stay for only twenty minutes, and then they must decompress carefully for ninety minutes on their way back to the surface. The interior of the seven-hundred-foot-long ship is also vast and dark, so divers can get disoriented while inside. During the summer of 1998 alone, three divers died while exploring the wreck. Despite the danger, though, divers are attracted to the hunt for treasure aboard the doomed liner.

a. time order
b. simple listing
c. definition
d. cause and effect
e. comparison and contrast
f. classification

---

*capsized: overturned.

▶ **TEST 7**   **Recognizing Mixed Patterns in Longer Readings**

DIRECTIONS   Circle the appropriate letter to identify the pattern or patterns. Then answer the question about what's important in the reading.

1. The Difference Between Data and Information

1   Many people use the terms *data* and *information* interchangeably, but the two differ in important ways. **Data** are numerical or verbal descriptions that usually result from some sort of measurement. (The word *data* is plural; the singular form is *datum*.) Your current wage level, the amount of last year's after-tax profit for Hewlett Packard Computers, and the current retail prices of Honda automobiles are all data. Most people think of data as being numerical only, but they can be nonnumerical as well. A description of an individual as a "tall, athletic person with short, dark hair" certainly would qualify as data.

2   **Information** is data presented in a form useful for a specific purpose. Suppose that a human resources manager wants to compare the wages paid to male and female employees over a period of five years. The manager might begin with a stack of computer printouts listing every person employed by the firm, along with each employee's current and past wages. The manager would be hard-pressed to make any sense of all the names and numbers. Such printouts consist of data rather than information.

3   Now suppose that the manager uses a computer to graph the average wages paid to men and to women in each of the five years. . . . The result is information because the manager can use it for the purpose at hand—to compare wages paid to men with those paid to women over the five-year period. When summarized in the graph, the wage data from the printouts become information.

4   Large sets of data often must be summarized if they are to be useful, but this is not always the case. If the manager in our example had wanted to know only the wage history of a specific employee, that information would be contained in the original computer printout. That is, the data (the employee's name and wage history) already would be in the most useful form for the manager's purpose; they would need no further processing.

5   The average company maintains a great deal of data that can be transformed into information. Typical data include records pertaining to personnel, inventory, sales, and accounting. Often each type of data is stored in individual departments within an organization. However, the data can be used more effectively when they are organized into a

data   numerical or verbal descriptions that usually result from some sort of measurement

information   data presented in a form that is useful for a specific purpose

database a single collection of data stored in one place that can be used by people throughout an organization to make decisions

database. A **database** is a single collection of data stored in one place that can be used by people throughout an organization to make decisions. Today, most companies have several different types of databases. Often the data and information necessary to form a firm's databases are the result of business research activities. (Pride, Hughes, and Kapoor, *Business*, pp. 501–2.)

1. a. time order
   b. simple listing
   c. definition
   d. cause and effect
   e. comparison and contrast
   f. classification

2. Based on the pattern or patterns you chose, what should your notes on the reading record?

_____

_____

2. Grievance Procedures

grievance procedure a formally established course of action for resolving employee complaints against management

1 A **grievance procedure** is a formally established course of action for resolving employee complaints against management. Virtually every labor contract contains a grievance procedure. Procedures vary in scope and detail, but they may involve all four steps described below.

2 **Original Grievance** The process begins with an employee who believes that he or she has been treated unfairly, in violation of the labor contract. For example, an employee may be entitled to a formal performance review after six months on the job. If no such review is conducted, the employee may file a grievance. To do so, the employee explains the grievance to a

shop steward an employee elected by union members to serve as their representative

shop steward, an employee elected by union members to serve as their representative. The employee and the steward then discuss the grievance with the employee's immediate supervisor. Both the grievance and the supervisor's response are put in writing.

3 **Broader Discussion** In most cases the problem is resolved during the initial discussion with the supervisor. If it is not, a second discussion is held. Now the participants include the original parties (employee, supervisor, and steward), a representative from the union's grievance committee, and

the firm's industrial-relations representative. Again, a record is kept of the discussion and its results.

4 **Full-Scale Discussion** If the grievance is still not resolved, a full-scale discussion is arranged. This discussion includes everyone involved in the broader discussion, as well as all remaining members of the union's grievance committee and another high-level manager. As usual, all proceedings are put in writing. All participants are careful not to violate the labor contract during this attempt to resolve the complaint.

arbitration the step in a grievance procedure in which a neutral third party hears the two sides of a dispute and renders a decision

5 **Arbitration** The final step in a grievance procedure is arbitration, in which a neutral third party hears the grievance and renders a binding decision. As in a court hearing, each side presents its case and has the right to cross-examine witnesses. In addition, the arbitrator reviews the written documentation of all previous steps in the grievance procedure. Both sides may then give summary arguments and/or present briefs. The arbitrator then decides whether a provision of the labor contract has been violated and proposes a remedy. The arbitrator cannot make any decision that would add to, detract from, or modify the terms of the contract. If it can be proved that the arbitrator exceeded the scope of his or her authority, either party may appeal the decision to the courts. (Pride, Hughes, and Kapoor, *Business*, pp. 355–56.)

1. a. time order
   b. simple listing
   c. definition
   d. cause and effect
   e. comparison and contrast
   f. classification

2. Based on the pattern or patterns you chose, what should your notes on the reading record?

   _____

   _____

▶ **TEST 8**   **Developing Your Textbook Vocabulary**

DIRECTIONS   Fill in the blanks with one of the words listed below.

paramount	transient	entail	symbiotic	allocating
denounced	injunction	fertile	contention	denigrated

1. The judge issued a(n) _____ against the strike, insisting that a suspension of labor by the dockworkers could cause economic chaos.

2. With the coming of the locust, what had once been a(n) _____ plain now looked like a dried-up wasteland.

3. If it didn't _____ great difficulty, the plan was to move the meeting up a week so that everyone could attend.

4. The lawyer's _____ was that his client had been driven to violence by spousal abuse.

5. _____ in the minds of nineteenth-century Cuban rebels was the desire to break the grip of Spanish rule.

6. Not all _____ relationships are harmful; some actually benefit both sides or do no harm to either.

7. The young tourist tried hard to speak French, but the Parisians generally _____ her efforts; in the countryside, however, people seemed genuinely delighted by the girl's attempts to speak their language.

8. After the general was _____ as a traitor, several attempts were made on his life.

9. For one _____ moment, peace in the Middle East almost seemed possible, but the fighting resumed almost immediately.

10. When essential resources are scarce, _____ them fairly should be the key role of government.

From Comprehension to Critical Reading

IN THIS CHAPTER, YOU WILL LEARN

● how to identify informative and persuasive writing.

● how to tell the difference between fact and opinion.

● how to identify tone.

● how to evaluate bias.

To thoroughly understand a piece of writing, you almost always have to do more than understand the message. You also have to determine the author's purpose in writing. Is the author's primary purpose mainly to inform readers? Or did the author hope to persuade readers to share a particular point of view? Because the writer's choice of a persuasive or an informative purpose influences everything from content to word choice, that's where this chapter begins.

Informative versus Persuasive Writing

Overall, most writing falls into three categories: (1) writing meant to inform, (2) writing meant to persuade, and (3) writing meant to entertain. Writing intended to entertain is fairly easy to identify. Even if it doesn't amuse you, you can usually tell that it was written to make people laugh or at least smile. Knowing the difference between informative and persuasive writing can be a bit trickier. Sometimes what looks like informative writing actually has a pinch of persuasion mixed in. Thus, it's worth your while to have a clear understanding of the difference between informative and persuasive writing.

Characteristics of Informative Writing

Writers whose main purpose is to inform want to describe people, events, or ideas without judging them. Here, for example, is a passage where the author's intention is to inform, not judge:

> In December 2001, police in Cooper City, Florida, entered Audrey Weed's house after neighbors had complained that it was overrun by animals. According to the neighbors, Weed adopted stray cats and dogs. Based on the dirt and the smell, the neighbors were convinced that the strays had taken over the household. And they were right. Upon entry, police found sixty-seven dead kittens and cats in Audrey Weed's refrigerator. Numerous other cats and dogs were running loose in the house. In four similar cases in January 2002, police in North Miami-Dade County responded to complaints about pet-ridden homes in an area close to Weed's. As a result of these raids, police confiscated 201 cats and dogs, some of them terribly undernourished and obviously ill. In the end, ninety of the animals were put up for adoption. The remainder were destroyed. Both the raids and the results are not unusual. Incidents of "animal hoarding" are on the rise across the nation. (Source of information: Chris Colin, "Loving Animals to Death," *Salon*, March 8, 2002, www.salon.com.)

This passage has all the earmarks, or typical characteristics, of informative writing. When an author's writing is intended mainly to inform, it has the following features:

1. **The tone is impersonal. Tone** in writing is like a tone of voice in speech. It's a means of conveying a feeling, an attitude, or an emotion. Writers who want to persuade choose their tone carefully. They might choose to be friendly, puzzled, sarcastic, or sympathetic (for more words describing tone, see the chart on page 434). But writers who want mainly to inform usually keep their feelings to themselves and maintain an objective, neutral tone. Their language, in other words, reveals no emotion.

2. **The language is denotative. Denotative language** carries little or no emotional punch. Thus, relying on denotative language is perhaps the best way to maintain a neutral tone that describes events without making the reader react to them emotionally. The following sentence, for instance, relies on denotative language: "Both the raids and the results are not unusual." Sentences like this one are not meant to have a powerful emotional effect. For this reason, the writer tries to keep the language as denotative, or coolly factual, as possible.

3. **More facts than opinions are present. Facts** can be verified or checked for accuracy. Factual statements report on people, places, ideas, or events without evaluating or judging them. The first sentence of the sample paragraph on page 427 is a fact: "In December 2001, police in Cooper City, Florida, entered Audrey Weed's house after neighbors had complained that it was overrun by animals." This fact can be verified. You can look it up in archives, or collections of historical records.

Facts
◆

1. can be verified for accuracy.
2. rely on denotative or unemotional language.
3. are not shaped or affected by a writer's personality, background, or training.
4. frequently use numbers, statistics, dates, and measurements.
5. name and describe but do not evaluate.

4. **Main ideas describe but don't evaluate.** Purely informative writing generally does not evaluate the topic or issue under discussion. Thus, topic sentences like "William Randolph Hearst is widely considered the father of tabloid* journalism," "Scientists express concern about the future of the Amazon rainforest," and "Hollywood's star system began in the 1920s" could well turn up in writing meant purely to inform. These topic sentences are different from those likely to appear in persuasive pieces of writing—for example, "William Randolph Hearst made his fortune from tabloid journalism, and the newspaper industry has never recovered from his success," "If we lose the Amazon rainforest, we lose an untold number of remedies that might well have saved countless lives," and "The originality of American movies began to diminish in the 1920s when the star system took hold."

---

*tabloid: sensationalist newspaper, interested in gossip more than news.

Now compare the opening sentence of the sample paragraph on page 427 with the following one, which blends a little opinion in with the facts. "In December 2001, police in Cooper City, Florida, entered Audrey Weed's house and were confronted by a horrifying sight." In this sentence, the author doesn't merely describe events; she also tells readers how to view or respond to them. A house overrun with animals might be horrifying to some, merely unpleasant to others. It depends on the individual. That's why **opinions** can't be checked in reference books. There's never been an opinion that every single person in the world could agree on in the way that everyone agrees on the fact that water freezes at 32 degrees Fahrenheit.

Opinions
◆

1. cannot be verified for accuracy.
2. can only be labeled valid or invalid, sound or unsound, informed or uninformed, depending on the amount and type of support offered.
3. rely on emotionally charged language.
4. are affected by a writer's personality, background, and training.
5. frequently express comparisons using words such as *more*, *better*, *most*, and *least*.
6. often make value judgments suggesting that some action or event has a positive or negative effect.
7. are often introduced by verbs and adverbs that suggest doubt or possibility, such as *appears*, *seems*, *apparently*, *probably*, *potentially*, and *possibly*.

---

5. **Titles make no judgments.** In longer pieces of writing, the title often tells you a good deal about the author's purpose. Informative titles usually identify the subject matter without implying a point of view. Thus, titles like "Five Ways to Deal with Conflict," "Culture and Communication," and "Common Herbal Remedies" are typical of writing meant to inform.

6. **The writer remains distant from the audience.** Writers with an informative purpose in mind tend to keep their audience at a distance. They don't refer to themselves or their personal lives. Nor do they speak directly to the audience. They write as if they were speaking to people they did not know and whom they had just met at a business meeting or some other formal event.

⊶ **READING KEYS**

◆ Writers with an informative purpose are likely to use a cool, impersonal tone.

◆ Writers with an informative purpose do not use emotionally charged or highly connotative language.

◆ Informative writing relies heavily on factual statements that can be checked for accuracy and don't vary according to person or location.

◆ In informative writing, neither the title nor the main idea suggests a judgment.

IDIOM ALERT: Sacred cow

In parts of India, cows have a religious significance and are viewed as sacred. Thus they are objects of respect, even worship. That view of holy or sacred cows is the origin of the idiom *sacred cow*, which refers to a belief or an institution so widely viewed with respect that people get upset if someone criticizes it. Here's an example of how the idiom is used: "For those who worship the economist Milton Friedman, belief in the free market is a *sacred cow*, and even a hint of government intervention in the marketplace sends Friedmanites into a tizzy."

◆ **EXERCISE 1**   **Separating Fact from Opinion**

DIRECTIONS   Label each statement *F* (fact) or *O* (opinion).

EXAMPLE

__F__   a. The longest game in the history of Monday Night Football lasted four hours and ten minutes.

__O__   b. *The Fellowship of the Ring* was a wonderful book, but it was made into an even better movie.

EXPLANATION   Statement *a* is a fact. Its accuracy can be verified, or checked, against the *World Almanac and Book of Facts*. Any statement that can be verified true or false, correct or incorrect, is bound to be factual. Statement *b* is an opinion. There is no way to check every reader's opinion of *The Fellowship of the Ring*. Nor is it possible to survey every single person who saw the film.

_____ 1. On January 11, 2005, Venezuelan President Hugo Chavez signed a land reform decree.

_____ 2. Bears usually hibernate for a period of three to five months.

_____ 3. Nurses who have three years of advanced training in anesthesia are allowed to give anesthesia without a doctor's supervision.

_____ 4. Making tobacco companies pay for the damage caused by cigarettes is a superb form of justice.

_____ 5. Cervantes' *Don Quixote* can be read and enjoyed by both children and adults.

_____ 6. Parents whose children participate in organized sports have a responsibility to model good sportsmanship on the sidelines.

_____ 7. The collected letters of John Adams and Thomas Jefferson[†] reveal that Adams wrote two letters to every one of Jefferson's.

_____ 8. Smokers in this country are treated like second-class citizens.

_____ 9. In rejecting motherhood, she knew that she was challenging one of her family's sacred cows: All women want to have children.

_____ 10. The halfpipe is a snow-covered, U-shaped course that allows snowboarders to launch off a wall and perform tricks in the air.

VOCABULARY EXTRA

There's a big difference between holding a strong opinion and being *opinionated*. People who are *opinionated* often believe that their opinion is the only one that matters. But it's possible to hold a strong opinion and still listen to opposing points of view. In fact, that's what most of us strive for.

[†]Adams was the country's second president, Jefferson the third.

> **CLASS ACTION**
>
> Think of at least three more sacred cows that people are not inclined to criticize because belief in their value is so deeply entrenched in our society.

Characteristics of Persuasive Writing

In terms of topic, the following passage resembles the one on page 427. But because the writer intends to persuade rather than inform, there are differences in tone, word choice, selection of details, and relationship to the audience. As you read the passage, see if you can identify some of the characteristics of persuasive writing.

When people like Audrey Weed get their name in the paper, most of us react with knee-jerk sympathy. However, like most knee-jerk reactions, this may be a mistake. A self-proclaimed animal lover, Weed took in every stray animal she could find until neighbors' complaints brought the police to her door. When the police arrived, they found Weed's home overrun with cats and dogs. Some of the animals in the house were dead. For some unknown reason, Weed had stored their bodies in the refrigerator. Upon hearing Weed's story, we may be shocked and appalled, but we are more than likely to assume that Weed's behavior was motivated by good intentions. We view her as an eccentric* woman who went too far in her love for animals. At least, that's the traditional line of reasoning. However, people like Gary Patronek at the Center for Animals and Public Policy at Tufts University rightly want us to change our thinking. They argue convincingly that what's now called "animal hoarding" is a serious psychological malady. From this perspective, animal hoarding has negative effects on both the hoarders and the animals they claim to protect. Certainly, four similar raids conducted on homes not far from Weed's confirm that point of view. Of the 201 cats and dogs confiscated, only 90 of those animals were healthy enough to be adopted. The rest had to be destroyed. Audrey Weed was no animal lover.

---

*eccentric: odd.

Now compare your list of characteristics to the one that follows:

1. **The facts serve opinions.** Although informative writing can rely solely on facts, persuasive writing invariably includes an opinion. Certainly in the sample passage above, we can quickly identify the opinion the writer wants readers to share: Feeling sympathy for "self-proclaimed" animal lovers like Audrey Weed is probably a big mistake. Note, too, how the key opinion statement ("However, like most knee-jerk reactions, this may be a mistake") uses the words *may be*.

   Such phrases acknowledge that the writer is not dealing with hard facts. On the contrary, the phrases signal the presence of opinions. While facts can and do appear in persuasive writing, they are usually included to support the author's opinion.

2. **Language is emotionally charged.** Connotative language—language that calls up an emotional response—is one of several tools writers use to create a persuasive tone meant to make readers agree with their point of view. For instance, in the previous passage, Audrey Weed isn't just an animal lover, she is a "self-proclaimed," or self-titled, animal lover. This phrase suggests others might or might not agree with Audrey's view of herself. And those who support her might be doing so on the basis of a "knee-jerk reaction. A knee-jerk reaction is one that is based more on instinct and habit than on thought, and it is generally considered a poor way to evaluate behavior, events, or ideas. Thus, it discourages readers from sympathizing with Audrey Weed.

3. **Opinions are mixed in with facts.** Writers don't necessarily keep facts and opinions neatly separated. Writers mix the two together, by including a word or phrase that encourages a particular point of view, as in this example: "The revered* and recklessly brave civil rights activist Fannie Lou Hamer started life as a sharecropper who picked cotton instead of going to school." Hamer did pick cotton as a child. That's a fact. But not everyone revered her. Some people hated her. They didn't consider her "recklessly brave"; they thought she didn't know her place in the then-segregated South. The author, however, is clearly an admirer, and his opening words nudge readers into sharing his admiration.

---

*revered: treated or thought of with great respect.

4. **The tone expresses a feeling or an attitude.** Occasionally, authors persuade by assuming an impersonal tone while, at the same time, piling up facts that favor their side. But most persuasive writing employs a tone that conveys an attitude or feeling. For example, in the passage about Audrey Weed on page 432, the author's tone is critical, even slightly sarcastic.

And, yes, it's possible for different people to label tone in different ways—you might say "disbelieving," I might say "irritated"—the point is that the writer's words convey an attitude or emotion. When the words convey a feeling, the writing's purpose is likely to be persuasive.

Words That Describe Tone ◆		
admiring	disgusted	patriotic
amazed	doubtful	proud
angry	enthusiastic	puzzled
anxious	friendly	regretful
arrogant	humorous	respectful
breezy	insulted	rude
bullying	insulting	sarcastic
cautious	ironic (saying the opposite of what is intended)	self-pitying
challenging		serious
comical	neutral	shocked
confident	nostalgic (longing for a past time)	skeptical
critical		solemn
curious	objective	spiteful
cynical	outraged	sympathetic
determined	passionate	worried

5. **Titles take a stand.** If the title indicates a point of view, it's all but guaranteed that the writer has persuasion in mind. Thus, titles like "Boxing Needs Reform," "Whatever You Do, Don't Call the Psychic Hotline!" and "Internet Censorship Bound to Fail" all announce a persuasive purpose.

6. **Main ideas evaluate.** Main ideas like the following are tip-offs to a persuasive intent: "Our voting system needs to be revised so that there is a paper count of every vote cast"; "Movies like *Alexander* and *Troy* offer audiences a ridiculously distorted view of ancient history"; and "Fingerprint evidence is prone to more errors than most people realize." If the stated or implied main idea suggests how you should view the topic, then you can be sure you are dealing with persuasion.

7. **The writer's background reveals a personal connection.** Any time you have information about the writer's personal and professional background, you are in a better position to judge the writer's purpose as well as his or her **bias**, or personal leaning. If the writer of a magazine article seems to be objectively criticizing efforts to improve the inspection of beef and lists the National Beef Association as her affiliation, you should probably assume a persuasive purpose and a bias in favor of the beef association.

8. **Persuasive writers try to connect to the audience.** Writers who want to persuade are likely to address the audience—"How would you feel in this situation? Wouldn't you be outraged too?"—or assume a set of shared assumptions: "We Americans don't like rigid rules." They write as if they and the audience share a personal relationship or an understanding.

⊶ **READING KEYS**

◆ Writers who are trying to persuade focus on developing an opinion and use facts only to serve that opinion.
◆ Writers with a persuasive purpose are likely to use emotionally charged language.
◆ In persuasive writing, even seemingly factual statements are likely to include some opinion.
◆ In persuasive writing, both titles and main ideas take a stand.
◆ If the author's background suggests that he or she has a personal connection to the topic under discussion, the writing is probably persuasive.
◆ Writers with a persuasive purpose try to connect with their audience.
◆ Inferring purpose is like drawing any other inference. You have to study what the author actually says or reveals. Then you have to use that information as the basis for inferring the purpose.

◆ **EXERCISE 2** **Separating Opinion from Fact**

DIRECTIONS Read each statement. Then label each one *F* (fact), *O* (opinion), or *B* (both).

EXAMPLE

_____B_____ a. A jury justly convicted a pair of dog owners for murder when the owners' dogs attacked and killed someone.

_F_ b. After the September 11, 2001, attack on New York's World Trade Center, the actress Julia Roberts donated $1 million to the fund set up for victims' families.

EXPLANATION Statement _a_ doesn't just tell you that a jury convicted two dog owners of murder. With the word _justly_, it also tells you how to feel about that conviction. Statement _b_, however, limits itself to who, when, and how much. There's no attempt to evaluate the generous action.

_____ 1. In his book _Blink_, writer Malcolm Gladwell correctly asserts that snap judgments deserve more respect.

_____ 2. The Supreme Court ruled that the Americans with Disabilities Act does not require companies to alter assembly lines in order to suit disabled workers.

_____ 3. Surprising as it may seem, Oprah Winfrey is probably the most influential woman in America.

_____ 4. The Chinese government sentenced Christian pastor Gong Shengliang to death for the supposed "crime" of practicing Christianity.

_____ 5. Oddly enough for a state so liberal, Massachusetts has the lowest divorce rate in the nation.

_____ 6. A federal judge has ruled that fingerprinting, a respected tool of crime fighting, has never been proven to be scientifically valid.

_____ 7. Photographer Robert Frank's book _The Americans_ was first published in France because no American publisher wanted it.

_____ 8. Every minute, 149 acres of rainforest are destroyed through clear-cutting of trees.

_____ 9. For close to 15 percent of the American population, Spanish is the mother tongue.

_____ 10. The record weight for a black bear is 880 pounds.

◆ **EXERCISE 3**   **Identifying Tone**

DIRECTIONS   Read each passage. Then identify the author's tone.

EXAMPLE   Though it's been off the air for six years now, *Buffy the Vampire Slayer* lives on, in the theses of hundreds of culture studies grad students, in a series of comic books by creator Joss Whedon . . . in seemingly countless spin-off novels, and . . . in fan fiction. But Buffy persists in other, less obvious ways as well. Whedon's original idea, to take "the little blonde girl who goes into a dark alley and gets killed in every horror movie" and make her the hero of the story, mutated into a remarkably flexible and inventive* way to portray the terrors of adolescence. The supernatural elements of the stories provided Buffy and her friends with more than just monsters to kill; they served as metaphors for everyday identity crises and social anxieties, most famously when Buffy and her boyfriend, the redeemed* vampire, Angel, consummate their love, whereupon a gypsy curse renders him suddenly cruel and hateful. (Laura Miller, "The Spirit of the Vampire Slayer Lives On," *Salon*, www.salon.com/books/feature/2009/06/23/vampire_fiction/.)

The writer's tone is

a. critical.

b. objective.

c. solemn.

d. admiring.

EXPLANATION   The author clearly expresses her admiration in calling the television program *Buffy the Vampire Slayer* "a remarkably flexible and inventive way to portray the terrors of adolescence." Calling a story line "flexible" and "inventive" is already high praise. But when the author adds the modifier "remarkably," the tone becomes even more positive. The tone is not just in the word choice, though. It's also in the author's careful selection of details chosen to support her opinion: "The supernatural elements of the stories provided Buffy and her friends with *more* than just monsters to kill." In other words, *Buffy* was no ordinary horror story.

---

*inventive: original.
*redeemed: saved from sin.

1. Hunters hotly defend their right to kill wildlife. However, the reasons they offer to justify their "sport" are all self-serving myths. For instance, hunters claim that they pursue and shoot animals for meat. The Humane Society of the United States does not support this claim. The society's research shows that only 25 percent of hunters say they kill animals for the meat. A large number, 43 percent, say they kill purely for recreation. In America, most hunters are not killing to put food on the table for their families, no matter what they claim. Hunters would also like us to believe that they help to control wildlife populations. However, the majority of animal species—both those that are hunted and those that are not—rarely become overpopulated. When left alone, Nature herself corrects species overpopulation. She doesn't require the bloodthirsty help of hunters. Claiming to be doing an animal a favor by shooting it is another flimsy reason offered by those who love the hunt. Yet hunters don't gun for weak, sick animals—the ones most likely to succumb in a harsh winter. Instead, they aim for the large, strong, trophy* animals, despite the fact that these are the ones that would be least likely to starve to death. Finally, hunters want us to believe that they know what they're doing. But if they do, how is it that they accidentally kill or injure thousands of people every year? They also wound or kill livestock and family pets. During hunting season, the woods aren't safe for anyone. Thanks to hunters on the prowl, hikers and campers must fear for their lives if they want to enjoy the outdoors.

   The writer's tone is
   a. objective.
   b. angry.
   c. puzzled.
   d. relaxed.

2. In 1989, North Dakota state senator Tim Mathern proposed that his state's name be shortened to just plain "Dakota." Unfortunately, his suggestion was defeated by the state legislature. Still, the idea is a good one and deserves reconsideration. Words are powerful. They influence people's perceptions.* The word *North* suggests to many that the state's primary characteristic is its cold weather. As a

---

*trophy: prize.
*perceptions: thoughts, views.

result, most people avoid visiting or even passing through the state. Because of its frigid image, North Dakota ranks forty-ninth in tourist revenues and does not attract much industry. Mathern was smart to try to combat the state's image with a name change.

The writer's tone is

a. objective.

b. annoyed.

c. admiring.

d. concerned.

3. Normally, there's something about a dog show that deeply offends me. Maybe it's the sight of smirking poodles being combed, primped, and fluffed till they look less like dogs and more like ruffled lampshades. Or maybe it's just that having owned mutts for most of my life, I don't like the idea that none of my dogs would have been allowed in the ring, never mind awarded a ribbon. However, I must say that on at least one night, Westminster Kennel Club Dog Show at Madison Square Garden was something special. The night was in February of 2002, only a few short months after the September 11, 2001, terrorist attack that changed our country, maybe even the world, forever. The night I attended, the guests of honor were the human and canine members of the K-9 rescue unit. Together, the dogs and their masters had risked their lives to search for victims of the tragedy. The dogs present that night included German shepherds, retrievers, and one lone border collie. And no, the dogs probably weren't prize winners when it came to size of paw or length of ear. But I have to give the normally fussy audience credit. They knew better than to care about such trivia. They knew heroes when they saw them. As the dogs came trotting out, making sure to stay close to their handlers, the crowd went wild. Ten thousand people rose in unison to give the dogs and their trainers a standing ovation. The human members of the rescue unit smiled proudly. Even the dogs seemed to be pleased with themselves. There probably wasn't a dry eye in the house.

The writer's tone is

a. objective.

b. admiring.

c. surprised.

d. cynical.

4. Thankfully, many schools across the nation are finally deciding to enforce "zero tolerance" policies that dictate harsh, automatic punishments for students who bring drugs or weapons to school. Some mistakenly criticize these policies as too harsh or unreasonable. However, the policies are both effective and fair, and schools must keep them in place, despite pleas from soft-hearted parents. With zero tolerance policies in effect, students know that they will be expelled and placed in another school if they bring guns or illegal drugs to campus. As a result, most choose to refrain from breaking the rules, making schools safer places for everyone. If schools did not have zero tolerance policies in place, their halls would be filled with students carrying guns, selling drugs, and fighting. No one would be able to learn a thing in the resulting chaos. Maintaining a tough stance on serious infractions is not only effective but also much fairer than previous policies. In the past, school discipline has been arbitrary* and inconsistent. Zero tolerance, however, is based solely on behavior and not on other factors, such as the student's race, past record, or relationships with school employees. Therefore, it is more just. Establishing a universal zero tolerance policy also protects schools against lawsuits. Parents are less likely to sue schools for not keeping their children safe. Furthermore, parents of children who violate the rules cannot claim that their kids are victims of discrimination.

The writer's tone is

a. objective.

b. good-natured.

c. confident.

d. outraged.

◆ **EXERCISE 4**   **Determining Purpose**

DIRECTIONS   Read each pair of thesis statements. Label each one *I* (informative) or *P* (persuasive).

_____

*arbitrary: determined by chance.

EXAMPLE

_P___ a. Consumers do not want a world of endless and confusing choices.

_I___ b. From deodorant to cereals, consumer choices have tripled in the last ten years.

EXPLANATION   Statement _a_ is persuasive because it does more than describe events; it offers a point of view on them: Consumers don't want a lot of confusing choices. Statement _b_, however, simply describes how events have unfolded over the last decade.

_____ 1. a. In his prison memoir _You Got Nothing Coming: Notes from a Prison Fish_, Jimmy A. Lerner, a former marketing executive, claims that life in corporate America was the perfect preparation for survival in prison.

_____   b. Not surprisingly, Jimmy A. Lerner's critically acclaimed memoir, _You Got Nothing Coming: Notes from a Prison Fish_, suggests there are many similarities between criminal and corporate behavior.

_____ 2. a. Karl Marx and Max Weber disagreed as to how they viewed power. Marx linked it to wealth; Weber thought power could be independent of wealth.

_____   b. When it comes to the relationship between power and wealth, Karl Marx has been proven correct and Max Weber wrong.

◆ EXERCISE 5   Determining Purpose

DIRECTIONS   Read each passage. Then identify the purpose, using _P_ for persuasive and _I_ for informative.

EXAMPLE

a. One major goal of the animal rights group People for the Ethical Treatment of Animals (PETA) is to get everyone on the planet to become a vegan, a person who does not eat animal products of any kind. To achieve this goal, PETA conducts anti-meat campaigns.

By means of TV commercials, billboards, bumper stickers, and leaflets, the organization educates people about the virtues of a meatless diet. The group also makes presentations to schoolchildren, often bringing with them descriptions and photographs of slaughterhouses, as well as literature about the dangers of eating meat. Although they have been criticized for terrorizing children with pictures of animal slaughter, PETA members say they do not want to frighten children. The goal is to make them aware of how animal products arrive on their plate. The organization's hope is that children will then choose not to eat meat. (Sources of information: Jill A. Kennedy, *An Introduction to Ethics*, p. 188; Center for Consumer Freedom, "PETA Denies 'Traumatizing' Kids," June 3, 2004, www.consumerfreedom.com; Philip Brasher, "Hates Meat, Loves Animals," *Des Moines Register*, March 7, 2004.)

____ I

b. We members of the National Poultry Producers Association support and always strive for the humane treatment of animals. Just like animal rights groups such as People for the Ethical Treatment of Animals (PETA), we are concerned about animal welfare and are careful to avoid any form of animal cruelty. However, that's where the similarity ends. While it's understandable that some people object to eating meat on ethical grounds, PETA's anti-animal products campaigns often go too far in trying to win converts. For example, the organization's campaign coordinator Matt Rice has claimed, "We would never use shock tactics with children; it wouldn't be right." Yet, in reality, Rice's organization aims some of its most ghastly campaigns directly at kids. In 2004, for example, PETA announced its plan to distribute "Buckets of Blood" to children outside middle schools and KFC fried chicken restaurants. These "toys"—which might well horrify an adult, let alone a vulnerable child—included a bloody plastic chicken and a caricature of a blood-splattered Colonel Sanders threatening a frightened bird with a butcher knife. (Sources of information: *Animal News*, December 12, 2004, p. 26; Center for Consumer Freedom, "PETA Denies 'Traumatizing' Kids," June 3, 2004, www.consumerfreedom.com; Philip Brasher, "Hates Meat, Loves Animals," *Des Moines Register*, March 7, 2004.)

____ P

EXPLANATION   Paragraph *a* is guided by an informative purpose. The language is largely denotative and the author's tone neutral. Overall, the author describes PETA's anti-meat campaign without passing judgment. Paragraph *b* is quite different. Here the author's purpose is persuasive. This is clear from the presence of words with strong connotations, such as "ghastly campaigns," "horrify," and "vulnerable child." The opinion the author wants readers to share is also clearly stated: "While it's understandable that some people object to eating meat on ethical grounds, PETA's anti-animal products campaigns often go too far in trying to win converts."

1. Beginning in the 1960s, the religious movement known as "liberation* theology"* has had widespread influence in Latin America and the Caribbean. The former president of Haiti, Jean-Bertrand Aristide, is a well-known practitioner, as was the former archbishop of El Salvador, Oscar Romero. At its core, liberation theology insists on linking Christianity to political activism in the service of social justice and human rights. Thus, Haiti's Aristide came to office vowing to improve the lives of Haiti's poor, while Romero was shot to death for using his pulpit to speak out against the government's use of violence against the poor. Focusing on the role of Jesus as liberator, supporters of liberation theology quote those portions of the Bible that emphasize Jesus' attempts to help the poor and the downtrodden. Before his death in 2005, Pope John Paul II openly spoke out against liberation theology and ordered its followers, most of whom were Catholics, to cease their activities or risk excommunication from the church.

2. Archbishop Oscar Romero was probably the most famous practitioner of liberation theology. But it was Gustavo Gutiérrez who, in the 1960s and 1970s, gave the movement its start. Gutiérrez argued for committed Christian action in response to the poverty and pain of the millions barely earning a living in Third World countries. And there were many who heard Gutiérrez's call. It became commonplace, especially in Latin America and the Caribbean, for priests and nuns to take part in trade union politics and community organizations. From the perspective of these Catholic workers, it was sinful

*liberation: the act of setting free.
*theology: study of religion.

to care for people's souls without paying attention to their need for food, shelter, and dignity. Living, and often dying, in service to the poor, liberation theologians have become the true disciples of Jesus.

―――

3. Colleges and universities should no longer use the Scholastic Aptitude Test (SAT) to determine whether to accept an applicant for admission. The test is unable to assess what students have actually studied and learned. As one university president put it, "The SAT sends a confusing message. It says that students will be tested on material that is unrelated to what they study in their classes." It makes no sense to rely so heavily on a test score that measures only a small fraction of the knowledge and skills students have acquired. Getting rid of the SAT would force colleges and universities to more thoroughly evaluate each applicant. The SAT makes it too easy for admissions officers to look only at test scores when deciding whom to accept. Without SAT scores, schools would put more weight on each applicant's grades, participation in extracurricular activities, special talents, and accomplishments outside school. Eliminating the test would encourage college officials to develop a more complete portrait of each individual. Then they would make fairer admissions decisions.

―――

4. One of the architects of modern American education, Harvard President James Bryant Conant, wanted to develop a test that could identify those who would do well in elite colleges. With this type of test Conant believed that admission to school could be based on natural ability rather than wealth or class privilege. In 1933 Conant assigned two assistants, Wilber Bender and Henry Chauncey, the task of developing a test that could be used to select students for college. They, in turn, got in touch with Carl Brigham, who had developed the Scholastic Aptitude Test, a college admissions test, which was not widely used. State universities, in particular, used no standardized test at the time. But it wasn't until the end of World War II that Conant really pushed through the nationwide use of the SAT and the establishment of the Educational Testing Service.

―――

◆ **EXERCISE 6**   **Determining Purpose**

DIRECTIONS   Read each passage. Then identify the purpose, using *I* for informative or *P* for persuasive.

EXAMPLE   Many schools believe it's a good idea to keep children in kindergarten if their academic performance is weak. However, there are good reasons not to hold back kids who struggle in school. One of these reasons is the educational leap children often experience toward the end of their kindergarten year. A child who struggles throughout kindergarten may very well make up his or her lack of progress at the end of kindergarten, over the summer, or even during first grade. Another reason is the lack of progress kids make when they are held back. Sandra Rief, author of *Ready . . . Start . . . School!*, says, "Children who are retained may do better at first, but many fall behind again if their areas of weakness haven't been addressed." Being held back also carries a social stigma, which aggravates the problem. Children who are teased by their peers for being held back begin to dislike school. If teachers insist on retaining kindergarteners, they should prepare themselves for soaring dropout rates as these kids fall behind, become frustrated, and start thinking they can't learn. (Source of quotation: Vicky Mlyniec, "Should Your Child Repeat Kindergarten?" *Parents*, February 2002, pp. 137–38).

  P
  ———

EXPLANATION   The author has a definite opinion: Keeping kids back in kindergarten is not a sound practice. She then offers readers some reasons for her position. In other words, her goal is to convince.

1. The last time several different European countries had a single currency was in the eighth century. At that time, Charlemagne[†] commanded all members of the Holy Roman Empire to use the silver penny. As the empire weakened and fragmented, though, local rulers took over the power to mint coins. Over the next several centuries, different countries created different currencies. The French used the franc, the Germans the deutsche mark, the Spanish the peseta, the Italians the lira, and the Greeks the drachma. Not until January 1999

[†]Charlemagne (742?–814): founder of the first empire in Western Europe after the fall of Rome.

did Germany, France, Belgium, Luxembourg, Spain, Italy, Portugal, Ireland, Austria, Finland, and the Netherlands officially adopt a new common currency, the euro. Two years later, Greece joined the group. On January 1, 2002, the individual currencies of these twelve nations disappeared, replaced by euro notes and coins.

———

2. In January 2005, a 66-year-old Romanian woman delivered a baby girl and became the oldest woman in the world to ever give birth. Although no longer fertile, Adriana Iliescu was artificially made pregnant by having sperm and eggs from anonymous donors injected into her body. Although it's hard not to applaud the birth of a child, this does seem the time to ask a crucial question: Has science gone too far? True, the artificial impregnation was successful and Iliescu initially carried triplets. But she lost one fetus after nine weeks, and a second baby died in the womb. The one surviving child was born six weeks premature. Weighing just over three pounds, the infant was less than half the weight of a typical newborn and had to begin her life in the hospital's intensive care unit. Bishop Ciprian Campineanul, a member of the Orthodox Church's bioethics committee, not surprisingly, pronounced Iliescu's decision to have a child "selfish." Iliescu's daughter will probably still be young when her mother dies or becomes incapable of taking care of her. Of course, there is no guarantee that any child will not become an orphan, but this infant's chances are certainly much higher than normal. (Source of quotation: Associated Press, "Romanian Woman, 66, Gives Birth to Baby Girl," MSNBC.com, January 17, 2005, www.msnbc.msn.com/id/6835044.)

———

3. While serving almost forty-four years in prison for murder, Wilbert Rideau became a self-educated, award-winning journalist. At age 19, Rideau, an eighth-grade dropout, decided that bank robbery was his ticket out of poverty. On February 16, 1961, he held up a Louisiana bank and took three employees hostage, shooting all three of them and stabbing bank teller Julia Ferguson to death. Police arrested him about eighty minutes later. Rideau gave a videotaped confession the next day and has never denied committing the crime. However, he claimed that panic drove him to do what he did. Nevertheless, he was convicted and sentenced to death. On death row at the Louisiana

State Penitentiary, he spent his time reading and learning to write. "I didn't want a criminal act to be the final definition of me," Rideau said. "I picked up a pen and tried to do something good." In 1976, he became editor of *The Angolite*, the prison magazine. A year later, it became the first prison publication to be nominated for the National Magazine Awards, and it went on to win several other awards, including the Robert F. Kennedy Journalism Award. Rideau also wrote and narrated an award-winning National Public Radio documentary and co-directed the Oscar®-nominated prison documentary *The Farm*. Throughout these years, Rideau's conviction was overturned three separate times. Juries in three new trials still found him guilty, but his sentence was commuted to life in prison when the Supreme Court outlawed existing death penalty laws in 1972. In his fourth and final trial, a jury convicted him of the lesser charge of manslaughter, and he was released in 2005 because of the time he had already served. (Source of quotation: Janet McConnaughey, "Wilbert Rideau's Complex Path to Freedom," Newsday.com, January 16, 2005, www.newsday.com/news/nationworld/nation/ wire, sns-ap-prison-journalist-profile,0,1170940.story.)

———

4. A recent study conducted by the National Institute for Health Care Management indicates that heavy advertising of prescription medicines causes consumers to spend billions more dollars on those drugs. Such advertising is obviously unethical. The U.S. Food and Drug Administration must revise the laws that allow big drug companies to take advantage of people in this way. Drug companies want us to believe that they are doing us all a favor by turning heavily promoted drugs like Vioxx, Celebrex, Zocor, Paxil, and Prozac into household words. Honestly, though, the companies know that this advertising significantly increases their sales. That's the only reason they spend more on advertisements than PepsiCo spends to advertise Pepsi. As a result, the drug companies' ads encourage consumers to self-diagnose. Some patients visit their doctors mainly to request a certain medication by name.

———

5. In the United States, the Homeland Security Advisory System classifies the potential for terrorist attacks according to five color-coded levels. The "low" level of threat, green, indicates no threat of attack.

The "guarded" level, blue, indicates a general risk for terrorist attacks. When officials gather information suggesting the increased possibility for terrorist attacks, they raise the threat level to "elevated," designated by yellow. If intelligence indicates an even greater potential for attack, the risk level goes to "high," coded orange. At this level, evidence may indicate that terrorists are targeting a specific building. The fifth and highest level, red, indicates the "severe" level of threat. Officials use the red level when they have gathered specific, trustworthy information suggesting that an attack is imminent. (Source of information: "Homeland Security Advisory System," http://en.wikipedia.org/wiki/Homeland_Security_Advisory_System.)

When Bias Goes Overboard

The word *bias* has already been mentioned in this chapter. But it's time now to really focus on that subject. Bias, after all, is hard to escape. When a writer of a textbook says, "A 15-year-old teenager's social immaturity makes commitment difficult," there's a bit of personal bias tucked away in the statement. Not everyone would agree with it—particularly not most 15-year-olds. The point is *not* that you should refuse to read anything reflecting a bias. Instead, you should be on the lookout for bias, in order to evaluate its degree. You have to decide, that is, if the writer's bias interferes with his or her judgment and purpose. Writers who openly try to persuade need to be fair to the opposition, while writers who claim to inform should not express their personal point of view.

In evaluating bias, keep in mind the following criteria for judgment.

Writers with a bias that doesn't cloud their judgment or ability to be fair
1. will mention opposing points of view.
2. explain why they do not share the opposing points of view.
3. refuse to claim that everything on their side is good and everything on the opposition's side is bad.
4. readily acknowledge that the opposition has some good points.
5. use a confident tone that doesn't bully or badger.
6. never engage in name calling or sarcasm.

> Writers with a bias so strong you should double-check their facts
>
> 1. won't acknowledge an opposing point of view or may insist that the opposition is stupid, unpatriotic, crazy, weak, and so on.
> 2. will tell you that the opposition is wrong or misinformed without telling you why this is true.
> 3. insist that everyone feels the same way.
> 4. use an overconfident tone that tries to browbeat you into seeing things the same way.

Here are two passages on the same subject. Both express a bias. However, only one is so biased you might start to wonder if the author's claims are even accurate.

In the past few years, several people have filed lawsuits against fast food companies. Those filing suits claim that eating fast food has made them obese and caused other health problems as well. While it would be all but impossible to argue that fast food companies have done all they can to supply their customers with healthful fare, those claiming that eating cheeseburgers is the cause of their health problems have a tough case to make. Obesity, after all, has a strong genetic* component.* This means that if you have several relatives who are overweight, you too are inclined to be overweight. Someone lacking your genetic makeup might eat cheeseburgers without gaining weight. But those blaming the fast food business for their weight gain are bound to face an unpleasant question. Critics might well ask: Did someone put a gun to your head to make you eat those French fries? Yes, advertising has promoted the pleasures of fast food without ever mentioning the health risks involved. For that reason alone, the fast food companies deserve strong criticism. But advertising is not brainwashing. The people who consumed mountains of fried food made a choice. They chose to eat food that, given its fatty nature, was obviously high in calories. Having made that choice, it hardly seems fair to then blame someone else for the unpleasant consequences.

The current spate of lawsuits against fast food companies is symbolic of everything that currently is wrong with this country. In short, Americans don't take responsibility for their own actions any more. In the case of fast

*genetic: based on biological inheritance.
*component: element.

food companies, all the companies do is sell a product. It's up to the consumer to decide if he or she wants that product. The makers of fast food obviously don't hold a gun to consumers' heads. Nor do they force-feed them French fries and onion rings. Anyone who makes cheese-burgers and fried foods a steady diet and then complains about obesity doesn't deserve any sympathy. These people should practice self-control and not clog up the legal system with frivolous lawsuits.

The writer of the first passage is critical of lawsuits against fast food companies. However, he is willing to acknowledge that those bringing the lawsuits have some legitimate grievances. The writer is even some-what sympathetic. He certainly does not vilify those suing. In other words, his bias hasn't made him put blinders on. It hasn't made him be-have as if there were simply no opposing points of view that made any sense. He can see merit in the arguments of those who disagree. He just doesn't think there is enough merit to convince.

The writer of the second passage speaks with so much confidence it's almost hard not to agree with her. But generally, you would do well to hold off sharing the opinion of a writer who seems unable to even consider that there might be some merit in the opposition. This kind of writer probably hasn't given you a fair description of opposing points of view.

Writers who really want readers to understand and evaluate an issue will usually tell you about the opposition. Then they'll point out what's wrong with it. Or they will say something along the lines of "yes, that's a good point, but . . ." They won't act as if any disagreement is silly and pointless. If they do, experienced readers draw the correct inference and assume that such writers are excessively biased and probably aren't supplying accurate enough information for readers to form a sound judgment.

A Three-Step Strategy for Responding to Bias
◆

1. Determine the direction of the author's bias, asking what the author is in favor of or against.

2. Look to see how the author handles opposing points of view.

3. If you can't find any indication of the opposing point of view or if the author treats it as nonsense, hold off forming a definite opin-ion even if you are inclined to agree with the author.

⊶ **READING KEY**

◆ There's nothing wrong with a writer revealing a bias. The question readers have to ask themselves is: Does the writer's bias overwhelm his or her ability to be fair and balanced?

> **IDIOM ALERT: Whirlwind courtship**
>
> Whirlwinds are rapidly moving air masses. Link the word *whirlwind* to *courtship*, and you have an idiom describing a very speedy romance. *Whirlwind courtships* usually end in an impulsive and unplanned marriage—for instance, "After a *whirlwind courtship*, the couple decided to elope."

◆ **EXERCISE 7   Evaluating Bias**

DIRECTIONS   Read each passage. Then circle the appropriate letter to indicate if the writer is (1) biased but fair, (2) excessively biased and incapable of being fair to the opposition, or (3) reveals no bias at all.

EXAMPLE   Mail order brides are considered the subject of jokes in the U.S. But they are no joke. Every year more men search print and online ads looking for women to marry—the right kind of women, that is. Russian, Eastern European, and Asian women are in particularly hot demand because they are famous for pampering their men. Or at least that's what the men who search for brides overseas believe. It never occurs to them that the women willing to, in effect, put themselves up for sale are really just desperate to escape the circumstances of their lives. No, these gentlemen prefer to think that women from other countries, countries that are often enormously poor, are really just dying to live out women's true role—to love, honor, and obey some man. Desperate to be the master of the house, these men meet and marry women they barely know. Then they are shocked and surprised when the women are not forever grateful. After a two-year probation period, the women can legally stay in the country. When they abandon their marriages, their loving husbands are stunned. But what did these men think? Did they really believe that women from poor countries don't want personal independence? These men deserve what they get. They do not deserve our sympathy. The time when men were masters of the household is gone. They should just accept it and prepare to treat women as their equals.

Bias a. The author expresses a bias but still seems trustworthy.

ⓑ. The author expresses a bias so strong that he or she may not be providing readers with accurate information.

c. The author does not reveal a personal bias.

EXPLANATION   Answer *b* is the only one that seems appropriate in this instance. Men who want mail order brides may want women to worship them. But many claim that they just want a woman to take care of. They want someone willing to assume a role once considered traditional and appropriate for all women, that of full-time housewife. Although some openly admit they are not fond of the stereotypical feminist, they also don't want women afraid to stand up for themselves. However, the author of this passage so obviously despises men who look overseas for a bride that you can't assume you are getting an accurate picture of what either the men or the brides really think.

1. In 1998, Ukrainian-born Nataliya Derkach met Natasha Spivack, the Russian-American owner of Encounters International, an international matchmaking service. At the time, Spivack seemed to offer the young Ukrainian woman the answer to her prayers. Spivack had arranged for Nataliya to meet an American named James Fox, whose objective was marriage. The couple did indeed hit it off and were married after a whirlwind courtship. But according to Nataliya, Fox began beating her shortly after they married, at one point so badly that she landed in the hospital. When the new Mrs. Fox complained to the owner of Encounters, Spivack supposedly told her there was nothing to be done because American men were "crazy." Nataliya Fox headed first for a women's shelter and then took her case to a judge. A jury awarded her $433,500 from Encounters International after finding that the company failed to give her a crucial piece of information. Immigration law protects foreign women who leave abusive husbands, and they cannot be deported. Fox also eventually sued her husband, who settled the case for $115,000. (Source of information: Daren Briscoe, "Mail-Order Misery," *Newsweek*, February 7, 2005, p. 54.)

Bias
    a. The author expresses a bias but still seems trustworthy.
    b. The author expresses a bias so strong that he or she may not be providing readers with accurate information.
    c. The author does not reveal a personal bias.

2. It's hard to understand why the debate over global warming continues. How do you debate a fact of life? We are in the midst of a global warming that will radically alter the face of the earth and life as we know it. For instance, hurricanes are growing more common and

more intense. This fact was noted by scientist Kevin Trenberth, in a report prepared for the Intergovernmental Panel on Climate Change. However, Trenberth's suggestion that there might be a connection between the intensity of hurricanes and global warming was met with expressions of outrage. Critics claimed, incorrectly, that Dr. Trenberth's comments were not justified by the scientific evidence. Yet Trenberth's data does show a clear connection between hotter ocean temperatures and hurricane intensity. Clearly, there are those who do not want the issue of global warming addressed. They don't want it addressed because to do so might affect business as usual. In debates over the environment, there are far too many people who care more about making money than they do about the quality of life on earth.

Bias

a. The author expresses a bias but still seems trustworthy.

b. The author expresses a bias so strong that he or she may not be providing readers with accurate information.

c. The author does not reveal a personal bias.

3. In *American Rebels*, a collection of brief essays about men and women who broke with established traditions, writer Patricia Bosworth eulogizes Congresswoman Bella Abzug of New York, giving her credit for three crucial pieces of legislation: the Freedom of Information Act, the Sunshine Law (government bodies were required to meet publicly), and the Right to Privacy Act. From Bosworth's point of view, Abzug was an enlightened and exciting legislator, whose presence in Congress is still deeply missed. Yet it's hard to imagine how Bosworth could have such fond memories of a woman whose main claim to fame was her bad taste in hats and loud grating voice. President George H. W. Bush was right to express his sympathy for the Chinese when Abzug was there on a visit. She was, as Bush claimed, someone who always represented the extremes of the women's movement. (Source of information: Newfield, *American Rebels*, p. 212.)

Bias

a. The author expresses a bias but still seems trustworthy.

b. The author expresses a bias so strong that he or she may not be providing readers with accurate information.

c. The author does not reveal a personal bias.

4. The United States should replace its current income tax with a national sales tax. It's high time to challenge the status quo* and make this change. Forward-thinking politicians know that getting rid of the income tax is the right thing to do for this country. They recognize that the current system needs to be revised. Failing to make the necessary changes would mean continuing to live with an unsolved and long-standing problem that must be addressed. Yet the people we have elected to office are loath to take action. They are obviously fearful that whatever action they take will lose them a vote. It is time for them to overcome their indecisiveness and replace the income tax with a national sales tax.

Bias
   a. The author expresses a bias but still seems trustworthy.
   b. The author expresses a bias so strong that he or she may not be providing readers with accurate information.
   c. The author does not reveal a personal bias.

5. America should remove the penny from circulation and eliminate the one-cent coin from daily cash transactions. The penny isn't worth keeping because its cost almost equals its value. The costs of manufacturing, transporting, and distributing each penny add up to more than nine-tenths of a cent. Thus, the U.S. Mint does not make enough on the coin to justify continuing its production. Besides, people don't carry and use these coins anyway. They're too heavy to lug around in pockets or purses. As a result, people just keep them at home in jars rather than circulate them. Pennies were successfully eliminated at U.S. military bases in Europe. Similarly, other nations, including France, Spain, and Britain, all stopped producing low-value coins. These examples suggest that it's time for the United States, too, to retire the penny.

   a. The author expresses a bias but still seems trustworthy.
   b. The author expresses a bias so strong that he or she may not be providing readers with accurate information.
   c. The author does not reveal a personal bias.

*status quo: existing state of affairs.

ROUNDING UP THE KEYS

Here is a list of all the reading keys introduced in the chapter. Use them to review for the test on page 463. If a particular reading key doesn't make sense on its own, go back to the page where it appeared and review the section preceding it.

READING KEYS: Characteristics of Informative Writing

- ◆ Writers with an informative purpose are likely to use a cool, impersonal tone. (p. 430)
- ◆ Writers with an informative purpose do not use emotionally charged or highly connotative language. (p. 430)
- ◆ Informative writing relies heavily on factual statements that can be checked for accuracy and don't vary according to person or location. (p. 430)
- ◆ In informative writing, neither the title nor the main idea suggests a judgment. (p. 430)

READING KEYS: Characteristics of Persuasive Writing

- ◆ Writers who are trying to persuade focus on developing an opinion and use facts only to serve that opinion. (p. 435)
- ◆ Writers with a persuasive purpose are likely to use emotionally charged language. (p. 435)
- ◆ In persuasive writing, even seemingly factual statements are likely to include some opinion. (p. 435)
- ◆ In persuasive writing, both titles and main ideas take a stand. (p. 435)
- ◆ If the author's background suggests that he or she has a personal connection to the topic under discussion, the writing is probably persuasive. (p. 435)
- ◆ Writers with a persuasive purpose try to connect with their audience. (p. 435)
- ◆ Inferring purpose is like drawing any other inference. You have to study what the author actually says or reveals. Then you have to use that information as the basis for inferring the purpose. (p. 435)

READING KEY: When Bias Goes Overboard

- ◆ There's nothing wrong with a writer revealing a bias. The question readers have to ask themselves is: Does the writer's bias overwhelm his or her ability to be fair and balanced? (p. 450)

Ten More Words for Your Textbook Vocabulary

1. **transactions:** actions, communications, or exchanges that have been carried out by two different parties

   Transactions that involve business customers differ from consumer transactions in several ways. (Pride and Ferrell, *Marketing*, p. 238.)

2. **socialization:** the passing on or training in a society's attitudes, traditions, and morals

   Through the process of *socialization*, we develop our ideas of what it means to be male or female.

3. **proliferate:** to grow or multiply rapidly

   The cells were *proliferating* at an alarming rate.

4. **jurisdiction:** extent of authority or control

   Those particular South Sea islands are under France's *jurisdiction*.

5. **deform:** to spoil or ruin an existing shape

   Arthritis had badly *deformed* the elderly man's hands.

6. **consolidate:** to combine separate things into a larger whole

   The trend in school districts follows the theory that fewer is better: Small districts are so expensive to maintain that *consolidations* have occurred throughout the nation. (Adapted from Bowman and Kearney, *State and Local Government*, p. 255.)

7. **congruent:** fitting with; matching up; appropriate to

   The type and mix of taxes imposed should be *congruent* with citizen preferences. (Bowman and Kearney, *State and Local Government*, p. 275.)

8. **cognitive:** related to thinking

   The psychologist was a believer in *cognitive* therapy, and she encouraged her patient to change harmful thought patterns.

9. **deft:** quick and skillful

   In one *deft* move, the dealer palmed the card that would have given the woman a winning hand.

10. **prominent:** famous

    When Johns Hopkins University discovered that the *prominent* psychologist John B. Watson was having an affair with his research assistant, the school didn't care how famous he was, they forced him to resign.

◆ **EXERCISE 8**   **Building Your Academic Vocabulary**

DIRECTIONS   Fill in the blanks with one of the words listed below.

cognitive	deformed	jurisdiction	transactions	consolidate
socialization	prominent	congruent	deft	proliferation

1. After the investigators carefully studied the bank's financial _____ for the previous year, they were convinced that someone had been falsifying the figures.

2. The acid rain had worn away the original rock, leaving it completely _____.

3. With _____ and knowing fingers, the surgeon sliced through the damaged muscle.

4. The _____ of special districts makes it hard to find solutions to public problems. (Bowman and Kearney, *State and Local Government*, p. 255.)

5. Although some therapists insist that rediscovering one's childhood memories is the key to improving psychological health, Aaron Beck

argues that recognizing and altering negative _____ patterns is far more useful.

6. The sheriff wanted to arrest the runaway for her own good, but he had no _____ in that county.

7. _____ is not always a conscious process; in some instances, we unthinkingly absorb our society's beliefs without realizing it's happening.

8. The workshop would have been a lot better if all the topics had seemed more _____; instead, nothing seemed related to anything that came before.

9. Although the heart specialist was one of the most _____ doctors in the field, she was very down-to-earth and friendly to everyone at the conference.

10. He hopes to _____ all of his debts into one and pay it off month by month.

DIGGING
DEEPER

Archbishop Oscar Romero

Looking Ahead This reading re-introduces Archbishop Oscar Romero, mentioned on page 443. As you read, apply what you have learned about detecting purpose, tone, and bias.

1 On March 24, 1980, Archbishop Oscar Romero stood in the pulpit of a chapel in El Salvador while, outside, from a car across the street, an assassin took aim. As Romero was finishing his sermon, a bullet pierced Romero in the heart, silencing once and for all one of Latin America's most powerful and influential voices.

2 Just three years before, Romero had been a most unlikely martyr. A predictable, orthodox, timid bookworm, Romero wasn't expected to make any waves. After all, he had criticized clergy who argued that God's abundance was for everyone, not just for a handful of flamboyantly affluent people. He had spoken out against "liberation theology" and its notion that wealth should be spread around to feed, clothe, and shelter *all of* God's people. Naturally, El Salvador's conservative upper classes considered him a safe choice. Their soft-spoken new archbishop would surely work with them to maintain the status quo.

3 They were wrong. At first, Romero had no intention of challenging his country's ruling elite. Then, a priest named Rutilio Grande was ambushed and killed. Grande was murdered for publicly insisting that wealthy landowners' dogs ate better than the families who worked those landowners' fields. He had also supported peasants' right to organize farm cooperatives. For daring to speak up for the poor, he was killed in cold blood.

4 Romero went to see the corpses of Grande and the old man and 7-year-old boy murdered with him. From there, he went to a church packed with local peasants. That night, he stood before the terror-stricken faces of his congregation while their eyes silently pleaded for his help. Suddenly, Romero realized that liberation theology had it right: No true Christian could turn his back upon the poor and suffering. His voice firm with new resolve, he urged his audience to become the "masters and protagonists of their own struggle for liberation."

5 He couldn't—and didn't—promise them that the atrocities would cease. In war-torn El Salvador, 3,000 people were killed every month. Corpses sometimes lay in the streets and were tossed onto garbage dumps and into streams. Two hundred of the people Romero had addressed in that country church would be dead within a year, along with 75,000 others.

While violence ripped the country apart, rich and powerful Salvadorans refused to acknowledge that many of their countrymen went to bed hungry night after night.

6   But Romero refused to close his eyes to the suffering of his people. Every week, in his Sunday sermon, he pleaded with those in power to stop the vicious repression of anyone questioning their authority. Above all, he called for an end to social and economic inequality. All the while, he assured those who believed in him that the church would not be silent no matter how dangerous the situation became.

7   Away from the pulpit, he begged for help from the international community. Appealing to President Jimmy Carter, he asked the U.S. to end its annual $1.5 million in aid. The money, he said, was being used to hurt the very people it was meant to help. But his letters were ignored. Even the Salvadoran bishops, with only one exception, turned their backs on him.

8   Although Romero knew he was alone in his fight, he continued to speak out. Despite death threats, he defied those in power who demanded his silence. Romero knew the price for such defiance would be high, but he was ready to pay it. "I am bound, as a pastor, by divine command," he said, "to give my life for those whom I love, and that is all Salvadorans, even those who are going to kill me."

9   For his enemies, the last straw was Romero's public criticism of the Salvadoran military. The day before he was murdered, Romero accused the army of violating God's law against killing. Then, he encouraged the soldiers to mutiny: "No soldier is obliged to obey an order that is contrary to the will of God." His sermon, which was broadcast throughout the country, was punctuated by thunderous applause. But the next day, Romero was dead, probably killed by a soldier's gun.

10   In 2000, on the twentieth anniversary of Romero's death, thousands of people marched through the streets of El Salvador to honor Romero's memory. The men and women of El Salvador had not forgotten the man they called the "people's saint." (Sources of figures and quotations: The Romero Society, www.romerosociety.org/index.htm; James R. Brockman, "The Spiritual Journey of Oscar Romero," www.spiritualitytoday.org/spir2day/904242brock.html; "Remembering the Assassination of Archbishop Oscar Romero," www.creighton.edu/CollaborativeMinistry/romero.html.)

Sharpening Your Skills

DIRECTIONS   Answer the following questions by filling in the blanks or circling the letter of the correct response.

1. Based on the context, how would you define *orthodox* in paragraph 2?
   a. unreliable
   b. traditional
   c. rebellious
   d. fierce

2. Based on the context, how would you define *resolve* in paragraph 4?
   a. determination
   b. puzzlement
   c. joy
   d. defeat

3. Based on the context, how would you define *protagonists* in paragraph 4?
   a. enemies
   b. friends
   c. heroes
   d. defeatists

4. Which statement best expresses the main idea of paragraph 2?
   a. Romero hid his rebellious spirit behind the mask of a bookworm.
   b. Romero's heroism was unexpected.
   c. Romero did not ever come to accept liberation theology.
   d. Romero originally expected to earn great wealth in his new office.

5. What cause and effect relationship is implied in paragraph 4?

   _____

6. What's the implied main idea of the entire reading?

   _____

   _____

7. The sentences in paragraph 9 are connected by which type of transition?

   a. contrast

   b. time order

   c. cause and effect

   d. comparison

8. How would you describe the author's tone?

   a. doubtful

   b. quietly supportive

   c. admiring

   d. slightly suspicious

9. What is the author's purpose?

   _____

10. Based on the reading, how do you think the author would react to the idea of naming a bridge or a building in honor of Bishop Romero?

    _____

    _____

► **TEST 1**   **Reviewing the Key Points**

DIRECTIONS   Answer the following questions by filling in the blanks or circling the letter of the correct response.

1. An informative purpose means that the author wants to _____

   _____.

2. Informative writing relies heavily on _____ language, which carries little _____.

3. Tone in writing is like _____; it's a way of conveying _____.

4. Writers who want mainly to inform usually use a neutral, objective

   _____.

5. Informative writing relies more on _____ than on opinions.

6. Which of the following is likely to be the main idea of an informative piece of writing?
   a. The number of caesarian section deliveries has sharply increased over the last decade.
   b. Women should not be so ready to have caesarian deliveries.
   c. Whether to have a caesarian section is a personal decision, but you would never know that from the current controversy on the subject.

7. Most persuasive writing uses a tone that conveys _____

   _____.

8. Which title is most likely to introduce a piece of persuasive writing?
   a. "Alfred Kinsey: The Making of a Sexual Revolutionary"
   b. "The Kinsey Report"
   c. "The Controversy Over the Kinsey Report"

9. Which main idea would be more likely to appear in a piece of persuasive writing?

    a. Archbishop Oscar Romero was assassinated after he used the church pulpit to speak out against the treatment of the poor in El Salvador.

    b. Archbishop Oscar Romero courageously spoke out against the exploitation of the poor and willingly became a martyr to his cause.

10. Identify the four signs of excessive bias introduced in this chapter.

    _____

    _____

    _____

    _____

    _____

    _____

To correct your test, turn to page 554. If one or more of your answers is incorrect, re-read the Rounding Up the Keys section of the chapter to find out where your mistakes might be.

▶ **TEST 2**   **Distinguishing Between Fact and Opinion**

DIRECTIONS   Read each statement. Then label it *F* (fact), *O* (opinion), or *B* (both).

_____ 1. Putting a sky marshal on each of 30,000 flights per day is impractical and unrealistic.

_____ 2. The annual Consumer Electronics Show showcases thousands of new cutting-edge gadgets.

_____ 3. The ability to manage one's emotions is an essential ingredient of effective leadership.

_____ 4. If you don't eliminate poverty and homelessness, you can't decrease the crime rate.

_____ 5. Today, Americans' life expectancy has increased to seventy-eight years, thirty years longer than the outlook for their ancestors living in 1900.

_____ 6. A defective O-ring caused the tragic explosion of the space shuttle *Challenger* on January 28, 1986.

_____ 7. An astonishing 61 percent of all Americans are overweight.

_____ 8. The largest Indian land claim in U.S. history was the $247.9 million a judge ordered the state of New York to pay the Cayuga Indians in 2001.

_____ 9. Many European and Asian countries have a better organ donation system than does the U.S.: Unless an individual objects to being an organ donor, he or she is considered to be one.

_____ 10. America is the world's mightiest power—militarily, economically, politically, and culturally.

▶ **TEST 3**   **Distinguishing Between Fact and Opinion**

> **DIRECTIONS**   Read each statement. Then label it *F* (fact), *O* (opinion), or *B* (both).

_____ 1. Alan Mathison Turing (1912–1954) was an English mathematician whose brilliant career was senselessly destroyed when it was discovered that he was a homosexual.

_____ 2. A carcinogen is any agent that increases the chances of a cell's becoming cancerous.

_____ 3. During World War I, Chile remained neutral.

_____ 4. Home shopping networks encourage viewers to engage in mindless consumerism.

_____ 5. Although most people don't realize it, eyewitnesses to crimes are extremely unreliable.

_____ 6. The music of rapper 50 Cent is offensive and disgusting.

_____ 7. A new species of land mammal has been discovered in the forests of Vietnam.

_____ 8. The pop singer Michael Jackson died in 2009 at the age of 50.

_____ 9. When he pardoned the fugitive financier Marc Rich, William Jefferson Clinton disgraced his presidency.

_____ 10. The Japanese mushrooms called *maitake* sometimes grow as big as footballs.

▶ **TEST 4** **Recognizing Tone and Purpose**

DIRECTIONS   Circle the appropriate letters to identify the author's tone and purpose.

1. The Miss America pageant is a throwback to a time when women were oppressed. Therefore, we need to end this dinosaur competition once and for all. After all, the contest encourages Americans to treat women as objects. There is no difference between parading a group of pretty girls wearing swimsuits in front of a panel of judges and rating cattle at a country fair or dogs in a dog show. Also, pageants encourage young girls to focus on their bodies and their appearance above all else. As a result, too many women suffer a loss of self-esteem when they cannot achieve perfect Barbie-doll figures and faces like those of the contestants.

The writer's tone is
a. objective.
b. disgusted.
c. comical.
d. puzzled.

The writer's purpose is
a. to inform.
b. to persuade.

2. Botox, which paralyzes facial muscles and makes wrinkles disappear, has become the latest fad of the rich and excessively vain. Not surprisingly, many people with too much money for their own good are clamoring for this new procedure. But those in pursuit of permanent youth should probably think twice before having this poison injected into the skin. For one thing, it's potentially dangerous. Botox is derived from botulin, a substance that can cause fatal poisoning when it's ingested in food. Although it's not common, one woman in California died after receiving her Botox injection. Also, Botox immobilizes the muscles. Thus, people who submit to this procedure occasionally lose some facial expression. For example, they lose the ability to frown or move their foreheads. In the end, they may have wrinkle-free skin, but they also look like robots.

Yet for those who refuse to submit to time, looking like a robot apparently doesn't matter as long as they look like youthful robots.

The writer's tone is

a. optimistic.

b. scornful.

c. objective.

d. admiring.

The writer's purpose is

a. to inform.

b. to persuade.

3. In many ancient kingdoms such as Bengal and Sumatra, a king did not rule for long. After a king had ruled for a few years, his subjects would execute him so that he didn't become too powerful. The king would be beaten to death or executed in an elaborate ritual. Once their ruler was no longer alive and capable of letting power go to his head, his subjects worshipped him as a god. In the meantime, they waited for a new king to prove himself strong enough to take power. Somehow new heroes always seemed to arrive on the scene, eager to take the throne and ready to believe that they would escape the fate of the previous kings. Few, however, did.

The writer's tone is

a. horrified.

b. disgusted.

c. friendly.

d. objective.

The writer's purpose is

a. to inform.

b. to persuade.

4. Every poll about young people and their heroes seems to suggest that celebrities are the main heroes of today's preteens and teens. This seems a shame because our heroes when we are young play an important role in how we behave as adults. If young people today worship

celebrities, who—or, more to the point, what—are they imitating? To give an example, my 10-year-old daughter worships Britney Spears. The nubile* Ms. Spears is, in fact, her expressed hero. "I wanna be just like Britney," she announced over breakfast the other morning. Hearing my daughter make that claim gave me goosebumps. After all, the charming Ms. Spears doesn't seem to have any talent, so what does my daughter find worthy of admiration? Specifically, what kind of behavior is she likely to imitate? I certainly hope she does not aspire to displaying her navel or performing suggestive dance routines. Unfortunately, many of today's hottest celebrities are known more for their notoriety* than for their talent. So if our kids consider them heroes, are they saying they want to grow up to have no talent, make a lot of money, and behave badly in public? How I wish we were back in the days when kids thought people like Muhammad Ali, John F. Kennedy, and Billie Jean King were heroes worthy of imitation.

The writer's tone is

a. objective.

b. mournful.

c. lighthearted.

d. disapproving.

The writer's purpose is

a. to inform.

b. to persuade.

5. The babies in China's orphanages are a sad and disturbing reminder of a persistent Chinese tradition concerning the value of female life. Most of the orphaned babies are healthy girls. The few orphaned boys usually suffer from a physical handicap of some sort. For girls, being born female seems to be handicap enough. This unfortunate prejudice against girls is especially strong in rural areas, where farming is a major source of income. On a farm, strength is highly valued. Because girls are not as physically strong as boys, a female child's birth is often greeted with disappointment, even anger. Some parents will simply abandon a baby girl. They hope to try again to

---

*nubile: sexually mature and attractive.
*notoriety: fame earned for the wrong reason.

have a child and, with any luck, produce a boy. For years, the Chinese government has tried to stamp out this negative attitude toward females. But the rows of healthy baby girls lying abandoned in orphanages suggest the government's lack of success. What *has* been successful, in general, is adoption. Childless couples in the city are ready and willing to adopt baby girls. So, too, are foreigners. In 1988, the government loosened restrictions on foreign adoptions. As a result, couples from Canada, France, and the United States began arriving in the hopes of adopting a healthy baby girl who otherwise would have no home but the orphanage.

The writer's tone is

a. objective.

b. discouraged but hopeful.

c. lighthearted but serious.

d. angry.

The writer's purpose is

a. to inform.

b. to persuade.

▶ TEST 5   **Evaluating Bias**

DIRECTIONS   Circle the appropriate letter to identify the author's degree of bias.

1. Harvard psychologist Dan Kindlon says that parents who always protect their children from the consequences of their actions are shortchanging their kids. First, parents who cover for their kids' mistakes or keep them from unpleasant situations are inhibiting their children's character development. A father who inconveniences himself by retrieving an item his child forgot loses an opportunity to help that child develop a sense of personal responsibility. Likewise, parents who don't want their teenagers to work during the summer or after school rob teens of a chance to develop a work ethic. Overprotective parents also prevent their kids from growing up as a result of difficult experiences. Kindlon says that children who have never faced hardship or pain do not learn the right lessons about life. When they grow up, they are likely to blame other people when things don't go right.

    a. The author expresses a bias but still seems trustworthy.
    b. The author expresses a bias so strong that he or she may not be providing readers with accurate information.
    c. The author does not reveal a personal bias.

2. The owner of the mall in the center of town has leased one of the storefronts to the owner of an adult bookstore. Understandably, the townspeople are furious, and they have a right to be. Everyone knows what kind of people patronize an adult bookstore. And no one wants those kinds of people hanging around and driving customers away from the other stores in the mall. Aware of the anger among his other tenants and those who live nearby, the owner has begun to talk about the free speech issue. But this is just an attempt to sidestep responsibility for a terrible mistake.

    a. The author expresses a bias but still seems trustworthy.
    b. The author expresses a bias so strong that he or she may not be providing readers with accurate information.
    c. The author does not reveal a personal bias.

3. Anyone who believes that law-abiding citizens should have the right to own a gun needs to call his or her representatives immediately. Our government should know that we do not require any more gun-control legislation. We already have too much legislation. Yet now the federal government is again trying to extend the waiting period for the purchase of a handgun. Everyone knows where this will lead. By the time the government is through, no one will be able to buy a handgun for protection or a rifle for hunting. Even gun clubs will be outlawed. Target practice will be severely punished with stiff fines, even jail time. Supposedly, the laws controlling the purchase of guns are designed to ensure that guns don't fall into inappropriate hands. But the truth is, these laws are supported by people who believe that no one should have guns. They don't even want honest citizens to keep a gun for their own protection.

a. The author expresses a bias but still seems trustworthy.
b. The author expresses a bias so strong that he or she may not be providing readers with accurate information.
c. The author does not reveal a personal bias.

4. States should not execute convicted felons who are mentally retarded. People with extremely low IQs who commit crimes cannot fully understand the nature of their actions or the moral implications of those actions. This means that imposing the death penalty on them violates the Eighth Amendment of the Bill of Rights, which prohibits cruel and unusual punishment. Then, too, it is important to remember that people suffering from severe mental retardation often lack impulse control. Even if they could grasp the consequences of their actions, they may be emotionally and physiologically unable to control themselves. Thus, it's not fair or just to take their lives when they never possessed the ability to restrain the behavior they are being punished for.

a. The author expresses a bias but still seems trustworthy.
b. The author expresses a bias so strong that he or she may not be providing readers with accurate information.
c. The author does not reveal a personal bias.

▶ **TEST 6**   **Developing Your Textbook Vocabulary**

DIRECTIONS   Fill in the blanks with one of the words listed below.

> socialized   jurisdiction   consolidate   cognitively   deft
> prominent   deformed   congruent   proliferated   transaction

1. The teenager was _____ very sophisticated, but emotionally he was still a child.

2. Because she was one of the town's most _____ citizens, the support of the widow for the new proposal made a powerful impression on the audience.

3. When it came to making excuses, the lawyer was both quick and _____.

4. Born with a _____ right arm, the little girl refused to let it stop her from leading a normal life.

5. The judge's _____ was much more limited under the new guidelines.

6. After completing a small _____ at the teller's window, the bank robber pulled out a gun.

7. Overnight the little red beetles had _____ wildly and they covered every single lily in the garden.

8. Japanese children are _____ to consider the group more important than themselves.

9. Based on the shape, the carpenter could tell that the two planks of wood were not _____ no matter what the lumber company manager claimed.

10. The town council voted to _____ the different bureaus into one large department.

Combining Your Skills

As the title suggests, this is your chance to combine all the skills you mastered in Chapters 1 through 9. The questions accompanying the following readings give you additional practice on everything from using context clues to recognizing purpose, bias, and tone.

◆ **READING 1** **The Seven-Day Antiprocrastination Plan**

Dave Ellis

Looking Ahead Many college students procrastinate, or put off, doing their assignments until the very last minute. And guess what? Students who wait until the last minute often don't do their best work. Author Dave Ellis describes seven sound tips for managing time and breaking the procrastination habit.

Word Watch You probably know most of the words in the reading. The ones you don't know can mostly be defined from context. The words that follow, however, cannot be fully understood from either context or analysis of word parts. For this reason, their meanings are supplied here. Look them over before you begin reading.

> **irregular verbs (5):** verbs that do not follow the usual rules for forming the past tense—for example, *ring, rang, rung*
>
> **legitimately (6):** rightfully
>
> **immersion (7):** sinking into; submerging
>
> **ponder (9):** consider or think about
>
> **imminent (9):** immediate, just about to happen

Reading Tip To make sure you remember the author's seven pointers, paraphrase and list them in the margins of your text. Also, consciously evaluate each suggestion by deciding which ones you are most likely to use.

1 Here are seven strategies you can use to eliminate procrastination. The suggestions are tied to the days of the week to help you remember them.

Monday: Make It Meaningful

2 What is important about the job you've been putting off? List all the benefits of completing it. Look at it in relation to your goals. Be specific about the rewards for getting it done, including how you will feel when the task is complete.

Tuesday: Take It Apart

3   Break big jobs into a series of small ones you can do in 15 minutes or less. If a long reading assignment intimidates you, divide it into two-page or three-page sections. Make a list of the sections and cross them off as you complete them, so you can see your progress.

Wednesday: Write an Intention Statement

4   Write an Intention Statement on a 3 × 5 card. For example, if you can't get started on a term paper, you might write, "I intend to write a list of at least 10 possible topics by 9 p.m. I will reward myself with an hour of guilt-free recreational reading." Carry the 3 × 5 card with you or post it in your study area where you can see it often.

Thursday: Tell Everyone

5   Announce publicly your intention to get it done. Tell a friend you intend to learn 10 irregular* French verbs by Saturday. Tell your spouse, roommate, parents, and children. Include anyone who will ask whether you've completed it or who will suggest ways to get it done. Make the world your support group.

Friday: Find a Reward

6   Construct rewards carefully. Be willing to withhold them if you do not complete the task. Don't pick a movie as a reward for studying biology if you plan to go to the movie anyway. And when you legitimately* reap your reward, notice how it feels. You might find that movies, new clothes, or an extra hour on the bicycle are more fun when you've earned them.

Saturday: Settle It Now

7   Do it now. The minute you notice yourself procrastinating, plunge into the task. Imagine yourself at a mountain lake, poised to dive. Gradual immersion* would be slow torture. It's often less painful to leap. Then be sure to savor the feeling of having the task behind you.

Sunday: Say No

8   When you keep pushing a task into the low-priority category, reexamine the purpose for doing it at all. If you realize you really don't intend to do something, quit telling yourself that you will. That's procrastinating. Just say NO! Then you're not procrastinating, and you don't have to carry around the baggage of an undone task.

9   If you are going to procrastinate, there are three good reasons why you should do it consciously. First of all, if you recognize that you are procrastinating, you can decide if you really, really do want to put things off. After all, if you choose to procrastinate, you can also choose not to. Consciously thinking about the process of procrastination is also important. In effect, you need to think like a scientist and observe what you are doing and why. Ponder* the question of why you might be postponing important tasks. Second, consider the consequences of postponing. Seeing the cost of procrastination clearly may just help you kick the habit. And finally, ask yourself straight out if procrastination actually works in your favor. Some people really do thrive under pressure, and if you do your best work when you are pushing hard against an imminent* deadline, you may be one of those people.

Combining Your Skills **DIRECTIONS**   Answer the following questions by circling the appropriate letter or filling in the blanks.

Context 1. Based on the context, what is a good approximate definition for the word *intimidates* in paragraph 3?

   a. encourages

   b. frightens

   c. irritates

2. Based on the context, what is a good approximate definition for the word *savor* in paragraph 7?

   a. forget

   b. imagine

   c. enjoy

3. Based on the context, what is a good approximate definition for the word *thrive* in paragraph 9?

   a. grow stronger

   b. grow weaker

   c. fail

Sentence Sense 4. What is the connection between the sentences in paragraph 3?

   a. comparison

   b. cause and effect

c. addition

d. time order

Main Idea **5.** In your own words, what's the main idea of the entire reading?

_____

_____

Inference **6.** In paragraph 3, the author tells readers what to do if they feel intimidated by a long reading assignment. But he doesn't say why someone would feel intimidated. What's your guess, or inference?

_____

_____

7. In paragraph 4, the author tells you to post your Intention Statement where you can see it. Why do you think this would be important?

_____

_____

8. In paragraph 5, the author encourages those who would kick the procrastination habit to "publicly" announce what they expect to get done. Again, he doesn't say why this should work. What is your guess, or inference?

_____

_____

Purpose **9.** Do you think the author wants to

a. describe techniques for time management?

b. convince readers that managing time is really possible?

Tone **10.** How would you describe the author's tone?

a. friendly and natural

b. serious and formal

c. objective

Drawing Your Own Conclusions Procrastination has often been linked to fear of failure. Explain what you think might be the connection between the two.

_____

_____

Thinking Through Writing Start your paper by explaining which of the seven tips in the reading is the best. Be sure to explain how you arrived at your decision. Conclude by describing the tip you personally consider the *least* useful or valuable. Again, make sure to give the basis for your opinion.

◆ READING 2   Culture, Subcultures, and the Marketplace

William M. Pride and O. C. Ferrell

Looking Ahead   The following excerpt offers definitions for the terms *culture* and *subculture*. It also describes how companies analyze the needs and desires of three key American subcultures in order to promote their products.

Word Watch   You probably know most of the words in the reading. The ones you don't know can mostly be defined from context. The words that follow, however, cannot be fully understood from either context or the analysis of word parts. For this reason, their meanings are supplied here. Look them over before you begin reading.

> **per capita (3):** per person
> **designations (5):** places
> **demographic (5):** identifying characteristics of populations
>
> **retailer (9):** someone involved in direct selling to consumers
> **vignettes (11):** pictures

Reading Tip   Just a glance at the headings tells you that the reading is going to describe three separate subcultures—African-American, Hispanic, and Asian-American.

culture The accumulation of values, knowledge, beliefs, customs, objects, and concepts of a society

1   **Culture** is the accumulation of values, knowledge, beliefs, customs, objects, and concepts that a society uses to cope with its environment and passes on to future generations. Examples of objects are foods, furniture, buildings, clothing, and tools. Concepts include education, welfare, and laws. Culture also includes core values and the degree of acceptability of a wide range of behaviors in a specific society. For example, in U.S. culture, customers as well as businesspeople are expected to behave ethically.

2   Culture influences buying behavior because it permeates our daily lives. Our culture determines what we wear and eat and where we reside and travel. Society's interest in the healthfulness of food affects food companies' approaches to developing and promoting their products. Culture also influences how we buy and use products and our satisfaction from them. In the U.S. culture, makers of furniture, cars, and clothing strive to understand how people's color preferences are changing.

3   Because culture determines product purchases and uses to some degree, cultural changes affect product development, promotion, distribution, and pricing. Food marketers, for example, have made a multitude of changes in their marketing efforts. Thirty years ago, most U.S. families ate at least two meals a day together, and the mother spent four to six hours a day preparing those meals. Today more than 75 percent of women between ages 25 and 54 work outside the home, and average family incomes have risen considerably. These shifts, along with scarcity of time, have resulted in dramatic changes in the national per capita* consumption of certain food products, such as take-out foods, frozen dinners, and shelf-stable foods.

4   When U.S. marketers sell products in other countries, they realize the tremendous impact those cultures have on product purchases and use. Global marketers find that people in other regions of the world have different attitudes, values, and needs, which call for different methods of doing business as well as different types of marketing mixes. Some international marketers fail because they do not or cannot adjust to cultural differences.

subculture A group of individuals whose characteristics, values, and behavioral patterns are similar within the group and different from those of people in the surrounding culture

5   A culture consists of various subcultures. A **subculture** is a group of individuals whose characteristics, values, and behavioral patterns are similar within the group and different from those of people in the surrounding culture. Subcultural boundaries are usually based on geographic designations* and demographic* characteristics, such as age, religion, race, and ethnicity. U.S. culture is marked by many different subcultures. Among them are West Coast, teenage, Asian American, and college students.

6   Within subcultures, greater similarities exist in people's attitudes, values, and actions than within the broader culture. Relative to other subcultures, individuals in one subculture may have stronger preferences for specific types of clothing, furniture, or foods. Research has shown that subcultures can play a significant role in how people respond to advertisements, particularly when pressured to make a snap judgment. It is important to understand that a person can be a member of more than one subculture and that the behavioral patterns and values attributed to specific subcultures do not necessarily apply to all group members.

7   The percentage of the U.S. population consisting of ethnic and racial subcultures is expected to grow. By 2050, about one-half of the U.S. population will be members of racial and ethnic minorities. The U.S. Census Bureau reports that the three largest and fastest-growing ethnic U.S.

subcultures are African Americans, Hispanics, and Asians. The population growth of these subcultures interests marketers. Businesses recognize that to succeed, their marketing strategies will have to take into account the values, needs, interests, shopping patterns, and buying habits of various subcultures.

African American Subculture

8 In the United States, the African American subculture represents 12.4 percent of the population. Like all subcultures, African American consumers possess distinct buying patterns. For example, African American consumers spend more money on utilities, footwear, children's apparel, groceries, and housing than do white consumers. The combined buying power of African American consumers is projected to reach $1.1 trillion by 2012.

9 Like many companies, Procter & Gamble Company has hiked its marketing initiatives that are aimed at the African American community, spending $52.5 million last year. By including African American actors in its ads, the company believes it can encourage a positive response to its products, increasing sales among African American consumers while still maintaining ties with white consumers. Many other corporations are reaching out to the African American community with targeted efforts. Wal-Mart, for example, has adjusted the merchandising of 1,500 stores located in areas with large black populations to include more products favored by African American customers, such as ethnic hair-care products and large selections of more urban music offerings. The retailer* has also included more African American actors in its advertising campaigns. Another retailer, Target, launched a yearlong campaign called "Dream in Color" to celebrate diversity. The campaign included numerous Martin Luther King Day events, guest appearances by poet Dr. Maya Angelou, free posters for schools, and a unique online curriculum to provide access to historical and contemporary African American poets. McDonald's launched 365BLACK, a program that celebrates Black History all year-round. The following year, it introduced 365BLACK Awards, which honor African Americans for their outstanding achievements.

Hispanic Subculture

10 Hispanics represent nearly 15 percent of the U.S. population, and their buying power is expected to reach $1.2 trillion by 2012. When considering the buying behavior of Hispanics, marketers must keep in mind that this

subculture is really composed of nearly two dozen nationalities, including Cuban, Mexican, Puerto Rican, Caribbean, Spanish, and Dominican. Each has its own history and unique culture that affect consumer preferences and buying behavior. They should also recognize that the terms *Hispanic* and *Latino* refer to an ethnic category rather than a racial distinction. Because of the group's growth and purchasing power, understanding the Hispanic subculture is critical to marketers. Like African American consumers, Hispanics spend more on housing, groceries, telephone services, and children's apparel and shoes. But they also spend more on men's apparel and appliances, while they spend less than average on health care, entertainment, and education.[†]

11   To attract this powerful subculture, marketers are taking Hispanic values and preferences into account when developing products and creating advertising and promotions. For example, a growing number of retailers, including Wal-Mart, are promoting the Hispanic holiday of Three Kings Day on January 6 in markets with a significant concentration of Latino consumers. American Airlines has launched a Spanish-language advertising campaign to encourage more Latinos to fly across the country during the holiday. The *destinó* campaign, which includes ads on television, radio, online, and out-of-home, includes vignettes* showing Latinos' lives to illustrate how the airline can help them fulfill their destinies.

Asian American Subculture

12 The term *Asian American* includes people from more than 15 ethnic groups, including Filipinos, Chinese, Japanese, Asian Indians, Koreans, and Vietnamese, and this group represents 4.4 percent of the U.S. population. The individual language, religion, and value system of each group influences its members' purchasing decisions. Some traits of this subculture, however, carry across ethnic divisions, including an emphasis on hard work, strong family ties, and a high value placed on education. Asian Americans are the fastest-growing U.S. subculture. They also have the most money, the best education, and the largest percentage of professionals and managers of all U.S. minorities, and they are expected to wield $670 billion in buying power by 2012.

13   Marketers are targeting the diverse Asian American market in many ways. Kraft, for example, learned from marketing research that its Asian American customers were not interested in having "Asian" products from Kraft but rather in learning how to use well-known Kraft brands to create

---

[†][By 2020,] Hispanics will become the largest ethnic group in the United States.

healthy Western-style dishes. Targeting immigrant mothers trying to balance between Eastern and Western cultures, the company therefore launched a new ad campaign in Chinese and Mandarin—the two most commonly spoken Asian dialects—and offered samples and demonstrations in Chinese as well as a website with recipes and healthy tips. Retailer JCPenney likewise used an advertising campaign to tout its competitive prices to Chinese and Vietnamese women, particularly during cultural holidays.

Combining Your Skills **DIRECTIONS** Answer the following questions by circling the appropriate letter or filling in the blanks.

Main Idea 1. Which statement best expresses the main idea of the entire reading?

    a. Businesses are well aware that their marketing campaigns in the United States must take into account the needs and desires of the influential subcultures that make up the U.S. population.

    b. If marketers do not address the fact that the Hispanic subculture is made up of nearly two dozen different nationalities, they are unlikely to do well marketing to its members, who have unique preferences depending on their origins.

    c. Marketers have probably been most successful at targeting the Asian-American community.

    d. Ethnic and racial subcultures in the United States are expected to grow dramatically, and, by 2050, about one-half of the U.S. population will belong to a racial or ethnic minority.

Supporting Details and Paraphrasing 2. How would you paraphrase the author's definition of *culture*?

_____

_____

_____

3. In your own words, what makes a group a subculture?

_____

_____

_____

4. The author says in paragraph 8 that African Americans spend more money on utilities and footwear than white Americans do. This supporting detail is used to develop which main idea?

    a. African Americans are more concerned with appearances than white Americans are.

    b. African Americans are more willing to spend money than white Americans are.

    c. There is evidence of distinct purchasing patterns among African-American consumers.

    d. Targeted by banks, African Americans were encouraged to take subprime mortgages even if they qualified for mortgages with a better rate.

Sentence Sense 5. In paragraph 9, the references to Procter & Gamble and Wal-Mart are illustrations of which phrase from the opening sentence?

    a. many companies

    b. marketing initiatives

    c. African-American community

Inference 6. In paragraph 10, the authors say that marketers have to keep in mind that the Hispanic culture in the United States is actually composed of two dozen nationalities. But they don't say why marketers have to keep that in mind. What inference do they expect readers to draw?

_____

_____

Supporting Details 7. In paragraph 11, the *destinó* campaign is used to make what point?

_____

_____

Patterns of 8. Which of the following patterns does *not* organize the reading?
Organization
    a. definition

    b. comparison and contrast

    c. simple listing

    d. cause and effect

    e. classification

Supporting Details **9.** In paragraph 12, the authors point out that Asian Americans, like Hispanic Americans, come from many different ethnic groups. However, the authors also suggest that Asian Americans, *unlike* Hispanic Americans, are

a. not interested in having products that are Asian.

b. less affected by their differences in ethnic origin.

c. not affected at all by religious differences.

d. not being targeted by marketers.

Purpose **10.** How would you describe the authors' purpose?

a. The authors are describing the ways in which marketers target specific subcultures to sell products.

b. The authors are arguing that the targeting of subcultures to market products is unethical.

Drawing Your Own Conclusions In paragraph 6, the authors make a point of saying how important it is to understand that "the behavioral patterns and values attributed to specific subcultures do not necessarily apply to all group members." Why do you think the authors make it a point of mentioning this fact? What are they concerned about?

_____

_____

Thinking Through Writing Write a few paragraphs discussing whether marketers should or should not target products to specific subcultures. State your opinion in the opening paragraph. Then give at least one reason (two is even better) why you hold that opinion.

◆ **READING 3**   **The Demise* of Dating**

Charles M. Blow

Looking Ahead   When it appeared in the *New York Times*, the following article stirred up a good deal of controversy. Although some people praised the author, others claimed he was out of step with the times and out of touch with youth today.

Word Watch   You probably know most of the words in the reading. The ones you don't know can mostly be defined from context. The words that follow, however, cannot be fully understood from either context or analysis of word parts. For this reason, their meanings are supplied here. Look them over before you begin reading.

> **demise (title):** death, disappearance
> **paradigm (1):** pattern
> **norm (2):** average, tradition
> **stigma (4):** negative association; mark
>
> **inequity (4):** inequality
> **momentum (5):** forward movement

Reading Tip   The title suggests that dating has disappeared. Read to learn what's taken its place.

1   The paradigm* has shifted. Dating is dated. Hooking up is here to stay. (For those over 30 years old: hooking up is a casual sexual encounter with no expectation of future emotional commitment. Think of it as a one-night stand with someone you know.) According to a report released this spring by Child Trends, a Washington research group, there are now more high school seniors saying that they never date than seniors who say that they date frequently. Apparently, it's all about the hookup.

2   When I first heard about hooking up years ago, I figured that it was a fad that would soon fizzle. I was wrong. It seems to be becoming the norm.* I should point out that just because more young people seem to be hooking up instead of dating doesn't mean that they're having more sex (they've been having less, according to the Centers for Disease Control and Prevention) or having sex with strangers (they're more likely to hook up with a friend, according to a 2006 paper in the *Journal of Adolescent Research*).

3   To help me understand this phenomenon, I called Kathleen Bogle, a professor at La Salle University in Philadelphia who has studied hooking up among college students and is the author of the 2008 book, *Hooking Up: Sex, Dating, and Relationships on Campus*. It turns out that everything is the opposite of what I remember. Under the old model, you dated a few times and, if you really liked the person, you might consider having sex. Under the new model, you hook up a few times and, if you really like the person, you might consider going on a date.

4   I asked her to explain the pros and cons of this strange culture. According to her, the pros are that hooking up emphasizes group friendships over the one-pair model of dating, and, therefore, removes the negative stigma* from those who can't get a date. As she put it, "It used to be that if you couldn't get a date, you were a loser." Now, she said, you just hang out with your friends and hope that something happens. The cons center on the issues of gender inequity.* Girls get tired of hooking up because they want it to lead to a relationship (the guys don't), and, as they get older, they start to realize that it's not a good way to find a spouse. Also, there's an increased likelihood of sexual assaults because hooking up is often fueled by alcohol.

5   That's not good. So why is there an increase in hooking up? According to Professor Bogle, it's the collapse of advanced planning, lopsided gender ratios on campus, delaying marriage, relaxing values, and sheer momentum.* It used to be that "you were trained your whole life to date," said Ms. Bogle. "Now we've lost that ability—the ability to just ask someone out and get to know them." Now that's sad.

Combining Your Skills   DIRECTIONS   Answer the following questions by circling the appropriate letter or filling in the blanks.

Main Idea **1.** Which statement best expresses the main idea of the entire reading?

   a. Young people currently favor hooking up over dating, and it's easy to see why they would make that choice.

   b. Although hooking up may be the way students currently form relationships, it won't be long before they return to more traditional ways of meeting and getting to know one another.

   c. Unfortunately, hooking up has replaced dating as a way of forming relationships, and much has been lost in the process.

   d. Dating was always an artificial and anxiety-producing experience, so it's no surprise that students don't want to do it anymore.

2. The main idea is
   a. stated.
   b. implied.

Supporting Details 3. The study done by Child Trends and referred to in paragraph 1 is mentioned in order to prove what claim made by the author?

_____

4. Why does the author consult Kathleen Bogle?

_____

_____

Paraphrasing and Supporting Details 5. Paraphrase the author's description of the differences between hooking up and dating.

_____

_____

_____

_____

6. In your own words, according to the reading, what are the pros of hooking up as opposed to dating?

_____

7. In your own words, according to the reading, what are the cons?

_____

_____

Patterns of Organization 8. Which pattern of organization do you see at work in paragraph 5?
   a. time order
   b. cause and effect
   c. comparison and contrast
   d. classification

Purpose **9.** Which statement accurately describes the author's primary purpose?

    a. The author wants to tell readers about how young people are revising traditional dating patterns.

    b. The author wants to convince readers that the practice of hooking up rather than dating is a serious mistake.

Tone **10.** How would you describe the author's tone?

    a. objective

    b. worried

    c. lighthearted

    d. sarcastic

Drawing Your Own Conclusions How do you think the author would react if he had a daughter and she told him that she wasn't into dating because she thought hooking up was a more practical approach to socializing with the opposite sex?

_____

_____

Thinking Through Writing Do you think the author is right or wrong to feel as he does about the current trend away from dating? Start by making your agreement or disagreement clear. Then give your reasons.

◆ **READING 4** **Good Grief**

Richard Lederer

Looking Ahead Though used a good deal, the word *oxymoron* is often used incorrectly. After reading "Good Grief," however, you will be able to use the word with confidence.

Word Watch You probably know most of the words in the reading. The ones you don't know can mostly be defined from context. The words that follow, however, cannot be fully understood from either context or analysis of word parts. For this reason, their meanings are supplied here. Look them over before you begin reading.

> **emporium (1)**: store
>
> **incongruous (7)**: not fitting together
>
> **pianoforte (8)**: a musical direction that asks for the music to be played softly but not too softly
>
> **sophomoric (8)**: showing a lack of judgment because of immaturity

Reading Tip If you finish this selection knowing exactly what an oxymoron is and can come up with a few of your own, you've met your reading goal.

1   Not long ago, a couple that I know tooled down to a local car emporium* to look over the latest products. Attracted to the low sticker price on the basic model, they told the salesman that they were considering buying an unadorned automobile and had no inclination to purchase any of the long list of options affixed to the side window of the vehicle they were inspecting.

2   "But you will have to pay $168 for the rear window wiper," the salesman explained.

3   "But we don't want the rear wiper," my friends protested.

4   And the salesman said: "We want to keep the sticker price low, but every car comes with the rear window wiper. So you have to buy it. It's a mandatory option."

5   *Mandatory option* is a telling example of the kind of push-me/pull-you doublespeak that pervades the language of business and politics these days. It is also a striking instance of an oxymoron.

6   "Good grief!" you exclaim. "What's an oxymoron?"

7   An oxymoron (I reply) is a figure of speech[†] in which two incongruous,* contradictory terms are yoked together in a small space. As a matter of fact, *good grief* is an oxymoron.

8   Appropriately, the word *oxymoron* is itself oxymoronic because it is formed from two Greek roots of opposite meaning—*oxy*, "sharp, keen," and *moros*, "foolish," the same root that gives us the word *moron*. Two other examples of foreign word parts oxymoronically drawn to each other are *pianoforte*,* "soft-loud," and *sophomore*, "wise fool." If you know any sopho-moric* sophomores, you know how apt that oxymoron is.

9   I have long been amused by the name of a grocery store in my town, West Street Superette, since *super* means "large" and *-ette* means "small." If you have a superette in your town, it is a "large-small" store.

10   Perhaps the best-known oxymoron in the United States is one from comedian George Carlin's record *Toledo Window Box*, the delightful *jumbo shrimp*. Expand the expression to *fresh frozen jumbo shrimp*, and you have a double oxymoron.

Combining Your Skills   **DIRECTIONS**   Answer the following questions by circling the appropriate letter or filling in the blanks.

Using Context Clues   1. Based on the context, *tooled* in paragraph 1 means

_____.

2. Based on the context, *unadorned* in paragraph 1 means

_____.

3. Based on the context, *inclination* in paragraph 1 means

_____.

4. Based on the context, *affixed* in paragraph 1 means

_____.

[†]figure of speech: an expression that uses language in a nonrealistic way. "It's raining cats and dogs" is a figure of speech. In reality, such a thing could never happen.

Sentence Sense 5. Identify the relationship that connects these two sentences from paragraph 7: "An oxymoron . . . is a figure of speech in which two incongruous, contradictory terms are yoked together in a small space. As a matter of fact, *good grief* is an oxymoron."

    a. statement and example

    b. time order

    c. contrast

Main Idea 6. Which statement expresses the main idea of the entire reading?

    a. Oxymorons are going out of style.

    b. Car salesmen are the people most likely to use oxymorons.

    c. Oxymorons are expressions linking seemingly contradictory terms.

    d. Oxymorons should be avoided because they don't make sense.

Supporting Details 7. Explain why the word *oxymoron* is itself *oxymoronic*.

_____

_____

8. Why is *fresh frozen jumbo shrimp* a double oxymoron?

_____

_____

9. Give an example of an oxymoron you have either seen or heard, such as "new preowned cars." If you wish, you can create your own.

_____

_____

Tone 10. How would you describe the author's tone?

    a. annoyed

    b. solemn

    c. amused

    d. neutral

Drawing Your Own Conclusions In a section of his essay titled "Good Grief" (not included in the excerpt on pp. 492–493), Richard Lederer lists other oxymorons like the following:

old news
even odds
pretty ugly
civil war
awful good

Working with your classmates, see if you can come up with five more.

1. _____

2. _____

3. _____

4. _____

5. _____

◆ **READING 5**   **Backlash: Women Bullying Women in the Workplace?**

Mickey Meece

Looking Ahead   The author of this reading, who is herself female, suggests that women, having struggled to overcome sexism in the workplace, may face another obstacle: themselves.

Word Watch   You probably know most of the words in the reading. The ones you don't know can mostly be defined from context. The words that follow, however, cannot be fully understood from either context or analysis of word parts. For this reason, their meanings are supplied here. Look them over before you begin reading.

> **sabotaging (1):** ruining, encouraging failure
>
> **elephant in the room (2):** an idiom that refers to an embarrassing or troublesome event that, for some reason, no one wishes to acknowledge
>
> **glass ceiling (2):** prejudice against women that has kept them from reaching the same high positions as men do in the business world
>
> **corporate (3):** related to large businesses or corporations
>
> **jeopardizing (4):** endangering
>
> **confrontative (5):** ready to fight or openly oppose and argue
>
> **dynamic (6):** cause and effect relationship
>
> **litigation (10):** turning to the legal system; lawsuits
>
> **immersion (13):** getting deeply into something
>
> **mentoring (13):** teaching and offering advice to someone less experienced
>
> **nurturing (13):** caretaking, supporting

Reading Tip   The question in the title should be your guide in this case. Does the author offer compelling evidence that women are bullying one another in the workplace? If so, does she explain why?

1   Yelling, scheming, and sabotaging:* all are tell-tale signs that a bully is at work, laying traps for employees at every pass. During this downturn, as stress levels rise, workplace researchers say, bullies are likely to sharpen their elbows and ratchet up their attacks. It's probably no surprise that most of these bullies are men, as a survey by the Workplace Bullying

Institute, an advocacy group, makes clear. But a good 40 percent of bullies are women. And at least the male bullies take an egalitarian approach, mowing down men and women pretty much in equal measure. The women appear to prefer their own kind, choosing other women as targets more than 70 percent of the time.

2   In the name of Betty Friedan and Gloria Steinem,[†] what is going on here? Just the mention of women treating other women badly on the job seemingly shakes the women's movement to its core. It is what Peggy Klaus, an executive coach in Berkeley, California, has called "the pink elephant" in the room.* How can women break through the glass ceiling* if they are ducking verbal blows from other women in cubicles, hallways and conference rooms? Women don't like to talk about it because it is "so antithetical to the way that we are supposed to behave to other women," Ms. Klaus said. "We are supposed to be the nurturers and the supporters."

3   Ask women about run-ins with other women at work and some will point out that people of both sexes can misbehave. Others will nod in instant recognition and recount examples of how women—more so than men—have mistreated them. "I've been sabotaged so many times in the workplace by other women, I finally left the corporate* world and started my own business," said Roxy Westphal, who runs the promotional products company Roxy Ventures Inc. in Scottsdale, Arizona. She still recalls the sting of an interview she had with a woman 30 years ago that "turned into a one-person firing squad" and led her to leave the building in tears. Jean Kondek, who recently retired after a 30-year career in advertising, recalled her anger when an administrator in a small agency called a meeting to dress her down in front of co-workers for not following agency procedure in a client emergency. But Ms. Kondek said she had the last word. "I said, 'Would everyone please leave?'" She added, "and then I told her, 'This is not how you handle that.'"

4   Many women who are still in the work force were hesitant to speak out publicly for fear of making matters worse or of jeopardizing* their careers. A private accountant in California said she recently joined a company and was immediately frozen out by two women working there. One even pushed her in the cafeteria during an argument, the accountant said. "It's as if we're back in high school," she said. A senior executive said she had "finally broken the glass ceiling" only to have another woman gun for her job by telling management, "I can't work for her, she's passive-aggressive."

[†]Betty Friedan and Gloria Steinem were pioneers of the feminist movement, which reemerged in the 1960s. The slogan for this movement was "Sisterhood Is Powerful."

The strategy worked: The executive said she soon lost the job to her accuser.

5   One reason women choose other women as targets "is probably some idea that they can find a less confrontative* person or someone less likely to respond to aggression with aggression," said Gary Namie, research director for the Workplace Bullying Institute, which ordered the study in 2007.

6   But another dynamic* may be at work. After five decades of striving for equality, women make up more than 50 percent of management, professional and related occupations, says Catalyst, the nonprofit research group. And yet, its 2008 census found, only 15.7 percent of Fortune 500 officers and 15.2 percent of directors were women. Leadership specialists wonder, are women being "overly aggressive" because there are too few opportunities for advancement? Or is it stereotyping and women are only perceived as being overly aggressive? Is there a double standard at work?

7   Research on gender stereotyping from Catalyst suggests that no matter how women choose to lead, they are perceived as "never just right." What's more, the group found, women must work twice as hard as men to achieve the same level of recognition and prove they can lead. "If women business leaders act consistent with gender stereotypes, they are considered too soft," the group found in a 2007 study. "If they go against gender stereotypes, they are considered too tough." "Women are trying to figure out the magical keys to the kingdom," said Laura Steck, president of the Growth and Leadership Center in Sunnyvale, California, and an executive leadership coach. Women feel they have to be aggressive to be promoted, she said, and then they keep it up. Then, suddenly, they see the need to be collegial and collaborative instead of competitive.

8   Cleo Lepori-Costello, a vice president at a Silicon Valley software company, came to the center for training. She got off to a bumpy start when she stormed into her new role "like a bull in a china shop," Ms. Steck said. In gathering feedback about Ms. Lepori-Costello, Ms. Steck heard comments like: "Cleo is good at getting things done but may have come on too strong in the beginning. She didn't read the different cultural unspoken rules like she could have." So Ms. Steck and Kent Kaufman, another coach at the center, began a one-year, once-a-week individual coaching program. It included role-playing and monthly group discussions with other female executives who acknowledged that they also had major blind spots about being politic at work. (The group was once nicknamed the Bully Broads.) When she came to the center, Ms. Lepori-Costello said, she thought her colleagues were not initially open to her ideas. Through coaching and conflict role-playing, she came to realize that her behavior was

perhaps "too much overkill" and that she was not always attending to all the people around her.

9   Joel H. Neuman, a researcher at the State University of New York at New Paltz, says most aggressive behavior at work is influenced by a number of factors associated with the bullies, victims and the situations in which they work. "This would include issues related to frustration, personality traits, perceptions of unfair treatment, and an assortment of stresses and strains associated with today's leaner and 'meaner' work settings," he said. Mr. Neuman and his colleague Loraleigh Keashly of Wayne State University have developed a questionnaire to identify the full range of behaviors that can constitute bullying, which could help companies uncover problems that largely go unreported.

10   Bullying involves verbal or psychological forms of aggressive (hostile) behavior that persists for six months or longer. Their 29 questions include: Over the last 12 months, have you regularly been glared at in a hostile manner, been given the silent treatment, been treated in a rude or disrespectful manner, or had others fail to deny false rumors about you? The Workplace Bullying Institute says that 37 percent of workers have been bullied. Yet many employers ignore the problem, which hits the bottom line in turnover, health care and productivity costs, the institute says. Litigation* is rare, the institute says, because there is no directly applicable law to cite and the costs are high.

11   Two Canadian researchers recently set out to examine the bullying that pits women against women. They found that some women may sabotage one another because they feel that helping their female co-workers could jeopardize their own careers. One of the researchers, Grace Lau, a Ph.D. candidate at the University of Waterloo, said the goal was to encourage women to help one another. She said: "How? One way we predicted would be to remind women that they are members of the same group." "We believe that a sense of pride in women's accomplishments is important in getting women to help one another," Ms. Lau said. "To have this sense of pride, women need to be aware of their shared identity as women."

12   In the workplace, however, it is unlikely that women will constantly think of themselves as members of one group, she said. They will more likely see themselves as individuals, as they are judged by their performance. "As a result, women may not feel a need to help one another," she said. "They may even feel that in order to get ahead, they need to bully their co-workers by withholding information like promotion opportunities, and that women are easier to bully than men because women are supposedly less tough than men."

13   What better place to be a bully than in a prison? Even so, that is exactly where Televerde, a company in Phoenix that specializes in generating sales leads and market insight for high-tech companies, set up shop. About 13 years ago, the company created four call centers in the Arizona state prison in Perryville, employing 250 inmates (out of 3,000). Through immersion* training, mentoring* and working with real-world clients, these women can overcome their difficult circumstances, said Donna Kent, senior vice president at Televerde. "Often, they will win over bullies and we see the whole thing transform. That's what gives us inspiration and our clients inspiration."

14   Today, about half of Televerde's corporate office is made up of "graduates" from Perryville, including Michelle Cirocco, the director of sales operations. She has seen how women treat one another in other settings and she thinks the root cause is that women are taught to fight with one another for attention at an early age. "We're competing with our sisters for dad's attention, or for our brother's attention," Ms. Cirocco said. "And then we go on in school and we're competing for our teachers' attention. We're competing to be on the sports team or the cheer squad."

15   To be sure, the Televerde experience is not for every inmate, and those who are in it still must work hard to maintain a highly competitive position. "As we get into the corporate world," Ms. Cirocco added, "we're taught or we're led to believe that we don't get ahead because of men. But, we really don't get ahead because of ourselves. Instead of building each other up and showcasing each other, we're constantly tearing each other down." Televerde reversed that attitude in Perryville, Ms. Cirocco said, by encouraging women to work for a common cause, much like the environment envisioned by the Canadian researchers.

16   "It becomes a very nurturing* environment," Ms. Cirocco said. "You have all these women who become your friends, and you are personally invested in their success. Everyone wants everyone to get out, to go on to have a good healthy life." If the level of support found at Televerde were found elsewhere, Ms. Klaus said, it would solve a lot of problems. "The time has come," she said, "for us to really deal with this relationship that women have to women, because it truly is preventing us from being as successful in the workplace as we want to be and should be. We've got enough obstacles; we don't need to pile on any more."

Combining Your Skills   **DIRECTIONS**   Answer the following questions by circling the appropriate letter or filling in the blanks.

Main Idea   1. Which of the following statements best expresses the main idea of the entire reading?

    a. Although women do occasionally bully other women in the workplace, it's still men who think that the only way to get things done is to push people around and browbeat them.

    b. Women have had to struggle for years to win equal access to good jobs, and it's no surprise that as a result of that struggle they have turned mean and bitter.

    c. There is some evidence that women, for a number of reasons, do bully one another in the workplace, but there's also evidence that once they understand what they are doing, they stop.

    d. Although much has been written about how women, if they got into positions of power, would humanize the workplace, the opposite is true: Women in the workplace are actually tougher and more overbearing than men are, and this is especially true when it comes to how they treat their female colleagues.

Supporting Details   2. In your own words, why is "the pink elephant in the room" mentioned in paragraph 2?

_____

_____

3. Why are the names Betty Friedan and Gloria Steinem mentioned in paragraph 2?

_____

_____

_____

Supporting   4. What kind of evidence does the author offer to support her claim
Details and Fact   that women bullying one another in the workplace is a significant
and Opinion   problem?

    a. facts

    b. opinions

    c. a mixture of both

Supporting Details **5.** Why is Gary Namie quoted in paragraph 5?

_____

_____

Sentence Sense **6.** Paragraph 6 opens with the sentence: "But another dynamic may be at work." The function of that sentence is

a. to provide background.

b. to state the main idea.

c. to make a transition.

7. In paragraph 6, the author cites leadership specialists who wonder if women are aggressive with one another because "there are too few opportunities for advancement." This reference is the author's attempt to explain which phrase from the previous sentences?

a. striving for equality

b. another dynamic

c. nonprofit research

d. related occupations

Supporting Details **8.** In paragraph 7, the author cites Laura Steck, president of the Growth and Leadership Center. Steck says, "Women are trying to figure out the magical keys to the kingdom." What does she mean by "the magical keys to the kingdom"?

_____

_____

Purpose **9.** Which statement best describes the author's purpose?

a. The author wants to tell readers that some people believe women bullying women in the workplace is a significant problem.

b. The author wants to persuade readers that women bullying women in the workplace is a significant problem.

Bias **10.** Which statement best describes the author's attitude toward the subject?

a. The author does not believe that women bullying women in the workplace is a significant problem.

    b. The author believes that women bullying women in the work-
       place is a significant problem.

    c. It's impossible to determine the author's personal opinion.

Drawing Your Own Conclusions Why does the author end with a discussion of women in prison?

_____

_____

_____

Thinking Through Writing Write a paper in which you explain why you do or do not believe that the author has painted an accurate picture of women in the workplace.

◆ READING 6   Nonjudgmental and Critical Listening

Joseph DeVito

Looking Ahead   The author, Joseph DeVito, describes two kinds of listening, which at first glance look as if they might be in conflict. Read to discover if they truly are.

Word Watch   You probably know most of the words in the reading. The ones you don't know can mostly be defined from context. The words that follow, however, cannot be fully understood from either context or analysis of word parts. For this reason, their meanings are supplied here. Look them over before you begin reading.

> **integrate** (2): make part of; combine
>
> **embellished** (2): added to; made bigger or more important
>
> **incidental** (2): casual, happening by chance
>
> **fallacious** (2): false, incorrect

Reading Tip   In this case, the title gives you clear guidance. Read to define nonjudgmental and critical listening. Jot the definitions along with the examples, both the author's and your own, in the margins. Make sure you understand why the author thinks combining these two types of listening is important.

1   Effective listening includes both nonjudgmental and critical responses. You need to listen nonjudgmentally—with an open mind with a view toward understanding. You need to listen critically—with a view toward making some kind of evaluation or judgment. Clearly listen first for understanding while suspending judgment. Only after you've fully understood the relevant messages should you evaluate or judge.

2   Supplement open-minded listening with critical listening. Listening with an open mind will help you understand the messages better; listening with a critical mind will help you analyze and evaluate the messages. In adjusting your nonjudgmental and critical listening, focus on the following guidelines:

- Keep an open mind. Avoid prejudging. Delay your judgments until you fully understand the intention and the content the speaker is communicating. Avoid both positive and negative evaluation until you have a reasonably complete understanding.

- Avoid filtering out or oversimplifying complex messages. Similarly, avoid filtering out undesirable messages. You don't want to hear that something you believe in is untrue, that people you care for are unkind, or that ideals you hold are self-destructive. Yet, it's important that you reexamine your beliefs by listening to these messages.

- Recognize your own biases. These may interfere with accurate listening and cause you to distort message reception through the process of assimilation—the tendency to integrate* and interpret what you hear or think you hear with your own biases, prejudices, and expectations. For example, are your ethnic, national, or religious biases preventing you from appreciating a speaker's point of view?

- Be sure to listen critically to the entire message when you need to make evaluations and judgments. Recognize and combat the normal tendency to sharpen—a process in which one or two aspects of the message become highlighted, emphasized, and perhaps embellished.* Often the concepts that are sharpened are incidental* remarks that somehow stand out from the rest of the message.

- Recognize some of the popular but fallacious* forms of reasoning such as the following (Lee & Lee, 1972, 1995; Pratkanis & Aronson, 1991):

  - *Name-calling* involves giving an idea, a group of people, or a political philosophy a bad name ("atheist," "Neo-Nazi," "cult"). In the opposite of name-calling, the speaker tries to make you accept some idea by associating it with things you value highly ("democracy," "free speech," "academic freedom"). Remember that labels are useful most of the time but can often obscure the actual person or idea. Listen first to evidence and argument; never take labels as evidence or reasons for judgment.

  - *Testimonial* involves using the image associated with some person to gain your approval (if you respect the person) or your rejection (if you don't respect the person). This technique is used by advertisers who use people dressed up to look like doctors or plumbers or chefs to sell their products. Listen carefully to the person's credentials; be suspicious when you hear such phrases as "experts agree," "scientists say," "good cooks know," or "dentists advise." Ask yourself exactly who these experts are and what the source of their expertise is.

  - *Bandwagon* is a technique that tries to persuade you to accept or reject an idea or proposal because "everybody is doing it," so "jump on the bandwagon." You'll hear this technique used frequently during election time where results of polls are used to get you to join the group and vote for one person or another. Again, listen to the evidence; 50,000 Frenchmen—as the saying goes—can be wrong.

- *Agenda-setting* involves claiming that a particular issue is crucial and all others are unimportant and insignificant. This technique is used frequently in interpersonal conflict situations where each person may claim that her or his viewpoint is the accurate and important one and that the other person's is less accurate and less important. In almost all situations, and especially in interpersonal conflict situations, there are many issues and many sides to each issue.
- *Attack* involves accusing another person (usually an opponent) of some serious wrongdoing so that the issue under discussion never gets examined as in the argument, "How can I ever believe you after you lied." Although a person's reputation and past behavior are often relevant, listen most carefully to the issue at hand. When personal attack draws attention away from other issues, then it becomes fallacious.

Combining Your Skills   **DIRECTIONS**   Answer the following questions by circling the appropriate letter or filling in the blanks.

Context **1.** In paragraph 1, what kind of context clue does the author use?

    a. restatement

    b. contrast

    c. example

    d. general knowledge

He uses it to define which words or phrases?

_____

Sentence Relationships **2.** What relationship connects these two statements from paragraph 2: "Listening with an open mind will help you understand the messages better; listening with a critical mind will help you analyze and evaluate the messages"?

    a. agreement and modification

    b. time order

    c. contrast

    d. statement and example

Main Idea **3.** Which of the following statements best expresses the main idea of the entire reading?

    a. Keeping an open mind while listening is extremely important, but listening critically is more important.

    b. Critical listening is one of the main reasons why people from different cultures so often have difficulty communicating.

    c. To be a good listener, you need, at times, to be both open-minded and nonjudgmental; however, you also need to be ready to evaluate what you hear.

    d. Good listeners always analyze and evaluate what they hear; they do not simply absorb uncritically everything they hear.

Patterns of Organization **4.** The two paragraphs that make up this reading rely on which two patterns of organization?

    a. cause and effect *and* time order

    b. definition *and* comparison and contrast

    c. cause and effect *and* classification

    d. definition *and* time order

Supporting Details **5.** Use your own words to explain the natural tendency to "sharpen" what we hear.

_____

_____

6. According to the author, why is recognizing your own biases an essential part of effective listening?

_____

_____

Inferences **7.** Read the following description of a conversation and identify the kind of behavior it illustrates.

Doris and Anna are long-time friends who are having some problems. Anna has a new job. She feels she has to prove herself and has been working overtime. As a result, she has cancelled most of their usual activities together. Now Doris feels that the friendship is being neglected. She tells Anna that the most important thing about their friendship has always been their shared activities. Thus, it's rude and disrespectful to cancel their plans. Doris responds by saying that the most essential element of their friendship has been their mutual support of one another. She insists that Doris's failure to support her when she feels under stress is a serious betrayal. It appears that both women are engaging in

    a. the bandwagon technique.

    b. name calling.

    c. agenda-setting.

    d. testimonials.

Purpose 8. How would you describe the author's purpose?

    a. He wants to describe the differences between nonjudgmental and critical listening.

    b. He wants to convince readers that critical listening is essential to effective listening.

Bias 9. Which statement best describes the presence or absence of bias in the reading?

    a. The author considers nonjudgmental listening more important than critical listening.

    b. The author considers critical listening more important than nonjudgmental listening.

    c. The author reveals no bias in favor of one or the other.

Tone 10. How would you describe the author's tone?

    a. cool and distant

    b. friendly and relaxed

    c. self-important

    d. confident to the point of arrogance

Drawing Your Own Conclusions Gerald and Miguel are having a heated discussion about a new law that makes it harder to eliminate debt by declaring bankruptcy. When Gerald tries to explain why he thinks the new law will benefit credit card companies but further burden those people already in debt, Miguel quickly responds. He says, "Anyone dumb enough to use plastic when they don't have cash doesn't deserve my sympathy."

What is Miguel doing that Joseph DeVito, the author of the reading, cautions against?

_____

_____

Thinking Through Writing Write a description of another conversation that illustrates one of the fallacies DeVito warns readers about. Read it aloud to classmates to see if they can spot the error.

◆ READING 7 What Makes a Hero?

Ted Tollefson

Looking Ahead Author Ted Tollefson believes that the heroic character can be defined. Read to see if his description of a hero matches yours.

Word Watch You probably know most of the words in the reading. The ones you don't know can mostly be defined from context. The words that follow, however, cannot be fully understood from either context or analysis of word parts. For this reason, their meanings are supplied here. Look them over before you begin reading.

> **orator (1)**: speaker
>
> **transformers (3)**: devices used to transfer electricity from one circuit to another
>
> **zest (3)**: excitement, enthusiasm
>
> **abundant (3)**: rich, full, varied
>
> **catalysts (4)**: people or substances that cause a change
>
> **charismatic (4)**: possessed of personal magnetism or charm
>
> **universal (5)**: common to all people
>
> **tutelage (5)**: teaching, education
>
> **disdained (5)**: disliked, disregarded
>
> **unbridled (7)**: uncontrolled
>
> **purveyors (7)**: people who hand out or give out something
>
> **grandiose (9)**: grand, great
>
> **pious (9)**: saintly
>
> **naïveté (9)**: innocence
>
> **collage (10)**: a picture created out of pieces from other pictures

Reading Tip As you read, keep asking yourself how you would define a hero if you were to write an essay similar to this one. List some key traits of a hero in the margins of the reading. Think, too, about people who do or do not match Tollefson's description.

1 For several years, a picture of Warren Spahn of the Milwaukee Braves hung on my closet door, one leg poised in midair before he delivered a smoking fastball. Time passed and Spahn's picture gave way to others: Elvis, John F.

Kennedy, Carl Jung,[†] Joseph Campbell,[†] Ben Hogan.[†] These heroic images have reflected back to me what I hoped to become: a man with good moves, a sex symbol, an electrifying orator,* a plumber of depths, a teller of tales, a graceful golfer. Like serpents, we keep shedding the skins of our heroes as we move toward new phases in our lives.

2　　Like many of my generation, I have a weakness for hero worship. At some point, however, we all begin to question our heroes and our need for them. This leads us to ask: What is a hero? Despite immense differences in cultures, heroes around the world generally share a number of traits that instruct and inspire people.

3　　*A hero does something worth talking about.* A hero has a story of adventure to tell and a community who will listen. But a hero goes beyond mere fame or celebrity. *Heroes serve powers or principles larger than themselves.* Like high-voltage transformers,* heroes take the energy of higher powers and step it down so that it can be used by ordinary mortals. *The hero lives a life worthy of imitation.* Those who imitate a genuine hero experience life with new depth, zest,* and meaning. A sure test for would-be heroes is what or whom do they serve? What are they willing to live and die for? If the answer or evidence suggests they serve only their own fame, they may be celebrities but not heroes. Madonna and Michael Jackson are famous, but who would claim that their adoring fans find life more abundant?*

4　　*Heroes are catalysts* for change.* They have a vision from the mountain-top. They have the skill and the charm to move the masses. They create new possibilities. Without Gandhi,[†] India might still be part of the British Empire. Without Rosa Parks[†] and Martin Luther King Jr., we might still have segregated buses, restaurants, and parks. It may be possible for large-scale change to occur without charismatic* leaders, but the pace of change would be glacial, the vision uncertain, and the committee meetings endless.

5　　Though heroes aspire to universal* values, most are bound to the culture from which they came. The heroes of the Homeric Greeks wept loudly for their lost comrades and exhibited their grief publicly. A later

---

[†]Carl Jung (1875–1961): Swiss psychologist.
[†]Joseph Campbell (1904–1987): a collector of myths who was heavily influenced by Carl Jung.
[†]Ben Hogan (1912–1997): one of the greatest golfers in the history of the game.
[†]Mohandas Gandhi (1869–1948): Indian leader who used nonviolent disobedience to gain India's independence from Great Britain.
[†]Rosa Parks (1913–2005): African-American Rosa Parks refused to give up her bus seat to a white man in 1955. In doing so, she helped ignite the civil rights movement.

generation of Greeks under the tutelage* of Plato disdained* this display of grief as "unmanly."

6   Though the heroic tradition of white Americans is barely three hundred years old, it already shows some unique and unnerving features. While most traditional heroes leave home, have an adventure, and return home to tell the story, American heroes are often homeless. They come out of nowhere, right what is wrong, and then disappear into the wilderness. Throughout most of the world, it is acknowledged that heroes need a community as much as a community needs them.

7   And most Americans seem to prefer their heroes flawless, innocent, forever wearing a white hat or airbrushed features. Character flaws—unbridled* lust, political incorrectness—are held as proof that our heroes aren't really heroes. Several heroes on my own list have provided easy targets for the purveyors* of heroic perfectionism.

8   The ancient Greeks and Hebrews were wiser on this count. They chose for their heroes men and women with visible, tragic flaws. Oedipus'[†] fierce curiosity raised him to be king but also lured him to his mother's bed. King David's unbounded passion made him dance naked before the Ark *and* led him to betray Uriah so he could take Bathsheba for his wife.

9   American heroes lack a sense of home that might limit and ground their grandiose* ambitions. American heroes avoid acknowledging their own vices, which makes them more likely to look for somebody else to blame when things go wrong. Our national heroes seem to be stuck somewhere between Billy Budd[†] and the Lone Ranger:[†] pious,* armed cowboys who are full of energy, hope, and dangerous naïveté.*

10   Here are some exercises to give you insights into your own ideas about heroes and villains:

1. Draw a time line with markings every five years in your life. For each era, name an important hero (male or female). Identify three core qualities each stands for. Look at the overall list for recurring qualities. Who or what do your heroes serve?

2. Make a list of enemies, the people who really push your buttons. For each, specify three qualities that make your blood boil. Now look for

---

[†]Oedipus: the hero of a Greek tragedy who was determined to know the secret of his birth. When he found it out, he was so horrified that he blinded himself.
[†]Billy Budd: a character from a short story by Herman Melville. Young Billy is so innocent he arouses the hatred of the ship's cynical master-of-arms, John Claggart.
[†]Lone Ranger: the white-hatted hero of a television western.

recurring qualities. What emerges is your "shadow," parts of yourself that you fear, loathe, and therefore loan to others. What does your shadow know that you don't?

3. Make a collage* of your heroes, leaving room for their tragic flaws and holy vices.

Combining
Your Skills

DIRECTIONS   Answer the following questions by circling the appropriate letter or by filling in the blanks.

Main Idea **1.** Which paragraph introduces the main idea of the entire reading?

    a. paragraph 1

    b. paragraph 2

    c. paragraph 3

2. Which statement accurately paraphrases the main idea of the entire reading?

    a. In different stages of our lives, we need different heroes on whom to model ourselves.

    b. No matter where they come from or what their era, heroes are likely to share similar traits that are admired and imitated by others.

    c. All too often, Americans confuse celebrities with heroes.

    d. There are many differences between American and European heroes.

Supporting Details **3.** In paragraph 3, which of these sentences is a minor detail?

    a. "Those who imitate a genuine hero experience life with new depth, zest, and meaning."

    b. "Madonna and Michael Jackson are famous, but who would claim that their adoring fans find life more abundant?"

Inference **4.** Based on what the author says in paragraph 3, which inference is appropriate?

    a. He thinks the words *heroes* and *celebrities* mean the same thing.

    b. He thinks heroes should not be confused with celebrities.

    c. He believes Americans have replaced European royalty with celebrities.

Main Idea 5. Gandhi, Rosa Parks, and Martin Luther King Jr. are illustrations of which main idea?

    a. Heroes always suffer for their beliefs.

    b. Heroes bring about change in the world.

    c. Heroes are made, not born.

    d. Ordinary people are capable of great heroism.

6. What's the main idea of paragraph 6?

    a. Generally, heroes leave home and return to tell the story of their adventures.

    b. American heroes often feel homeless.

    c. Although it's only a few centuries old, the American heroic tradition already has some disturbing traits.

    d. Heroes almost always disappear into the wilderness and return completely transformed.

Patterns of 7. Which pattern do you recognize in paragraphs 7 and 8?
Organization
    a. sequence of events

    b. comparison and contrast

    c. cause and effect

    d. classification

Paraphrase 8. Which statement most effectively paraphrases the difference between American heroes and those belonging to the ancient Greeks and Hebrews?

    a. Unlike the Greeks and Hebrews, Americans don't require their heroes to be innocent.

    b. Americans seem to require their heroes to be politically correct, but the Greeks and Hebrews didn't care about political correctness.

    c. Whereas Americans expect their heroes to be flawless, the ancient Greeks and Hebrews knew better.

Inference 9. In paragraph 1, what simile—comparison using *like* or *as*—does the author use to convey the point that we have different heroes at different points in our lives?

_____

_____

Tone 10. What tone do you hear in this reading?

    a. friendly and personal

    b. angry and annoyed

    c. solemn and serious

    d. cool and distant

Drawing Your Own Conclusions The author lists his heroes. Who are your heroes? Do they fit the author's description? How are they similar or different? Do you think you are capable of being a hero? Why or why not?

_____

_____

_____

_____

Thinking Through Writing Write an essay in which you define the characteristics of a hero. Begin with a brief description of someone you consider heroic. Then describe the characteristics that make that person a hero to you.

Note: Your hero doesn't have to be a famous person; he or she just has to be someone you admire.

◆ **READING 8**   **Raoul Wallenberg: A Lost Hero**

Laraine Flemming

Looking Ahead   During World War II, the Nazis, under the leadership of Adolf Hitler, inspired terror in people, so much so that few were willing to interfere. As a result, millions of men, women, and children went to their deaths in the concentration camps of Dachau, Bergen-Belsen, Auschwitz, and others. Raoul Wallenberg, however, was not willing to look away from the suffering of others. Armed with nothing more than charm, intelligence, and courage, Wallenberg challenged the Nazis and frequently won.

Word Watch   Some of the more difficult words in the reading are defined below. The number in parentheses indicates the paragraph in which the word appears. An asterisk marks its first appearance in the reading. Preview the definitions before you begin reading and watch for the words while you read.

> **cultivated (1):** refined by training and education
>
> **atrocities (5):** acts of cruelty and violence
>
> **callously (10):** without feeling or pity
>
> **unorthodox (11):** untraditional
>
> **sanctuary (12):** a place of safety
>
> **dismantled (17):** taken apart

Reading Tip   Read the section titled Word Watch. Then read the first paragraph, all of the headings, and the last paragraph of the selection. Based on your survey, make one or two predictions. What points do you expect the author to make? In addition to making predictions, jot down one or two questions you will try to answer as you read.

1   In 1937, Raoul Wallenberg was a young man who seemed to have everything. Born into one of Sweden's richest and most respected families, he was cultivated,* handsome, and charming. His future seemed assured. After a few years spent learning the family business, he would follow in his grandfather's footsteps and become a banker.

2   But the young Wallenberg was not content. In a letter to his grandfather, he made it clear that something was missing: "To tell the truth, I don't feel especially bankish. . . . I think it is more in my nature to work positively for something."

3   Wallenberg's words were prophetic. By 1944, he was indeed working positively for something. He was risking his life to save the Jews of Budapest, Hungary. Members of the last large Jewish community in Europe, the Jews of Budapest had been targeted for extinction. Without their death, Nazi Germany could not claim that the "Final Solution," their plan to eliminate all the Jews in Europe, was a success. And, as the world now knows, the Nazis were determined to be successful.

4   Adolf Eichmann, one of the architects of Hitler's Final Solution, openly proclaimed his enthusiasm for the Hungarian "project." He personally organized the transportation of Jews to Auschwitz and insisted that the job be completed as swiftly as possible. But Eichmann had reckoned without the arrival of Raoul Wallenberg. Almost single-handedly, Wallenberg saved over 100,000 Hungarian Jews. Then, in one of the great mysteries of all time, he vanished. To this day, his disappearance remains unexplained and his whereabouts, alive or dead, are unknown.

Wallenberg's American Connection

5   By late 1942, most of the world's leaders knew that the German government was determined to make all of Europe *judenrein*, or free of Jews. Although reports of atrocities* had been circulating for months, government officials had viewed them as isolated events. As 1942 drew to a close, however, both the American State Department and the British Foreign Office had to confront the terrible truth hidden behind the euphemism *Final Solution*. The Nazis were systematically killing, or, in their words, "exterminating," the Jews of Europe.

6   By 1944, the American government had decided to organize the War Refugee Board. Its goal was to block "Nazi plans to exterminate all the Jews." This goal clearly required intervention in Hungarian affairs, because Hungary was the only remaining country with a large Jewish population. The country was also under German occupation.

7   As a result, Iver C. Olsen, a member of the U.S. Treasury Department, was sent to neutral Sweden. His task was to find a Swedish representative who could enter Hungary and somehow stop deportations to the concentration camps. Within days of meeting Olsen, Raoul Wallenberg was ready to travel.

A Powerful Piece of Paper

8   Raoul Wallenberg arrived in Budapest on July 9, 1944. When he entered the Swedish embassy, he saw a long line of people wearing the yellow Star of David that proclaimed their status as Jews. Word had gotten out that the

Swedes were giving travel documents or citizenship papers to Hungarian Jews who were planning to become Swedish citizens or residents. In several cases, those documents had offered protection against deportation and death.

9   One Jewish businessman had even gone to court, claiming his Swedish citizenship protected him from deportation. To everyone's surprise, he had won his case. Another man had escaped deportation to Auschwitz, the most dreaded of all concentration camps, by showing a Swedish document. The German officer in charge had simply let him go, obviously intimidated by the sight of an official document.

10   Quick to infer a valuable lesson from these incidents, Wallenberg realized immediately that the same people who could callously* inflict suffering and death could also be intimidated by a piece of paper. Inhumanity did not disturb them, but failure to follow the rules did. Inspired by that knowledge, Wallenberg designed an impressive-looking document, bearing the symbol of the Swedish government. More important, it announced that anyone carrying the document was under the protection, or *Schutz*, of the Swedish government. The document was signed by Raoul Wallenberg.

11   Wallenberg's next step was to set up a small network for the distribution of the *Schutz* passes. He then visited members of the Hungarian government and showed them a letter from King Gustav of Sweden. He made it clear to all present that Sweden was committed to protecting the Jews against further aggression. Other Swedish diplomats were a bit taken aback by Wallenberg's unorthodox* efforts, citing questions of procedure and legality. But Wallenberg managed to brush all such considerations aside with one answer: "It will save lives."

12   By October 1944, Wallenberg had been in Budapest just three short months. During that time, he had purchased a number of houses with the money provided by Olsen. Draping them with Swedish flags, Wallenberg claimed the houses were Swedish property and therefore not subject to German or Hungarian law. In effect, they became "safe houses," places of sanctuary* for Jewish refugees.

13   When, on one occasion, Hungarian troops tried to force their way into one of Wallenberg's safe houses, he blocked their way, saying, "No one leaves this place as long as I live." The troops withdrew.

14   On October 15, 1944, Hungarian radio announced that the war was lost, and the announcer openly blamed the Germans for dragging Hungary into a losing battle. In the Jewish quarter, there was dancing in the streets. Unfortunately, the dancing was premature. Shortly after the first

announcement came another more ominous broadcast. The Hungarian Nazi Party, the hated and feared *Arrow Cross*, had taken over. Along with the German Nazis still in Hungary, members of the *Arrow Cross* would continue to be loyal to Adolf Hitler. Above all, they would continue to work toward the Final Solution.

The *Arrow Cross*'s Reign of Terror

15 The notorious Adolf Eichmann was again in Budapest, and fifteen members of the *Arrow Cross* roamed the streets hunting down and shooting Jews on sight. At one point, a small band of Jewish laborers and a handful of Communists got hold of arms, and they fought back. Immediately the German SS[†] and the Hungarian police were at the scene of the fighting. They rounded up hundreds of suspected sympathizers and executed them where they stood. A nightmare world prior to October 15, Budapest had now become a living hell.

16 As Soviet tanks drew closer, the Nazis became more violent and more vicious. They barged into Wallenberg's "safe" houses and dragged out the "protected" Jews. They tortured their victims, shot them, and then threw their bodies into the Danube River.

17 Eichmann, however, was furious that his plans for exterminating the Hungarian Jews were being interrupted. Nazi officials had become anxious about what was going to happen when the war ended. With good reason, they were afraid of being tried as war criminals. Auschwitz was being dismantled,* and orders had been given to stop the extermination program. But Eichmann was not to be stopped; he devised yet another scheme.

18 Jews now were to be rounded up to work on the "East Wall" in Vienna. The wall would supposedly be protection against the advance of the Russians. But, more important, Eichmann knew that most of the Jews who would be marched on foot to Vienna would not survive. The cold, starvation, and hunger would do their work.

19 Wallenberg also knew that the "labor march," as it was called, was bound to be a death march. He tried to have the march postponed but succeeded only in getting exemptions for those Jews bearing *Schutz* passes. On November 9, the march began.

20 Shivering for lack of clothing and starving for food, the Jews were marched toward the Austrian border. Anyone who stumbled or fell out of line was shot. The marchers were without hope. But then Wallenberg

---

[†]SS: *Schutzstaffel* (protective units), the elite guard of the Nazi party, notorious for their brutal tactics.

miraculously began to turn up at points along the way. Susan Tabor, a survivor of the march, described lying on the floor of a shed so crowded she could neither stand up nor move. Suddenly she saw Wallenberg stride in, carrying a briefcase. Through a megaphone he announced that food and medical supplies would soon arrive. When he left, the marchers had new hope. As Susan Tabor was to say long after the march was over, "He made me feel human again. For the first time I had hope."

21   As always, true to his word, Wallenberg returned the next day with food and medicine. He also brought a stack of protective passes. Within minutes, he had created chaos by telling the marchers to assemble in various lines. As Wallenberg biographer Elenore Lester later wrote:

> The Jews ran helter-skelter around the brick factory. They changed lines and jostled one another to get a good place as Wallenberg backed his trucks into the yard. The *Arrow Cross* guards lost control. . . . In the confusion many Jews simply walked away or bribed individual guards to let them escape.

This scene was repeated many times as Wallenberg worked tirelessly to save as many Jews as he could.

The Russians Arrive

22   By January 1945, the Russians were closing in on Budapest, and it was clear to everyone that the war was truly coming to an end. On January 13, 1945, a small group of Russian soldiers broke through the wall of a house where Wallenberg was staying. He explained who he was, and the soldiers examined his documents. But something about Wallenberg or his papers seemed to make them suspicious. A few hours later, some high-ranking Soviet officials arrived to question him, in the first of several interrogations by the Russian secret police. Nevertheless, Wallenberg was permitted to move freely through the now-liberated city of Budapest.

23   On January 17, Wallenberg dropped in on friends before leaving to visit Soviet headquarters. He was in high spirits, convinced that the Soviets wanted his advice on postwar relief and reconstruction: "The Russians are certain to respect the suggestions of a Swedish diplomat."

24   Shortly after the visit, Wallenberg left Budapest under Russian escort. As he looked at the soldiers who were to accompany him, he made a cruelly prophetic joke: "I still don't know if they're coming along to protect me or guard me. Am I a guest, or a prisoner?"

25   Even today, no one is really sure what happened to Raoul Wallenberg after he left with his Soviet escorts. When he failed to return to Budapest as

planned, the Swedish Foreign Office sent the Russians a series of messages asking for an investigation. There was no reply. After repeated refusals of requests for information, the Soviets claimed to have no knowledge of his whereabouts. Then, in 1957, Andrei Gromyko, the Soviet deputy foreign minister, claimed Wallenberg had died in 1947. According to Gromyko, Wallenberg had suffered a heart attack at the age of thirty-four. Despite Soviet claims, however, rumors persisted that Raoul Wallenberg was still alive.

26   Whether he is alive or dead, the file on Wallenberg needs to be opened. Wallenberg deserves to be remembered and honored. As Frederick E. Werbell and Thurston Clarke have pointed out, Wallenberg's life is an important source of inspiration: "If the Holocaust is to be taken as evidence that human nature is essentially evil, then Wallenberg's life must be considered as evidence that it is not."

Combining Your Skills Answer the following questions by filling in the blanks or circling the letter of the correct response.

Overall Main Idea 1. Which statement best expresses the overall main idea of the entire reading?

   a. Raoul Wallenberg, whose mysterious disappearance has never been explained, may have been working for the Russians all along.

   b. Despite the actions of men and women like Raoul Wallenberg, the Nazis' treatment of the Jews during World War II contradicts any illusions we might have that human beings are generally good rather than evil.

   c. To this day, no one knows for sure what happened to Raoul Wallenberg.

   d. After risking his life to save thousands of Hungarian Jews, Raoul Wallenberg mysteriously vanished, and, to this day, no one knows what happened to him, but his heroic example lives on.

Supporting Details 2. Which of the following details is *not* essential to developing the main idea of the entire reading?

   a. "In 1937, Raoul Wallenberg was a young man who seemed to have everything" (paragraph 1).

   b. "Raoul Wallenberg arrived in Budapest on July 9, 1944" (paragraph 8).

   c. "Wallenberg's next step was to set up a small network for the distribution of *Schutz* passes" (paragraph 11).

Inferences 3. Based on paragraph 11, which inference fits the information provided?

    a. Wallenberg held other Swedish diplomats in contempt.

    b. Wallenberg was impatient with questions of procedure and legality when they concerned human lives.

    c. Wallenberg was a true hero, but that didn't mean he was without flaws; he could be rude and arrogant.

4. When the Russians first arrived, Wallenberg was convinced that

    a. they would kill him.

    b. they wanted his advice.

    c. they would leave him alone.

Sentence Sense 5. The following sentence appears in paragraph 14: "Unfortunately, the dancing was premature." Which statement most accurately describes the function of that sentence?

    a. It helps to introduce the topic sentence.

    b. It sums up the main idea.

    c. It functions as a transition.

Patterns of 6. Which two patterns help organize the supporting details in this
Organization   reading?

    a. time order

    b. simple listing

    c. comparison and contrast

    d. cause and effect

Fact and Opinion 7. Label each of the following statements *F* (fact), *O* (opinion), or *M* (a mix of both).

    a. "In 1937, Raoul Wallenberg was a young man who seemed to have everything" (paragraph 1). _____

    b. "By 1944, the American government had decided to organize the War Refugee Board" (paragraph 6). _____

    c. "Raoul Wallenberg arrived in Budapest on July 9, 1944" (paragraph 8). _____

    d. "Whether he is alive or dead, the file on Wallenberg needs to be opened" (paragraph 26). _____

Tone **8.** How would you describe the author's tone?

a. angry

b. admiring

c. emotionally neutral

Purpose **9.** How would you describe the author's primary purpose?

a. The author wants to inform readers about the role Wallenberg played in the fight against the Nazis.

b. The author wants to persuade readers that they need to know about and remember Raoul Wallenberg.

Bias **10.** Many people now believe that the United States did not act quickly enough to help those being persecuted during World War II. Re-read paragraphs 5, 6, and 7. Then decide which statement you think is accurate.

a. The author leans toward the belief that the United States did not act quickly enough.

b. The author is inclined to believe that the United States acted as quickly as possible.

c. It's impossible to determine the author's personal feelings on this subject.

Drawing Your Own Conclusions Paraphrase the quotation that ends the reading. In your own words, what does it mean? How do you think someone who disagrees with the point of the quotation might respond to it?

_____

_____

Thinking Through Writing Write a paper explaining why you think Raoul Wallenberg was willing to risk his life for people he did not know. Focus on trying to explain what you think was his motivation or, more to the point, the motivation of people like him, who risk their lives for others. Conclude by saying if you think you would or would not be capable of such self-sacrifice.

◆ **READING 9**   **Online Therapy Clicks**

Marilyn Elias

Looking Ahead   People use the Internet for everything from booking airline tickets to meeting a potential spouse. Some even go online for psychological counseling. But does online therapy really work? This reading explores the pros and cons.

Word Watch   You probably know most of the words in the reading. The ones you don't know can mostly be defined from context. The words that follow, however, cannot be fully understood from either context or analysis of word parts. For this reason, their meanings are supplied here. Look them over before you begin reading.

> **sibling (1):** brother or sister
>
> **cyberspace (1):** the network of computers that makes up the online environment
>
> **advocate (2):** supporter
>
> **credential (2):** qualification
>
> **obese (4):** overweight
>
> **inhibition (6):** sense of holding back
>
> **impending (8):** about to happen

Reading Tip   Much of this reading focuses on the advantages and disadvantages of online therapy. As you read, highlight or underline each of these pros and cons. You may also want to list the arguments for each side in the margins. Then, evaluate the various reasons provided by supporters and critics of online therapy. In your opinion, which side of the debate makes more sense?

1   Pat Underwood was reeling from a hard slap of midlife emotional pain when she began therapy three months ago. She was grieving over her father's recent death. Old sibling* conflicts had resurfaced. After remarrying, she had left good friends behind in Tennessee and moved with her new husband to Madison, Georgia, where she had no job or friends. The therapy, she says, "has been a great help. I've been able to work through a lot of problems." She has never met her counselor, though, because he lives 2,100 miles away. He's Peter Chechele (Check-a-lee), a San

Francisco marriage and family therapist who treats many clients at his "office" in cyberspace.*

2   Online counseling is the hottest and certainly the most controversial new trend in therapy, many experts say. Five years ago, six therapists practiced online. Now there are more than 500, says consumer advocate* Martha Ainsworth, whose Web site, www.metanoia.org, provides information and independent credential* checks of therapists doing e-therapy. "The field has just exploded," she says.

3   Therapists practicing on the Net are primarily psychologists, licensed clinical social workers, marriage and family counselors and other licensed professional counselors; very few are psychiatrists. About 90 percent of the counseling is done by e-mail, she says. Clients send therapists e-mails any time of the day or night. Counselors typically respond within a day or two, sometimes within hours. Most charge by the e-mail response, but some allow unlimited e-mails over a specific time for a single fee. Chechele, for example, offers varied plans, including unlimited e-mails over 30 days for $200.

4   E-therapy is not suited for people with severe mental disorders, such as schizophrenia or bipolar disorder (manic-depression). Medication is not generally prescribed by therapists on the Net because anyone with a problem serious enough to need drugs also needs a face-to-face counselor. But for many others, boosters say, the advantages of Net therapy abound:

- It's tailor-made for business travelers and employed parents who find it hard to carve out daytime hours or keep weekly appointments in one city.
- It costs less. E-mails average $25 to $50 each, Ainsworth says. Even rates of $90 an hour fall below typical therapy charges of $125 to $165.
- It can work faster. There is evidence that people self-disclose more quickly using a computer than they do face-to-face, says Johns Hopkins University psychologist Patricia Wallace, author of *The Psychology of the Internet*.
- It may attract those too embarrassed to face a therapist: childhood sexual-abuse victims, the obese,* those with physical deformities or painful secrets.

5   Jessica Bride, 26, marketing and communications director for a restaurant chain, had been seeing therapist Mark Sichel in his New York office last year when her work started to require a lot of travel. As the youngest director her firm had ever had and a woman to boot, "I found I had a lot of challenges on the job," Bride says. A painful romantic breakup added to the stress. When she's on the road or even at work in New York, e-mail exchanges with Sichel "offer great immediacy. As a problem comes

up, you can deal with it right away. I like the rapid response. It heads off trouble when you're right at the edge of blowing," says Bride.

The Net's Downside

6 But is such online support truly psychotherapy? No way, critics argue. And can it hurt rather than help? Absolutely, says the chorus of opponents. The downside of all that lack of inhibition* online is greater potential for deception, Wallace says. Either the patient or the therapist may not be who he says he is.

Deception by Patients May Not Even Be Deliberate

7 "Often, a patient will not think they're suicidal or that their problems are serious, and they turn out to be. The Net is packed with depressed people," says San Diego psychologist Marlene Maheu, who runs Netpsych, the largest Internet professional discussion list for U.S. therapists.

8   She points to therapists' moral responsibility to report impending* suicides to emergency agencies and their legal duty to report child abuse or other violence. "Some of these online therapists don't even have the client's address, or the address may not be real. So how can you prevent tragedy?"

9   So far, no "tragedies" or lawsuits have surfaced, says Russ Newman, executive director for professional practice at the American Psychological Association. But it's debatable whether Net therapy is even legal, he adds. Therapists are licensed to practice in a specific state, so is it all right to treat clients living in another state through the medium of cyberspace? "We just don't know. This is frontier territory," says Newman, an attorney and psychologist.

Combining Your Skills   **DIRECTIONS**   Answer the following questions by circling the appropriate letter.

Main Idea   1. What's the main idea of the entire reading?

   a. Online therapy may well have its boosters, but it also has its critics.

   b. Online therapy is far superior to traditional face-to-face therapy.

   c. Online therapy is far too dangerous, and potential users should be very, very careful about talking to a therapist online.

   d. Online therapy is growing in popularity for a number of reasons.

2. What's the implied main idea of paragraph 5?

   a. Busy professionals are under more stress than anyone else.

   b. More female professionals than male professionals prefer online therapy to traditional face-to-face therapy.

   c. Online therapy allows professionals with busy schedules to get the help they need.

   d. Dealing with a problem right away is better than ignoring it and allowing it to become worse.

Supporting Details 3. The expert opinion of psychologist Patricia Wallace in paragraph 4 is a supporting detail that develops what point?

   a. Most psychologists support the use of online therapy.

   b. Computers have improved our lives in many ways.

   c. Online therapy has many advantages.

   d. Online therapy has many disadvantages.

Transitions 4. Paragraph 2 contains what type of transitions?

   a. cause and effect

   b. time order

   c. comparison and contrast

Inference 5. What's the implied main idea of paragraph 6?

   a. It is impossible to provide therapy online.

   b. Critics say online therapy encourages deception on both sides.

   c. Online therapy encourages patients to be deceptive with their therapists.

   d. Online therapy has both advantages and disadvantages.

Paraphrase 6. Which statement most effectively paraphrases the implied main idea of paragraphs 7 and 8?

   a. Online therapists have a poor track record when it comes to identifying suicidal patients.

   b. Online therapists can readily disguise their lack of expertise when it comes to diagnosing suicidal patients.

   c. Online patients don't necessarily realize how serious their condition is.

   d. Online therapists are not in a position to recognize or intervene in a possibly tragic situation.

Inference 7. What can you conclude from paragraphs 7 and 8 about Marlene Maheu's opinion of online therapy?

   a. She probably supports the use of online therapy.

   b. She probably opposes the use of online therapy.

Fact and Opinion 8. How would you label the following statement from paragraph 4—*fact, opinion,* or *a blend of both*? "Medication is not generally prescribed by therapists on the Net because anyone with a problem serious enough to need drugs also needs a face-to-face counselor."

   a. fact

   b. opinion

   c. a blend of both

Purpose 9. Which of the following statements more effectively describes the author's purpose?

   a. The author wants to tell the readers about the pros and cons of online therapy.

   b. The author wants to convince readers that online therapy is dangerous.

Tone 10. How would you describe the author's tone?

   a. neutral

   b. critical

   c. admiring

   d. humorous

Drawing Your Own Conclusions Do you think that online counseling could be improved so that it's less subject to deceptiveness, safer, and more effective overall? Explain.

_____

_____

Thinking Through Writing Would you try online therapy? Why or why not? Write a paper that presents the reasons for your decision.

◆ **READING 10** **Checking the Stats**

Laraine Flemming and Ann Marie Radaskiewicz

Looking Ahead Many people think statistics are the kind of hard factual evidence that can't be questioned. This reading, however, based largely on the work of Joel Best, the best-selling author of numerous books on misleading statistics, suggests that statistical evidence, like any other form of evidence, needs to be examined with a critical eye.

Word Watch You probably know most of the words in the reading. The ones you don't know can mostly be defined from context. The words that follow, however, cannot be fully understood from either context or analysis of word parts. For this reason, their meanings are supplied here. Look them over before you begin reading.

> **legitimate (2):** proper or reasonable
>
> **manipulation (3):** tampering with something for personal gain
>
> **allegedly (8):** supposedly
>
> **abducted (9):** carried off by force; kidnapped
>
> **surrogate (10):** stand-in or substitute
>
> **testimony (10):** statements in favor of or against
>
> **dictum (13):** saying
>
> **skeptical (15):** suspicious, unsure

Reading Tip The author mentions five questions you can use to evaluate statistical evidence. To help you remember what they are, write a brief list in the margins. Then, practice evaluating an actual statistic. Locate a statistic mentioned in a newspaper article, in a television news report, or on an Internet website. Answer the five questions for determining if that statistic can be trusted.

1   Activists who want to draw the public's attention to a previously ignored social problem—for example, stalking, domestic violence, teenage gambling, or media bias—frequently use statistics as part of their argument. They'll often point to a large figure that supposedly identifies the number of people affected by the problem or situation. The size of the statistic is meant to impress. It suggests that the problem has to be solved or the situation altered. It's urgent. Something must be done!

2   Now, the use of statistics is a perfectly legitimate* way to get the public's attention. Yet, as Joel Best has pointed out in his book *Damned Lies and Statistics*, statistics are not simple facts. They are the product of human decisions. It's people who decide what should be counted and what forms of measurement to use.

3   Because statistics are the invention of humans, they are subject to conscious or unconscious manipulation.* In short, statistics can mislead. This is particularly true, says Best, because so many of us suffer from *innumeracy*, confusion about the use of numbers. Faced with statistical evidence, we accept it without question, mainly because we don't know how to evaluate it with an informed and critical eye.

4   What follows are some possible pitfalls associated with statistical evidence along with some suggestions for evaluating such evidence with a more informed and critical eye.

Hard Facts Can Really Be Educated Guesses

5 There are usually no accurate records available to define the extent of previously unrecognized social problems. At one time this was certainly true, for instance, of domestic violence. Ashamed and embarrassed, families tended to keep the problem under wraps. As a result, the reality of domestic violence in the home was generally not acknowledged. Few records were kept, except perhaps by the police who had been called to the scene of a particularly violent domestic quarrel.

6   However, when social—or, for that matter, political—activists work to draw attention to a problem they think needs to be addressed, the first thing they are asked is "Exactly how big is this problem?" Often what activists offer is an educated guess, which reporters, in turn, report as if the guess were an established fact based on careful statistical research. Scott Adams, the cartoonist who draws Dilbert, explained how this could happen in two brief sentences: "Reporters are faced with the daily choice of painstakingly researching stories or writing whatever people tell them. Both approaches pay the same."

7   Once a statistic about a social problem turns up on the news, the number tends to get reported over and over again. Unfortunately its simple beginnings as an educated guess are forgotten.

Definitions Need to Be Clearly Explained

8 You can't talk about social problems without defining them first. (Well, you can, but you shouldn't.) The definition makes a huge difference in the

numbers ascribed to the problem. For instance, statistics on sexual harass-ment in the workplace can skyrocket or sink, depending on how harass-ment is defined. Does it exist when employers offer promotions in exchange for sexual favors, or is it present when there are sexual pictures on display in the workplace? How a problem is defined can increase or decrease reports of its existence. Despite that fact, statistical evidence allegedly* proving that a problem is (or is not) serious is quite likely to appear without a description of the definition used to gather the evidence.

The Method of Measurement Should Be Clear

9 The definition of a problem dictates what should be counted. However, the next step in acquiring statistical evidence is just as crucial. Researchers have to decide how they will measure the problem, and the form of measurement they choose involves choices. Those choices can shape the results. For example, several years ago a national survey reported that nearly four million people claimed to have been abducted* by aliens. Most people reading about the survey would assume that the researchers got that figure by asking a direct question such as "Have you ever been abducted by aliens?" But, in fact, researchers picked five characteristics typical of stories about alien abduction. Then they asked their subjects questions related to those characteristics—for example, "Have you ever woken up and felt that there was a strange and powerful presence in the room?" Anyone whose answers matched four out of five typical signs of alien abduction became part of the four million people who believed themselves to have been abducted by aliens. The researchers had chosen a method of measurement that encouraged the production of an impressive figure as the outcome of their research.

The Sample Should Be Representative

10 Because it is all but impossible to count every instance of a specific social problem or condition, most statistics are based on a sample, or representa-tive portion, of the larger population. An article on surrogate* mothers, for example, might claim that studies show 90 percent of all surrogate moth-ers have few regrets about their decision to give up the children they bore. What the article might not report, however, is that the sample used consisted of only ten women. In other words, the statistical evidence in favor of surrogate motherhood consists of testimony* from *only* nine women.

11   And there is an even bigger problem associated with sampling. Many samples—even big ones—don't necessarily reflect or represent the larger population. Say, for example, that a researcher wanted to discover how people 18 to 25 feel about premarital sex. That researcher could have tens of thousands of people fill out questionnaires. But if the names of those people came from the subscription rolls of magazines such as *Cosmopolitan, Playboy,* and *Maxim,* the responses would be biased. They would probably be much more liberal than those from readers of more conservative magazines. Thus, the researcher could come up with an impressive figure, such as 80 percent of men and women between the ages of 18 and 25 do not consider premarital sex to be wrong. The figure might be impressive, but it hardly reflects the population at large.

12   As Darrell Huff, author of the best-selling *How to Lie with Statistics,* points out, "The result of a sampling study is no better than the sample it is based on." Samples are supposed to be representative and *random.* That means members of the sample have been selected by chance from the larger group of which the sample is a part. The test of a random sample is whether every member of the larger group being studied has a chance to be in the sample.

Studying Statistical Evidence

13   We've seen some of the ways statistical evidence can mislead. However, knowing some of the problems associated with using statistics doesn't mean you should unquestionably accept Mark Twain's famous dictum,* "There are lies, damned lies, and statistics." Knowing the problems should make you better at sorting out good statistics from bad. At the very least, it should make you unwilling to accept statistical evidence without evaluating it carefully and posing some critical questions.

14   The following questions will also help you determine which statistics are to be trusted and which cannot be taken at face value:

1. Who is using the statistic? Do they have a bias that might encourage them to seek out large or small numbers that put their cause in a good light?
2. How was the statistic arrived at? What method of measurement was used?
3. Could the problem being studied have hidden numbers that can't adequately be accounted for? For example, accurately counting the number of runaway children is nearly impossible. Unfortunately, not all the children who run away from home are reported missing to

authorities. Do you count only children who run away for more than six months, or only those who do not come back voluntarily?

4. What definition was used to count incidents of the particular problem under study?

5. How was the sample drawn? Is it random enough to represent the general population?

15   Overall, keep in mind the words of Joel Best: "One sign of good statistics is that we're given more than a number; we're told something about the definitions, measurement, and sampling behind the figure—about how the number emerged. When that information remains concealed, we have every reason to be skeptical."* Excellent advice to rely on the next time someone offers you statistical "evidence." (Sources of information: Best, *Damned Lies and Statistics*; Huff, *How to Lie with Statistics*.)

Combining Your Skills   **DIRECTIONS**   Answer the following questions by circling the appropriate letter or filling in the blanks.

Context   1. Based on the context, how would you define the word *pitfalls* in paragraph 4?

_____

2. Based on the context, how would you define the word *painstakingly* in paragraph 6?

_____

3. Based on the context, how would you define the word *ascribed* in paragraph 8?
   a. described
   b. attributed
   c. clarified
   d. drawn

Sentence Sense   4. Identify the relationship that connects these two sentences from paragraph 2: "Now, the use of statistics is a perfectly legitimate way to get the public's attention. Yet, as Joel Best has pointed out in his book *Damned Lies and Statistics*, statistics are not simple facts."
   a. comparison
   b. contrast

c. general statement and specific example

d. agreement and modification

5. Identify the relationship that connects these two sentences from paragraph 2: "They are the product of human decisions. It's people who decide what should be counted and what forms of measurement to use."

a. comparison

b. contrast

c. general statement and specific example

d. agreement and modification

Main Idea 6. What's the main idea of the entire reading?

_____

_____

Supporting Details 7. According to the author, statistics should be based on a _____ sample that _____

_____.

8. According to the author, what often happens when political activists are asked to make an educated guess?

_____

_____

Inference 9. What does the quote in paragraph 6 from Scott Adams imply about how journalists report statistics?

a. Journalism is hard work that requires reporters to evaluate complex statistical evidence.

b. Because journalists don't get paid more for researching the accuracy of statistics, they may not do the research.

c. Reporters are careless about how they use statistics, and a misinformed public pays the price for their carelessness.

d. Journalists will invent statistics if they need to.

Tone **10.** How would you describe the author's tone?

    a. warning

    b. comical

    c. neutral

    d. angry

Drawing Your Own Conclusions Based on what you know from the reading, why would handing out questionnaires to everyone riding the trains in New York, Chicago, Detroit, and San Francisco *not* give you a representative sample on which to draw conclusions about the larger population?

_____

_____

Which of the following populations is most likely to have a hidden number that can't adequately be accounted for?

a. people arrested for drinking while driving

b. the homeless

c. children not promoted to second grade

Please explain your answer.

_____

_____

Appendix for Dictionaries: Online and in Print

IN THIS APPENDIX, YOU WILL LEARN

- how to choose the right dictionary.
- how to look up unfamiliar words.
- how to understand a dictionary entry.

Dictionaries are filled with information. However, to make use of that information, you need to know how dictionaries are organized. You also need to know what kinds of information dictionaries contain. After reading this appendix, you'll know everything you need to about the organization and content of dictionaries, both online and in print.

Online and Print Dictionaries: You Need Both

As you probably know, online dictionaries are a terrific resource for looking up words. However, if you are thinking of abandoning print dictionaries altogether, think again. All dictionaries have their strengths and weaknesses. Some have a clearer layout than others. Some have more precise definitions. This is true of online dictionaries as well as print ones, and there are benefits and drawbacks to both.

Then, too, although you might be one of the lucky people who has access to a dictionary on your phone, not everyone is so fortunate. Even if you are addicted to looking up words online, there will be times when you are without access to a computer, and, for those times, you'll need a print dictionary. Thus buying yourself a good paperback or hardback dictionary, even if you do rely heavily on an online one, is a good idea.

As far as mastering dictionary skills, in general whatever you learn about print dictionaries can be applied to online ones and vice versa. The one major exception is the role of Guidewords, which we will cover first; then we will move on to those skills applicable to both online and print dictionaries.

 ## Using Guidewords

When you look up words in a print dictionary, you automatically make use of **guidewords** like the following: **experiment/exploit**.* The guideword on the left identifies the first entry on the page. The guideword on the right identifies the last entry. All other words on the page are listed alphabetically between these two guidewords.

Because dictionary entries are alphabetically ordered, guidewords live up to their name. They guide you in your search for a word. For example, would the word *expire** appear between the guidewords **experiment/exploit**? It certainly would. Alphabetically, the *i* in *expire* comes after the second *e* in *experiment* and before the *l* in *exploit*. Thus, *expire* would appear somewhere between the words *experiment* and *exploit*. Now, what about the word *explore*? Would that appear on the same page? No, it would not. Alphabetically, the letter *r* in *explore* comes after the letter *i* in *exploit*. As you know from the guidewords, *exploit* is the last word on the page. Words coming after it appear on later pages.

> Guidewords on the left identify the first entry on the page. Guidewords on the right identify the last entry on the page. All other words on the page are ordered alphabetically between the two guidewords.

♦ **EXERCISE 1** **Using Guide Words**

DIRECTIONS Look at each set of guidewords. Then look at the four words below them. Circle the two words that would appear on a dictionary page with these guidewords.

---

*exploit: to use unfairly.
*expire: to die or give out.

EXAMPLE comeback/comfort

(comedy)   comic   commander   (comet)

EXPLANATION Because all four words start with the letters *com*, you need to concentrate on the fourth letter in each guideword (*e* and *f*). Now look at the fourth letter in each of the remaining words. The letters *i* in *comic* and *m* in *commander* do not fall between the letters *e* and *f* in the guidewords, **comeback/comfort**. Thus, you would not circle *comic* or *commander*, but you would circle *comedy* and *comet*.

1. **madhouse/magazine**

   madman   maggot   madras   mayor

2. **mirthless/misconduct**

   mischief   miscarry   miserable   misquote

3. **blockade/bloodless**

   blood   bloodhound   blooper   blimp

4. **clean/clear-sighted**

   clench   clearing   cleanse   client

5. **enter/enthusiasm**

   entertain   enthrone   envy   error

Reading Entries

In whatever form they appear, dictionary entries contain several different kinds of information. Here's what you can expect to find in a typical entry.

Correct Spelling

Every dictionary entry opens with a word printed in **boldface**. That boldfaced entry word provides the correct spelling or spellings for a word. In print dictionaries, if a word has more than one correct spelling, you'll find it here. For example, this is how the entry for *theater* in the *American Heritage Dictionary* starts off: **the•a•ter** or **the•a•tre**. This entry tells you that the preferred spelling is *theater* because it is the first of the two spellings. However, *theatre* is also acceptable.

Note that some online dictionaries don't provide the alternative spellings, which is another reason you should consider using both print and online dictionaries.

Breaking Words into Syllables

Most dictionary entries will tell you how many syllables there are in a word and where the syllable breaks occur. In general, syllables are separated using dots. For example, here's the way the *American Heritage* breaks the word *contemporary* (from Chapter 7) into syllables: **con•tem•po•rary**. And here's how the *Merriam-Webster Online Dictionary* divides *saturate* (from Chapter 6): **sat•u•rate**.

Please note, though, that although print dictionaries just about uniformly break words into syllables, some online dictionaries do not. Currently, the entries for *Webster's Online Dictionary*, for instance, do not break words into syllables.

◆ **EXERCISE 2**   **Choosing the Correct Spelling**

DIRECTIONS   Use a print or an online dictionary to choose the correct spelling. Circle the letter of the correct answer.

1. a. rhinestone   b. rhine stone

2. a. tender foot   b. tenderfoot

3. a. tickertape   b. ticker tape

4. a. ammnesia   b. amnesia

5. a. comittee   b. committee

◆ **EXERCISE 3**   **Dividing Words into Syllables**

DIRECTIONS   Use a dictionary to divide the following words into syllables. The first one has been done for you.

1. efficient   ef•fi•cient _____

2. emergency   _____

3. industry   _____

4. lasagna   _____

5. roulette   _____

6. soprano   _____

7. tenancy   _____

8. valentine   _____

9. veterinarian   _____

10. weather   _____

Pronunciation Guides

Although you don't need to think twice about pronouncing words like *movie* or *childhood*, what about the word *dirge*? A dirge is a hymn sung at funerals, and it's not exactly a household word. So how do you pronounce the *g*? Do you pronounce it like the *g* in *gun* or the *g* in *sponge*?

To help you answer such questions, most entry words in print dictionaries are followed by a pronunciation guide in parentheses. Look, for example, at the pronunciation guide for *dirge*. The pronunciation guide (dûrj) clearly indicates that the *g* in *dirge* is pronounced like the *j* in *joke*:

dirge (dûrj) *n.* **1.** *Music* **a.** A funeral hymn. **b.** A slow, mournful* musical composition. **2.** A mournful poem or other literary work. **2.** *Roman Catholicism* The Office for the Dead.[1]

Using the Pronunciation Key: To further help readers pronounce unfamiliar words, print dictionaries like the *American Heritage Dictionary* also include a **pronunciation key**. Look, for example, at this pronunciation key from the *American Heritage Dictionary*:

---

*mournful: sad.

[1]This entry and all remaining ones illustrating print entries are adapted from those found in the *American Heritage Dictionary*.

ă pat	ĭ pit	oi boy	th **thin**
ā pay	ī **pie**	ou **out**	*th* **this**
âr **care**	îr **pier**	ŏŏ **took**	hw **which**
ä father	ŏ pot	ōō **boot**	zh vision
ĕ pet	ō **toe**	ŭ **cut**	ə† about, item
ē be	ô paw	ûr **urge**	◆ regionalism*

Imagine now that you had looked up the word *bilk*, which means "to cheat." You might not know how to pronounce the *i*. Should it sound like the *i* in *pie* or the *i* in *pit*?

To find the answer, look first at the pronunciation guide included in the entry: (bĭlk). Now find the symbol ĭ in the pronunciation key. There's your answer. The ĭ in *bilk* should be pronounced like the *i* in *pĭt*.

Online Pronunciation Guides

For the most part, online dictionaries use letters of the alphabet to indicate how words are pronounced. Here, for example, is the pronunciation guide *Dictionary.com* provides for the word *anemia* (introduced in a footnote in Chapter 3): [uh-nee-me-uh]. *Dictionary .com*, like other online dictionaries, also includes a spoken version of the word. Click on this megaphone icon (◀») and you can hear the word pronounced. Providing readers with a spoken version of the word is one of the big bonuses of using an online dictionary, particularly if you are looking up words you want to use in conversation.

◆ **EXERCISE 4**   **Using a Dictionary for Pronunciation**

DIRECTIONS   Using a dictionary of your choice, answer the following questions.

EXAMPLE   The *u* in *cusp* sounds like the *u* in

(a.) cup.   b. cute.

EXPLANATION   The pronunciation guide in the *American Heritage Dictionary* (kŭsp) tells us that ŭ sounds like the *u* in *cut*. Thus, *a* is the correct answer.

---

†ə: This symbol is called a *schwa*.
*regionalism: used only in a particular area of the country.

1. The *u* in *mute* (myo͞ot) sounds like the *u* in
    a. but.   b. cute.

2. The *i* in *winch* (wĭnch) sounds like the *i* in
    a. will.   b. hike.

3. The *u* in *brunt* (brŭnt) sounds like the *u* in
    a. sun.   b. June.

4. The *g* in *surge* (sûrj) sounds like the *g* in
    a. gun.   b. sponge.

5. The *g* in *gnat* (năt) is
    a. silent.   b. pronounced.

Accent Marks

Whenever you look up words with more than one syllable, you'll discover **accent marks** in the pronunciation guide. In print dictionaries, accented syllables are indicated with dark apostrophes. They tell you which syllable to stress, or emphasize, when saying the word aloud. Syllables with the darker mark (′) get the primary, or strongest, emphasis. Syllables with the lighter mark (′) get secondary, or less, emphasis. Syllables without a mark are not stressed at all.

For an illustration, look at the accent mark in the word *community* (kə•myo͞o′•nĭ•tē). Say the word aloud. Can you hear that only the second syllable is stressed? But what about the word *pronunciation* (prə•nŭn′•sē•ā′shən)? In this case, the second syllable is stressed but not as strongly as the fourth.

To understand the importance of accent marks, say the word *effort* aloud. Do you hear how the accent falls on the first syllable (**ef**′•fort)? Now say *effort* again. This time, emphasize the second syllable (ef•**FORT**′). The word should sound strange. Now you understand why accenting the right syllable is important.

Accent marks tell you which syllable to stress, or emphasize, when you pronounce a word.

Online Accent Symbols

Online dictionaries vary in how they indicate accented syllables. *YourDictionary.com*, for instance, uses accent marks like print dictionaries do. However, *Dictionary.com* uses boldface to tell you what syllable you need to accent. Here, for instance, is *transformer* (from Chapter 2): trans-**fawr**-mer. What's good about both dictionaries is that they include the megaphone icon, meaning you can hear the words pronounced. Again, particularly if English is not your first language, this is an excellent feature of online dictionaries.

◆ **EXERCISE 5** **Accenting the Correct Syllable**

DIRECTIONS   Answer each question by filling in the blanks.

EXAMPLE   **a•gree•ment** (ə-grē′mənt)

a. The word *agreement* has __3__ syllables.

b. The _____second_____ syllable receives the primary accent.

EXPLANATION   The entry word clearly divides *agreement* into three syllables. The primary accent appears over the second syllable.

1. **in•spec•tor** (ĭn-spĕk′tər)

    a. The word *inspector* has _____ syllables.

    b. The _____ syllable receives the primary accent.

2. **sim•i•lar•i•ty** (sĭm′ə-lăr′ĭ-tē)

    a. The word *similarity* has _____ syllables.

    b. The _____ syllable receives the primary accent.

3. **un•be•liev•a•ble** (ŭn′bĭ-lē′və-bəl)

    a. The word *unbelievable* has _____ syllables.

    b. The _____ syllable receives the primary accent.

4. **no•ti•fy** (nō′tə-fī′)

    a. The word *notify* has _____ syllables.

    b. The _____ syllable receives the primary accent.

5. **im•por•ta•tion** (ĭm′pôr-tā′shən)

    a. The word *importation* has _____ syllables.

    b. The _____syllable receives the primary accent.

Parts of Speech

After the pronunciation guide following each word, both print and online dictionaries usually tell you if the word is a noun, an adjective, an adverb, and so on. If a word can be used as more than one part of speech, the dictionary will provide separate definitions for each part of speech. Look, for example, at the following entry for *hoe* from the *American Heritage Dictionary*. It indicates that the word *hoe* can be both a noun (*n.*) and a verb (*v.*):

> **hoe** (hō) *n.* A tool with a flat blade attached at a right angle to a long handle, used for weeding and gardening. **hoe** *v.* **hoed**, **hoe•ing**, **hoes** To weed or dig with a hoe.

The following chart lists the most commonly used abbreviations for parts of speech.

Parts of Speech ◆		
n.	noun	a person, place, or thing—for example: *dog, tent, foot.*
pl.	plural	refers to more than one noun—for example: *dogs, tents, feet.*
adj.	adjective	a word that describes a noun—for example: *pretty, kind, difficult.*
adv.	adverb	a word that modifies a verb—for example: *slowly, wildly, fast.*
v.	verb	a word that describes an action or a state—for example: *fight, kiss, be.*
tr. v.	transitive verb	a verb that takes an object—for example: "I *kicked* the *football.*" *v.* *o.*
intr. v.	intransitive verb	a verb that cannot take an object—for example: "She always *procrastinates.*"

> If a word can be used as more than one part of speech, the dictionary will provide separate definitions for each part of speech.

◆ **EXERCISE 6**   **Identifying Parts of Speech**

DIRECTIONS   Each of the following words can function as more than one part of speech. Use the dictionary of your choice to identify each part of speech. The first one is done for you.

Word	Parts of Speech
1. fume	*noun, verb*
2. grate	
3. honeymoon	
4. lowly	
5. main	

Meanings of a Word

As you know, many words have several different meanings. To help you identify those meanings quickly, online and print dictionaries usually separate them with boldface numbers. Look, for example, at this entry for the adjective *evil*. It contains five separate meanings.

> **e•vil** (e′vəl) *adj.* **e•vil•er, e•vil•est. 1.** Morally bad or wrong; wicked. **2.** Causing ruin, injury, or pain. **3.** Indicating future misfortune. **4.** Bad by report: *an evil reputation.* **5.** Characterized by anger or spite: *an evil temper.*

Online Lists of Meanings

Online dictionaries are more inclined to list the meanings, as *Dictionary.com* does here:

i•de•al•ize ◀)) [ahy-**dee**-*uh*-lahyz] *verb,* *-ized, -iz•ing.*

1. to make ideal; represent in an ideal form or character; exalt to an ideal perfection or excellence. *–verb (used without object).*

2. to represent something in an ideal form. Also *especially British,* i•de•al•ise.

Origin: 1780–90; ideal + -ize.

Related forms: **i•de•al•iz•er,** *noun.*

Online dictionaries are also likely to provide definitions drawn from several different dictionaries. This is both a plus and a minus. On the one hand, you get a range of meanings that will undoubtedly provide you with the one you need. On the other hand, you may also have to sift through many meanings to find the clearest definition. Here, for instance, is the list you'll find at *Dictionary.com* for *allocation* (from Chapter 8):

al•lo•ca•tion ◀)) [al-*uh*-**key**-sh*uh* n] *-noun.*

1. the act of allocating; apportionment.

2. the state of being allocated.

3. the share or portion allocated.

4. *Accounting,* a system of dividing expenses and incomes among the various branches, departments, etc., of a business.

Origin: 1525–35; < ML *allocātiōn-* (s. of *allocātiō*), equiv. to *allocāt(us)* (see ALLOCATE) + *-iōn-* -ION.

Related forms: **al•lo•ca•tive,** *adjective.*

Dictionary.com Unabridged
Based on the Random House Dictionary,
© Random House, Inc. 2009.

Related Words for : allocation
allotment, apportioning, apportionment, assignation, parceling
View more related words »

al•lo•cate (āl′lo-kāt′)

tr. v.   **al•lo•cat•ed, al•lo•cat•ing, al•lo•cates**

1. To set apart for a special purpose; designate: *allocate a room to be used for storage.*

2. To distribute according to a plan; allot: *allocate rations for a week-long camping trip.*

[Medieval Latin allocāre, allocāt- : Latin ad-, *ad-* + Latin locāre, *to place* (from locus, *place*).]

al′lo•cat′a•ble *adj.,* **al′lo•ca′tion** *n.,* **al′lo•ca•tor** *n.*

Synonyms: These verbs mean to set aside for a specified purpose: *allocated time for recreation; appropriated funds for public education; designated a location for the new hospital; money earmarked for a vacation.*

Allocation

Al`lo*ca″tion\, *n.* [LL. allocatio: cf. F. allocation.]

1. The act of putting one thing to another; a placing; disposition; arrangement. —Hallam.

2. An allotment or apportionment; as, an allocation of shares in a company.

The allocation of the particular portions of Palestine to its successive inhabitants. —A. R. Stanley.

3. The admission of an item in an account, or an allowance made upon an account; —a term used in the English exchequer.

Choosing the Correct Meaning

If you look up a word and find several different meanings, don't get discouraged. Instead, pay close attention to the word's original context. Use that context to choose the right meaning.

Imagine that you weren't familiar with the word *nimble* in the following passage:

The gymnast was extremely nimble on the balance beam, and the coach expected her to do well in the balance beam event.

Puzzled, you looked up the word and found two different meanings:

1. Quick, light in movement or action. **2.** Quick and clever in understanding.

Which meaning should you choose? Because the original sentence clearly refers to physical activity, we can eliminate meaning number 2. Meaning number 1, however, is a perfect match.

It doesn't matter how many meanings there are in an entry. You can usually pick the right one by paying close attention to the original context of the word.

◆ EXERCISE 7   **Choosing the Right Definition**

DIRECTIONS   Read each sentence. Decide which meaning for the italicized word best fits the sentence. Fill in the blank with the number of that definition.

EXAMPLE   Sean was the *beneficiary* of his grandmother's excellent advice.

beneficiary 1. One who receives a benefit. **2.** The receiver of funds, property, or other benefits.

Meaning number ___1___ best fits the sentence.

EXPLANATION   The context refers to a nonfinancial benefit. Thus, meaning 2 is eliminated.

1. Nothing could *pacify* her rage.

    pacify 1. To ease someone's anger. **2.** To end war or establish peace.

    Meaning number _____ best fits the sentence.

2. The mountains were covered in a *shroud* of fog.

    shroud 1. A cloth used to wrap a body for burial. **2.** Something that conceals, protects, or screens.

    Meaning number _____ best fits the sentence.

3. The climbers were frightened by the mountain's dangerous *ascent*.

> **ascent 1.** The act or process of rising or going upward. **2.** An advancement, especially in social status. **3.** An upward slope. **4.** Going back in time.

Meaning number _____ best fits the sentence.

4. The teacher was *impervious* to all forms of student sarcasm.

> **impervious 1.** Incapable of being penetrated, The casing was *impervious* to rust. **2.** Incapable of being affected, The reporter was *impervious* to insult.

Meaning number _____ best fits the sentence.

5. A *flock* of noisy reporters asked a flood of annoying questions.

> **flock 1.** A group of animals that live, travel, or feed together. **2.** A group of people under the leadership of one person. **3.** A large crowd or number.

Meaning number _____ best fits the sentence.

Word Histories

Many dictionary entries include in brackets an **etymology**, or history, of the word defined. Entries for the word *fatigue*, for example, usually end with the following information: [French, from Old French, from *fatiguer*, to *fatigue*, from Latin *fatigare*]. This bracketed history tells you that *fatigue* was originally a Latin word. In time, it found its way into French. Finally, it became part of the English language.

To save space, almost all dictionaries use abbreviations when tracing word history (**ME** for Middle English, **Gr** for Greek, **Fr** for French, and the symbol < for the word *from*). Don't worry, however, about memorizing these abbreviations. They are always explained in the dictionary's opening pages.

◆ **EXERCISE 8** **Learning About a Word's History**

DIRECTIONS   Use the dictionary of your choice to choose the correct answer. *Note*: If you don't find the answer in one dictionary, look up the same word in another dictionary.

EXAMPLE   The origins of the word *formal* are

a. Greek.

(b.) Latin.

EXPLANATION   The etymology for *formal* [Middle English, from Latin *formalis*] says that the word has Latin origins.

1. The origins of the word *domino* are
    a. Spanish.
    b. French.

2. The word *silhouette* came from the name of a French finance minister
    named _____.

3. The word *sinister* now means "threatening" or "evil," but it comes
    from the Latin word for _____.

4. The word *gamble* comes from
    a. Latin.
    b. Old English.

5. The word *piano* comes from
    a. Greek.
    b. Italian.

Answer Key: Reviewing the Key Points

Chapter 1 (page 43)

1. F
2. T
3. F
4. F
5. T
6. F
7. F
8. F
9. F
10. T

Chapter 2 (page 79)

1. F
2. F
3. T
4. F
5. F
6. T
7. T
8. F
9. F
10. T

Chapter 3 (page 129)

1. T
2. F
3. F
4. T
5. T
6. F
7. F
8. T
9. T
10. T

Chapter 4 (page 171)

1. but; however
2. c
3. specific; general
4. example; general
5. c

Chapter 5 (page 230)

1. misinterpretation or misunderstanding; supporting details
2. F
3. make the main idea clear and convincing
4. the main idea
5. F
6. (1) to further explain major details
   (2) to add emphasis
   (3) to add a colorful fact or detail
7. explain a major detail
8. T
9. *Answers will vary.* reasons, advantages, goals, studies, programs, categories, groups
10. I mean this, not that

Chapter 6 (page 284)

1. F
2. look at the evidence supplied by the author; infer a main idea about what was unsaid but implied
3. F
4. the author's topic sentence would
5. confusion or miscommunication
6. what the writer actually says
7. overshadow the author's
8. F
9. you need to revise the main idea you inferred
10. be contradicted by the author's actual statements

Chapter 7 (page 354)

1. the order of the steps or stages
2. steps, stages, or phases
3. sequence of dates and events
4. order; author; content
5. the word or term being defined
6. one thing, idea, or event leads to or produces another
7. d
8. a
9. The topic sentence gives it away by announcing that a large group can be subdivided.
10. the method used to create the categories

Chapter 8 (page 403)

1. the main idea
2. the main idea
3. F
4. T
5. F

Chapter 9 (page 463)

1. describe a person, an idea, or an event without passing judgment
2. denotative; emotional punch, feeling, or attitude
3. tone of voice; feeling or attitude
4. tone
5. facts
6. a
7. an emotion or a feeling, a personal point of view
8. a
9. b
10. (1) The writer can't acknowledge that the opposing point of view has a point.
    (2) The writer doesn't explain why the opposition is wrong.
    (3) The writer insists that everyone feels as he or she does.
    (4) The writer tends to browbeat the reader by using an overly confident or bullying tone.

Acknowledgments

American Heritage College Dictionary excerpt. Copyright © 2006 by Houghton Mifflin Harcourt Publishing Company. Reproduced from *The American Heritage College Dictionary*, 4th Edition.

Charles M. Blow. "The Demise of Dating" by Charles M. Blow from *The New York Times*, December 13, 2008. Copyright © 2008 The New York Times Co. Reprinted by permission.

Anne O'M. Bowman and Richard Kearney. From *State and Local Government*, 5th Edition. © 2002 Wadsworth, a part of Cengage Learning, Inc. Reproduced by permission. www.cengage.com/permissions.

Joseph DeVito. "Nonjudgmental and Critical Listening." From *The Interpersonal Communication Book*, 10th Edition. Published by Allyn and Bacon/Merrill Education, Boston, MA. Copyright © 2004 by Pearson Education. Reprinted by permission of the publisher.

Dictionary.com excerpt. From Dictionary.com, Unabridged. Based on the *Random House Dictionary*, © Random House, Inc. 2009.

Marilyn Elias. "Online Therapy Clicks" by Marilyn Elias from *USA Today*, May 22, 2001, p. 1D. Copyright © 2001. Reprinted with permission.

Dave Ellis. "The Seven-Day Antiprocrastination Plan." From *Becoming a Master Student*, 8th Edition. © 1997 Wadsworth, a part of Cengage Learning, Inc. Reproduced by permission. www.cengage.com/permissions.

Dave Ellis. "Muscle Reading." From *Becoming a Master Student*, 12th Edition. © 2009 Wadsworth, a part of Cengage Learning, Inc. Reproduced by permission. www.cengage.com/permissions.

Dana Jennings. "Life Lessons from the Family Dog" by Dana Jennings from *The New York Times*, March 31, 2009. Copyright © 2009 the New York Times Co. Reprinted by permission.

Richard Lederer. Reprinted with the permission of Atria Books, a Division of Simon & Schuster, Inc., from *Crazy English: Revised Edition* by Richard Lederer. Copyright © 1989, 1990, 1998 by Richard Lederer.

Mickey Meece. "Backlash: Women Bullying Women in the Workplace?" by Mickey Meece from *The New York Times*, May 10, 2009. Copyright © 2009 The New York Times Co. Reprinted by permission.

William M. Pride. From *Business*, 8th Edition. (2005) South-Western, a part of Cengage Learning, Inc. Reproduced by permission. www.cengage.com/permissions.

William M. Pride and O. C. Ferrell. "Cultures, Subcultures, and the Marketplace." From *Marketing*, 15th Edition. © 2010 South-Western, a part of Cengage Learning, Inc. Reproduced by permission. www.cengage.com/permissions.

Ted Tollefson. "What Makes a Hero?" from "Is a Hero Really Nothing but a Sandwich?" by Ted Tollefson as appeared in *Utne Reader*, May/June 1993, pp. 102–3. Reprinted by permission of the author.

Index

AN ACTIVE READER'S CHECKLIST (continued)

	Yes	No
10. Do you make it a point to paraphrase (put into your own words) the most important ideas of each chapter section?	☐	☐
11. Do you mark difficult passages for a second reading and then make sure to go back and re-read them?	☐	☐
12. Do you monitor, or check, your comprehension by trying to recite the key points of a chapter section without looking at the text or your marginal notes?	☐	☐
13. If you realize you haven't understood the author's message, do you look for a "fix-up strategy," a different reading approach that could help you bring the author's meaning into better focus?	☐	☐
14. Do you make a list of and routinely review any textbook vocabulary that is printed in boldface, colored ink, or italics?	☐	☐
15. If the text you are reading has a lot of illustrations and visual aids, do you study those carefully to determine what they add to your understanding of the text?	☐	☐
16. If the course includes outside readings, do you try to figure out how the outside readings relate to what you are learning from your textbooks?	☐	☐
17. Are you always ready to adapt your reading strategies to the material, for example, drawing diagrams to understand your science text but using timelines to master what you are learning in history?	☐	☐
18. Do you adapt your reading rate to the material, slowing down for difficult passages and speeding up for easier ones? (See the reading rate chart opposite.)	☐	☐
19. If the author seems determined to convince you of his or her point of view, do you double check the author's reasoning, making sure it is sound?	☐	☐
20. Once you feel you have understood the author's point, do you ask yourself why you agree or disagree?	☐	☐